*Christian Bernstorff*
*and Prussia*

# Christian Bernstorff and Prussia

## Diplomacy and Reform Conservatism
### 1818-1832

*Lawrence J. Baack*

Rutgers University Press
New Brunswick, New Jersey

**Library of Congress Cataloging in Publication Data**

Baack, Lawrence J
Christian Bernstorff and Prussia, 1818–1832.

Bibliography: p.
Includes index.
1. Prussia—Foreign relations—1815–1870.
2. Bernstorff, Christian Günther, Graf von, 1769–1835.
I. Title.
DD429.B2     327.43     79–19574
ISBN 0–8135–0884–3

To Peter Paret
and to the memory of
Raymond J. Sontag

✠✠✠✠✠✠✠✠✠✠✠✠✠✠✠

# Contents

✠ ✠ ✠ ✠ ✠ ✠ ✠ ✠ ✠ ✠ ✠ ✠ ✠ ✠

# Preface

Scholars have again begun to investigate the period that has been called the Age of Reaction, the Restoration, or the Era of Metternich. The works of Werner Conze, Reinhard Koselleck, Peter Paret, Wolfram Fischer, and others have led to a quiet renaissance in the study of German history during the era following the Congress of Vienna.[1] Thus far, however, little attention has been paid to the foreign relations of Prussia and Germany during this period. The only comprehensive study is still Heinrich von Treitschke's five-volume *Deutsche Geschichte im Neunzehnten Jahrhundert.*[2]

Treitschke's work is the product of a prodigious amount of research and is written in a dynamic and insightful style. Although it justly ranks as one of the classics of German historiography and can command the respect of those who have worked in the period, it still contains obvious deficiencies. The most notorious is Treitschke's strong bias in favor of Prussia, which at times seriously distorts his presentation of historical developments and hinders the usefulness of his interpretations. His almost exclusive reliance on German, especially Prussian, documents for source material is an equally important flaw. Treitschke's work is thus a one-sided description of the period, rather than an integrated understanding of Prussian developments within the wider European framework.

1. For example, Werner Conze, ed., *Staat und Gesellschaft im deutschen Vormärz;* Reinhard Koselleck, *Preussen zwischen Reform und Revolution;* Peter Paret, *Clausewitz and the State;* and Wolfram Fischer, *Der Staat und die Anfänge der Industrialisierung in Baden, 1800–1850.*

2. This study will use the English translation, *History of Germany in the Nineteenth Century.*

In view of these deficiencies and of the noticeable gaps in the literature on the subject, the need to reexamine this period of Prussia's diplomatic history is clear. This book describes the nature of Prussian foreign policy during the ministry of Count Christian von Bernstorff. Its organization has been determined by the characteristics of the subject. After an extended introduction, the study proceeds chronologically. For the sake of clarity, Prussia's European and German policies have been examined separately. Naturally this introduces a certain artificiality, for neither aspect of Prussia's foreign relations was conducted in isolation from the other. In fact, there was usually a close interaction between these two spheres of diplomatic activity, and I have attempted to delineate this relationship where appropriate. However, Prussia did exist within two separate systems: the European and the German. Each had different characteristics and posed different kinds of problems to policy makers in Berlin.

This study focuses on Prussia's function within the European Concert and its relationship to political changes that occurred in Europe during the early 1830s. For Germany, military affairs and the development of the *Zollverein,* and attitudes toward the press and constitutional movements in the period of the Carlsbad Decrees and after, will be of special interest. The question of what happened to the Prussian reformers after 1819 is also related to these issues. This problem cannot be treated comprehensively in a study that concentrates on foreign affairs, but significant insights into the activities and the ideas of the reformers in the 1820s and 1830s can be gained from an examination of Prussia's European and German policies. A final aim of this book is to analyze aspects of Prussian conservatism during the early nineteenth century.

As Klaus Epstein has noted, the period after the Congress of Vienna was the classic age of conservative rule in Central Europe, and, as he demonstrated in *The Genesis of German Conservatism,* the need to relate conservatism as a mode of thought to concrete historical conditions and to differentiate the major categories of conservative thought is essential to any meaningful understanding of the phenomenon.[3] In a period when foreign policy in Central Europe was closely connected with domestic political concerns, the analysis of diplomatic activity provides an opportunity for this kind of differentiation. I find Epstein's typology of three kinds of conservatives—the reactionary, the defender of the status quo,

3. Klaus Epstein, *The Genesis of German Conservatism.*

and the reform conservative—to be basically accurate and useful.[4] The terminology I have used in this book therefore conforms to Epstein's definitions, although variants, such as the term "ultraconservative" for "reactionary," are employed.

This book does not pretend to be comprehensive. It concentrates only on those aspects of Prussia's diplomatic activities that seem central to an understanding of its foreign relations. It also relies on a great number of previous works, most of which are excellent. Where these accounts seemed confused or contain significant gaps, I have not hesitated to return to the archives in an effort to reconstruct a more accurate picture of this period of Prussian history. Although Bernstorff was an important person, he was not a dominating figure in Prussia and Europe during this era. He shared the historical stage with a number of other significant leaders. Events in which he played only a subsidiary role have been examined in considerable detail if they are essential to a coherent understanding of Prussian policy. Similarly, developments in other European states have been discussed so that events in Prussia could be placed within a broader European context. While this means that Bernstorff will not always be the main figure in every section of this study, he is the theme about which it is organized. Thus this book is biographical to the extent that Bernstorff is the prism through which the international activities of the period are generally viewed and by which developments are differentiated.

Bernstorff had a varied and rich career that stretched from the end of the *ancien régime* into the fourth decade of the nineteenth century. He knew the European system prior to the outbreak of the French Revolution. As the foreign minister of Denmark, he confronted the power of Napoleon and England. He participated in the reestablishment of peace at the Congress of Vienna. As Prussia's foreign minister, he was present at the meetings in Aachen, Carlsbad, Troppau, Laibach, and Verona. He played an important role in the creation of the German *Zollverein,* and he was a key European and German statesman during the turbulent years from 1830 to 1832. His career provides a continuity and a perspective that opens up analytical relationships that might not be apparent in a more topical approach.

4. Ibid., pp. 3–22.

✠✠✠✠✠✠✠✠✠✠✠✠✠✠

# Acknowledgments

This study would not have been possible without the help of many institutions and individuals, and it is a pleasure to acknowledge the assistance I have received. I am very grateful to the staffs of the following archives and libraries: the *Zentrales Staatsarchiv*, Merseburg; the *Rigsarkiv*, Copenhagen; the *Haus-, Hof-, und Staatsarchiv*, Vienna; the Public Record Office, London; the *Archives du Ministère des Affaires Étrangères*, Paris; the *Geheimes Staatsarchiv Preussischer Kulturbesitz*, Berlin; the *Geheimes Staatsarchiv*, Munich; the *Niedersächsisches Staatsarchiv*, Osnabrück; the *Kongelige Bibliotek*, Copenhagen; the *Friedrich Meinecke Institut* and the University Library of the *Freie Universität*, Berlin; the *Staatsbibliothek der Stiftung Preussischer Kulturbesitz*, Berlin; the *Staatsbibliothek*, Munich; and the libraries of Stanford University, the University of California, Berkeley, and the University of Nebraska. I would also like to thank Count Carl Johan von Bernstorff-Gyldensteen for permission to use the Bernstorff papers deposited in the *Rigsarkiv*, Count Albrecht von dem Bussche-Ippenburg for letting me consult manuscripts at Ippenburg and in the *Niedersächsisches Staatsarchiv*, Count Andreas von Bernstorff and the late Count Hugo von Bernstorff for the use of the archives at Gartow and Wotersen, and Frau Marie-Agnes von Heinz for access to the collections at Tegel.

I am also very grateful to Professor Gordon A. Craig for his valuable suggestions and assistance throughout the course of this project. Herbert F. Mann and Margaret L. Christ of Rutgers University Press carefully supervised the editing and production of this book and made my work much easier. In addition, Count Joachim von Bernstorff, Count Werner von Bernstorff, Frau Marie-Louise von Bethmann Hollweg, née Countess

xiii

Reventlow, Professor Georg Nørregård of the University of Århus, and Dr. Hans Branig were also helpful in a variety of ways.

Financial assistance from several institutions enabled me to make three research trips to Europe. I would like to acknowledge the support of the Department of History and the Center for Research in International Studies, Stanford University; the *Historische Kommission zu Berlin;* and the Research Council of the University of Nebraska. In particular, I want to mention the help of Professor Otto Büsch of the *Historische Kommission.*

Finally, I would like to mention two individuals who have had a prime influence on my study of history. The late Professor Raymond J. Sontag first introduced me to the study of diplomatic history and encouraged my interest in the field at a time when graduate school seemed very far away. In its earliest stages, this work benefitted greatly from his criticism. From the beginning of my graduate studies, I was most fortunate to receive the guidance and warm encouragement of Professor Peter Paret, my doctoral advisor. His penetrating criticism, great ability to stimulate thought in others, and extremely kind support not only contributed immensely to the completion of this book but made my years at Stanford a memorable educational experience. I would like to express my special sense of gratitude to him.

*Christian Bernstorff
and Prussia*

# *Chapter 1*

# Introduction

Christian Bernstorff's career as Prussia's foreign minister was clearly shaped by four elements. First, his personal values and political philosophy were largely determined by the rich political and cultural heritage of his family. Second, as a result of thirty years of diplomatic experience in Denmark, he had formulated certain definite views on international and domestic affairs. Third, the European political environment in the wake of the Congress of Vienna included characteristics that no statesman could afford to ignore. Fourth, the Prussian state had certain capabilities, limitations, and objectives that restricted and shaped the conduct of its foreign policy.

## BERNSTORFF'S FAMILY HERITAGE

The Bernstorff family tradition of public service emerged as a product of the political careers of three members of the family: Andreas Gottlieb von Bernstorff (1649–1726), Hanoverian *Premierminister* and chief German advisor to George I of Great Britain; Johann Hartvig Ernst von Bernstorff (1712–1772), *Obersecretaire* of the German Chancellery and foreign minister of Denmark from 1751–1770; and Andreas Peter von Bernstorff (1735–1797), holder of the same two offices in Denmark (1773–1780 and 1784–1797).[1] Although the beliefs and political activities of each man varied, over time, certain commonalities took shape. The combination of values and approaches developed by these three men inspired four

1. For a full discussion of the political development of the Bernstorffs in the eighteenth century, see Lawrence J. Baack, "State Service in the Eighteenth Century."

more generations of Bernstorffs, who served Prussia and Germany into the twentieth century.

The Bernstorffs were devout Protestants. The family testament, written by A. G. Bernstorff as a strict guide for future generations, emphasized the importance of Christianity as the spiritual and ethical foundation for the family's daily lives. J. H. E. Bernstorff lived up to his grandfather's expectations and, throughout his life, retained an absolute faith in God. He believed that the requirements of the divine creator were quite simple: "To love God above all things with all one's might and to hold him even closer than oneself."[2] A. P. Bernstorff was closely associated with the pietist movement and married into the Stolberg family, which was at the center of religious life in Denmark. A sense of Christian responsibility was a prime inspiration for his official activities, and he repeatedly used Christian values as the basis for his political judgments.

The Bernstorffs were also keenly aware of the intellectual and cultural developments of their age. While he was minister to the court of Louis XV, J. H. E. Bernstorff frequented the literary salons of Paris and met some of the leading thinkers of the period—Maupertuis, Montesquieu, Bernis, Fontenelle, and Voltaire. Later in his life, he encouraged the work of scientists, historians, and literary figures in Denmark and helped to stimulate a revival of cultural activity in Copenhagen. For example, he secured a yearly pension from Frederick V for Friedrich Gottlieb Klopstock, the pietistic, preromantic German poet; thereafter, the Bernstorff family was closely linked to new developments in German literature. A. P. Bernstorff shared his uncle's interests. As a young man, he studied the works of Voltaire, Montesquieu, Rousseau, Diderot, d'Alembert, Locke, and Hume and concluded that "the study of philosophy is the study of reason and what can instruct us better in the duties of religion and human society."[3] Through his marriage to Henrietta Stolberg, and later to Auguste Stolberg, he came into close contact with the world of Goethe, an association that made him sensitive to new literary themes in Germany. More than anyone else in the family, A. P. Bernstorff personified the conservative but enlightened outlook that has been associated with those Bernstorffs who were active in government.

Above all, the family tradition incorporated the concept of political

2. Aage Friis, *Die Bernstorffs*, p. 253.

3. A. P. Bernstorff to A. G. Bernstorff, 10 February 1755, Aage Friis, ed., *Bernstorffske Papirer*, 1:121.

service. Although the Bernstorffs could trace their lineage back to the twelfth century and had held estates in Mecklenburg and Lower Saxony for centuries, their record of service was insignificant until the seventeenth century. The career of A. G. Bernstorff first made the name prominent in Europe and created an example of distinguished political servce for his family. His testament emphasized the importance of service and argued that a rigorous education and a true respect for God would make the Bernstorffs capable servants "of the general public and of the world."[4] His career and personal concern inspired his grandson, J. H. E. Bernstorff, to devote his entire life to administration and politics in the service of Denmark. As a young man, A. P. Bernstorff quite openly decided to follow in the footsteps of his uncle, to whom he once wrote: "I would like to try to make myself worthy so that I can be entrusted with public affairs, in short I would like to follow your example. . . . So inspired and with such a model before me, I do not doubt that with God's help, I will be a useful member of human society."[5]

During the eighteenth century, except for A. G. Bernstorff, who was a stout defender of the privileges and institutions of the provincial aristocracy, the politically active members of the family turned their attention toward reform. As the teachings of the Enlightenment and of pietism awakened their social conscience, and as experience broadened their perspective on political affairs, J. H. E. and A. P. Bernstorff became associated with social and economic innovation in Denmark. Johann Hartvig Ernst Bernstorff was a humanitarian. He enthusiastically supported numerous charitable and educational causes; he allowed Andreas Peter Bernstorff to implement pioneering agrarian reforms on his estate outside of Copenhagen; and he was the first president of the Royal Agricultural Society of Denmark, which advocated a progressive approach to the rural problems that plagued Denmark and most of Europe. But, for him, reform remained a personal matter; it was not related to government policy. His ideal of the state was not dynamic. Instead, he visualized a just and paternal Danish absolutism "administered by conscientious ministers according to the law."[6]

His nephew, A. P. Bernstorff, became an active reformer. During his ministry (1784–1797), Danish society was transformed: The peasantry

4. Friis, *Die Bernstorffs*, p. 17.
5. A. P. Bernstorff to J. H. E. Bernstorff, Friis, *Bernstorffske Papirer*, 1:187–188.
6. Aage Friis, *Die Bernstorffs und Dänemark*, p. 180.

was emancipated, and a successful program of land reform was begun. Fundamental improvements in the legal, educational, and welfare systems made social arrangements more rational and just. Practically every aspect of Danish society underwent some significant change. Throughout this period of innovation, A. P. Bernstorff was Denmark's de facto leading minister. He commanded the respect of the crown and dominated the *Staatsrad,* through which the reform measures had to pass. Although progressive, he was a monarchist. He was critical of Louis XVI, but he also condemned the French Revolution. He did not believe in a democratic form of government. "It is contrary to the nature of man," he wrote, "to believe the people will obey when they believe they are the source of the law." He felt that the National Assembly was guided by impassioned men who erroneously believed in the infallibility of their own ideas. He believed that the interests of the individual would be trampled on by the masses and predicted in 1791 that a democracy "will become a horrible despotism, the antithesis of the liberty toward which they aspire."[7] In other words, A. P. Bernstorff could be called a reform conservative. Change and innovation were tolerated and even encouraged as long as they took place within existing institutional procedures. As he once remarked, "I think that the gardener is most clever who lets a tree remain and does not try to remove it when it is unhealthy, but rather puts fresh earth around its roots and scrapes off the moss."[8]

The Bernstorffs also developed a generally ethical, rational, and peaceful approach to politics. For example, J. H. E. Bernstorff wrote to his nephew that "the conduct of affairs of state makes great demands, it requires an honest heart and mind not to make out of politics what others make out of it—an art of lying and deception, unworthy of a man and ruinous for a Christian."[9] The Bernstorffs began to think of the state as a separate entity and strove to determine is interests in a rational manner—that is, on the basis of specific geographical, economic, financial, and military factors or of certain qualities of political leadership. They were devoted to the cause

7. Renate Erhardt-Lucht, *Die Ideen der Französischen Revolution in Schleswig-Holstein,* p. 21.

8. Fernando Linderberg, *Staatsminister Andreas Peder Bernstorff,* p. 71. The most important Danish reforms are analyzed in Lawrence J. Baack, *Agrarian Reform in Eighteenth-Century Denmark.*

9. J. H. E. Bernstorff to A. P. Bernstorff, August 1754, Friis, *Bernstorffske Papirer,* 1:116.

of peace. Echoing his uncle, A. P. Bernstorff once said, "Even the most fortunate war is the greatest disaster a nation can encounter."[10] Although he believed that the rule of law and moral energy ought to prevail over the use of force, he realized that this was rarely the reality of European politics. He condemned the spirit of bitterness and self-seeking ambition that characterized international affairs and was particularly bothered by the impending partition of Poland. "A mania for aggrandizement," he wrote, "has corrupted nearly all the powers. May God keep Denmark from ever having anything to do with these seductive plans, compatible neither with religion, nor with true morality."[11] He believed ultimately that all peoples belonged to one nation. The phrase *Patria ubique* (Everywhere is fatherland), which he found so appealing, is indicative of his sense of international brotherhood.

Those Bernstorffs who served in government in the late eighteenth century were not provincial noblemen whose perspectives were restricted to considerations based on the *Stände* and the region. They had a broad knowledge of Europe, were aware of the intellectual developments of the age, were dedicated to the service of the state, and no longer retained any significant identification with corporate and local institutions. Although cautious and in many ways conservative, they were receptive to change. Above all, they believed that the conduct of politics should not normally conflict with basic religious and ethical truths. Finally, they were tied together by a strong feeling of family solidarity and tradition. As J. H. E. Bernstorff told A. P. Bernstorff, "The sense of family has been a fervent one for a long time with the Bernstorffs; it is one of the greatest blessings that God has given to your grandfather and his brothers, and to your father and me. May it continue to be handed down among us and may it never leave us so long as our name and our family exist."[12] Christian Bernstorff shared this belief. As a result, the tradition of his family helped him to interpret political reality throughout his career and provided a system of values that could be applied to the day-to-day conduct of government affairs.

10. Alexander Scharff, *Schleswig-Holstein in der Europäischen und Nordischen Geschichte*, p. 28.

11. A. P. Bernstorff to Schack-Rathlou, 16 March 1793, Th. Thaulow and J. O. Bro Jørgensen, *Udvalgte Breve, Betænkninger og Optegnelser af J. O. Schack-Rathlous arkiv, 1760–1800*, pp. 159–160.

12. Friis, *Die Bernstorffs*, p. 411.

## YOUTH AND EARLY CAREER

Christian Günther von Bernstorff was born in Copenhagen on 3 April 1769. His youth was dominated by the powerful personality of his father and by the environment of the Bernstorff home. A private tutor was hired to instruct him in the sciences, history, and modern languages, but the course of study was not rigorous. His education was further enriched by the Stolberg brothers, who frequently read poetry to the family, and by Klopstock and other writers who continued to have contact with the Bernstorffs. The atmosphere within the family was warm and affectionate. The family was a close-knit social unit.[13] By the time Christian Bernstorff was thirteen, his father had already decided that his son should pursue a career in politics.[14] In fact, in his insistence on preparing Christian for diplomacy, A. P. Bernstorff ignored other aspects of the young man's education. In violation of the family testament, Christian Bernstorff was not allowed to attend a German university or to travel extensively through Europe. Instead, he opened his official career at the age of eighteen when his father sent him as Denmark's observer to the Swedish *Riksdag*. Soon thereafter, he was sent to Berlin to assist his uncle, Friedrich Stolberg, the Danish minister to Prussia.

For Bernstorff, Berlin was a cultural, rather than political, experience. Although his uncle guided his studies of classical and contemporary literature, his chief intellectual stimulation came from his association with the Jewish salons of the city. The impact of such women as Rahel Levin and Henrietta Herz on a number of Bernstorff's contemporaries—Wilhelm von Humboldt and Friedrich Gentz, for instance—is well known. Their taste in the arts and in literature was unconventional, and they played an important role in introducing new literature and art forms to the higher social circles of Berlin. Most of those who participated in the various reading sessions at the house of Markus Herz or in Levin's apartment on the Jäger Strasse responded to their stimulating and informal atmosphere and were often seduced by the emotionalism and sensitivity

13. Manuscript of biographical fragment on Christian Bernstorff by Johann Rist, RA Stintenburg 5128/54; and extract from the *Allgemeine Preussische Staatszeitung* (1835) entitled "Christian Günther Graf von Bernstorff, Königl. Geheimer Staats- und Kabinetts Minister," in the possession of Count Werner von Bernstorff.

14. Undated statement by Bernstorff's sister, Charlotte, in Elise von Bernstorff, notes, Private Archives, Gartow. It was probably written in 1797. Also A. P. Bernstorff to Bernstorff, 17 October 1782, RA Ober Ellguth 5127/4.

that pervaded them.[15] Bernstorff was no exception. By early 1791, he was a regular member of one of the reading groups, the so-called *Theekränzchen,* hosted by Herz, and was reading the works of Goethe with enjoyment.[16]

We know little of Bernstorff's inner thoughts during this period; his letters are vague about his personal life. But we do have information about one relationship that sheds light on his total experience in Berlin. Early in 1790, he met Marianne Meyer, the daughter of a wealthy Jewish merchant. She was a central figure in the salons and knew Goethe later in life. Beautiful, lively, and a gifted conversationalist, she seems to have been perfect company for Bernstorff. He fell deeply in love with her and, after two years, proposed marriage. It is inconceivable that he was unaware of the political consequences of this decision. A career in the highest ranks of government would have been closed to him forever. Therefore, his father strongly disapproved of the whole affair. On 12 December 1792, by letter, he tried to convince his son to abandon the idea of marrying Marianne. He told Bernstorff to think carefully about the course of action he was proposing, and he reminded him ominously at the end, "My career is drawing to a close, yours is just beginning."[17]

The issue was not only obedience to his father. Devotion to state service and, perhaps, to the entire ethos of the Bernstorffs was at stake as well. While Bernstorff may not have arrived at any specific philosophical conclusions as a result of his Berlin experiences, he must have perceived that the salons propagated a free, individualistic, romantic view of life that was not entirely compatible with a one-sided devotion to government. He must have realized the difference between the purposeful acquisition of knowledge (the approach of the Bernstorffs) and the immersion of oneself in culture with the goal of self-fulfillment and aesthetic refinement that was represented by the salons. A. P. Bernstorff had developed an affinity for

15. Bernstorff to J. F. Bernstorff, 3 April 1789, RA Ober Ellguth 5127/18; and J. F. Bernstorff to Bernstorff, 2 January 1790, RA Ober Ellguth 5127/7. Also see Johannes Janssen, *Friedrich Leopold Graf zu Stolberg,* 1:228–229, and 250–251. For an interesting discussion of the role of the Jewish salons in the intellectual life of Berlin, see Karl Hillebrand, "Die Berliner Gesellschaft in den Jahren 1789 bis 1815," pp. 13–81; and Ingeborg Drewitz, *Berliner Salons.*

16. J. F. Bernstorff to Bernstorff, 2 May 1792, RA Ober Ellguth 5127/7; and Julian Fürst, ed., *Henrietta Herz,* p. 102.

17. A. P. Bernstorff to Bernstorff, 12 December 1792, Elise von Bernstorff, notes, Private Archives, Gartow. On Marianne Meyer, see Hillebrand, "Die Berliner Gesellschaft," p. 15; and Fürst, *Henrietta Herz,* p. 143.

the *Humanitäts-ideal* central to the thought of Weimar, but in other ways he was far distant from the world of Goethe. Andreas Peter Bernstorff's fervent piety and the dominant role of Christian values in his life constrast sharply with Goethe's non-Christian views and pagan tendencies. The Bernstorffs' personal behavior was still governed by the kind of strict and formal moral code from which Goethe believed an individual had to be liberated to truly experience life. In short, because Christian Bernstorff's life up to this point had been narrow and sheltered, these social and intellectual associations must have given him a sense of emancipation from his more disciplined past. Nevertheless, he bowed to his father's dictates and did not marry Marianne Meyer.[18]

This episode provides important insights into Christian Bernstorff's personality. Although he obeyed his father in this matter, it would be wrong to overestimate his commitment to his father's tradition. There is ample evidence that both Marianne and the intellectual values of the period continued to be present in his mind for years to come and may have instilled in him a certain discontent with a life of service.[19] Bernstorff sometimes demonstrated a lack of intensity in his approach to politics, and this shortcoming may have kept him from becoming a statesman of the first rank. He was less devoted than his father to the day-to-day business of government and several times expressed a desire to be free of his duties. This may have been a result of normal frustration and fatigue, but it may also be attributed to his truncated youth and to the attractiveness of the life he had briefly experienced in the salons of Berlin. Too much influence, however, should not be ascribed to the distracting effects of this early period in Prussia. The Bernstorff tradition, even when buffeted by conflicting intellectual and moral values, remained intact. Throughout his life, Bernstorff was devoutly pious. Government service dominated all other aspects of his activities, and a clearly defined ethical code governed both his private and public existence. The years 1789–1794 have a twofold significance: They exposed him to the beginnings of German idealism and neo-humanism, and they demonstrated his continuing affirmation of the Bernstorff family tradition.

18. Bernstorff to A. P. Bernstorff, n.d., Elise von Bernstorff, notes, Private Archives, Gartow.

19. On Bernstorff's continued affection and concern for Meyer, see Fürst, *Henrietta Herz*, p. 147; and L. T. A. Bobé, ed., *Efterladte Papirer fra den Reventlowske Familienkreds*, 6:490–493.

In 1791, at the age of twenty-one, he succeeded his uncle as Danish minister to Prussia. Three years later, he was appointed Denmark's envoy to Sweden, his country's most sensitive diplomatic post. In May 1797, while on a special mission to St. Petersburg, he was ordered to return to Denmark. His father was dying, and Bernstorff was to assume responsibility for directing Denmark's foreign policy. On 2 June 1797, he made his first report to Crown Prince Frederick (who had been the active ruler of the state since 1784). On 21 June 1797, Andreas Peter Bernstorff died. Later that year, Bernstorff and his brother, Joachim, agreed that "the way of virtue has been prescribed for us more strongly than for anyone else; however, his example, his memory and his blessing will give us courage and strength to follow him without deviation or fatigue."[20]

In 1800, a French official wrote that, by 1789, "there had long ceased to exist any maxims of government, any federal union, any fixed political principles in Europe. . . . An imaginary principle of aggrandizement . . . had fascinated all governments. . . . The Revolution was only a loud and formal announcement of its long-determined dissolution."[21] This sense that the European system had already collapsed by the first decade of the eighteenth century was widespread, and, for many people, seemed to be symbolized by the partitions of Poland in 1793 and 1795. With the signing of the Treaty of Lunéville on 9 February 1801, France achieved a position of predominance in Europe that was unmatched during the eighteenth century, and the dislocation of the European equilibrium was confirmed. A feeling of confidence in the rationality of the European order, which had never been very great, was now completely lost. As a result, bitterness, fear, desperation, and the willingness to use power without traditional "European" restrictions characterized the conduct of international affairs during the first years of the nineteenth century.

The destruction of the European system threatened Denmark's position as a small neutral state and called the principles that governed the Bernstorffs' approach to diplomacy into question. When Bernstorff became Denmark's Secretary of State for Foreign Affairs, the political mood of Europe was not compatible with the interests of the state he served nor with his family's philosophy of statecraft. From 1797 to 1810,

20. J. F. Bernstorff to Bernstorff, 1 July 1797, RA Ober Ellguth 5127/7, and Bernstorff to J. F. Bernstorff, 18 July 1797, RA Ober Ellguth 5127/18.
21. Quoted in F. H. Hinsley, *Power and the Pursuit of Peace*, p. 186.

he struggled unsuccessfully to overcome this basic conflict.[22] The French Revolution and the Napoleonic era did not force or inspire domestic reform—that had already been initiated. However, they did destroy Denmark's security as a sovereign nation. The consequences of this development had a profound effect on Bernstorff.

He was only twenty-eight when he took over the foreign department. Andreas Peter Bernstorff had been thirty-eight, and Johann Hartvig Ernst Bernstorff, thirty-nine, when they assumed similar positions. Thus, in comparison with his father and great-uncle, Bernstorff lacked experience as well as education. In addition, he faced a more difficult situation in 1797 than his predecessors had faced in 1751 or 1773, without having inherited his father's strong position within the government. After A. P. Bernstorff's death, the influence of the enlightened ministers who had dominated Denmark since 1784 began to decline. Crown Prince Frederick no longer deferred to them and began to take an active and leading role in government. Although he was a humane man and favored reform, he thought of himself primarily as a military leader, and, over the years, he became more authoritarian. He was typically inflexible or impulsive during important crises, and he sometimes let considerations of honor take precedence over political reality.[23] Edvard Holm, the eminent historian of eighteenth-century Denmark, called Bernstorff the country's most capable diplomat and the logical choice to direct Danish foreign affairs.[24] This evaluation is sound, but it cannot be denied that the Crown Prince's personal attributes and Bernstorff's immaturity introduced a certain instability and lack of judgment into the formulation of Danish policy.

When Bernstorff took office, Denmark's most pressing foreign problem was the maltreatment of her ocean-going commerce in the War of the First Coalition. Faced with repeated seizures of Danish vessels by French privateers and the British navy, the Crown Prince decided to establish a convoy system. This immediately led to incidents at sea, to diplomatic controversy with Great Britain, and, ultimately, to Danish participation in the Russian Pact of Armed Neutrality of 1801. In retaliation, British

22. In 1800, Bernstorff became Minister of State and foreign minister.

23. Axel Linvald, *Kronprins Frederik og hans Regering, 1797–1807,* pp. 22–55; and Otto Brandt, *Geistesleben und Politik in Schleswig-Holstein um die Wende des 18. Jahrhunderts,* pp. 71–75.

24. Edvard Holm, *Danmark-Norges Historie fra den store Nordiska Krigs Slutning til Rigernes Adskillelse, 1720–1814,* 6:2:602–628.

naval units attacked and defeated Danish warships, blockships, and forts in the harbor of Copenhagen on 2 April 1801. In the armistice signed five days later, Denmark agreed to suspend all affiliation with the Armed Neutrality and acceded reluctantly to the British interpretation of the maritime rights of belligerents and neutrals in time of war.[25]

Throughout this period, Bernstorff had tried to follow the basic guidelines of his father's policy of neutrality and to avoid a confrontation with Great Britain. But, because the British were determined to control the seas and to check the westward expansion of Russian influence, it was nearly impossible to maintain a delicate balance between East and West and still meet the demands of Denmark's maritime community. During this period, Bernstorff opposed the introduction of convoys and other major decisions made by Frederick, but he could not overcome the Crown Prince's prejudices and the influence of Danish commercial interests and rival government officials. In general, Bernstorff's position was vindicated, but this was little compensation for the disastrous series of events that led to the bombardment of Copenhagen.

Although the British attack was distasteful and humiliating for many Danes, it did not affect the basic course of national policy. Bernstorff quickly resumed Denmark's neutral stance, and indeed the years 1802–1805 have been called the "quiet years." This period of tranquility came at a fortunate time, because family matters temporarily took precedence over political events. In 1805, Bernstorff decided to marry his niece, Countess Elise von Dernath, who was twenty years younger than he was. Attractive and high-spirited, the Countess was a hard-working person and came to place great value on creating a warm and stimulating environment for her family. Although intensely religious, she also had an open mind to the new literature of the day. She and Bernstorff were married in 1806, and, by all accounts, they had a very compatible marriage.[26]

<hr />

25. Ibid., pp. 289–313; Linvald, *Kronprins Frederik,* pp. 111–165; Ole Feldbæk, "The Anglo-Danish Convoy Conflict of 1800"; and Dudley Pope, *The Great Gamble.*

26. The Bernstorffs had six children—three boys and three girls—but only the girls lived beyond childhood. Their household was expanded in 1807 when they also began to take care of the three daughters of Bernstorff's brother Joachim, whose wife, Sophie von Blücher, niece of the Prussian general Gebhardt von Blücher, died. Countess Bernstorff's notes, which were compiled in later life, form the basis of her memoirs as they were published by her granddaughter. They are a useful portrait of the Bernstorffs' social and family life, but they contain practically

Between 1801 and 1807, as Bernstorff tried his utmost not to show favoritism toward either France or England, Denmark enjoyed a period of peace and commercial prosperity. But events in Europe that were beyond Copenhagen's control again intensified the climate of warfare. The ultimate consequences for Denmark were the British attack on Copenhagen in 1807 and Denmark's subsequent entry into an alliance with Napoleon. The British expedition to Copenhagen has been the subject of great dispute. It is not possible in this study, which concentrates on Bernstorff's career in Prussia, to untangle the confusing sequence of events that led to the British attack.[27] It is important to understand, however, that this act of hostility led Bernstorff to conclude that, as a result of the French conflict, the international system had become completely irrational. This conclusion made his later affiliation with the policies of the Restoration and the Concert of Europe after 1815 even stronger.

As a neutral state, Denmark was caught between the Continental System of Napoleon and the Orders in Council issued by Great Britain. When the British once again began to seize a significant number of Danish ships, relations between the two governments deteriorated. At the same time, French pressure on Copenhagen made the British government believe that soon Denmark would be forced to adopt policies that would be prejudicial to London's interests. Finally, Napoleon's victory at Friedland convinced George Canning that Denmark would soon succumb to French demands to enter the war as Napoleon's ally, a demand that in fact was contained in the secret articles of the agreement signed by Alexander I of Russia and Napoleon at Tilsit. The British became obsessed with the fear that Napoleon would seize the Danish fleet. Bernstorff's efforts to convince the British that Denmark was not going to abandon its policy of neutrality fell on deaf ears. As a result, the British fleet again attacked Copenhagen on 16 August 1807 in order to capture the Danish navy before Napoleon could get his hands on it.

The British bombardment made Denmark's affiliation with France

---

no information on political and intellectual developments. See Gräfin Elise von Bernstorff, *Aus ihren Aufzeichnungen.*

27. The best and most balanced account is A. N. Ryan, "The Causes of the British Attack upon Copenhagen in 1807." Also excellent, though pro-Danish, is Erik Møller, "England og Danmark-Norge i 1807."

practically inevitable. This change in Danish policy was made official by the signing of the Treaty of Fontainebleau on 31 October 1807. Bernstorff was opposed to Napoleon and could not reconcile himself to the French alliance. As a result, the next three years saw a series of conflicts between Bernstorff and Frederick over Denmark's foreign policy.[28] Bernstorff also opposed the crown's new administrative procedures for Schleswig-Holstein because they antagonized its German-speaking population. In time, these and many other tensions convinced Frederick that there was a fundamental difference between his aims and those of his German ministers. He became more inclined toward a monarchical government based on one nationality. After his coronation in 1808, he changed the spelling of his name from the German *Friedrich* to the Danish *Frederik*.[29] By 1810, Bernstorff had become extremely uncomfortable in his position as Minister of State, and it took only a minor incident, the Rist Affair, to make him resign.[30] He was replaced by the head of the so-called Danish party, Baron Niels Rosenkrantz.

In addition to his many disagreements with the King, Bernstorff was also depressed about his lack of success in office. As he wrote to his aunt and uncle on 26 May 1810, for a long time he had felt ashamed when he realized that he had done nothing to add to the luster of his family's brilliant heritage. But, he added, he knew that he still had to try to preserve the "sanctity of the tradition bequeathed and entrusted to me." He had sacrificed "the years of his youth, the prime of his life," and even his freedom in order to fulfill this obligation. He wondered whether, in view of all his past worries and burdens, it was still possible to find inner peace.[31] The business of government had become unattractive, and he felt inadequate when measured against his father and great-uncle. At the age

28. These are discussed in Holm, *Danmark-Norges Historie,* 7:2:5, 48, 69, 75, 156, 170.

29. Danish-German tensions in Schleswig-Holstein are discussed in Brandt, *Geistesleben und Politik in Schleswig-Holstein,* pp. 326–327; Aage Friis, "Holstens Indlemmelse i Danmark i Aaret 1806"; and Christian Degn, *Die Herzogtümer im Gesamtstaat, 1773–1830.*

30. Bernstorff to Frederick, 22 April 1810, RA Stintenburg 5128/52. The Rist Affair is discussed in Johann Georg Rist, Lebenserinnerungen, 2:74; Degn, *Die Herzogtümer im Gesamtstaat,* p. 321; and Roland Ruppenthal, "Denmark and the Continental System," p. 8.

31. Bernstorff to Christian and Louisa Stolberg, 26 May 1810, RA Stintenburg 5128/53.

of forty-one, he experienced a momentary crisis in his life and was re-evaluating the career that had been partly imposed on him.

In judging Bernstorff's ministry in Denmark, contemporaries and historians have naturally drawn a comparison between him and his father. Clearly, he was less effective than Andreas Peter Bernstorff. Although Christian Bernstorff had often shown courage and foresight, he was not as dynamic or diligent as his father.[32] But these differences in personal ability were not as important as the differences in the political environment within which each man operated. Christian Bernstorff's was much more demanding and vexing. The humane and rational tradition of the Bernstorffs' was entirely out of tune with the characteristics of the time.

## THE CONGRESS OF VIENNA

With his political career seemingly over, Bernstorff decided to retire to Dreylützow, his large estate located north of the Elbe in western Mecklenburg. However, financial need and disenchantment with country life made him ask the King for the post of minister to Vienna, which had become vacant in the spring of 1811. Despite their past differences, Frederick was pleased to have Bernstorff back in the diplomatic service, especially in a position where considerations of nationality were unimportant. Bernstorff went to Vienna with the highest recommendation of the Austrian ambassador in Copenhagen, Baron Frantz von Binders, who wrote that he was the most distinguished man in his country—a person of high principle who was also cultured and kind.[33]

For the most part, Bernstorff's tour in Vienna was depressing. Frederick's alliance with France made Denmark's position increasingly precarious after Napoleon's defeat in Russia. By 1813, Copenhagen was faced with a powerful coalition mobilized by Sweden, including Russia,

---

32. One official who knew both men well evaluated their abilities in this way: "The son was certainly superior to the father in terms of intellect and talent, but he was inferior with regard to the versatility of his training for government, his capacity for work, and the extent of his practical knowledge." He completed his comparison by saying that Christian Bernstorff was "without a doubt the most substantial in terms of character and the most kind individual that I have ever encountered in my life." Rist, *Lebenserinnerungen,* 1:133.

33. Bernstorff, *Aufzeichnungen,* 1:105–124; and Georg Nørregård, "Christian Bernstorffs afsked med Danmark," pp. 50, 59. Nørregård's article is the most detailed study of Bernstorff's personal career from 1810 to 1818.

Berlin's approach to the future arrangement of Germany. He believed that close cooperation between Austria, Great Britain, and Prussia was the only way to reduce the influence of France and Russia in Central Europe.

Initially, Metternich reluctantly agreed to Hardenberg's demands for the annexation of Saxony in exchange for Prussia's support of England and Austria in their opposition to Russia's claims to all of Poland. He also accepted Hardenberg's plan for the organization of Germany. In July 1814, Hardenberg proposed that the states of Germany be organized into a Confederation composed of nine *Kreise,* or circles.[39] Each *Kreis* would have one or two *Kreisobersten,* and Austria and Prussia would each hold three of these positions. The executive council of the Confederation, *Der Rat der Kreisobersten,* would contain twelve votes. Again, three would belong to Austria, and three to Prussia. This council was to have exclusive control over all matters concerning foreign policy and military affairs, and a majority vote was required for any decision. It also held the executive power for the entire federal assembly, which was to be made up of the remaining members of the Confederation. According to the voting system in Article 19 of Hardenberg's draft, there would be a total of forty-five votes, twenty-four of which would belong to the *Kreisobersten.* This arrangement would have concentrated power in Austrian and Prussian hands and would, in effect, have divided north and south Germany into two spheres of influence. It would have given Prussia the power it felt it deserved for its contribution to the defeat of Napoleon. It would have also enabled Austria to maintain its pivotal position in Germany and Central Europe in accordance with Metternich's desires. Finally, it would have greatly reduced the influence of the smaller states of Germany. Considerable attention was also given to the question of a federal German army. Each *Kreisobersten* would hold the supreme command over the military units of the *Kreis,* thus guaranteeing that Prussia would control the forces of northern and central Germany, while giving domination over those on the upper Rhine to Austria. Hardenberg's draft, inspired by the ideas of Stein and Humboldt, would have made Germany into a tightly organized confederation ruled by the two great German powers. It satisfied the needs of the balance of power in Europe, was predicated on the concept of peaceful dualism between Austria and

39. Hardenberg's plan is printed in Griewank, "Preussen und die Neuordnung Deutschlands," pp. 269–276.

Prussia, and also allowed for a strengthening of the German political fabric.

A modification of this draft might well have been adopted at Vienna if Frederick William had not forced Hardenberg to drop all opposition to the Tsar's plans for Poland. This shift in Prussian policy caused Metternich to reconsider his support for Prussia's annexation of Saxony and for Hardenberg's concept of a German Confederation. After much controversy that threatened to break up the Congress, a compromise territorial settlement was arranged. In return for relinquishing a portion of its former Polish territories to Russia, Prussia received two-fifths of Saxony and most of the left bank of the Rhine. At the same time, Austria's connections with Western Europe were reduced. Vienna did not reacquire the Austrian Netherlands, and, due to the opposition of Francis I, Metternich was unable to obtain Mainz and the Palatinate, which would have given Austria a secure foothold in western Germany and a major role in the defense of the area against France. Finally, instead of Hardenberg's more unified approach to the organization of Germany, the German Confederation, according to the Federal Act adopted by the German states on 8 June 1815, became a loose association of thirty-four (later thirty-five) states and four cities. This arrangement, which was backed by Metternich and the lesser states, created a defensive federation that aimed at increasing the security of Germany and preventing foreign interference in German affairs. The Confederation's major institution was the federal Diet, composed of diplomatic representatives from the member states, which was to meet in Frankfurt am Main. Its Select Council (*Engerer Rat*), which conducted most of the business of the Confederation, did not possess the executive power envisioned by Hardenberg for the *Rat der Kreisobersten*. Despite the absence of strong executive authority, the German Confederation clearly represented a more rational system of institutions and procedures than the Holy Roman Empire. But, according to the federal constitution, the institutionalized influence of Prussia within Germany was much less than Hardenberg had intended and felt was appropriate for Prussia, considering its position and strength.[40]

The German territorial settlement and the nature of the German Con-

---

40. For the German Confederation, see Holborn, *History of Modern Germany*, pp. 445–447; Ernst Rudolf Huber, *Deutsche Verfassungsgeschichte seit 1789*, 1:583–673; and Treitschke, *History of Germany*, 2:92–136.

federation set in motion a certain dynamic that was inherently unstable. The Prussian government was reluctant to accept new territories in the Rhineland and would have much preferred all of Saxony. The new possessions in the west placed Prussia opposite France and meant, as Castlereagh and Metternich had intended, that the direct defense of Germany in that region was now Prussia's responsibility. Insecurity in the west became a hallmark of Prussian policy for the next several decades. Prussia repeatedly sought to compensate for this weakness by strengthening the unity of Germany, particularly in military affairs. The new acquisitions in the Rhineland, combined with the restoration of earlier possessions there and in Westphalia, and the reduction of Prussian territories in Poland made Prussia much more of a German state. Prussia's basic interests in certain areas now coincided more closely with the interests of the German community as a whole. Similarly, because Prussia's western and eastern territories were not contiguous, a desire to compensate for this division by developing greater uniformity within Germany, especially in the areas of military and economic affairs, became a major aspect of Prussia's German policy.

Austria's position within the German system was weakened in one important respect. Metternich had successfully achieved his objective of controlling Germany and Central Europe, but Austria did not play a vital, visible role in the defense of Germany because it did not obtain major territorial acquisitions in western Germany. Austrian influence was now primarily dependent on Austria's position as the presiding power within the German Confederation. Metternich attempted to compensate for Austria's lack of tangible strength in Germany by using the presidential office and the institutions of the Confederation in general as a tool of Austrian policy. Any increase in German unity, except for conservative, repressive measures, would tend to accrue to Prussia's favor because of its basic interests and geographical position. Thus, Austria's position in Germany was dependent on the continued maintenance of the loose federal structure of the Confederation, while, in the future, Prussia would tend to pursue a policy that led in the opposite direction. Thus, underneath the concept of peaceful dualism—a principle that was often valid and useful to both German powers—an inherent tension already existed in the German state system.

As previously stated, Bernstorff's participation in these developments was peripheral. As Denmark's chief representative, he was involved in a number of negotiations, but only those that concerned the future of Germany are of interest to us. He opposed Hardenberg's plan for the organization of the Confederation because Holstein would have been part of the *Kreis* represented by the King of Hanover, who was also the King of England. Frederick refused to accept an arrangement that would allow Denmark's interests in Germany to be represented by his former enemy. Bernstorff tried to modify the Prussian proposal by suggesting a separate *Kreis* composed of Schleswig, Holstein, and Lauenburg, represented by the King of Denmark, but Frederick also unconditionally opposed having Schleswig included in any German institutions. Therefore, Bernstorff joined the representatives of the lesser states in supporting the loose arrangement that eventually became the German Confederation.[41]

In the middle of June, Bernstorff left Vienna for allied headquarters and then traveled north to Dreylützow. His task as minister to Austria and as Denmark's representative at the Congress of Vienna was over. The leading historian of Denmark's participation in the Congress has called Bernstorff an "extraordinarily fine diplomat" who represented Denmark's interests well.[42] Bernstorff's performance at Vienna, while minor, does appear to have been satisfactory. But he was clearly depressed and discouraged by Denmark's deplorable diplomatic situation. In 1814, he lamented that "our poor land is now threatened with new storms. For us there is no longer any justice or magnanimity."[43] Humboldt, who had frequent dealings with Bernstorff and liked him as a person, complained of his apathy and absentmindedness, which Humboldt theorized were partly due to Bernstorff's representation of a country that had made serious errors in policy and had contributed to its own diplomatic isolation.[44]

Humboldt's remarks help us to understand why Denmark, which eighty-five years earlier had seemed an attractive country to serve, should now become a burden for Christian Bernstorff. In 1731, when J. H. E. Bernstorff had entered Danish service, Denmark was a respected medium-sized power, important in the affairs of Northern Europe. In the 1790s,

41. Degn, *Die Herzogtümer im Gesamtstaat,* p. 350; and Nørregård, *Danmark og Wienerkongressen,* p. 160.

42. Nørregård, *Danmark og Wienerkongressen,* p. 214.

43. Bernstorff, *Aufzeichnungen,* 1:143.

44. W. von Humboldt to Caroline, 18 December 1815, Anna von Sydow, ed., *Wilhelm und Karoline von Humboldt in ihren Briefe,* 5:156. Also see W. von Humboldt to Caroline, 9 June 1815 and 8 March 1814, ibid., 4:570, 265.

the Danish *Gesamtstaat* was prosperous, progressive, and tolerant. But, in the years that followed, international crises, bad luck, and unwise foreign policy decisions ruined Denmark's economy and broke many of the bonds that held the *Gesamtstaat* together. As the federal kingdom began to fall apart, Bernstorff's affinity for Denmark also declined. Denmark's predicament also taught Bernstorff that, regardless of the efficiency and justice of internal administration, fiscal and military pressures resulting from international conflict could have a disastrous effect on the fortunes of the state. He saw his father's belief—that war under any circumstances was a great misfortune—reaffirmed. The events of 1797–1815 also intensified his conservatism. The French Revolution had precipitated the general crisis in Europe that resulted in Denmark's defeat. The revolutionary period contradicted the Bernstorffs' belief in harmony, peace, political stability, and rational, tolerant administration, as well as their attachment to the monarchical form of government. In view of what the French Revolution had done to those ideas and principles, and what it had done indirectly to Denmark, it is no wonder that an active antirevolutionary outlook, which for a time submerged some of the more progressive aspects of the family's philosophy, should come to characterize Bernstorff's approach to Europe in 1815.

## BERNSTORFF AND THE PRUSSIAN STATE
## IN 1818

The breakdown in the traditional relationship between the Bernstorff family and the Danish state was soon reflected by Bernstorff's transfer to the service of Prussia. Although nationalism, the complexity of state administration, and mass political movements have made shifts from a high position in one state to a high position in another almost unthinkable in the twentieth century, moves of this kind were not unusual in the seventeenth and eighteenth centuries. However, by 1818, it is possible to see a changing attitude in Prussia toward international civil servants such as the Bernstorffs. Since Bernstorff's transfer highlights an alteration in European attitudes toward government service and reveals major aspects of Prussia's political developments at the time, his move to Berlin has more than purely biographical significance.

The pressures of work and the fate of the Danish state seem to have taken a heavy toll on Bernstorff. He complained of poor health and was depressed over the prospect of having to return to Vienna as Danish minister. He finally decided to send a subordinate official to Austria while he traveled to his estate. While relaxing at Dreylützow, he began the lengthy correspondence with Rosenkrantz that led to his appointment as Danish minister to Prussia.[45] In her memoirs, Countess Bernstorff wrote that friends were commenting on her husband's reverse pattern of advancement; first, he had been Minister of State, then minister to an imperial court, and now only minister to a royal court.[46] But Bernstorff had reasons for preferring Berlin. He thought that the climate would be better for his health and the cultural and social environment more appealing to his family. More important, he hoped that the move would improve his deteriorating financial situation.[47]

When Bernstorff reported to Berlin in the spring of 1817, he entered a society he already knew. Many of his friends from the 1790s were in positions of responsibility. As a result of his family connections with Blücher, he was quickly reintroduced into the social circles of the city.[48] Bernstorff's spirits seem to have revived in Berlin. His official reports to Rosenkrantz were crisply written and demonstrate that he was well informed on political developments in the country.[49] This assignment also brought him to the attention of Prussian officials at a time when they were contemplating a reorganization in government. On 10 April 1818, Prince Wilhelm Ludwig Sayn-Wittgenstein, the Minister of Police and a long-time ultra-conservative official of the court, asked Bernstorff to become the foreign minister of Prussia.[50] Bernstorff evidently rejected the offer, but finally accepted after repeated approaches.[51]

45. See Bernstorff to J. F. Bernstorff, 30 July, 11 August, and 21 August 1815, RA Ober Ellguth 5127/20; J. F. Bernstorff to Bernstorff, 11 August 1815, RA Ober Ellguth 5127/9; Bernstorff to Rosenkrantz, 15 September 1816, and J. F. Bernstorff to Rosenkrantz, 15 October 1816, RA Niels Rosenkrantz arkiv 6128/1.

46. Bernstorff, *Aufzeichnungen*, 1:212.

47. Bernstorff to J. F. Bernstorff, 21 September 1815, RA Ober Ellguth 5127/20; and Nørregård, "Christian Bernstorffs afsked fra Danmark," p. 51.

48. Bernstorff to Rosenkrantz, 3 and 31 December 1816 and 3 January 1817, RA Niels Rosenkrantz arkiv 6128/1; and Bernstorff, *Aufzeichnungen*, 1:218–219.

49. Depecher 1817 and 1818, RA DfuA 1771–1848, Preussen II.

50. Bernstorff to J. F. Bernstorff, 15 June 1818, RA Ober Ellguth 5127/20.

51. Bernstorff to C. D. F. Reventlow, 10 October 1818, Bobé, *Efterladte Papirer fra den Reventlowske Familienkreds*, 6:42; Caroline to W. von Humboldt, 24 October 1818, in Sydow, *Briefe*, 6:352; and Bernstorff to Rosenkrantz, 28 May 1818,

Obviously the appointment was a new challenge and meant financial security, but Prussia was also an attractive state to work for. After a decade of reform, it was relatively progressive. Many of the innovations carried out after 1806 paralleled the similar but more extensive developments in Denmark during the late eighteenth century. Moreover, Frederick William III—quiet, unassuming, and responsible—typified the kind of monarch under whom the Bernstorffs had preferred to serve. He was a conservative force in the state, and measures could not be implemented in opposition to his views. But, generally, he let the chief ministers take the initiative in government affairs. However, a more important question than why Bernstorff decided to enter the service of Prussia is why the post of foreign minister was given to Bernstorff instead of a Prussian. Bernstorff's nomination reflected the existence of very serious political and economic tensions within the Prussian government and state, which were the result of a decade of reform and innovation following Prussia's defeat by Napoleon in 1806.

As the eighteenth century came to a close, a growing discrepancy had begun to develop in Prussia between the nature of the Prussian state and the intellectual themes and economic and political requirements of the age.[52] The institutional structure of Frederician Prussia had been progressive, but was now ossified. The mechanistic attitude that governed its operation stood in opposition to certain aspects of the German Enlightenment and to the developing concepts of German idealism. Similarly, new economic developments in the West could not be easily accommodated by a hierarchical society that restricted the economic activities of its composite groups and kept a majority of its members in a state of servitude. A discrepancy of the same magnitude was not present within the composition of Prussian society. The bourgeoisie was not numerous. It did not possess significant economic power and, as a group, did not exert dynamic

---

RA DfuA Preussen Id, Korrespondancesager vedr. det danske Gesandtskab i Preussen, II, Danske Gesandter 1808–1846. The original draft of the same letter is located in RA Stintenburg 5128/52. It is unclear whether Wittgenstein approached Bernstorff under instructions from Hardenberg, or on his own. Probably it was cleared through Hardenberg, for Bernstorff wrote to Rosenkrantz that he had been contacted through the "double channel of Prince Wittgenstein and Prince Hardenberg." Bernstorff to Rosenkrantz, 28 May 1818, RA DfuA, Preussen Id.

52. The following analysis is heavily indebted to the excellent work of Reinhard Koselleck, *Preussen zwischen Reform und Revolution.*

leadership within the national community. The nobility was the most powerful social group within the state, not simply because it had retained its privileged position under Hohenzollern absolutism and thereby continued to dominate the countryside, but also because it effectively served the state in the military and bureaucracy. Prussia, therefore, was socially and economically backward. However, the organization of Frederick's state, despite its many problems, gave Prussia a toughness and a potential for development that was unusual in view of its limited resources. Like many developing nations, the dynamic element within Prussian society was tied to the state. A progressive group of both noble and bourgeois government officials, who were often non-Prussian in nationality, became the prime carriers of new ideas and the stimulators of change. The high bureaucracy tried to remove or at least reduce the gap between the state and the times.

Their first attempt in this direction, already begun during Frederick's reign, was the implementation of the *Allgemeines Landrecht,* the Prussian law code. The chief author of the code, Karl Gottlieb Svarez, hoped to synthesize Frederician absolutism and the *ständisch* residue that continued to survive with the need to create a more modern society that served the general welfare and was governed by the rule of law. In its final form, promulgated in 1794, the law code fell far short of this goal; it tended to codify and regularize existing arrangements and conditions rather than to reform the nature of the Prussian state. Nevertheless, it pointed Prussia in the direction of becoming a modern society by rationalizing certain procedures and social relationships.[53]

Until 1806, government officials continued to attempt to complete, expand, and eventually go beyond the basic accomplishments of the code. The pressure of events in France added an urgency to their work and gained them the support of reformist military leaders, who were inspired by similar ideas and were impressed by the new military energies developing in France. However, their attempts met with little success, and, with a few exceptions, the Prussian state of 1806 scarcely differed in structure

---

53. For the *Allgemeines Landrecht,* see, in addition to Koselleck, Hermann Conrad, *Die Geistigen Grundlagen des Allgemeinen Landrechts für die preussischen Staaten von 1794;* C. G. Svarez, *Vortäge über Recht und Staat;* Gerd Kleinheyer, *Staat und Bürger im Recht;* and Klaus Epstein, *The Genesis of German Conservatism,* pp. 372–387.

from that of 1786.[54] By themselves, the reformist bureaucrats were too weak to carry out extensive innovation against the opposition of conservative elements in government and the landed aristocracy. Their efforts were guided by a concern for the power of the state, humanistic interests, and economic need, but they still lacked a social base. Georges Lefebvre, writing about the French nobility and clergy prior to 1789, noted that "these groups preserved the highest rank in the legal structure of the country, but in reality economic power, personal abilities, and confidence in the future had passed largely to the bourgeoisie. Such a discrepancy never lasts forever. The Revolution of 1789 restored the harmony between fact and law."[55] The bourgeoisie in Prussia did not possess the power and expertise of their counterparts in France. The experience of defeat by a foreign power, rather than the bourgeoisie's opposition, ultimately caused parts of the old order in Prussia to crumble.

Napoleon's victories at Jena and Auerstedt and the consequences of the Peace of Tilsit demonstrated the validity of the reformers' critique of the Prussian state. Even such a cautious monarch as Frederick William III saw the necessity of turning over some power to capable and creative individuals. Defeat called the traditional fabric of Prussian society into question, it loosened its structure, and it enabled reformers in the bureaucracy and the army to seize the opportunity to implement their ideas. Stein, Hardenberg, Humboldt, and, in the military, Scharnhorst, Gneisenau, Boyen, Clausewitz, and Grolmann were the leaders of this movement. Together they introduced innovations that represent the most extensive and intensive attempt in Prussia during the nineteenth century to meld the intellectual currents and economic characteristics of the age with the political and military requirements of the state.[56] In the course of a

54. See the article by Otto Hintze, "Prussian Reform Movements before 1860"; and Peter Paret, *Yorck and the Era of Prussian Reform, 1807–1815,* pp. 47–110.

55. Georges Lefebvre, *The Coming of the French Revolution,* p. 2.

56. The literature on the reform era is very extensive. See, for example, Friedrich Meinecke, *The Age of German Liberation, 1795–1815;* and Walter M. Simon, *The Failure of the Prussian Reform Movement, 1807–1819.* Important studies of individual reformers include Gerhard Ritter, *Stein;* Peter G. Thielen, *Karl August von Hardenberg, 1750–1822;* Siegfried A. Kaehler, *Wilhelm von Humboldt und der Staat;* Bruno Gebhardt, *Wilhelm von Humboldt als Staatsmann;* Friedrich Meinecke, *Das Leben des Generalfeldmarschalls Hermann von Boyen;* Peter Paret, *Clausewitz and the State* and his *Yorck;* and G. H. Pertz and Hans Delbrück, *Das Leben des Feldmarschalls Grafen Neithardt von Gneisenau.*

decade, they achieved important successes. By the edict of 9 October 1807, the three legal estates of Prussia were abolished, thereby emancipating the peasantry. Many impediments to the free development of the economy were removed, the educational system was expanded and reformed, and municipal self-government was reestablished in urban communities. The cabinet system was abolished, and functional, centralized ministries were introduced. Crucial financial reforms were initiated, and popular military institutions that theoretically would allow all elements in society to participate on a more equal basis were established.

Much remained to be done by 1815. The permanence of some of the reforms was still in question. Above all, a system of national representative institutions in which some groups in society would have at least a consultative voice in the political life of the country needed to be implemented. Comprehensive social and economic legislation that would make the Prussian peasant not only free legally, but also more secure economically and socially, was also needed. The future of the new reformed army was uncertain. An environment that encouraged the growth of a free citizenry inspired by an integrated sense of public spirit had not yet been created. Thus, the accomplishments of the reform era were uneven. Its most successful efforts were those aspects that aimed directly at the reestablishment of Prussian military and financial strength. Changes that tried to develop the people's capacity to participate in politics and establish freer, more humane social conditions were either less successful or failed entirely.

The reasons for this outcome are not difficult to find. First, the reform movement lacked unity. Because there were no political parties or even cohesive factions, the politics of reform was an intensely personal activity. The reformers differed among themselves in their goals and methods. The movement was fragmented, and in the absence of party programs, each issue that faced the government presented a new occasion for the rearrangement of political forces within the state.[57] The same, of course, could be said for the opponents of reform. But it was the reformers who were trying to change society and that effort required a more forceful organization and more concentrated energy than was sometimes present in the reform movement.

Second, the continued vitality of traditional elites inside and outside of government blocked essential aspects of the reform program. The native

57. See Paret, *Clausewitz*, pp. 264–265.

Prussian aristocracy still played a dominant role in the life of the state. To be sure, middle-class officials had held important positions in the bureaucracy since the early part of the eighteenth century, and foreigners had been drawn to Prussia to serve in the state apparatus. Stein, Hardenberg, Gneisenau, and Scharnhorst, all non-Prussians, had few personal attachments to land, locality, and privilege in a traditional sense. They were able to bring a broader perspective to public affairs than many men who were indigenous to the country. Native Prussians also played an important role in the reforms, but they often came from the lesser or, in some cases, even impoverished nobility. In a larger sense, their identification with state and society superseded their local ties. In general, however, the numerous landed aristocracy, despite economic and career problems of its own, remained powerful in the countryside, was integrally connected with the army and the bureaucracy, and was strongly supported by neo-feudal elements associated with the court. It formed a powerful, conservative, even reactionary force in Prussia. Provincial aristocrats such as Marwitz and Finckenstein might be defeated on isolated issues, but, when backed by the old nobility, they were able to impede the progress of reform in crucial areas. Ultraconservatives within the government—such as Schuckmann, Kamptz, Kircheisen, and General Knesebeck—performed a similar function and were reinforced by the court figures—Prince Wittgenstein, Johann Peter von Ancillon, and Duke Charles of Mecklenburg, the King's brother-in-law. Thus, although true political factions did not exist, two groups with generally opposing views are identifiable: on the one hand, a small reformist coalition constantly changing in its membership; and what was usually termed by contemporaries a "feudal" or "ultra" conservative opposition, on the other.[58]

The reform movement never had sufficient strength to overwhelm the opposition forces in Prussia. The elements of their program that were implemented were those that helped to extricate Prussia from its position of subservience to France. A free, educated citizenry mobilized in a new, reformed army was clearly required to eject the foreign conqueror. Government agencies had to be reorganized so that the energies of the population could be more directly tapped by the state. The economy had to be allowed to develop and the finances of the state had to be reformed if the French indemnity and the costs of war were to be covered. Opposi-

---

58. Werner Frauendienst, "Das preussische Staatsministerium in vorkonstitutioneller Zeit," p. 147.

tion could generally be overcome only in those areas where the need was obvious, even to the King.

If the Prussian reformers found it difficult to implement essential aspects of their program while the desire to defeat France was paramount, their problems increased after 1815. The necessity for renewal and renovation seemed less pressing once Napoleon's power had been overcome. The priorities of the state changed after 1815 from waging war to establishing peace and stability in Europe and Germany. Napoleon was the single greatest stimulus to reform, and, after his death, opponents to reform found that their objections were received with greater sympathy by the crown. At the same time, some reformers realized that, under these conditions, compromise on important issues was inevitable if the reform movement were to continue at all, and, as a result, the slight unity of the movement began to disintegrate. This was the situation that faced Chancellor Hardenberg in the years after Waterloo.

Hardenberg was a Hanoverian nobleman with extensive administrative and diplomatic experience in Prussia since 1790. He had been a strong supporter of enlightened absolutism, but he now realized that new provisions for the more active participation of individual citizens in the life of the state were both necessary and desirable if Prussia were to become a strong and progressive nation. He shared the basic goals of many of the reformers, but, as Ernst Klein has pointed out, he was more concerned with the reorganization of the Prussian state than with its regeneration, which was the prime objective of Stein and others.[59] This distinction should not be drawn too sharply. There were elements of both approaches in the work of these two men, but Hardenberg's political interests, both of necessity and by inclination, did revolve more around economic and administrative reform than around political change. He placed less emphasis on the development of a sense of community and personal attachment to the state than on the smooth and rational operation of the state and society as a whole. A parallel could be found in the area of foreign policy where, in contrast to many of the reformers, Hardenberg tended to deemphasize considerations based on German nationalism and instead concentrated on reestablishing the balance of power in Europe and strengthening Prussia's influence within the European community.[60]

59. Ernst Klein, *Von der Reform zur Restauration.*
60. Walter M. Simon, "Variations in Nationalism during the Great Reform Period in Prussia," pp. 307–310.

In general, political ideologies were less important than practical measures that contributed to the reconstruction of the Prussian state. The conflict between Hardenberg's approach to reform and that of those members of the reform group who were burdened with fewer political responsibilities was accentuated still more by the necessity to cope with certain unavoidable characteristics of the postwar period in Prussia and Europe.

The second decade of the nineteenth century inaugurated a prolonged period of chronic depression in Germany. All parts of Prussia shared in this economic stagnation. In the years immediately following the reestablishment of peace, agricultural prices were extremely low, and, as a consequence of peasant emancipation, rural society was in a state of flux. In urban areas, artisans found it difficult to sell their products at a profit. In some trades, unemployment was as high as 50 percent. From 1806 to 1816, most urban communities in Prussia lost a significant percentage of their population, except for Berlin whose population swelled. But even in Berlin, this increase was due to the influx of penniless peasants from the provinces; the number of artisans and skilled laborers declined significantly during the same period as did production for the entire city. As a result, large numbers of workers were employed by the government in road construction and other projects, and there was an increased fear of growing unrest among large sections of the urban population. In the newly acquired Rhineland, commercial activity, already depressed in 1816, declined still further in the next two years, and many categories of trade suffered from strong English competition. Leading statesmen—most especially Hardenberg and the Minister of Finance, Count Hans von Bülow—were made aware of the deteriorated state of the economy through detailed reports by government officials and by petitions for government assistance submitted by landowners, employers, and craftsmen from around the country. The liberal economic reforms of the period from 1818 to 1821 were in part a direct response to these problems.[61]

The financial condition of the state was no better. Prussia was saddled with a huge state debt that amounted to 187,971,521 talers at the beginning

---

61. For the best treatment of economic conditions in Prussia during this period, see Wilhelm Treue, *Wirtschaftzustände und Wirtschaftpolitik in Preussen, 1815–1825*, pp. 1–159. Also see Wilhelm Abel, *Geschichte der deutschen Landwirtschaft vom frühen Mittelalter bis zum 19. Jahrhundert*, pp. 312–315. For a general bibliographic discussion of the problem of poverty in Germany during the period, see Frederick D. Marquardt, "Pauperismus in Germany during the Vormärz."

of 1819. This sum was over four times the total revenues of the state. Instead of declining or even holding steady after 1815, it continued to grow from a deficit of over 8 million talers in 1818 to almost 13 million in 1819. In the eighteenth century, Prussia had based much of its security on financial solvency and on a buildup of government reserves. Thus, the condition of Prussian finances was a serious governmental and psychological problem for Prussian officials.[62] By the spring of 1818, Hardenberg, Bülow, and Christian Rother, Chief of the Central Directory of the Ministry of Finance, were all aware that the state was on the verge of bankruptcy. Only the negotiation of loans from foreign banking houses eased the country through this financial crisis.[63]

Foreign policy reflected the instability of Prussia's domestic economy. Hardenberg felt that Prussia needed to maintain the firm support of Austria and Russia and could not tolerate any disturbance of the tranquility of Europe or Germany. The slightest exertion could seriously complicate the state's financial troubles. Financial and economic weakness, which demanded a change in the economic status quo, thus resulted in a foreign policy that reinforced Prussia's commitment to maintaining existing political and territorial arrangements in Europe. Furthermore, Prussia needed international support against France. The acquisition of the Rhineland placed Prussia in an exposed defensive position in the west, based upon territories not yet fully integrated governmentally or attitudinally into the Prussian state. Such vulnerability made a close alliance with Austria all the more advisable. This in turn implied a relatively passive Prussian foreign policy vis-à-vis the eastern powers. Prussia often had to accede to Metternich's more conservative viewpoint.[64] Hardenberg's

62. See Hans Haussherr, "Hardenbergs Reformdenkschrift Riga 1807," p. 301: "In Hardenberg there still survived Frederick the Great's maxim that the power and freedom of movement of a state depend on two things, a full treasury and a battle-ready army." Prussia followed a fiscal policy of extreme frugality down to the 1840s; this policy was directly related to the government's precarious financial situation in the years 1815–1820. See Richard Tilly, "The Political Economy of Public Finance and the Industrialization of Prussia, 1815–1866," p. 495.

63. On the general question of Prussian finances, see especially Klein, *Von der Reform zur Restauration,* pp. 1–99; W. O. Henderson "Christian von Rother als Beamter, Finanzmann und Unternehmer im Dienste des Preussischen Staates, 1810–1848," pp. 527–529; Bernard Brockhage, *Zur Entwicklung des Preussisch-deutsche Kapitalexports,* pp. 102–111; and Hildegard Theirfelder, "Rother als Finanzpolitiker unter Hardenberg, 1778–1822."

64. Paul Haake, "König Friedrich Wilhelm III, Hardenberg und die preussische Verfassungsfrage, IV," p. 331.

policy was supported by ultraconservatives in the government. These men valued the concepts of legitimacy and stability and were extremely pro-Austrian.[65]

Hardenberg's foreign policy made clear his divergence from the reformers' general approach to external policy and increased their depression following the disappointing outcome of the Congress of Vienna.[66] After having failed to achieve the "German" goals of the movement at the Congress, Hardenberg had been forced to accept an ill-defined duality with Austria in Germany.[67] This policy contrasted with the ideas of Humboldt and Gneisenau, who still wanted Prussia to mount a moral offensive in Germany that, because of the exemplary nature of Prussia's progressive ways, would complete a degree of consolidation of Germany around Prussia.[68] Because of Hardenberg's divergent perception of political reality, the reformers were increasingly critical of the Chancellor's conduct of foreign policy.[69]

The question of the future of Prussia's reformed military establishment, in particular the organization and size of the *Landwehr,* reflected a similar mixture of political and economic concerns. In 1817, Bülow proposed a sizable reduction in military expenditures, which at the time consumed about one-half of all government revenues.[70] As a part of these economy measures, he proposed reducing the size of the *Landwehr* and reestablishing the pre-Jena furlough system. Bülow was not an inveterate opponent of the Landwehr, but he felt that reducing the size of the military budget was more important than questions of military structure and philosophy.[71] His rationale for eliminating part of the militia found prompt support among such ultraconservatives as Knesebeck, Wittgenstein, and Duke Charles, who were all opposed to a popular military force. As Wittgenstein wrote, "To arm a nation means merely to organize and facilitate opposition and disaffection."[72] At the very least, the reaction-

65. Simon, *Failure of the Prussian Reform Movement,* p. 117.

66. Thielen, *Hardenberg,* pp. 324–328.

67. Hans Haussherr, "Stein und Hardenberg," p. 278.

68. Simon, "Variations in Nationalism," pp. 308–310; and Kaehler, *Wilhelm von Humboldt,* p. 330.

69. The only account of Prussian foreign policy during this period is in Treitschke, *History of Germany,* 2:369–444.

70. Meinecke, *Hermann von Boyen,* 2:300. The best analysis of the issues involved is found in Paret, *Clausewitz,* pp. 286–298.

71. Meinecke, *Hermann von Boyen,* 2:306, 302.

72. Gordon Craig, *The Politics of the Prussian Army, 1640–1945,* p. 69.

aries wanted to eliminate the *Landwehr's* bourgeois officers corps and to abolish the *Landwehr* cavalry.[73] They recognized the connection between the military and the political structure of the state and, as in other aspects of Prussia's political and social organization, favored a return to the pre-reform period.[74]

Hermann von Boyen, who was the Minister of War and the author of the Prussian defense law of 1814 that had established the organization of the postwar militia, vigorously defended the concept of the *Landwehr* against the attack of Bülow and the reactionaries.[75] For the reformers, the militia was more than a fighting force that had made useful contributions during the War of Liberation; it was a symbol of the blending of national and local life and a vehicle for the participation of all classes in the political and military activities of the nation.[76] At the same time, because the *Landwehr* increased the number of men under arms that could be quickly mobilized in the event of international conflict, it helped to compensate for the comparatively small size of Prussia's active-duty army. Boyen threatened to resign over the *Landwehr* issue, but the King refused to accept his resignation.[77] Subsequently, a compromise was arranged in which the funds allotted to the *Landwehr* were slightly reduced. This had an adverse effect on the efficiency of the organization, but its basic structure survived unchanged until 1819.[78]

The greatest political issue facing the government in 1818 was the implementation of Frederick William's promise to constitute a national representative assembly for Prussia.[79] Once again, Hardenberg found him-

---

73. Meinecke, *Hermann von Boyen*, 2:305, 311.

74. Gerhard Ritter, *Staatskunst und Kriegshandwerk*, 1:138.

75. Boyen showed that in 1817 the military consumed a smaller percentage of state revenues than the old Prussian system, which Bülow held up as being more economical. Boyen, however, somewhat understated the size of the military expenditures.

76. Paret, *Clausewitz*, p. 289; and Ritter, *Staatskunst und Kriegshandwerk*, 1:135.

77. Meinecke, *Hermann von Boyen*, 2:306. Frederick William's letter to Boyen, while emphasizing the confidence which he still had for his Minister of War, also stated that "the times teach us and will continue to teach us with increased frequency, that measures adopted partly in haste now and then must be modified or even abandoned."

78. Ibid., p. 307; Craig, *Politics of the Prussian Army*, p. 74.

79. The Royal Decree of 22 May 1815 promised the establishment of provincial estates and of a national assembly that would have consultative powers in matters

self between the forces of progress and those of reaction. Hardenberg was in favor of some kind of representative body, but he was also against any reduction of monarchical authority or of his own power. His original proposal viewed elected representatives as being part of the central administration, not as a separate branch of government. At all times, he foresaw only consultative power for this national body.[80] Hardenberg was most interested in representative institutions as a means of mobilizing financial support for the state by tapping the financial strength of the bourgeoisie. Representative bodies may be viewed, in a way, as a kind of financial *Landwehr,* a mustering of national energy by the central government to answer the country's financial as well as military needs.[81] To accomplish this objective, Hardenberg was willing to make concessions to the liberal spirit of the times, while making sure that the concessions did not alter the fundamental distribution of political power in the state. This does not mean that he was less dedicated to the concept of a constitution than other reformers—he, too, saw it as a vital tool for strengthening the state—but the foundation for this desire was more financial and administrative than political and moral.[82]

The practical underpinning to Hardenberg's constitutional ideas differed markedly from the outlook of Stein, Humboldt, and Gneisenau. These men held divergent concepts of what a constitution should be, but they all tended to view the constitution as an essential institution for involving the people in the political processes of the state and for strengthening the moral character and progressive image of the nation. Political representation was a necessary and parallel follow-up to military participation by all citizens, which the reformers had already implemented.[83] Hardenberg's

---

affecting personal property rights and taxation. Simon, *Failure of the Prussian Reform Movement,* p. 109.

80. Klein, *Von der Reform zur Restauration,* pp. 170–172.

81. Ibid., pp. 166–240.

82. For example, as Boyen later wrote in his memoirs, "the production of money, this was in general Hardenberg's great assignment. If he was to accomplish this through new taxes, for loans for Prussia (thank God) at this time could not be considered, then he had to sweeten this imposition of new taxes upon the nation with added concessions and with a recognition of the new spirit of the times voiced since the French Revolution." See Hermann von Boyen, *Erinnerungen aus dem Leben des Generalfeldmarschalls Hermann von Boyen,* 2:86.

83. Stein to Eichhorn, 2–3 January 1818, Heinrich Friedrich Karl Freiherr vom und zum Stein, *Briefe und Amtliche Schriften,* 5:687.

flexibility, based on his desire to achieve very pressing needs, was interpreted by some reformers as inconsistency, weakness, insincerity, or even opposition.[84]

Hardenberg's constitutional policy was further complicated by the insecurity of his position. Since 1815, Hardenberg's favor with the King had been declining. As the immediate pressures of war disappeared, Frederick William's willingness to support progressive change that increased the vitality of the state but promised to reduce the power of the monarch also diminished. In terms of its ultimate goals, the entire reform movement became suspect in the King's eyes. His cautious attitude was reinforced by the activities of liberal journalists throughout Germany, by political conflicts over the question of constitutional rule in southern Germany, and by the nature of the nationalistic student movement. All these events and the sinister interpretations given them by Wittgenstein, Ancillon, and Duke Charles weakened the King's already doubtful commitment to a constitutional body.[85] At the same time, Ancillon was emphasizing to the King that, as long as the finances of the state were in such disorder, it would be unwise to elect a national assembly that could take advantage of the state's fiscal difficulties to wring further concessions from the King. For dramatic effect, he cited the case of Louis XVI.[86]

Hardenberg knew that this conservative camarilla exerted a decisive influence on the King. From 1817 on, he had clear indications of Frederick William's declining confidence.[87] He could not afford to antagonize the conservatives completely without endangering his political program and personal power. Therefore, he found it necessary to control the activities of so-called revolutionaries and to tighten press censorship, for which he was criticized by reformers.[88] These repressive policies,

84. In 1817, for example, several high-ranking liberals complained directly to the Chancellor about his dilatory tactics in setting up a constitutional government. Klein, *Von der Reform zur Restauration*, p. 190.

85. Paul Haake, "König Friedrich Wilhelm III, Hardenberg und die preussische Verfassungsfrage, III," pp. 341–342.

86. Haake, "König Friedrich Wilhelm III, . . . IV," p. 324.

87. For example, the King's Cabinet Order of 12 April 1817 showed great distrust of Hardenberg; see Klein, *Von der Reform zur Restauration*, p. 192. On 5 February 1818, the King reproached Hardenberg for a statement on the government's constitutional policy; see Simon, *Failure of the Prussian Reform Movement*, p. 133.

88. Stägemann, Stein, and Humboldt criticized Hardenberg's press policy. See Gebhardt, *Wilhelm von Humboldt*, 2:224; Klein, *Von der Reform zur Restauration*, pp. 214–217; and Stein, *Briefe und Ämtliche Schriften*, 5:710.

which he pursued out of inclination as well as necessity, placed him in alliance with the same reactionaries who were opposing his plans for a constitution. Thus, Hardenberg's position within Prussia was extraordinarily difficult and required an acute sense of balance, careful tactics, and great perseverance.[89]

Superimposed on this matrix of political and economic pressures were additional tensions resulting from the nature of the Chancellor's office. Since early in his career, Hardenberg had shown a clear preference for the concept of one all-powerful minister who directed the entire policy of the state and who alone had direct access to the King. When he became Chancellor in 1810, he required that the ministers, with the exception of the Minister of War, submit all communications intended for the King to him so that he alone would present them to Frederick William. This rule was officially restated in 1814 and again in 1817 and was enforced throughout Hardenberg's office.[90] The *Staatskanzlersamt,* established in 1811 as the Chancellor's executive staff, grew in size and power over the next decade.[91] Such centralized authority was necessary if the government's energies were to be concentrated and the various agencies of the state controlled. But Hardenberg's domination reduced the responsibility of other officials and thus liberal and conservative opposition to his rule mounted. In 1817, a severe ministerial crisis occurred in which Bülow and Schuckmann objected strongly to the subordinate role assigned to the ministers and in turn were stripped of most of their influence.[92] During the same crisis, Hardenberg's administrative procedures came under heavy attack from Humboldt and Theodore von Schön, the liberal *Oberpräsident* for East Prussia.[93] The insecurity of Hardenberg's position was accentuated when he was forced to modify his dominant position in the new *Staatsrat* (Council of State).[94] On this issue, Hardenberg was opposed

89. Haake, "König Friedrich William III . . . IV, pp. 328–329.

90. Kaehler, *Wilhelm von Humboldt,* p. 289; Klein, *Von der Reform zur Restauration,* pp. 248, 252–253, 282; and Koselleck, *Preussen zwischen Reform und Revolution,* pp. 276–277.

91. Klein, *Von der Reform zur Restauration,* pp. 254–295; Frauendienst, "Das preussische Staatsministerium," pp. 140–144.

92. Klein, *Von der Reform zur Restauration,* pp. 283–285; see also Paul Haake, "König Friedrich Wilhelm III, Hardenberg und die preussische Verfassungsfrage, I," p. 198.

93. Thielen, *Hardenberg,* p. 341; Kaehler, *Wilhelm von Humboldt,* p. 346; and Frauendienst, "Das preussische Staatsministerium," p. 149.

94. Paul Haake, "Die Errichtung des preussischen Staatsrat im März 1817."

by Wittgenstein, Bülow, and Schuckmann and was supported by Boyen and the conservative Minister of Justice, Friedrich von Kircheisen. The entire problem of the Chancellor's power confused political issues in Prussia and increased personal animosities. It cut across factional lines and intensified the Chancellor's fear that, in the closing stages of his career, his power might be diminished.

In the tension-filled atmosphere of Prussian politics, the appointment of a new foreign minister assumed great importance. Up to 1818, Hardenberg had acted as his own foreign and treasury ministers. However, with his increasing age, the burden of work had become too great, and he had been unable to pay close attention to foreign affairs. It was therefore decided to name Count Carl von Lottum, a conservative but essentially colorless and apolitical individual, as treasury minister.[95] The appointment of a foreign minister was more difficult. Potentially a post of great significance, it was sought by numerous individuals and factions. Humboldt was a leading candidate for the position, but he was not the only possibility among the reformists. Conceivably either Boyen or Gneisenau could have been appointed, but the nomination of any reformer would have aroused the wrath of the reactionaries. In addition, the courts of Austria, France, and Russia would have viewed Humboldt's appointment with particular disapproval.[96] On the other hand, the appointment of an ultraconservative would have roused opposition from the reformers as well as from Hardenberg, who would not have welcomed an additional and strategically placed opponent to his plans. Furthermore, a talented Prussian appointee already associated in some way with the government could increase the power of the ministers opposed to Hardenberg's superior position within the state. It became apparent that any Prussian, except for a mere technician who would neither relieve Hardenberg of much of the work load nor add luster to Prussian policy, was unacceptable.

These considerations prompted Hardenberg to look outside Prussia. Bernstorff was ideally suited.[97] Although he did not share Hardenberg's

95. Treitschke, *History of Germany,* 3:94; and Thielen, *Hardenberg,* p. 344.

96. Kaehler, *Wilhelm von Humboldt,* pp. 334, 367. Rose to Castlereagh, 19 September 1818, PRO F.O. 64/114; and Pozzo di Borgo to Nesselrode, 8 September 1818, *Russkoe Istoricheskoe Obshchestvo Sbornik,* 119:819–820.

97. Hardenberg had known Bernstorff since 1791 and was familiar with the Bernstorff family's political philosophy and history of government service. See Bernstorff to A. P. Bernstorff, 4 June 1791, RA Ober Ellguth 5127/2: and Hans

wish for the implementation of representative institutions, he would support his program of reform and renovation within the Prussian administration and economy. Bernstorff was also cautious in foreign policy, yet he had been an opponent of Napoleon. He had excellent relations with Metternich and would be viewed with approval by the eastern powers. He was a capable and experienced diplomat, already familiar with political conditions in Germany. Finally, he was concerned about political instability in Germany and advocated strong action against potentially revolutionary activity.[98] This last consideration probably prompted Wittgenstein to play such a prominent role in Bernstorff's appointment. He had only known Bernstorff since 1815, when Bernstorff's conservatism became particularly pronounced. Wittgenstein saw Bernstorff as an ally in his attempts to block the activity of the reformers. Hardenberg, on the other hand, saw Bernstorff as a useful diplomat who could possibly aid him, but would not oppose him—a man who might be acceptable to all factions and would not further complicate Hardenberg's already difficult position. Bernstorff certainly posed no threat to the Chancellor's authority, for, as a foreigner, he had no political base inside the government. Although some contemporaries and historians have since interpreted Bernstorff's appointment as a victory for the ultraconservative faction led by Wittgenstein, in reality it was a neutral move.[99] Gneisenau and Clausewitz, for example, gave their qualified approval, and Stein distinguished clearly between Bernstorff and Wittgenstein. As he wrote in November 1818, "The Ministers Count von Bernstorff and von Altenstein can be trusted with everything. Prince Wittgenstein is an opponent of all excellent and progressive arrangements."[100] George Rose, the British minister to Prussia

---

Haussherr, *Hardenberg*, pp. 63–85. When Hardenberg met with Bernstorff in Berlin in 1806, he wrote, "I had the pleasure of finding in this admirable man, in the course of several private conversations, a for me very gratifying similarity of outlook." Leopold von Ranke, ed., *Denkwürdigkeiten des Staatskanzlers Fürsten von Hardenberg*, 2:455.

98. See Bernstorff to Rosenkrantz, 9 and 29 November 1817, RA DfuA 1771–1848, Preussen II, Depecher 1917; and Bernstorff to Rosenkrantz, 24 January and 14 February 1818, RA DfuA, Preussen II, Depecher 1818, for his attitude toward popular political activity.

99. For example, Treitschke, *History of Germany*, 3:95; and Kaehler, *Wilhelm von Humboldt*, p. 558.

100. Stein, *Briefe und Ämtliche Schriften*, 6:829; Gneisenau to Clausewitz, 8 November 1818, Pertz and Delbrück, *Neithardt von Gneisenau*, 5:355; and Clause-

and a High Tory, reported that "the Revolutionists consider the nomination of Count Bernstorff as a contrivance of Prince Wittgenstein to strengthen the party opposed to them. I anxiously hope it may have that effect, but there is nothing in the Count's opinions, or character that would justify an imputation upon him of head long party spirits blinding him as to the nature of the engagements the Sovereign has contracted or as to the exigencies of the state."[101]

Hardenberg and Wittgenstein were both pleased that Bernstorff's appointment was generally well received.[102] This was certainly true in diplomatic circles, though in Prussia the reaction was negative.[103] Humboldt and the other aspirants for the position naturally disapproved of the appointment.[104] In Humboldt's letters to his wife, he condemned Bernstorff on the basis of nationality as well as on personal grounds. Bernstorff was an able and honorable man, Humboldt wrote, but he was a Dane! How could a foreigner, who had no inner feeling for Prussia's people, work for the best interests of the nation?[105] Stein was also disappointed by the announcement. He agreed that Bernstorff was honorable and respected, but, he added, it was a sad commentary on the politics of Prussia, that all the really talented people like Humboldt were passed over.[106] The most bitter condemnation came from the individualistic reactionary, Friedrich August von der Marwitz, who stated that the Chancellor had looked around for a nonentity that he could easily control. He selected Bernstorff whose façade was admirable, but who had presided over

---

witz to Gneisenau, 7 November 1818, Pertz and Delbrück, *Neithardt von Gneisenau,* 5:358.

101. Rose to Castlereagh, 9 September 1818, PRO F.O. 64/114.

102. Hardenberg to Wittgenstein, 4 September 1818, Hans Branig, ed., *Briefwecshel des Fürsten Karl August von Hardenberg mit dem Fürsten Wilhelm Ludwig von Sayn-Wittgenstein, 1806–1822,* p. 236.

103. Nørregård, "Christian Bernstorffs afsked fra Danmark," pp. 56–57; and Rose to Castlereagh, 29 August 1818, PRO F.O. 64/114.

104. Moltke to Rosenkrantz, 6 September and 8 October 1818, RA DfuA 1771–1848, Preussen II, Depecher 1818.

105. Humboldt to Caroline, 25 September 1818, Sydow, *Briefe,* 6:322. Also see *Humboldt to Goltz,* 22 September 1818, in Albert Leitzmann, Bruno Gebhardt, and Wilhelm Richter, eds., *Wilhelm von Humboldts Gesammelte Schriften,* 17:259–260; and Kaehler, *Wilhelm von Humboldt,* p. 375.

106. Stein to Gagern, 16 September 1818, and Stein to Mirbach, 8 October 1818, Stein, *Briefe und Ämtliche Schriften* 5:820, 825.

Denmark's decline and destruction. Bernstorff only accepted the position, Marwitz contended, because the King paid off his debts of 100,000 talers, presented him with the Order of the Black Eagle, paid him a salary of 12,000 talers, and agreed to a 6,000 taler annual pension for Bernstorff's wife after her husband's death. "Thus it was," he wrote, "that there came to be such a scandal in this country and throughout Europe, that in the entire Kingdom of Prussia, no one was considered sufficiently capable to guide the foreign affairs of the country, and that a Dane had to leave the diplomatic service of his country one day in order to direct the policy of Prussia the next." Even if one credited such a changeling with great ability, he would still never possess what was needed most for such a post, "namely, Prussian character, Prussian honor, and a Prussian heart!"[107] Marwitz's remarks are an important example of the condemnatory attitude of one patriotic nobleman who was closely identified with the *ständisch* interests in Prussian society.[108] Although the appointment was not particularly well received, there was relatively little discussion of whether Bernstorff was a reactionary or a liberal. The appointment, therefore, seems not to have distorted the political lines of force in Prussia and did not add to the ministerial opposition to Hardenberg. The Chancellor's purpose in making the appointment had been fulfilled.

Bernstorff's transfer opened a new phase in his life. In beginning his second career in Prussia, Bernstorff brought with him the heritage of his family nurtured in the environment of the Danish state. He brought with him personal memories and political judgments developed during the

---

107. Friedrich Meusel, ed., *Friedrich August Ludwig von der Marwitz,* 1:676–678.

108. Bernstorff's financial difficulties were considerable, but Marwitz's statement is misleading. There is no evidence in Bernstorff's private papers or the relevant government files on Bernstorff's appointment that the Prussian government assumed Bernstorff's debts. This does not mean that this transaction did not take place, but the Prussian state had debts enough of its own without adding Bernstorff's. It is worth noting, however, that the government assumed a large amount of Hardenberg's debts when he became Chancellor, so it possible that Hardenberg would have been sympathetic to Bernstorff's problem. Klein, *Von der Reform zur Restauration,* p. 243. Bernstorff did receive the Order of the Black Eagle, but his salary was larger than even Marwitz anticipated: 18,000 talers, not 12,000 as Marwitz stated. Bernstorff's wife did receive a pension, but only 1,500 talers, not 6,000. See Frederick William to Bernstorff, 16 September 1818, printed in Bernstorff, *Aufzeichnungen,* 1:246–247; and Frederick William's Cabinet Order of 12 April 1835, RA Stintenburg, 5128/50.

Napoleonic era. These, together with the characteristics of the European international community and the nature of the Prussian state after 1815, formed the environment in which he worked as the foreign minister of Prussia.

*Chapter 2*

✠✠✠✠✠✠✠✠✠✠✠✠✠✠✠

# Preserving the
# Status Quo

## THE CONGRESS OF AACHEN

In Berlin, Bernstorff had little time to become familiar with his new position. In August, following a brief meeting in Vienna, he left for Aachen to join Frederick William and Hardenberg as one of Prussia's representatives at the upcoming congress of the powers.[1] Article VI of the treaty of 20 November 1815 called for periodic meetings of the four powers to discuss matters of common interest related to the European peace. That article was symbolic of the powers' desire to make a long-term commitment to the success of the Vienna settlement and to peacefully adjudicate crises among themselves. As Charles Webster pointed out, "The Conference of Aix-la-Chapelle was the first ever held by the Great Powers of Europe to regulate affairs in time of peace."[2] The main issues to be discussed at Aachen were the withdrawal of the allied army of occupation from France, the settlement of reparations, and the determination of the future relationship of France to the great powers.

In the months prior to the meeting, relations between Austria, Great

1. Gertrud Steckhan, *Preussen und die Neuorientierung der europäischen Staatengesellschaft auf dem Aachener Kongress 1818*, p. 43.
2. Webster, *The Foreign Policy of Castlereagh, 1812–1822*, 2:121. See Webster, pp. 121–172, for the most detailed account of the conference; see also Ernst Molden, *Zur Geschichte des österreichisch-russischen Gegensatzes*. Prussia's role is analyzed in the study by Steckhan, as well as in Eberhard Büssem, *Die Karlsbader Beschlüsse von 1819*, pp. 101–128; and Heinrich von Treitschke, *History of Germany in the Nineteenth Century*, 3:105–134.

Britain, and Russia had become increasingly strained. Alexander's unpredictable behavior, ambiguous pronouncements, and apparently contradictory approach to politics, as well as the extraordinary activity of his envoys in various European capitals, were disquieting to Metternich and Castlereagh, not only for ideological reasons, but more importantly because they feared the expansion of Russian power in Europe.[3] Their suspicions were somewhat assuaged by Alexander's willingness to agree to Austrian and British proposals concerning the form of the congress and by what they interpreted as his increasing conservatism.

The major concern of all the powers was France. Russia and England were anxious to accommodate the government of Richelieu to strengthen its internal position vis-à-vis the ultras and the liberals. Even Metternich, who, prior to the conference, had attempted to hinder the reestablishment of France's equality as a great power, was interested in developing close relations with Paris to disrupt the growing influence of St. Petersburg.[4] Of all the powers, Prussia was the least favorable to French interests. Although Hardenberg was willing to support Richelieu's regime, his primary concerns were Prussian security in the west and a favorable settlement of the reparations payment question, which would help to improve Prussia's financial situation. The willingness of the other powers to treat France leniently worked to Prussia's detriment and once again revealed the weakness of Prussia's European position.[5]

The question of the removal of allied troops, which was contingent on a satisfactory French guarantee of all outstanding financial obligations, was settled easily. The date set for the complete withdrawal of allied forces was 30 November 1818. An accompanying agreement established a payment plan for France's outstanding financial obligations to the allies.[6] Two-hundred-and-eighty million francs were still owed from the original 700,000,000 in war reparations. The evacuation agreement called for the

---

3. For a good discussion of Alexander I and his approach to international affairs, see Patricia Kennedy Grimsted, *The Foreign Ministers of Alexander I*, pp. 32–65.

4. Webster, *Foreign Policy of Castlereagh*, 2:126–127; and Heinrich Ritter von Srbik, *Metternich*, 1:572–574.

5. Guillaume de Bertier de Sauvigny, *Metternich et la France après le Congrès de Vienne*, 1:188–209; Alfred Stern, *Geschichte Europas seit den Verträgen von 1815 bis zum Frankfurter Frieden von 1871*, 1:460–480; and Peter G. Thielen, *Karl August von Hardenberg, 1750–1822*, pp. 346–347.

6. Bernstorff to Lottum, 1 October 1818, ZSA Me, AAI, Rep. 6, Nr. 335; Webster, *Foreign Policy of Castlereagh*, 2:145; Walter Alison Phillips, *The Confederation of Europe*, pp. 158–159; and Molden, *Zur Geschichte*, p. 136.

reduction of this sum by 15,000,000 francs for various reasons and for the payment by the French government and its agents, the banking houses of Hope and Baring, of the remaining 265,000,000 in nine monthly installments of French bonds and bank notes.

Prussia was not entirely satisfied with this arrangement. Because of its immediate need for operating funds, the Prussian government usually sold French bonds at a depressed level. Bank notes, because of repeated fluctuations in value, often worked against Prussian fiscal interests. Thus, Prussia wanted hard currency to meet her financial obligations. In order to tailor the French financial agreement to Prussian needs, Hardenberg negotiated a special arrangement with Baring and Hope to ensure a more stable method of payment.[7] Unfortunately, the new French financial settlement caused a crisis on the French bond market. The value of bonds dropped rapidly, and the French government faced a financial emergency. On 3 November, the French minister wrote Hardenberg that France would be unable to meet the recently concluded payment schedule and requested an extension of three months. At the same time, Baring and Hope found it impossible to meet their obligations. The Prussian government now looked in vain for diplomatic support to enforce the original timetable. Isolated, Hardenberg reluctantly agreed to accept a new payment schedule. According to the new agreement, the French government and Baring and Hope were to make payments in installments over eighteen months. Hardenberg was able to include the provision that the French government would have to make good any losses in market value resulting from the new system of payment.[8] The nature and period of payment were of little interest to the other powers. They were concerned with the overall effect of the agreements on the political situation in France. To Hardenberg and Bernstorff, on the other hand, who were bombarded with memoranda concerning the necessity of an advantageous financial settlement and were acutely aware of Prussia's poor financial situation, it was a matter of major importance.[9]

The most difficult question the congress had to face was the admittance of France into the European community of great powers. More specifically, France's relationship to the Quadruple Alliance needed to be clearly de-

---

7. Treitschke, *History of Germany,* 3:82–83, 106; Steckhan, *Aachener Kongress,* pp. 47–49; and Bernstorff to Lottum, 10 October 1818, ZSA Me, AAI, Rep. 6, Nr. 335.

8. Steckhan, *Aachener Kongress,* p. 49. Also see *British and Foreign State Papers, 1818–1819,* pp. 11–14.

9. Bernstorff to Lottum, 19 November 1818, ZSA Me, AAI, Rep. 6, Nr. 335.

fined.[10] On 8 and 9 October, Austria, Great Britain, and Russia submitted proposals concerning the future of the European alliance. Castlereagh called for the maintenance of the Treaty of Chaumont as it had been constituted and for a formal invitation to France to participate in all future reunions of the powers. Metternich, anticipating the Russian proposal, agreed that the Quadruple Alliance should be maintained and that France should not be admitted as a member. The Russian draft, first submitted on 8 October 1818, was far more expansive in scope and introduced confusion and disagreement into the proceedings of the conference. It was poorly written, imprecise, and difficult to interpret.[11] As Bernstorff said, its obscurity and bombastic style exceeded one's worst expectations.[12] The Russians recognized the Quadruple Alliance as the foundation of European peace, but at the same time they called for the creation of a general European alliance, including France and all other states, which would maintain the territorial status quo and the existence of monarchical rule. Although the proposal was favorable to France in many ways, it also contained provocative language concerning the French revolutionary threat to Europe. The entire arrangement was supposed to create a moral means of maintaining peace and order in Europe to replace the material guarantee (the armed occupation of France) that had just been dissolved. The Prussians also had a prepared draft that combined features found in the plans of the other three powers. It postulated the continued maintenance of the treaties of Chaumont and Paris, but also suggested the establishment of a general defensive treaty, supported by specific military agreements, that would guarantee the territorial arrangements of Europe.[13] This draft demonstrated Prussia's fear of France as well as its concern for the security of its eastern frontier. Interestingly, Hardenberg and Bernstorff did not present this proposal at the conference. In view of the friction between the other powers, Bernstorff reported that "we have found it advisable for our part to suppress an already prepared proposal and instead to concentrate when possible on mediation and conciliation."[14] This decision was symptomatic of the Prussian representatives' lack of

---

10. For Bernstorff's anticipation of problems in this area, see Bernstorff to Lottum, 1 October 1818, ibid.

11. The text is given in *Russkoe Istorischeskoe Obshchestvo Sbornik,* 119:832–844. See also Bernstorff to Lottum, 15 October 1818, ZSA Me, AAI, Rep. 6, Nr. 335.

12. Bernstorff to Lottum, 10 October 1818, ZSA Me, AAI, Rep. 6, Nr. 335.

13. Steckhan, *Aachener Kongress,* p. 64.

14. Bernstorff to Lottum, 10 October 1818, ZSA Me, AAI, Rep. 6, Nr. 335.

confidence. In fact, they would play a relatively passive role in most major questions at the congress.

Castlereagh and Metternich both objected to the language of the Russian draft and suspected that Russian influence in Europe would increase greatly if the Russian proposal were adopted. Castlereagh indicated that his government was absolutely opposed to any guarantee of the monarchical order in Europe.[15] When, after lengthy and even bitter discussions, it became clear that acceptance of the Russian proposal would mean the withdrawal of Great Britain from the alliance, the Russian position softened. A compromise draft was produced that on most essential points conformed to the Anglo-Austrian point of view.[16] Prussia apparently played no significant role in the negotiations, and even Bernstorff had to admit that Prussia's attempts at mediation were not very successful. Personally, Bernstorff was more sympathetic to the position of Metternich and Castlereagh and was suspicious of the influence of Capodistrias, the liberal Russian minister, on the Tsar.[17]

While these discussions were proceeding, the Russians introduced another paper that specifically discussed the establishment of a general pact to guarantee the territorial status quo in Europe. Bernstorff read the document with considerable interest and even greater surprise, for, as he wrote, its contents "appear, I do not know exactly during which period, to have come from a paper originating out of our cabinet."[18] Indeed, in the winter of 1815–1816, Ancillon, as an official in the foreign ministry, had composed a *Denkschrift* proposing a European security treaty; it had been sent to St. Petersburg by Hardenberg in the spring of 1816. Its ideas were an indication of the profound sense of insecurity by Prussia in the aftermath of the Congress of Vienna. Now the essence of Ancillon's paper was being presented by the Russian delegation at Aachen.[19] Although the Russian proposal was favorably received by the Prussian and Austrian representatives, neither the original draft nor its modifications were adopted at Aachen. Concerned with security as usual, Prussia also sug-

---

15. Bernstorff to Lottum, 10 and 22 October 1818, ibid. For a full exposition of Castlereagh's position, see his memorandum to the British Cabinet in Webster, *The Congress of Vienna, 1814–1815,* app. VIII, pp. 187–193.

16. Bernstorff to Lottum, 15 and 26 October 1818, ZSA Me, Rep. 6, Nr. 335.

17. Bernstorff to Lottum, 10 and 19 October 1818, ibid.

18. Bernstorff to Lottum, 1 November 1818, ibid.

19. See Werner Markert, "Preussisch-russische Verhandlungen um einer europäischer Sicherheitspakt im Zeichen der Heiligen Allianz."

gested the idea of a European army headquartered in Brussels, under the command of the Duke of Wellington and tried to get Great Britain to continue to maintain a contingent of troops in Belgium. Neither idea was approved.[20]

Castlereagh consistently felt that the Prussians exaggerated the French threat. "They reason," he wrote to the Foreign Office on 9 November, "as if Bonaparte was still on the throne of France and as if the French Army was capable of effectuating a *coup de main* as formerly. I really think their irritability and taste for demonstration is more likely to excite the military spirit in France and to augment our danger than to add security to the general interests."[21] A Prussian *Memoire,* apparently drafted by Bernstorff, presented the opposite case. "People who knew France's internal conditions intimately," it argued, "see new revolutions as entirely possible, one might say probable." In such a case, the paper went on to say, Prussia would be attacked immediately, while the other powers would be less directly threatened. "As France's neighbor, and as a state in possession of provinces which it wants, Prussia is and will remain for a long time, the only object of its revenge, hate, and plans for conquest."[22]

These worries over Prussia's security were not removed by the results of the Congress of Aachen. In the final documents, the allies agreed by a secret protocol to maintain the Quadruple Alliance, while they publicly invited France to participate in all future reunions of the great powers.[23] The only measure taken to strengthen the military defenses against France

20. For the position of Austria, Prussia, and Great Britain on the Russian proposal, see Metternich's comments in Clemens Lothar Wenzel Fürst von Metternich-Winneburg, *Aus Metternichs nachgelassenen Papieren,* 3:159–160; Bernstorff to Lottum, 1, 5, and 9 November 1818, ZSA Me, AAI, Rep. 6, Nr. 335; and Webster, *Foreign Policy of Castlereagh,* 2:160–164. Hardenberg's role in these discussions has repeatedly confused historians. Most standard accounts credit him with reviving the idea of a guarantee treaty; see Webster, *Foreign Policy of Castlereagh,* 2:161; Phillips, *Confederation of Europe,* p. 176; and Hans W. Schmalz, *Versuche einer gesamteuropäischen Organization, 1815–1820,* p. 44. However, it is clear from Bernstorff's correspondence, which never mentions any Prussian proposal, and from the archives at Vienna, that the idea was initially revived by the Russian delegation and then was formally modified by Metternich. See also Büssem, *Die Karlsbader Beschlüsse,* p. 556n 9.

21. Webster, *Foreign Policy of Castlereagh,* 2:163.

22. Steckhan, *Aachener Kongress,* p. 91.

23. See *British and Foreign State Papers,* pp. 14–20.

was the military protocol of 15 November 1818, calling for the continued maintenance of the system of fortifications (to be supervised by the Duke of Wellington) in the Low Countries opposite the French frontier.[24] With great skill, Castlereagh had saved the Quadruple Alliance and maintained the idea of the congress system. Yet he had not committed England to additional obligations in Europe. After Aachen, the question was whether "a salutary impression of 'surveillance,' " as Castlereagh phrased it, was to be viewed as sufficient to maintain European stability.[25] On the basis of their interests, the British government thought it would be. The eastern powers, however, increasingly sought a more substantial guarantee because of their geographical position and social-political arrangements.

To Hardenberg, Bernstorff, and Frederick William, the meaning of the Congress of Aachen was clear. The end of the occupation removed the only direct allied restrictions on French power. No obstacle to French expansion had been set up that could be mobilized on short notice or might act as a deterrent. The defenses of the Netherlands were notoriously weak; a French attack could immediately penetrate Prussia's western perimeter. Bernstorff was very much aware of Prussia's military weakness, and he knew that the final agreements were unsatisfactory from the standpoint of Prussian security.[26] Prussia had asserted itself in only two areas: defense

24. For the text, see Karl Hampe, *Das belgische Bollwerk*, pp. 180–182.

25. Webster, *Foreign Policy of Castlereagh*, 2:159–160.

26. Bernstorff to Lottum, 12 and 23 November 1818, ZSA Me, AAI, Rep. 6, Nr. 335. Gneisenau was also concerned about Prussia's position. He wrote to Gröben: "The Congress of Aachen has ended; our position for the future, however, is weak. The Kingdom of the Netherlands has over forty fortresses, but only 28,000 of the worst possible soldiers to defend them. The spirit in Belgium is strongly French. The French will be able to conquer and annex this land right at the outbreak of the war. The revolution in France is beginning anew, or rather is completing itself. The Bourbons will soon lose the throne. The republicans are clearly winning more influence and we Prussians may count on having to repulse the first attack, and perhaps also the last, if our allies are not faithful.

Our situation is not comforting. The finances are not in order, the bureaucracy is so involved, overburdened, and costly that the business of state is paralyzed and the strength of the state is wasted in useless paper work. The Rhine Province has turned away from us completely and looks upon us not as its older brother, but as a foreign exploiter, who is always asking for more." Gneisenau to Gröben, 18 December 1818, in G. H. Pertz and Hans Delbrück, *Das Leben des Feldmarschalls Grafen Neithardt von Gneisenau*, 5:363–364.

and French financial obligations. With slight exceptions, it had failed to carry its point in both instances because Prussian interests did not coincide with the interests of the other European powers. Because of Prussia's weakness as a great power, the leaders of Prussia were even more inclined toward Austria and Russia, their primary supports against France, and toward policies that would prevent any disturbance of the European political order.

The Congress of Aachen signified an important shift in the nature of European politics. Before 1818, stability was primarily equated with preventing France from disturbing the status quo through revolution or invasion. With the readmission of France into the European community, there was no longer any immediate means available to block the development of a second French Revolution. Instead, the concert, especially as far as the eastern powers were concerned, acquired a more general scope, namely, that of preventing *any* disturbance of the European territorial and political status quo. With the resurgence of revolutionary energy in France an ever-present possibility, and with the recognition of what revolutionary ideas could do to their own social and political arrangements, the eastern monarchies sought to suppress liberal and national movements from whatever source.

The Congress of Aachen also marked the zenith of allied cooperation after the Vienna settlement. The drift toward pronounced conservatism by the continental allies and their emphasis on the maintenance of the monarchical order in Europe presaged the split between England and the eastern monarchies, but the degree of unity among the great powers at the congress was remarkable. As Castlereagh wrote to Berlin, "I can assure you that much of the success which attended our labors is to be attributed to the fixed determination of the 5 cabinets and all their best endeavors to remove all difficulties and to conciliate every difference of opinion."[27]

## THE ONSET OF THE
## CONSTITUTIONAL STRUGGLE

The Prussian constitutional struggle and the issuance of the Carlsbad Decrees have long stood as the foremost indications of the beginning of

27. Castlereagh to Rose, 7 February 1819, PRO F.O. 64/117.

a period of reaction in Germany. The extent to which 1819 marked the end of the reform era is one of the questions this study intends to explore. There is no doubt that the events of that year signaled the momentary suppression of efforts at comprehensive reform and led to a permanent transformation of the reformers' political program. Bernstorff was not a major figure in all the developments associated with the constitutional struggle, but he was involved in some of them. In any case, this crisis is central to the context of his work for the next thirteen years.

The course of events in Prussia during 1819 was primarily determined by internal political factors, but international pressures were also important. Both Metternich and Alexander demonstrated a strong interest in the outcome of political reform in Prussia. Metternich's attitude toward the implementation of national representative institutions in Berlin was based on several considerations. His willingness to tolerate liberal reforms in Prussia was restricted by his failure to accomplish significant reforms inside the Austrian Empire. His arguments that Austria could only perform its duties as a major international power if "morally strong in our interior" fell on deaf ears.[28] By 1818, it was clear to him that, under Francis' rule, Austria's ability to match reforms in administration and government that had been achieved elsewhere in Europe was slight. In view of Austria's autocratic and multinational character, the alternative was to combat liberal political reform and nationalistic tendencies in an effort to repress developments incompatible with Austria's internal structure and international function. The failure of internal reform reinforced Metternich's determination to press forward with efforts to control progressive political developments in areas of Austrian interest.

Stability in Germany—the maintenance of the German Confederation and of the princely rule on which it depended—was crucial. In contrast to Italy where Austria had no indigenous rival for leadership, Prussia was one of the great powers of Europe. Austria could not maintain its influence in Central Europe without Prussian support. If the liberal movement in the various German states continued to develop and if the Prussian reformers achieved all their objectives, especially those involving representative in-

---

28. On Metternich's attempts at reform, see Arthur G. Haas, *Metternich, Reorganization, and Nationality, 1813–1818,* p. 147. Also see Alan J. Reinerman, "Metternich and Reform: The Case of the Papal State, 1814–1848"; Karl Otmar Freiherr von Aretin, "Metternichs Verfassungspläne"; and Alfred Stern, "L'Idée d'une Représentation Centrale de l'Autriche conçue par le Prince de Metternich."

stitutions, a natural coalition of constitutional states based on common political and economic interests and buttressed by Prussia's strategic geographical location could develop.[29] The ultimate result would be the reduction of Austrian influence in Germany, which could have serious repercussions for the domestic stability of the Austrian Empire itself. From the time constitutional systems were introduced in southern Germany, Metternich was on the offensive against liberal and nationalistic movements. By early 1818, he was describing the revolutionary threat to Germany to Hardenberg and Wittgenstein in the blackest possible terms and was trying to persuade them that Prussia was in fact the center of liberal activity in Germany.[30] Through flattery that played on a certain ideological compatibility, Metternich convinced Wittgenstein to work directly in support of Austria's efforts to halt political reform in Prussia.[31] Later, in private conversations with Frederick William at Aachen, Metternich not only painted a sinister picture of the revolutionary conspiracies rampant in Germany and even to a certain extent within the Prussian bureaucracy, but also emphasized that the granting of a constitution in Prussia would only give encouragement and power to the liberals.[32] To increase the effectiveness of his campaign, he gave Wittgenstein two papers: One was an argument against implementing a representative constitution, and the other was a proposal for strict measures to control the press, universities, and patriotic gymnastic organizations in Germany.[33] He told Wittgenstein that he would leave it to the Prince's judgment whether to lay the two papers confidentially before the King. But he left no doubt about what he really intended Wittgenstein to do, for he told him, "Time is pressing. What is possible today, may no longer be tomorrow, and remedy is possible only so long as complete freedom of action is retained by the King." He added in the same letter that "a

---

29. See Metternich to Zichy, 21 May 1818, HHSA, Stk., Preussen, Karton 106.

30. Metternich to Zichy, 28 January 1818, ibid. Metternich's activities during this period with regard to Germany are analyzed in the introductory sections of the excellent work by Büssem, *Die Karlsbader Beschlüsse.*

31. For example, Metternich to Wittgenstein, 18 April 1818, from the unpublished manuscript by Hans Branig, "Fürst Wittgenstein," p. 124.

32. For the importance of the Congress of Aachen for German affairs, see Büssem, *Die Karlsbader Beschlüsse,* pp. 101–128.

33. See "Über die Lage der preussischen Staaten," Metternich, *Papieren,* 3:172–178; and "Über Erziehung, Turnwesen und Pressefreiheit," ibid., pp. 178–181.

national assembly made up of representatives of the people means the dissolution of the Prussian state. This is so because such an innovation cannot be introduced in a great state without revolution or leading to revolution."[34]

At Aachen, Tsar Alexander reinforced Metternich's position by distributing fifty copies of Alexander Stourdza's "Memoire sur l'état actuel de l'Allemagne."[35] This pamphlet predicted that revolution was going to sweep Germany and called for the imposition of strict press censorship and numerous controls on German educational institutions. It is unknown what effect, if any, this paper had on Frederick William, but it is likely that because of it he became more aware of Alexander's increasing conservatism. Russian and Austrian concern over the political situation in Germany is representative of the pressure that the international system placed on Prussia and to which Prussia was particularly vulnerable. Metternich's efforts to undermine and isolate Hardenberg represent a continuing aspect of this influence on Prussia's domestic developments.

It would be more convenient if the outcome of the constitutional struggle in Prussia could be described as the result of a clear-cut conflict between two opposing ideological groups—the reformers and some enlightened conservatives, on the one hand, versus the feudal aristocrats and old absolutist courtiers, on the other. This basic division on the constitutional issue did theoretically exist, but the failure to implement national representative institutions in Prussia was not primarily determined on the basis of the constitutional question itself. Instead, peripheral political, international, and personal developments sapped and finally destroyed the energy of the constitutional movement.

In January 1819, Humboldt was named to head a conglomerate ministry concerned with constitutional arrangements, provincial affairs, and a number of other matters. Frederick William; General Job von Witzleben, the King's influential adjutant; Bernstorff; and even Hardenberg had all agreed on the appointment.[36] It was felt that, after nearly a year of stagnation, Humboldt's appointment would make progress on the constitution

34. Metternich to Wittgenstein, 4 November 1818, ibid., pp. 171–172.

35. Büssem, *Die Karlsbader Beschlüsse*, p. 111; Carl Brinkmann, "Die Entstehung von Stourdzas 'État actuel de l'Allemagne'"; Treitschke, *History of Germany*, 3:127–128; and Stern, *Geschichte Europas*, 1:477.

36. Siegfried A. Kaehler, *Wilhelm von Humboldt und der Staat*, p. 384.

possible. At the same time, the King issued a Cabinet Order, drafted by Hardenberg, that criticized the Council of Ministers for their lax administration of state affairs. He also called attention to the widespread political unrest and revolutionary activity that seemed to be present in Germany, ordered each minister to submit his opinion about the threat of revolution and the nature of internal political conditions in Prussia, and asked for suggestions on how the sad state of public opinion could be improved.[37] On the basis of these directives, it seems likely that Austrian and Russian anxiety over the political situation in Prussia did make the King more sensitive to the dangers of liberal activity, but, as demonstrated by his approval of Humboldt's appointment, did not alter his willingness to move forward with a constitution. Thus, the supposed threat of revolution, as conjured up by Metternich and others, did not represent an insurmountable block to the introduction of a constitution. Poor relations between Hardenberg and Humboldt, on the other hand, were a much more serious problem.

Humboldt was immediately suspicious of his appointment as Minister for Constitutional Affairs because Hardenberg's letter offering him the post indicated that the Chancellor himself was working on a constitutional draft, which he hoped would be issued soon. Humboldt viewed this as a clear invasion of his intended area of responsibility. He initially declined the appointment, but then took pains to try to secure direct access to the King and complete control over constitutional matters as a precondition for his appointment.[38] Witzleben and Bernstorff suggested to Humboldt that it was a mistake for him to try to seize sole control of a project that Hardenberg considered the crowning achievement of his own career.[39] They were right: The arrogant tone of Humboldt's replies aroused Hardenberg's hostility. As the Chancellor noted:

37. Büssem, *Die Karlsbader Beschlüsse*, p. 241; Ernst Klein, *Von der Reform zur Restauration*, pp. 232–233; Treitschke, *History of Germany*, 3:136–137; and Frederick William to Staatsministerium, 11 January 1819, ZSA Me, Rep. 92, Ancillon, Nr. 75.

38. Humboldt to Frederick William, 24 January 1819, and Humboldt to Witzleben, 24 January 1819, Albert Leitzman, Bruno Gebhardt, and Wilhelm Richter, eds., *Wilhelm von Humboldts Gesammelte Schriften*, 17:276–280; also see Humboldt's *Denkschrift*, "Über seinen Eintritt in das Ministerium," 9 February 1819, ibid., 12:296–306; Walter Simon, *The Failure of the Prussian Reform Movement, 1807–1819*, pp. 202–203; and Kaehler, *Wilhelm von Humboldt*, pp. 352–414.

39. Kaehler, *Wilhelm von Humboldt*, p. 409.

What kind of independence does he want? He is to have as much as all the other ministers. It is only me that he is attacking. Let the King decide whether I am dispensable. If I am not considered necessary, I will gladly retire without further ado. But so long as His Majesty deems my services useful, I shall maintain my authority.[40]

Forced to choose between Hardenberg and Humboldt, the King naturally chose the Chancellor and bluntly told Humboldt either to accept or to reject the appointment on the basis of the conditions offered. Humboldt accepted, but, as Simon has pointed out, "The establishment of representative government in Prussia went by default in 1819 because the two men most anxious to promote it were personally incompatible and divergent in their political background and heritage."[41]

In February, Humboldt drew up a long paper concerning a plan for a constitution. It called for a representative system of government based on communal, district, and provincial institutions. He proposed direct elections for all representative bodies, including the national assembly. In its concepts, Humboldt's proposal was a combination of Western European liberalism and allegiance to traditional institutions, embodied in the renovated old estates. It represented the culmination of constitutional thinking on the part of the reformers; the influence of Stein's ideas was readily apparent in the principles it contained.[42]

In May, Hardenberg also drew up a short draft for a constitutional form of government.[43] The Chancellor's plan coincided almost completely with Humboldt's; the only significant difference was that Humboldt favored direct elections based on a limited franchise to select members of the national assembly, while Hardenberg preferred having the provincial assemblies elect the deputies to the national representative body. This divergence was indicative of an important underlying political difference between the two men. Both posited a very limited form of constitutional rule; both stated the necessity for continued, basically unencumbered

---

40. Bruno Gebhardt, *Wilhelm von Humboldt als Staatsman*, 2:340–345. I have used the translation in Simon, *Failure of the Prussian Reform Movement*, p. 204.

41. Simon, *Failure of the Prussian Reform Movement*, p. 205. Kaehler has stated a similar conclusion in even stronger terms; see *Wilhelm von Humboldt*, p. 414.

42. "Denkschrift über Preussens ständische Verfassung," in Leitzman, Gebhardt, and Richter, *Wilhelm von Humboldts Gesammelte Schriften*, 12:225–296.

43. For the text, see Stern, *Geschichte Europas*, 1, app. IX, pp. 649–653.

monarchical authority; and both were interested in making the operation of government more effective and efficient. However, Humboldt also viewed the constitution as building a broader and revitalized national political community—a community that would slowly be educated to take on additional political responsibilities. Despite its corporate and provincial features, Humboldt's draft was essentially a progressive document. It was a further development of the reformers' political philosophy, and it aimed at moving Prussia into a new stage of political development.

Hardenberg, on the other hand, viewed the constitution more as a refinement of enlightened absolutism. He was interested in the constitution primarily in terms of enlarging the potential of central government. He approached the question of constitutional rule in very concrete terms. How would it aid the state's financial situation? How would it invigorate government administration at all levels of society? How would it strengthen the entire fabric of the Prussian state in the European context? The political intent behind Hardenberg's draft was more limited than Humboldt's. Hardenberg tended to think of the constitution in more of an administrative sense; Humboldt tended to view it more in an educational sense. The personal differences between Hardenberg and Humboldt and their slightly contrasting approaches to constitutional affairs were a major factor in determining the course of political events in 1819. Constitutional affairs were also affected by disturbing events outside of Prussia that, under the prevailing psychological atmosphere of Restoration Europe, had a detrimental effect on liberal innovations in Berlin.

The spring of 1819 saw the first gathering of representative assemblies in Bavaria and Baden. Considering the newness of these arrangements, the inexperience of the participants, and the usual nature of parliamentary proceedings, they do not appear to have been especially turbulent.[44] However, these bodies did come into repeated conflict with their rulers and governments and, in Baden, with the authority of the German Confederation as well. The sometimes unstable and free-wheeling nature of politics in the south (Württemberg had been going through a constitutional crisis since 1817) did not enhance the image of representative government in the eyes of Frederick William. This impression was reinforced when the King of Bavaria informed Frederick William that he

---

44. Treitschke's account should be compared with that of Eberhard Büssem. See Treitschke, *History of Germany*, 3:146–168; and Büssem, *Die Karlsbader Beschlüsse*, pp. 156–184.

might have to revoke the Bavarian constitution and asked how the Prussian King would react to such a decision.[45] Replying for the King, Bernstorff explained that, if Prussia had been consulted before Max Joseph's introduction of a constitution, Frederick William might well have had an opinion to offer, but, as the King of Bavaria had voluntarily granted it to his subjects, it was inappropriate for Frederick William to recommend any course of action. However, Bernstorff did suggest that any illegal suspension of the constitution could have serious consequences for the tranquility of Germany, and he inquired whether there were means available within the limits of the law for stabilizing the political situation in Bavaria.[46] Although neither Frederick William nor Bernstorff wanted to interfere in Bavaria's internal affairs, the Bavarian monarch's predicament did make the King less enthusiastic about introducing similar, if more limited, political institutions in Prussia.

Frederick William's anxiety over German political conditions was further increased by the murder of the conservative publicist, playwright, and sometime Russian informer, August von Kotzebue, by Karl Ludwig Sand, a young, mentally unstable student at the University of Jena. At first, Kotzebue might seem an unlikely target for such an attack, but in fact, he had become a central political figure in Germany. Because he was a symbol of conservative opposition to the liberal movement and the universities, as well as an inveterate opponent of the *Burschenschaften,* his death assumed unusual importance.[47] At the time of the murder, the universities came under heavy attack for their influence on the youth of Germany, although the existence of any serious conspiracy was later disproved. Those who had been preaching the threat of a Jacobin conspiracy found ready evidence in Sand's actions and associations. The fact that some newspapers and professors defended Sand's attack was equally disturbing.[48] Partly inspired by Wittgenstein, Frederick William viewed the

45. Zastrow to Frederick William, 31 March 1819, Anton Chroust, ed., *Gesandt-schaftsberichte aus München, 1814–1848: Abteilung III. Die Berichte der preussischen Gesandten,* 39:204–206.

46. Bernstorff to Zastrow, 11 May 1819, ibid., pp. 209–210.

47. See Treitschke, *History of Germany,* 3:168–180; Carl August Varnhagen von Ense, *Denkwürdigkeiten des eigenen Lebens,* 6:28–68; Stern, *Geschichte Europas,* 1:556–559; and Büssem, *Die Karlsbader Beschlüsse,* pp. 129–155. See also Clausewitz's essay "Umtriebe," Peter Paret, *Clausewitz and the State,* p. 300.

48. Zastrow to Frederick William, 14 April 1819, Chroust, *Gesandtschaftsberichte aus München: Abteilung III,* 39:207.

entire incident as confirmation of the threat of revolution in Germany. He ordered Prussian students to return home from the University of Jena and, on Hardenberg's advice, named a special commission to investigate demagogic activities in Prussia. He also directed Bernstorff to discuss with the Austrian envoy in Berlin the appropriateness of joint measures to bring the universities under closer control.[49] The murder of Kotzebue made a considerable impression on Bernstorff. He had dismissed Stourdza's paper as being shameful and groundless, but now he, too, urged measures to restrict the activities of the universities.[50]

It is difficult to assess the effect of Kotzebue's murder on the constitutional movement. By the end of May 1819, after Kotzebue's death, most of the ministers had sent their replies to Frederick William in response to his Cabinet Order of 11 January 1819. A majority of them did not believe that revolutionary conditions existed within Prussia.[51] Bernstorff, on the other hand, after apologizing for his lack of familiarity with domestic politics, wrote that the state of public opinion did appear to be unstable. In his view, this instability was caused primarily by the powerful but transitory feelings and energies aroused among the people by the war against Napoleon. However, the present period was also characterized by certain revolutionary tendencies, and to some extent Bernstorff felt that the public accurately reflected these as well. According to Bernstorff, the task of government was to reestablish a sense of balance and order within society. The King could do this by conciliating and mediating opposing views. The introduction of a constitution was a possible mechanism for accomplishing this objective. Bernstorff was not enthusiastic about this alternative and argued instead for the establishment of a forceful and independent government willing to gain both the respect and the trust of the nation. The government, he said, should be impartial to all classes and attentive to the needs of the people.[52] In Bernstorff's case, there appears to have been little open hostility to a constitution, but, as a result of Kotzebue's assassination and other developments, he certainly desired greater firmness on the part of government.

49. Treitschke, *History of Germany*, 3:182.

50. Stern, *Geschichte Europas*, 1:558–559: For Bernstorff's critical view of the universities, see Rose to Castlereagh, 19 May 1819, PRO F.O. 64/119. Also Bernstorff to Zastrow, 23 April 1819, Chroust, *Gesandtschaftsberichte aus München: Abteilung III*, 39:207–210.

51. Büssem, *Die Karlsbader Beschlüsse*, p. 241.

52. Bernstorff to Frederick William, n.d., ZSA Me, Rep. 93, Ancillon, Nr. 75.

The reaction to Sand's attack was much stronger in Vienna. For example, Gentz wrote to Metternich that "the murder of Kotzebue is an unmistakable symptom of the degree of malignity that the pestilential fever of our times in Germany has attained. For a long time, my opinion has been that Germany is incomparably more diseased than France."[53] On 1 April 1819, he suggested to Metternich that the major powers of Germany join together to establish controls over the activities of the press and universities in Germany.[54] Metternich agreed with Gentz's evaluation and answered: "For my part, there is no doubt that the murderer did not act out of individual motivation but rather because of a secret society. In this case, a true misfortune will produce some good, because poor old Kotzebue now represents an *argumentum ad hominem,* which even the liberal Duke of Weimar cannot defend. My concern is to make the most of the affair, to create the most support possible, and in this regard I will not proceed indifferently."[55]

By exploiting the fears of other conservatives in Germany, Metternich began to create an atmosphere that would accept the need to control the activities of the press, the student movement, and institutions of higher education. Gentz and Metternich singled out the universities as the primary contributors to the growth of a revolutionary spirit in Germany. As Gentz said with regard to the *Burschenschaften:*

> As is shown in its statutes, the *allgemeine Burschenschaft* is based expressly and essentially upon the idea of German unity, and, to be sure, not merely an idealistic or intellectual or literary unity, but rather a true political unity. It is also revolutionary in the highest and most frightful sense of the word. For regardless of what one may think theoretically or historically of the present political arrangement of the German states, the unity toward which these consummate Jacobins have been striving continuously for six years cannot be realized without the most turbulent of revolutions, without the overthrow of Europe.[56]

Metternich did not think the *Burschenschaften* were as dangerous as Gentz did—he called them "an impractical puppet show"—but he still

---

53. Gentz to Metternich, 9 April 1819, Friedrich Carl Wittichen and Ernst Salzer, eds., *Briefe von und an Friedrich von Gentz,* 3:1:386–388.
54. Gentz to Metternich, 1 April 1819, ibid., pp. 376–380.
55. Metternich to Gentz, 9 April 1819, ibid., pp. 388–391.
56. Gentz to Müller, 5 and 6 June 1819, ibid., pp. 456–464.

viewed the overall role of the universities in Germany with great suspicion. As he wrote in June, "I have never feared that the universities themselves will generate a revolution; that they will educate a whole generation of revolutionaries appears to me certain, however, if the evil is not controlled."[57] Both men envisioned a frontal assault on the humanistic and political disciplines of the universities that would fundamentally alter their educational role in German society.

Metternich's initial efforts to enact repressive legislation through direct action by the *Bund* were not successful. The Austrian representative at Frankfurt argued for a drastic curtailment of academic freedom and demanded that no German state hire a professor dismissed for political reasons by another member state, but the other governments were not as convinced as Vienna that the position of the universities should be fundamentally altered. At this time, officials in Berlin drafted two policy papers on the German universities: One was by Karl von Altenstein, the Minister of Education; the other was commissioned by Bernstorff, but was drafted by his assistant, Johann Albert Friedrich Eichhorn. Both documents viewed the basic structure of the university system as sound, but Eichhorn's in particular argued that illegal behavior should be severely disciplined.[58] The Prussian representative at Frankfurt, following the instructions in Eichhorn's paper, supported a proposal (made earlier by the government of Weimar) for new rules that would strengthen discipline at the universities without infringing on academic liberties.[59] Metternich wanted to neutralize the liberal effect of higher education in Germany once and for all. Prussia and others, on the other hand, favored temporary measures to cope with a serious, but hopefully transitory, situation and did not wish to impair the basic autonomy of the universities as educational institutions.

As the discussions at Frankfurt slowly proceeded, Metternich increasingly concentrated on the idea of having the major German powers gather at Carlsbad to discuss the implementation of repressive measures in Germany. To ensure the full cooperation of Prussia (by which Metternich meant Frederick William), he arranged to meet with the King beforehand at Teplitz, where the Prussian monarch was taking his usual

---

57. Metternich to Gentz, 17 June 1819, ibid., pp. 464–470.
58. Büssem, *Die Karlsbader Beschlüsse*, pp. 285–288.
59. Treitschke, *History of Germany*, 3:189.

summer vacation. The King's concern over revolutionary activity in Germany had been heightened by the unsuccessful assassination attempt on a high official in the government of Nassau.[60]

At Teplitz, Metternich met alone with Frederick William and Wittgenstein. Hardenberg and Bernstorff had also come to the spa, but they appear to have been unaware of this meeting. In the course of the conversation, of which Metternich's account is the only record, the Austrian leader painted a fearful picture for the King: Prussia was threatened with revolution, and only the help of Austria could save his throne. Prussia must act more effectively to combat all revolutionary tendencies within its borders.[61] Metternich systematically tried to destroy the King's confidence in Hardenberg. Metternich argued that the Prussian Chancellor had served his King faithfully in the past, but was now old and incapacitated. He still had good intentions, but he consistently supported ill-conceived ideas. Above all, he was surrounded by dangerous people who furthered the cause of revolution in Germany. Metternich presented an even more prejudiced description of the Prussian government to his own sovereign.

> When one considers that within the Prussian government most and precisely the most important positions in the central administration as well as in the provinces, and this is especially true in the Rhineland, are occupied by pure revolutionaries; so it is not surprising to be able to view *Prussia* as *completely ripe* for revolution. . . . [Hardenberg had] an unfortunate longing for the most miserable and base associations. He is in such a situation presently that one can assert without exaggeration that there is not a single man in his entourage who either would not be a supporter of the most pure democracy, or is already an active participant in the conspiracy against the Prussian throne.[62]

It is impossible to say whether Metternich really believed these fantastic statements. If he was using the word "revolutionary" in its normal sense, he was merely rationalizing a policy based on Austria's national interests by covering it with all-inclusive ideological characterizations that he knew

---

60. Ibid., pp. 206–207; and Hans Schneider, "Das Attentat des Apothekers Lönig auf den Präsidenten Ibell (1819)."

61. Büssem, *Die Karlsbader Beschlüsse*, pp. 263–268; and Metternich to Francis, 30 July and 1 August 1819, Metternich, *Papieren*, 3:258–270.

62. Büssem, *Die Karlsbader Beschlüsse*, p. 269.

to be false, but that would appeal to Francis's conservative inclinations. On the other hand, he may well have viewed the consequences of the reformers' activities in Prussia as being essentially "revolutionary," and thus he used this term (or the word "Jacobin") to describe indiscriminately (but, within his frame of reference, fairly accurately) any position to the left of his own. However, there can be little doubt that his purpose at Teplitz was to separate the Prussian King from his government and from Hardenberg in particular. How successful was he?

Frederick William did order Hardenberg, Wittgenstein, and Bernstorff to work with Metternich on a written statement concerning the suppression of liberal activity and the status of constitutional affairs in Prussia. These meetings resulted in the Teplitz convention of 1 August 1819, which recommended strict measures to control the press and universities and restated Austria's demand that discharged university professors not be rehired by another German government. Prussia had clearly modified its position on this issue.[63] The most controversial part of the convention was contained in the paragraph dealing with the Prussian constitution. It stated that

> Prussia is resolved not to apply this article [Article XIII of the federal constitution] in its literal sense to her domains until her internal financial affairs shall have been fully regulated; that is to say, she is determined that for the representation of the nation she will not introduce any general system of popular representation incompatible with the geographical and internal configuration of her realm, but that she will give her provinces representative constitutions, and will out of these construct a central committee of territorial representation.[64]

What exactly did the Teplitz convention imply? It meant that, because of his own convictions and because he wanted to pacify Frederick William and Metternich, Hardenberg had decided to take a much stronger position against the universities and the press. Hardenberg in fact had a strong personal inclination toward repressive measures before Teplitz. For example, in the Prussian government's campaign against the so-called demagogues, which began on 13 and 14 July, Kamptz carried out illegal house arrests, searches, and interrogations with Hardenberg's full

---

63. The original convention, signed by Hardenberg and Metternich, dated 1 August 1819, can be found in ZSA Me, AAI, Rep. 6, Nr. 338.

64. From Treitschke, *History of Germany*, 3:628–631.

knowledge. Jahn, Arndt, Welcker, and others were persecuted, and reformers such as Schleiermacher, Savigny, and even Eichhorn fell under
suspicion.[65] Hardenberg may have felt that these measures would calm
Frederick William, thus making the implementation of a constitution and
other reform legislation more possible. But he also saw no inconsistency
between repressive measures and the introduction of a constitution. He
simultaneously urged prompt action on constitutional matters, arguing that
the government's actions against the demagogues would be counter-
productive "if it was not demonstrated at the same time that the
legitimate desires of the people are being heeded."[66] However, it is clear
that Hardenberg also genuinely feared the popular national movement in
Prussia and, since 1817, considered repression of the liberal and national
movements to be entirely justified. According to Ernst Klein, the Chancellor was responsible for leading Prussia into an age of reaction and
persecution.

> There is no evidence that the policy which led to Carlsbad was forced
> upon Hardenberg against his will and better sense. If Prussia par-
> ticipated in the most ardent manner in the persecution of individuals
> of liberal political opinions in Germany, so that happened under Har-
> denberg's leadership and request, and not because he thought he could
> in this way strengthen his own position, but mainly out of the conviction
> that the forces which had been mobilized in 1813, because they were
> needed, threatened now to become dangerous to the monarchy.[67]

This judgment, while basically accurate, needs to be qualified in two ways.
As the censorship of the *Berliner Abendblatt* demonstrates, Hardenberg's
repressive measures were directed against the *alt-ständische* as well as the
liberal opposition. Hardenberg was against any opposition that might
endanger the implementation of his programs. It also seems quite clear
that, in addition to disliking Turnvater Jahn, the themes of the Wartburg
Festival, and the like, Hardenberg wanted to control these forces so that
they could not be exploited by the aristocratic opposition to block his
proposals. To that extent, concern for his own position and policies did
figure in Hardenberg's willingness to suppress liberal activity in Prussia.[68]

65. Ibid., pp. 194–199; Stern, *Geschichte Europas*, 1:565.
66. Paul Haake, "König Friedrich Wilhelm III, pp. 357–358.
67. Klein, *Von der Reform zur Restauration*, p. 238.
68. Büssem, *Die Karlsbader Beschlüsse*, pp. 209–210.

The Teplitz convention also meant that Austria had put limits on the nature of the Prussian constitution; the internal development of Prussia had been checked to some extent by considerations of international solidarity and stability. How crippling was the effect of the Teplitz convention on the implementation of a Prussian constitution? Walter Simon compared the two texts of Hardenberg's 5 May 1819 draft with that of his 11 August 1819 draft, which was written after Teplitz. Simon concluded that Hardenberg did not give in entirely to Metternich's demands, but he did modify his original draft in ways that weakened the strength and representativeness of the national assembly. However, the new draft was also vague and left many important issues open to interpretation.

The Teplitz convention did not have a decisive effect on Frederick William. For example, the King had announced the stipulation contained in the convention that ordered the stabilization of Prussia's finances prior to the implementation of a constitution before the meeting with Metternich.[69] He also did not hesitate to move forward once again on the constitutional question. On 23 August, after the Teplitz meeting, the King met with Hardenberg, Witzleben, Wittgenstein, and Bernstorff to discuss the constitution. Witzleben was a strong supporter of constitutional arrangements, while Wittgenstein was an adamant opponent. What was Bernstorff's position on this occasion?

In a draft dated 15 August 1819, he set forth his ideas on the appropriateness of a constitution for Prussia. Bernstorff wrote that it had been his firm conviction for a long time that the promise of either *ständische* or more truly representative institutions for Germany in general, and for Prussia specifically, had been made too hastily. He admitted that there was a strong desire for such arrangements on the part of the educated and middle classes, but he felt that, to protect the social order, the introduction of a new form of government had to be carried out with extreme caution. This was especially true of Prussia whose political-military and geographical position demanded a unified and forceful government. In theory, he opposed both *ständische* and representative institutions. As he said, "If nothing had been promised, I would still today be of the decided opinion that, instead of calling the *Stände* or creating a national representative body, the King should consider giving the administration more

69. Treitschke, *History of Germany,* 3, app. X, pp. 643–647; Simon, *Failure of the Prussian Reform Movement,* p. 216; and Haake, "König Friedrich Wilhelm III, . . . IV," p. 352.

unity and strength." However, Frederick William had repeatedly promised "publicly and voluntarily" to grant his people a constitution. Bernstorff believed that the King could not break his word and disappoint that part of the nation that was counting on the introduction of representative institutions. However, he felt that the competence of this body should be restricted and that unrealistic and unachievable political expectations should not be encouraged.[70] In other words, Bernstorff declared his commitment to a strong independent government, unencumbered by outside restrictions, and his belief that the imperatives of Prussia's international position made a constitution undesirable—a standard argument used then and later to oppose the wider distribution of political power in Prussia. He also demonstrated his sense of political ethics. The King had made a promise; he must keep it. However, it is unlikely that the opinion of Bernstorff—a newcomer to Prussia—carried much weight with the King. In any case, Bernstorff did not add to the opposition to Hardenberg's constitution, and, therefore, it is incorrect arbitrarily to classify him, even during this period, with the reactionary faction within the government.[71]

After concluding his discussions with his advisors, the King issued a Cabinet Order establishing a small commission to work on a draft of the constitution. The commission comprised Humboldt, Daniels, Eichhorn, Schuckmann, and Ancillon. The first three were strong supporters of a constitution, and, as recent research has demonstrated, the other two were not completely opposed to representative institutions.[72] Thus, despite the actions taken against nationalists in Prussia and the specifications of the Teplitz agreement on which Metternich had laid such great store, the momentum of the constitutional movement was not substantially broken.

As we have seen, Hardenberg considered the repressive measures ordered by the King to be compatible with the movement toward a constitution. He told the King in July that since the measures against the demagogues would be carried out strongly and effectively, "it was, on the other hand,

70. See Bernstorff's *Denkschrift* on the *Stände* in ZSA Me, Rep. 92, Ancillon, Nr. 75.

71. As was done in Ernst Rudolf Huber, *Deutsche Verfassungsgeschichte seit 1789*, 1:139–140; and in Werner Frauendienst, "Das preussische Staatsministerium in vorkonstitutioneller Zeit," p. 158.

72. Büssem, *Die Karlsbader Beschlüsse*, pp. 228–232; and Haake, "König Friedrich Wilhelm III, . . . IV," p. 357.

advisable to make well-thought-out progress on the constitutional question as soon as possible."[73] Hardenberg's conception is a classic example of a reform conservative's attempt to keep all popular movements under strict control, while carrying out measured, carefully restricted change. His task was made exceedingly difficult by the conservative nature of the European state system on which Prussia was dependent and was further complicated by the opposition that his repressive tactics aroused in his own government.

The police actions against the so-called demagogues were controlled almost exclusively by Hardenberg and Kamptz. The various ministries that would have normally been involved were ignored. On 16 July, the entire Council of Ministers except for Bernstorff and Wittgenstein, who were at Teplitz, formally complained to Frederick William about Hardenberg's high-handed methods. This protest, made by reformers and conservatives alike, was really over the issue of the power of the Chancellor.[74] The King rejected these complaints, but Humboldt, who finally joined the ministry on 11 August 1819, was able to build on this base of opposition. He drafted a memorandum attacking Hardenberg's extraordinary power and again called for a cabinet made up of ministers with full access to the King and complete responsibility for their own departments. He suggested that the Chancellor should be reduced to being the "first among equals." He also repeated the earlier protest against the actions of the police. The memorandum was again signed by nearly all the members of the ministry. Hardenberg defended himself vigorously before the King against Humboldt's attack and was largely successful in maintaining his position, for once again Frederick William reprimanded the ministers for their attitude. At the same time, Hardenberg yielded on the question of police activities and agreed to have the police investigations more closely coordinated with the relevant ministries. This concession did much to neutralize the opposition of Lottum, Schuckmann, and Kircheissen, the Minister of Justice.[75] However, the reformers' opposition in the ministry continued. The issue now shifted to Prussia's policy at the Carlsbad conference and the content of the Carlsbad Decrees.

73. Haake, "König Friedrich Wilhelm III, . . . IV," pp. 357–358.

74. Simon, *Failure of the Prussian Reform Movement*, pp. 217–218.

75. Ibid., p. 219; Gebhardt, *Wilhelm von Humboldt*, 2:396–398; and "Über die Kabinetsorder vom II. Januar 1819," Leitzmann, Gebhardt, and Richter, *Wilhelm von Humboldts Gesammelte Schriften*, 12:316–342.

## THE CARLSBAD DECREES AND THE DEMISE
## OF THE CONSTITUTIONAL MOVEMENT

On 6 August 1819, representatives of the nine major states of Germany met in Carlsbad to draw up regulations for the suppression of liberal activities in Germany. The basic agenda of the conference, which had already been determined by Metternich and Gentz, reflected the agreements made at Teplitz. Bernstorff was Prussia's representative at the meeting. From the start, he noted that a great spirit of unanimity with regard to the political problems that faced Germany existed among the ministers. Although he did not agree with the Austrian position on all points, he would avoid open conflict with Metternich in order to maintain the unity of the two major German powers. Nevertheless, he complained that the conference's work was being conducted so rapidly that he suspected that the general consensus did not always adequately reflect the individual feelings of the participants.[76] Although Bernstorff voiced more doubts than most of those present, he apparently felt that cooperation with Austria was the primary aim of his mission.

The conference concentrated its efforts in five major areas: press censorship, the enforcement rights of the Confederation, control of the universities, the establishment of a central investigatory commission, and the development of a restricted interpretation of Article XIII of the federal constitution. Gentz based his case for a drastic curtailment of freedom of the press on a highly questionable interpretation of Article XVIII of the Federal Act.[77] By 18 August, a draft of the press laws had been drawn up and was approved with few exceptions. It called for the censorship of all publications less than 240 pages long. At Hardenberg's specific request, Bernstorff had the length increased to 320 pages, which made the regulations even more extreme.[78] Every federal state was to be especially attentive to any criticism of the political institutions or administrative practices of the member states. The federal Diet had the right to suppress publications not censored by the individual state governments. The regulations were to be provisional and would last for five years.

The conference also agreed to coercive measures to impose the Carlsbad

76. Bernstorff to Hardenberg, 13 August 1819, ZSA Me, AAI, Rep. 6, Nr. 338.
77. The restrictions on the press are analyzed in Büssem, *Die Karlsbader Beschlüsse*, pp. 311–334.
78. Hardenberg to Bernstorff, 25 August 1819, ZSA Me, AAI, Rep. 6, Nr. 338.

regulations on member states. The alternatives open to the Confederation included the use of military force as a last resort. Bernstorff initially felt that this unnecessarily extended the authority of the *Bund* and that these punitive powers should be restricted.[79] However, Hardenberg said that the *Bund* needed strong measures to enforce its regulations and that Bernstorff should not oppose its right to intervene with force.[80] The law, therefore, enlarged the Confederation's power to interfere in the internal affairs of the member states and was an early example of the repressive politics of intervention that characterized European affairs in the following year.[81]

To regulate the universities, each government would appoint a commissar to oversee the political activities and teachings of the faculty and student body. In response to Bernstorff's intervention, it was agreed that, to preserve a small amount of the universities' autonomy, the curator could simultaneously hold the position of *Regierungskommissar*.[82] Any professor or teacher could be dismissed from his post for activities not consistent with the duties and nature of his position, and those so dismissed could not be rehired by any other federal state. All unauthorized student associations were forbidden, and students who were discovered to have been members of such groups "will not be accepted in any public office."[83] There was little discussion of these measures, although Bernstorff opposed the imposition of such far-reaching restrictions on the universities. He would have preferred a protocol agreement that stated basic principles in general terms.[84] As the representative of Nassau reported, "I have noticed that the Prussian minister has not acquiesced readily to the provisional regulations contained in the *Präsidialproposition* concerning the punishment of misconduct by teachers in the universities and schools. This appears to me to prove that in Prussia the faction that has taken over the system of public education in order to overthrow the state is still influential."[85]

79. Bernstorff to Hardenberg, 13 August 1819, ibid.

80. Hardenberg to Bernstorff, 17 August 1819, ibid.

81. See Büssem, *Die Karlsbader Beschlüsse,* pp. 339–345.

82. Bernstorff to Hardenberg, 25 August 1819, ZSA Me, AAI, Rep. 6, Nr. 338.

83. Büssem, *Die Karlsbader Beschlüsse,* pp. 371–379.

84. Bernstorff to Hardenberg, 25 August 1819, ZSA Me, AAI, Rep. 6, Nr. 338.

85. Marschall to Duke William of Nassau, 24 August 1819, in Albert Henche, "Die Karlsbader Konferenzen nach den amtlichen Berichten und der vertraulichen Briefen des Frh. von Marschall an den Herzog Wilhelm von Nassau," p. 95.

Metternich also tried to get the conference to adopt a more restrictive interpretation of Article XIII of the Federal Act. This article simply stated: "A representative constitution [landständische Verfassung] will exist in all federal states." Because of its brevity, it was open to varying interpretations. Did the article permit or intend modern national representative institutions, or was it restricted to those based exclusively on the old *Stände?* The course of the proceedings at Vienna in 1814 and 1815 shows that it was primarily designed to facilitate the erection of a counterweight to the absolutism of the Confederation of the Rhine.[86] However, its historical genesis and original intent had no legal bearing; only the actual wording of the article was relevant. Metternich and Gentz wanted the article expressly restricted to *Landständische* as opposed to *Repräsentativverfassungen.* Metternich said, that this was the most important of all the questions discussed at Carlsbad.[87] His ultimate desire was for the *Bund* to acquire the right to intervene in the affairs of the German states to suppress constitutions that did not conform to his interpretation of Article XIII.

Bernstorff was unsure of the position he should take on this issue. He hesitated to accept Metternich's interpretation, because it seemed to him that this would bring the Confederation into conflict with the constitutions of Bavaria and Baden. He requested instructions on this point from Hardenberg.[88] Hardenberg replied that Bernstorff should adhere to Metternich's version of Article XIII, but only in general terms. Details could be worked out later at the impending conference of the German ministers in Vienna.[89] Bernstorff anticipated Hardenberg's instructions and had already taken such a position. But he was still opposed to giving the *Bund* the power to alter the constitutional arrangements of a state except when the state's constitution prevented it from fulfilling its rights and obligations as a member of the Confederation.[90] In the end, the opposition of the south German states caused the question of Article XIII to be deferred to the Vienna ministerial conference. Finally, the conference decided to establish a central investigatory commission, *Die Zentrale Untersuchungs-*

86. Wolfgang Mager, "Dan Problem der Landständischen Verfassungen auf dem Wiener Kongress, 1814/15."
87. Büssem, *Die Karlsbader Beschlüsse,* p. 380.
88. Bernstorff to Hardenberg, 8 August 1819, ZSA Me, AAI, Rep. 6, Nr. 338.
89. Hardenberg to Bernstorff, 13 and 17 August 1819, ibid.
90. Büssem, *Die Karlsbader Beschlüsse,* pp. 388–390.

*Kommission.* Its purpose was to investigate and report on demagogic activity throughout Germany.[91]

The Carlsbad Decrees marked the zenith of Metternich's domination of Germany. His supremacy had been made possible not only by the great skill with which he managed the proceedings, but also because his program coincided with the attitudes held by most leading statesmen throughout Germany, including Hardenberg. Bernstorff may have been critical of certain details, but, like most who were present at Carlsbad, he praised Metternich's performance.[92] Treitschke has suggested that, being inexperienced in Prussian affairs, Bernstorff had been influenced by Ancillon's ideas and, as a consequence, unwittingly supported the reactionary policies of 1819.[93] Treitschke is probably incorrect; Bernstorff had known Ancillon since 1791 and was familiar with his political prejudices. Bernstorff supported repressive policies because, like Hardenberg, he believed that they were necessary, not because he was duped. He felt that some sort of federal disciplinary program was essential to maintain the political stability of Germany. The international imperative of cooperation with Austria merely reinforced this desire. His belief that some restrictions on liberal activity were needed was founded on experience more than ideology. However, there can be no doubt that this represented a departure from some of the basic values of the Bernstorff heritage. A. P. Bernstorff had extolled the virtues of a free press and believed in tolerating diverse political philosophies. When fear of revolution and war caused Christian Bernstorff to abandon these principles, some of his friends in Denmark viewed his activities as a betrayal of his family heritage.[94]

When Bernstorff returned to Berlin, he and Hardenberg were faced with opposition from Humboldt, who presented a *Denkschrift* attacking the Carlsbad Decrees on 5 October. He condemned them most for infringing the sovereignty of the Prussian state. He wrote: "It is no longer a question of temporary measures against the agitation of a number of deluded, misled, or deliberately troublesome persons, it is a question of the extension of the power of the federal Diet, a diminution of the rights of Your Royal Majesty over your subjects, and a decrease in the sovereignty

---

91. See Eberhard Weber, *Die Mainzer Zentraluntersuchungskommission,* pp. 5–18.
92. Bernstorff to Hardenberg, 2 September 1819, ZSA Me, AAI, Rep. 6, Nr. 338.
93. Treitschke, *History of Germany,* 3:97.
94. See Hegewisch to Bernstorff, 18 November 1821, RA Stintenburg 5128/50.

of the monarchy."[95] He was also critical of the content of the new regulations, but was willing to approve them as extraordinary measures valid for two years. Finally, he argued that the foreign minister should be required to consult with the ministry on any foreign policy decision that affected domestic policy.

Bernstorff defended himself against Humboldt's criticism in a detailed *votum* to the *Staatsministerium*. The conference had been based on the assumption, which Bernstorff believed to be valid, that serious problems existed in Germany. The states represented at Carlsbad had agreed that something must be done to control political excesses within the Confederation; the question was whether Prussia should be part of this general consensus. Bernstorff argued that Prussia was part of Germany. Because its domestic and foreign relations were integrally bound to the German state system, Prussia had to accede to special considerations based on the interests of the entire community. But Prussia also derived significant gains from doing so. The Confederation was predicated on Prussia's cooperation with Austria. "It would be in my opinion," he wrote, "a risky and inexpedient beginning for Prussia to isolate itself at the Diet in opposition to Austria, or in connection with other federal states to want to effect a systematic opposition to that same power." He denied that the Carlsbad Decrees exceeded the legal provisions of the Federal Act.[96]

Although the Cabinet did not agree to approve the Carlsbad Decrees, it did vote down Humboldt's proposal, with only Boyen and Beyme dissenting. None of the opposing ministers declared outright that the decrees were unnecessary or were based on false or exaggerated fears. The opposition to the Carlsbad Decrees was primarily anti-Austrian in tone and, because the King had done much to shape the basic orientation of Prussia's foreign policy, was pointed at Frederick William as well as Hardenberg. What was really at stake was the extent to which European and German considerations should be allowed to affect Prussia's internal policy.[97] Behind this issue loomed the larger question of the effect these measures would have on the national community in Prussia and

95. "Über die Karlsbader Beschlüsse," Leitzmann, Gebhardt, and Richter, *Wilhelm von Humboldts Gesammelte Schriften*, 13:364.

96. Bernstorff *votum* to *Staatsministerium*, n.d., ZSA Me, Rep. 92, Ancillon, Nr. 76.

97. Some of those with strong reformist tendencies conceded the need for some sort of repressive measures. Gneisenau, for example, who attempted to adopt a

Germany. For Humboldt, who was vitally concerned about popular attitudes toward the state, the Carlsbad Decrees fundamentally altered the progressive nature of Prussia's political institutions and represented a major infringement on important civil rights.

Already in disagreement over the Carlsbad Decrees, the disunity of the ministry, which was inhibiting work on the constitution, was further exacerbated by a second controversy over the future of the *Landwehr*. Duke Charles, General Borstell, and other opponents of the militia continued to argue that it was an unnecessary and dangerous organization. For various reasons since the 1817 financial crisis, the King's opinion of both the *Landwehr* and Boyen had declined. Therefore, early in the year, Frederick William, despite Witzleben's opposition, decided privately to amalgamate the line and *Landwehr*. In December, he ordered the disbanding of roughly one-fourth of the *Landwehr* regiments and a basic reorganization of the militia, which resulted in the loss of a considerable part of its independent status. Boyen immediately attacked the royal order. Such a reorganization, he said, in effect meant the end of a popular militia in Prussia. Rather than participate in a change that negated one of the key concepts of the entire reform program, he decided to resign. The King, probably resentful over Boyen's stand on the Carlsbad Decrees and concerned about his anti-Austrian feelings, allowed Boyen to leave office. Grolmann, Boyen's closest associate, resigned at the same time.[98] It appears that Hardenberg had no hand in Boyen's dismissal, but there can be no doubt he was happy over the resignation of the Minister of

---

position midway between Hardenberg and his critics, wrote in regard to the Carlsbad Decrees: "In view of the seriousness of the danger the ministers cannot be blamed for them since the investigations seem to show that there really has been talk of one indivisible German Republic, of this end justifying all means, even the most bloody, of the murders of German rulers. Every unprejudiced person must be struck by the frequency with which otherwise responsible people have defended Kotzebue's assassination." Gneisenau to Princess Radziwill, 20 November 1819. For Gneisenau's very detached but sound approach to the political controversies of 1819, see his letter to Princess Radziwill of 22 October 1819. Both are in Pertz and Delbrück, *Neithardt von Gneisenau,* 5:379–387.

98. Friedrich Meinecke, *Das Leben des Generalfeldmarschalls Hermann von Boyen,* 2:380–388; Gordon Craig, *The Politics of the Prussian Army, 1640–1945,* pp. 74–75; Simon, *Failure of the Prussian Reform Movement,* pp. 220–221; and Paret, *Clausewitz,* p. 292.

War. As Hardenberg wrote in his diary, "The Minister of War has gone; this is a big step, but to no avail if Beyme and Humboldt stay together. B. and H. must be dismissed."[99]

The resignation of Boyen severely weakened Humboldt's position in the government. His relations with Hardenberg declined further as a result of another conflict over the issue of taxation.[100] Hardenberg was in the final stages of pushing through a new law on taxation and on the regulation of the national debt. Along with the customs law of 26 May 1818, it comprised a major reorganization of the Prussian financial system. Humboldt, who continued to believe erroneously that there was no deficit in Prussia, considered the new taxes unnecessary. At the same time, he and Beyme had succeeded in passing a resolution in the ministry summoning the *Oberpräsidenten* to Berlin for consultation. Hardenberg knew that most of these senior officials opposed his financial reforms and that many would ally with Humboldt. This maneuver seemed like a clear-cut attempt not only to undermine his power, but also to block regulations that were essential for the fiscal stability of the state. Unless fiscal stability were achieved, the King would not allow a national representative assembly to be convened. Humboldt and his supporters were primarily concerned with not overtaxing the people, but by opposing Hardenberg on the taxation issue, they in effect allied themselves with the provincial aristocracy, Wittgenstein, and others who feared the consequences of Hardenberg's liberal economic and financial reforms. The impasse in the ministry was broken when Hardenberg asked the King to dismiss Humboldt and Beyme. He wrote Frederick William, "I am more convinced hourly . . . that there is no other solution but to either firmly maintain the present administration at whose head Your Royal Majesty's high confidence has placed me, or else to yield to those men and to dismiss me."[101] The King removed Humboldt and Beyme from office on 31 December 1819.

Bernstorff did not express any enthusiasm over the dismissal of Hum-

99. Eberhard Kessel, "Zu Boyen's Entlassung," pp. 51–54; and Simon, *Failure of the Prussian Reform Movement*, p. 221.

100. For an excellent analysis of the extraordinarily complicated financial, provincial, *ständische*, and constitutional factors, see Reinhard Koselleck, *Preussen zwischen Reform und Revolution*, pp. 311–332. Also see Treitschke, *History of Germany*, 3:273–274.

101. Simon, *Failure of the Prussian Reform Movement*, p. 222.

boldt and Beyme, and, in fact, Hardenberg appears to have feared that Bernstorff might be critical of the actions. But Bernstorff told him that the dismissal of the two ministers would not affect the relationship between Hardenberg and himself. He realized that the Chancellor had done what he felt was necessary.[102]

However, the removal of the three most powerful members of the reform movement meant that Hardenberg found himself without support for his plans for a constitution. As a result, the work of the constitutional committee was crippled. Based on the recommendation of a new committee dominated by Hardenberg's opponents, Frederick William notified the Chancellor on 11 July 1821 that no national assembly would be instituted and that Prussia would erect only provincial assemblies. The King said that the calling of such a body was abandoned because of "the times, experience, recent developments, and my concern as a sovereign."[103] In 1823, eight traditionally constituted provincial assemblies were erected in Prussia.

The idea of a constitution died quickly after Humboldt's dismissal. As we have seen, Humboldt's departure was the result of many developments. The change in the international system after 1818, the turbulent proceedings in the south German parliaments, two acts of violence, fiscal and military controversies as well as strong personal animosity between Hardenberg and Humboldt all contributed to the outcome of 1819. The Carlsbad Decrees, the repressive measures instituted in Prussia by Hardenberg, and Berlin's close association with Vienna did not directly block the implementation of a constitution, but they did disrupt the unity of the reformist movement and diverted attention away from constitutional affairs. While the cumulative effect of these developments was the creation of massive negative pressure against the basic thrust of the reform movement, the constitution per se was never the major political issue. For example, a memorandum on the ministerial crisis, written in December 1819 by Hardenberg, lists the Carlsbad Decrees, financial and tax matters, the actions of the *Oberpräsidenten,* and attacks on his administra-

---

102. Bernstorff to Hardenberg, 12 January 1819, ZSA Me, AAI, Rep. 1, Nr. 31. Bernstorff was also shocked by the earlier dismissal of Boyen. See Bernstorff to Hardenberg, 25 December 1819, ibid.

103. Paul Haake, "König Friedrich Wilhelm III, Hardenberg und die preussische Verfassungsfrage, V," p. 170.

tion as the primary causes of the crisis; the constitution is not mentioned at all.[104]

This is not to say there were no important connections between these controversies and the constitutional question. The Carlsbad Decrees are an obvious example, and, as Walter Simon has stated, the question of the Chancellor's power was intimately involved with the entire constitutional issue. He writes, "To Humboldt a national assembly was meaningful only if all the ministers were responsible to it; Hardenberg, on the other hand, would not hear of abolishing the office of the Chancellor which he occupied, even if it was an anomaly in a new constitution. While both men by their actions contributed to the sacrificing of the constitution, Humboldt sacrificed it for an idea, whereas Hardenberg sacrificed it, ultimately, to maintain his personal power."[105] This is certainly true, but Humboldt had political ambitions of his own, and Hardenberg was motivated by an idea as well. For him, a powerful executive, like a constitution, was an essential aspect of effective government administration. This emphasis on the power of central government set him apart from Humboldt and also caused feudal aristocrats initially to welcome Humboldt's appointment to the government in 1819 as a counterpoise to the Chancellor. As a result, Humboldt became an ally of the conservatives in the ministry in the fall of 1819. Hardenberg was defending a political concept as well as his personal position.

Historians have put forth various explanations for the demise of the constitutional movement in Prussia. Until recently, most of them have concentrated on Hardenberg's role. The most authoritative account has been that of Friedrich Meinecke, who argued that Hardenberg bears the chief responsibility for the failure of constitutionalism in 1819. "A liberal policy carried on by illiberal means was an intrinsic impossibility."[106] Walter Simon ended his examination of the Prussian reform movement with the same conclusion.[107] The basic validity of this argument cannot

104. Treitschke, *History of Germany*, 3, app. XI, pp. 647–648.
105. Simon, *Failure of the Prussian Reform Movement*, p. 223.
106. Meinecke, *Hermann von Boyen*, 2:370.
107. Simon, *Failure of the Prussian Reform Movement*, pp. 222–228. The contrasting contentions of Ernst Klein, that Hardenberg's commitment to liberal political reform lacked depth and of Paul Haake, that Hardenberg's repressive policies in 1819 actually enhanced the chances of implementing a constitution in

be denied. Hardenberg's tactics and prejudices led to the dissipation of the energy of the reform movement and played into the hands of his opponents.

On the other hand, Meinecke's explanation places too great an importance on Hardenberg as an individual. Other factors, broader in scope, were of equal importance. As Simon had noted, and as Reinhard Koselleck has exhaustively demonstrated, no true base for constitutionalism existed in Prussia.[108] The middle classes, needed to provide a foundation for political reform, could only acquire the requisite strength as a consequence of the economic and educational reforms that the enlightened bureaucracy was in the process of introducing. The middle classes could not create sufficient pressure on the monarchy to create a level of fear sufficient to convince Frederick William that there was no alternative to constitutional rule. On the other hand, the pressure of the *altständische* aristocracy and of neo-feudal elements within the government was substantial. The contradictory nature of Hardenberg's policies can be seen as a reflection of an underlying uncertainty that even the reformist bureaucracy entertained toward constitutional rule. Dependent on the state and the power of government, they were often ambivalent toward a development that could ultimately threaten their status and influence.

Simon and others have argued that Hardenberg should have fought with determination against the machinations of Wittgenstein and Metternich instead of adopting their approach to politics. That criticism overestimates both the security of Hardenberg's position as Chancellor and the security of the Prussian state as a member of the European community. Hardenberg did not possess the King's full confidence, and the fate of Boyen in 1819 demonstrates the risks of pursuing policies that were incompatible with the King's basic prejudices. Moreover, 1819 was not a good year for political reform. The Prussian constitutional movement was swimming against a tide of conservatism that was engulfing Europe. This change in the *Zeitgeist* need not have had a significant effect on the course of political reform in Berlin, but, when tied to the international insecurity of the Prussian state, it formed a powerful force against con-

---

1820, are both exaggerated. See Klein, *Von der Reform zur Restauration,* pp. 313–317; and Haake, "König Friedrich Wilhelm III, Hardenberg und die preussische Verfassungsfrage," parts 4 and 5.

108. Simon, *Failure of the Prussian Reform Movement,* pp. 236–237; and Koselleck, *Preussen zwischen Reform und Revolution,* pp. 283–332.

stitutionalism. For Frederick William, the introduction of new political arrangements was a step into the unknown, a step that could conceivably not only reduce the power of the monarchy, but could damage Prussia's close relations with its most important allies. Because no final guarantee for the territorial status quo in Europe had been created at Aachen, Prussia remained dependent on Austria and Russia. England was clearly reluctant to be involved in continental affairs, and France was the power that threatened Prussia the most. There appeared, therefore, to be little alternative to the orientation of Prussian foreign policy toward Austria and Russia. This orientation gave Metternich the opportunity to work with Wittgenstein and others to impede political reform in Berlin. Considerations of security made it difficult for Hardenberg, even if he had been so inclined, to openly oppose the policies of Vienna. England also contributed in small but significant ways to the conservative atmosphere that pressed on Berlin. For example, in 1819, when Clausewitz was proposed for the position of envoy to Great Britain, Rose, the British minister to Berlin, opposed the appointment on the grounds that Clausewitz held liberal political views and was personally unsuited for the post. He worked with the Austrian ambassador and conservative figures in the Berlin court, such as Wittgenstein, to create the impression that Britain viewed Clausewitz as politically dangerous—as a man whose appointment would damage relations between the two courts and hamper the operation of the international system. Rose's activities were the primary reason that Clausewitz did not receive the appointment, despite the fact that it was initially supported by Hardenberg, Bernstorff, and Gneisenau.[109]

109. See Paret, *Clausewitz,* pp. 319–323, and Paret, "Bemerkungen zu dem Versuch von Clausewitz, zum Gesandten in London ernannt zu werden." With regard to Clausewitz's suitability for an important diplomatic post, Rose wrote, "There is not that confidence in his being wholly free from revolutionary views on which such a nomination can safely repose in the present state of things, in which the tendency to anarchy and the destruction of all that is dear and sacred to man can be averted by no other means whatever than by the most cordial, energetic and simultaneous cooperation of the great Powers of Europe; that unless they can communicate together with the utmost confidence these qualities of the cooperation must be wanting; and that the mission of a person from this Court to that of London in whom complete reliance could not be placed as to his views and principles on that essential point, which is the basis and soul of the Alliance, could not but tend to inspire the most mischievous mistrust." See Rose to Castlereagh, 9 November 1819, PRO F.O. 64/120. This statement captures essential aspects of

Diplomatic appointments are a different kind of issue than questions of constitutional reform, but nevertheless Rose's activities are an example of the kinds of restraints placed on the conduct of Prussian policy by the conservative nature of Europe during this period. Thus the fate of the constitutional movement in Prussia in 1819 reflected the basic characteristics of the Prussian state and the international system in the immediate post-Napoleonic period as well as Hardenberg's imperfections as a leader. These factors in part determined and were in turn further complicated and reinforced by the peculiar course of history in 1819.

The failure of the constitutional movement had great, although not necessarily irretrievable, consequences for the development of Prussia and Germany. It meant that severe constraints had been placed on the work of the reformist bureaucracy at the very time when the educational and economic reforms they had enacted were slowly beginning to transform the nature of Prussian society. Many officials, seeing the change in the monarchy's official attitude, voluntarily suppressed their reformist feelings or else buried themselves in the routine of administrative procedure and derived satisfaction from their exalted positions within the state. A good example of this transition is Hardenberg himself, who wrote in December 1821:

> Two things are still required in order to consummate my love for King and fatherland.
>
> 1. To put our financial affairs completely in order.
> 2. To make suggestions for the simplification of administrative procedures.[110]

Both of these goals were worthwhile in themselves, but they were supremely apolitical. Nowhere is there any mention of the larger overriding themes of the reform movement or of the other areas in which its work was incomplete. The role of the bureaucracy was now greatly circumscribed. Its relationship to new ideas and social conditions was im-

---

the operation and mood of the international system in 1819 and reveals the way in which it could have an impact upon Prussia.

110. Hardenberg to Wittgenstein, 5 December 1821, Hans Branig, ed., *Briefwechsel des Fürsten Karl August von Hardenberg mit dem Fürsten Wilhelm Ludwig von Sayn-Wittgenstein, 1806–1822*, pp. 287–289.

paired, and its ability to inspire needed reform was greatly reduced. The tension between the political structure of Prussia and the intellectual, social, and economic characteristics of the age—already present in the eighteenth century—was in time intensified by the results of the Prussian reform movement and became one of the central themes of German history in the nineteenth and twentieth centuries. It would be a mistake, however, to think that all of this was predetermined by the outcome of 1819. On the contrary, other opportunities for development would occur, and elements of the reformist bureaucracy would reassert themselves during the next decade. However, an important opportunity was lost, and, as we shall see, the nature of the Prussian reform movement was fundamentally altered. The outcome of the constitutional conflict, like the Carlsbad Decrees and the congress of Aachen, was an indication that, within Europe, the German state system, and Prussia, the desire to maintain the political status quo had become the foremost characteristic of the age. It was an attitude that Bernstorff fully shared.

*Chapter 3*

✠ ✠ ✠ ✠ ✠ ✠ ✠ ✠ ✠ ✠ ✠ ✠ ✠

# European and German
# Affairs in
# the Early 1820s

## THE CONGRESSES OF TROPPAU
## AND LAIBACH

On 1 January 1820, units of the Spanish army assembled near Cadiz revolted against the government of Ferdinand VII. This precipitated further uprisings in other parts of Spain and led to the restoration of the constitution of 1812.[1] The spirit of revolution spread quickly throughout southern Europe during the early 1820s. This period of political unrest prompted the first direct intervention of the powers of restoration Europe in the internal affairs of the European states. As a result, the Congress system that had previously involved all five of the great powers disintegrated.[2]

Prussian diplomacy during the early 1820s has received little attention from modern scholars, and, when mentioned, it usually has been de-

1. The Spanish revolution of 1820 is discussed in Raymond Carr, *Spain, 1808–1939*, pp. 120–146; and in great detail in Hermann Baumgarten, *Geschichte Spaniens vom Ausbruch der französischen Revolution bis auf unsere Tage*, 2:244–394.

2. The best account of European diplomacy in the 1820s is Paul W. Schroeder, *Metternich's Diplomacy at Its Zenith, 1820–1823*. Also essential is Charles K. Webster, *The Foreign Policy of Castlereagh, 1812–1822*, 2:215–505. Useful discussions are found in Hans W. Schmalz, *Versuche einer gesamteuropäischen Organization, 1815–1820*, pp. 49–96; and Walter Alison Phillips, *The Confederation of Europe*, pp. 204–264.

scribed as a policy of nearly total subservience to Austria. The clearest formulation of this interpretation is by Hans Schmalz, who wrote that Prussia "renounced its own policy and allowed itself to be completely taken in tow by Austria."[3] This view has been echoed by Henry Kissinger, who referred to Prussia as a "diplomatic satellite of Austria" and described Bernstorff as "an appendage of Metternich."[4] Although Prussia did not play a predominant role in European politics during these years, Prussian policy was not necessarily determined by Vienna. Prussia's approach to international affairs was formulated on the basis of several political, economic, financial, and ideological factors. Metternich's influence was undeniably one of these factors, but it was not always the most important.

As in 1818, Prussia's economic and financial weakness, geographical disunity, and military vulnerability still placed fundamental constraints on external policy. Prussia's continued insecurity necessitated a policy that supported stability and peace in Europe. Bernstorff, who began to exert more control over Prussian policy during this period, was also profoundly influenced by the idealistic yet conservative nature of the international system. As he wrote in 1821:

> The basis of the system that governs Europe is the intimate union of the great powers, the identity of their guiding principles, the coincidence of their individual interests with the general interest, the maintenance of harmony, territorial existence, and the social order. Thanks to this system of solidarity, which has taken the place of the old system of countervailing forces, politics has assumed a lofty character, and its concurrence with morality has ceased to be a chimera. Everywhere justice has been substituted for force, good faith for artifice, moderation for projects of ambition, concurrence for divergence, reciprocal confidence for defiance and jealousy, and harmony for continually reviving divisions.[5]

This favorable description was typical of the views held by many states-

---

3. Schmalz, *Versuche einer gesamteuropäischen Organization*, p. 68.

4. See Henry Kissinger, *A World Restored*, pp. 247, 258, 272; also see Schroeder, *Metternich's Diplomacy*, pp. 47, 214; and René Albrecht-Carrié, *A Diplomatic History of Europe*, p. 23.

5. Bernstorff to Alopeus, 27 July 1821 (copy), HHSA, Stk., Collectiania Borussica Nr. 4.

men during these years.[6] Bernstorff was perhaps more optimistic than some, partly because avowed principles of the European system so closely matched the diplomatic values of his family. But, in general, the desire to conciliate national interests with broader European interests was pronounced on the part of most European governments.

Prussia formed part of the continental consensus and was not encouraged to forcefully enunciate an independent policy of its own. This was especially true during these years when few major issues involved vital Prussian interests. Prussian statesmen were unwilling to endanger their security by opposing Russia and Austria on questions about which they were not greatly concerned. On the other hand, Austria was directly involved with many of the problems of European diplomacy during the years 1820–1823, and it was natural that Metternich should have played a dominant role. Prussian weakness and preoccupation with internal affairs worked to Metternich's advantage in areas where Prussia had no specific state interests. On those occasions where important Prussian interests did come into play, Berlin did not hesitate to pursue its own independent policy. Thus, the description of Prussia as simply a satellite of Austria is neither entirely accurate nor enlightening.

The Spanish revolt naturally caught the attention of the conservative statesmen of Europe, particularly Alexander of Russia, who urged the members of the Quadruple Alliance to discuss ways of assisting the Spanish monarchy. Although Hardenberg endorsed Alexander's proposal, a lack of enthusiasm in Vienna and outright opposition in London forced the Tsar to drop the idea.[7] Then, in July, revolution broke out in the Kingdom of Naples.[8] Ferdinand I was forced to proclaim the liberal constitution of Spain, and once again a semipopular regime was established with amazing ease in a formerly absolutist state. This revolt was the first shock to Austria's hegemony in the Italian peninsula, and Metternich, who previously had been a noninterventionist, began looking for moral support from the other powers. Russia and France, however, suspected that unilateral action by Austria to crush the revolt would result in

6. See, for example, Richard B. Elrod, "The Concert of Europe," p. 162.

7. Webster, *Foreign Policy of Castlereagh*, 2:228–229, 236–242; Hardenberg to Castlereagh, 31 March 1820, Robert Stewart, Second Marquess of Londonderry, *Memoirs and Correspondence of Viscount Castlereagh, Second Marquess of Londonderry*, 12:223–224; and Schroeder, *Metternich's Diplomacy*, p. 26.

8. The Neapolitan Revolution is described in George T. Romani, *The Neapolitan Revolution of 1820–1821.*

the expansion of Austrian power in Italy, and they chose to regard the revolution as a European problem suitable for resolution at a congress or conference.[9] Castlereagh, on the other hand, preferred independent Austrian action to any intervention by the European alliance.[10] The Prussian government wanted Austria to have a free hand in quelling the revolt to ensure that no active involvement by Berlin in Italian affairs would be required. But, if Alexander insisted on the need for a conference, Bernstorff was willing to support him even though he felt that Russian suspicions of Austrian intentions in Italy were unwarranted.[11] However, Bernstorff also felt that Russia's continual attempts to pressure Great Britain into supporting a conference showed little understanding of Britain's domestic political situation. In early October, he expressed to Rose "his deep anxiety to prevent the supposition arising that there is a division in the councils of the Allies, since he was convinced that nothing prevents the revolutionary spirit in France from bursting forth out into rebellion, but the persuasion of the closest cooperation existing amongst the allies, and that if the French government is overturned the revolutionary cause must triumph in Europe."[12]

To avoid alienating Alexander, Metternich reluctantly agreed to the convening of a congress at Troppau, in Austrian Silesia, even though he knew that Castlereagh could not participate.[13] The congress of Troppau opened on 23 October 1820. Only Austria, Prussia, and Russia had official representatives; Britain and France sent observers. The Prussian delegation played a minor role in the proceedings. To briefly describe the course of the negotiations, Metternich succeeded in getting Russia to approve of Austrian intervention in Naples in return for a general, theoretical statement of antirevolutionary and interventionist principles that could only have reality when it coincided with the interests of the continental monarchies. This statement, the Troppau Preliminary Protocol, symbolized

9. Schroeder, *Metternich's Diplomacy*, pp. 45–50; and Patricia Kennedy Grimsted, *The Foreign Ministers of Alexander I*, pp. 46–47.

10. Webster, *Foreign Policy of Castlereagh*, 2:262–272; and Schroeder, *Metternich's Diplomacy*, pp. 46–47.

11. Rose to Castlereagh, 20 August, 9 September, and 12 September 1820, PRO F.O. 64/124; and Heinrich von Treitschke, *History of Germany in the Nineteenth Century*, 3:486.

12. Rose to Castlereagh, 26 September and 3 October 1820, PRO F.O. 64/124.

13. Schroeder, *Metternich's Diplomacy*, pp. 50–59; Guillaume de Bertier de Sauvigny, *Metternich and His Times*, pp. 141–142.

the reactionary eastern powers standing guard over the monarchical order in Europe and widened the gulf between England and these states. Castlereagh immediately condemned its contents as inadmissible.[14]

Hardenberg supported the Austrian position without any reservation, but according to La Ferronnays, the French observer at Troppau, Bernstorff indicated that this support had no great meaning and that he personally was not sympathetic to the reactionary policy that Austria was pursuing in Italy.[15] Rose also reported that Bernstorff felt that the Preliminary Protocol might damage the strength and vitality of the European alliance.[16] Bernstorff was convinced that the revolt in Naples had been caused by poor government as well as by liberal agitation. In his view, the key to eventual success for the restored regime would be the establishment of a reasonable government that could maintain order, rule in the national interest, and undertake gradual reform of the existing abuses.[17] In general, Bernstorff took little pride in Prussia's role at Troppau. He thought that the papers produced by the conference were mediocre. He concluded that Prussia's policy there had been determined by necessity, but, in his usual forthright manner, he told Frederick William, "I cannot hide the fact . . . that Prussia's influence here has been of absolutely no value."[18]

It was also agreed at the meeting that Ferdinand should be invited to meet with the powers at Laibach, where another congress of the eastern monarchs had been called for January 1821. There the details of Austria's intervention in Naples were to be worked out. The congress of Laibach was a continuation of Troppau.[19] Metternich was able to get quick approval for an Austrian expedition to quell the Neapolitan Revolution, and his instructions to Ferdinand stipulated the nature of the restored

14. Webster, *Foreign Policy of Castlereagh*, 2:298–306. The protocol is reproduced in René Albrecht-Carrié, ed., *The Concert of Europe*, p. 68.

15. Guillaume de Bertier de Sauvigny, *Metternich et la France après le Congrès de Vienne*, 2:373.

16. Rose to Castlereagh, 2 December 1820, PRO F.O. 64/124.

17. Bernstorff to Krusemarck, 12 January 1822, HHSA, Stk., Collectiania Borussica Nr. 5.

18. Bernstorff to Ancillon, 8 December, 23 December 1820, ZSA Me, AAI, Rep. 1, Nr. 44.

19. For the congress of Laibach, see Alfred Stern, *Geschichte Europas seit den Verträgen von 1815 bis zum Frankfurter Frieden von 1871*, 2:150–182; and Schroeder, *Metternich's Diplomacy*, pp. 104–128.

government. Hardenberg and Bernstorff allowed Metternich complete freedom of action until he asked the powers to jointly guarantee a loan enabling the Kingdom of Naples to pay for the costs of the Austrian operations in southern Italy. Prussia was especially sensitive to any added financial obligations and refused to participate in the guarantee. As Hardenberg and Bernstorff wrote to Frederick William, they were cognizant of the great burden that Austria had undertaken, "but we must on our part restrict ourselves all the more from merely accepting as a matter of course the proposal for a security agreement, which could easily become very burdensome, for as such it could become an important complication in the rearrangement of the state debt as ordered by Your Majesty.[20]

No sooner had the Austrians reestablished order in Naples, than a revolution broke out on 10 March in Piedmont, the one Italian state over which Austria had little influence. Once again, the revolt began among the military and, as in Naples, led to the introduction of the liberal Spanish constitution.[21] The news of the revolt came as a shock to the statesmen assembled in Laibach. On 15 March they decided to take immediate action to put down the uprising. Austria announced that it would reinforce its troops in Lombardy, and it was agreed that a Russian army of 60,000 men would be brought in by way of Hungary. It was expected that Prussia would also participate in this punitive expedition, but Bernstorff stated that, although Prussia supported the position taken by its two allies, it could not accept any obligations that were not specifically indicated in existing treaties. He told Frederick William that Prussia should not undertake any new responsibilities and asked the King for permission to return to Berlin. Continued participation in the conference could serve no direct interest of the state, "but could easily bring about new attempts to involve Your Highness more deeply in the present crisis than is consistent with your wishes and with the national interests of Prussia."[22] In any case, Prussian assistance was not essential; within a month, Austrian forces defeated the revolutionary army in Piedmont. The final declaration of the eastern powers at the conclusion of the congress of

20. Hardenberg and Bernstorff to Frederick William, 6 February 1821, ZSA Me, AAI, Rep. 6, Nr. 378.

21. Stern, *Geschichte Europas*, 2:162–170; and Schroeder, *Metternich's Diplomacy*, pp. 115–119.

22. Bernstorff to Frederick William, 15 March 1821, ZSA Me, AAI, Rep. 6, Nr. 378.

Laibach exalted in the success of their policy of intervention and restated their intention to maintain order and stability in Europe.[23] It is clear, however, that Berlin did not intend to expend any of its financial or military resources in support of this doctrine in areas that were not vital to Prussia's interests.

## THE EASTERN QUESTION:
## THE FIRST PHASE

On 7 March 1821, the peace of Europe was again broken when the Danubian principalities revolted against Turkish rule. Although the uprising was suppressed, it led to a second uprising in the Morea and soon developed into a bitter and brutal conflict between the Turks and Greeks. This revolution caught the imagination of Europe. In Germany, conservatives and liberals alike idealized Greece's efforts to gain her independence and organized campaigns to gather funds to support the uprising.[24] European statesmen, however, were less concerned about the Greek Revolution than about the threat of a Russo-Turkish war.

By the treaties of Kutchuk Kainjardji (1714) and Bucharest (1812), Russia had obtained the right to protect the religious rights of the Ottoman Empire's Greek Orthodox subjects. In addition, the Sultan had to obtain permission from the Tsar to send troops into the Danubian principalities and was required to obtain Russian approval for the appointment of the Turkish governors of these semiautonomous territories. At first, Russia officially observed neutrality toward the revolts. But, as the conflict became more intense, St. Petersburg found it more difficult to ignore. The Russian minister to Constantinople, Stroganov, who was strongly pro-Greek, received instructions from St. Petersburg to present an ultimatum to the Porte requiring the Turks to evacuate the principalities and to refrain from indiscriminate retaliation against those involved in the revolt. The Turks were also asked to protect Christian subjects in the Empire and to rebuild churches destroyed as a result of the recent fighting. In

23. For the text see Albrecht-Carrié, *Concert of Europe*, pp. 55–58.

24. For the opening phase of the revolt in the Ottoman Empire, see C. W. Crawley, *The Question of Greek Independence*, pp. 17–29; Webster, *Foreign Policy of Castlereagh*, 2:347–400; Schroeder, *Metternich's Diplomacy*, pp. 164–194; Stern, *Geschichte Europas*, 2:183–250; Douglas Dakin, *The Greek Struggle for Independence, 1821–1833*, pp. 1–90; and Treitschke, *History of Germany*, 3:528–532.

addition, Russia proposed a vague program for reforming the governmental structure of the Ottoman Empire to the advantage of its Christian subjects. The Turks' rejection of this ultimatum led to the recall of the Russian minister on 7 August 1821.[25]

Russian involvement made the Greek Revolution a European issue and revived the so-called eastern question. Austria, Britain, and France felt that a conflict between Turkey and Russia would almost surely result in an expansion of Russian power in the Balkans and the eastern Mediterranean. Although Prussia would be the least affected by the consequences of a Russo-Turkish war, such a conflict could have a detrimental impact on the vitality and strength of the European alliance system and on the general tranquility of Europe.[26] Bernstorff was willing to give theoretical support to Russian interests, as he had earlier to Austrian intervention in Italy, but he gave this support within the context of the European alliance and as the advocate of a peaceful resolution of the Russo-Turkish dispute. On 27 July 1821, following the Russian ultimatum, Bernstorff was careful to explain to Alopeus, the Russian minister in Berlin, that war against Turkey would threaten the individual interests of France and England and thus would further endanger the European alliance, which was the only guarantee for peace and order in Europe. While stating Prussia's full support of Russia's grievances against the Sultan, Bernstorff indicated his preference for using the mechanism of the European alliance to settle the eastern question.[27] In 1822, while again urging St. Petersburg to find a peaceful solution to the Turkish problem, he pointed out that it was Alexander's commitment to peace that allowed him to be "the keystone of the social order in Europe."[28]

Metternich's anti-Russian attitude posed particular difficulties for Bernstorff. In 1820, when Russia was trying to increase her influence in the Balkans and was pushing for intervention in Spain, Metternich asked Prussia to join Austria in a gentlemen's agreement to block future Russian ambitions in Europe. Bernstorff refused to accept such an arrangement. As he wrote to Ancillon:

25. John A. R. Marriot, *The Eastern Question*, p. 206.
26. Bernstorff to Alopeus, 10 October 1821, HHSA, Stk., Collectiania Borussica Nr. 4.
27. Bernstorff to Alopeus, 27 July 1821, HHSA, Stk., Collectiania Borussica Nr. 4.
28. Bernstorff to Schöler, 26 January 1822. On Bernstorff's other efforts to press for peace, see Bernstorff to Miltitz, 16 January 1822, and Bernstorff to Krusemarck, 4 March 1822, HHSA, Stk., Collectiania Borussica Nr. 5.

We must pursue a thoroughly upright policy toward Russia; we must not have to conceal or acknowledge an unrighteous action. Our friendship with Austria can never become too intimate or too strong, but it must be perfectly free, and remain a simple relationship of mutual confidence. The advantage we hope to secure from it would be frustrated by the first written word that should impose on us any formal and definite pledge.[29]

Bernstorff did support Austrian efforts to convene a European conference to discuss the eastern question. But, when these proposals broke down because of Russian and British opposition, he resisted attempts to include Prussia in the group of powers opposed to Russia's policy in the East.[30]

The efforts of Prussia and the other powers to impress on the Tsar the necessity of maintaining the peace may have tended to counteract Capodistrias' strongly pro-Greek sympathies, but Alexander himself was responsible for averting open conflict. He wanted to pursue a pacific policy in the Near East and to maintain the unity of the European alliance. "Heaven is my witness," he said in July 1821, "that my only wish, my sole ambition, is to conserve that peace that cost the world so much to attain."[31] On 23 April 1822, after new difficulties with Persia had forced Constantinople to stabilize its relations with Russia, the Turks agreed to evacuate the principalities by 5 May and to reestablish Turkish rule there in accordance with the terms of earlier treaties. Several questions remained unresolved, but the danger of immediate war was past.

## THE CONGRESS OF VERONA

While the powers repressed liberal movements in Italy and the crisis in the East passed, conditions in Spain worsened and approached a state

29. See Bernstorff to Ancillon, 16 April 1820, ZSA Me, AAI, Rep. 1, Nr. 44; and Treitschke, *History of Germany*, 3:481. He expressed the same view to Hardenberg, 17 April 1820, ZSA Me, AAI, Rep. 1, Nr. 31.

30. Irby C. Nichols, Jr., *The European Pentarchy and the Congress of Verona*, p. 9.

31. Grimsted, *Foreign Ministers of Alexander I*, p. 263; and Schroeder, *Metternich's Diplomacy*, pp. 186–192. Certainly Metternich also assisted in this process by clarifying and reducing Russia's demands on the Porte, thereby making ultimate agreement between the two powers more feasible.

of civil war.[32] Until the summer of 1821, Richelieu followed a policy of nonintervention in Spain. But, in August, the deterioration of conditions on the Iberian peninsula led him to establish an observation army along the Spanish border to prevent revolutionary agitation from spreading to France.[33] In December 1821, Richelieu fell from power. His moderate ministry was replaced by Villele's ultraconservative regime. Montmorency, who had close connections with royalist groups in Spain, became the foreign minister and immediately adopted a hostile attitude toward the constitutional government.[34]

At Laibach, Austria and Prussia had agreed to meet at a later date in Florence for a discussion of Italian affairs. This proposed meeting was transferred to Verona and was preceded by a meeting of the great powers in Vienna. These preliminary discussions in Austria revealed wide differences of opinion between the powers. France and Russia favored armed intervention in Spain, while Austria and Prussia opposed any such action and favored applying only diplomatic pressure to the government in Madrid. Britain naturally desired no direct interference by the powers in Spanish affairs.[35] There was also disagreement over Austria's policy toward Sardinia. France, Britain, and Russia suspected that Metternich was exploiting the instability there to enlarge Austrian influence in Italy, and even Bernstorff favored the prompt evacuation of Austrian troops from Naples and Sardinia.[36] Thus, from the beginning, the negotiations at Verona were clouded by considerable discord between Britain and the continental powers and among the continental powers as well.

By the middle of October, the representatives had assembled in Verona.

32. Schroeder, *Metternich's Diplomacy*, pp. 195–200; Carr, *Spain*, pp. 133–139; Baumgarten, *Geschichte Spaniens*, 2:366–376; and Stern, *Geschichte Europas*, 2: 251–287.

33. Nichols, *Congress of Verona*, p. 29.

34. Guillaume de Bertier de Sauvigny, *The Bourbon Restoration*, pp. 186–193; Schroeder, *Metternich's Diplomacy*, p. 198; and Nichols, *Congress of Verona*, pp. 31–32.

35. Schroeder, *Metternich's Diplomacy*, pp. 205–206; Webster, *Foreign Policy of Castlereagh*, 2:476–481. The Vienna meeting is discussed in Nichols, *Congress of Verona*, pp. 40–62; Bernstorff to Frederick William, 7, 8, and 14 September 1822, ZSA Me, AAI, Rep. 6, Nr. 395. Also see Gordon to Wellington, 22 September 1822, Arthur Wellesley, First Duke of Wellington, *Despatches, Correspondence and Memoranda of Field Marshall Arthur, Duke of Wellington, K. G.*, 1:566.

36. Bernstorff to Frederick William, 9 September 1822, ZSA Me, AAI, Rep. 6, Nr. 395.

Although the Prussian delegation included the King, Hardenberg (who died in Italy during this trip), and other notables, Bernstorff represented Prussia at nearly all of the discussions. On 20 October, during the first session of the congress, Montmorency immediately came to the heart of the matter. If France were forced to break relations with Spain, he asked, would the eastern powers follow suit? Were they willing to give moral support to France in the event of hostilities, and what kind of material aid could they provide if France asked them to intervene in a Franco-Spanish conflict?[37]

Bernstorff and Metternich had to take Russia's intentions into account because both Prussia and Austria were anxious to maintain the best possible relations with Alexander in order to retain their influence with him over the eastern question.[38] Bernstorff felt that France was not really threatened by developments in Spain. Furthermore, in view of the new French army's instability and lack of experience, he felt that France would probably be beaten if it attacked Spain. Metternich, Bernstorff, and Wellington all tried to counter the French proposal and to convince Alexander that armed intervention in Spain was unwise.[39] However, the Tsar would not be moved. On 29 October, Alexander expressed his willingness to sign a treaty with France offering material assistance in the event of war and announced his intention of moving 150,000 troops through Germany into Piedmont to be in position to help France.[40] If called on by the French government, Russia would break diplomatic relations with Spain and would provide moral and material support. Austria and Prussia also agreed to break diplomatic relations with Madrid and to provide moral support if necessary, but both hedged on the question of material assistance. Metternich stated that another congress would be required to determine the necessity of such aid, and Bernstorff noted that Prussia's geographical location and internal situation made any direct material assistance unlikely. Wellington refused to commit Great Britain to any action prejudicial to Spain and denounced the idea that France was in

---

37. Bernstorff to Ancillon, 21 October 1822, ZSA Me, AAI, Rep. 1, Nr. 44. For Montmorency's presentation, see Précis des Communications verbales faites par M. le Vicomte de Montmorency dans la réunion confidential de MM les Ministers d'Autriche, de Grande Bretagne, de Prusse et de Russe, à Verone, le 20me Octobre 1822, Wellesley, *Despatches of Wellington,* 1:403–404.

38. Nichols, *Congress of Verona,* pp. 87–88.

39. Ibid., pp. 89–90.

40. Ibid., pp. 93–94.

any danger.[41] Both Austria and Prussia wanted to avoid war and wished to maintain close relations with Britain. The eastern question and the importance of the solidarity of the eastern powers, however, forced them to succumb to Franco-Russian pressures to approve French intervention in Spain.[42]

On 4 November, at Russia's suggestion, the eastern powers agreed to send separate dispatches, of similar content, to their envoys in Spain. The instructions were to be written in a way that would automatically lead to a break in diplomatic relations. On 19 November, they signed a *procès-verbal,* which in effect sanctioned French intervention.[43] Thus, largely against his will, Bernstorff was forced to acquiesce to French armed involvement in Spain. When it became apparent that Alexander could not be convinced to withdraw support from France, Austria and Prussia had no choice but to support France and abandon Great Britain. As Bernstorff wrote, "In the end we were compelled to give up all idea of a common understanding with England, and in order to avoid a break with Russia, we had to adopt a middle course."[44]

On 22 November, Bernstorff sent his dispatch to the Prussian chargé d'affaires in Madrid. It was a blistering attack on the constitutional government in Spain and on the course of the revolution.[45] It demonstrated his complete disapproval of revolutionary activity and of liberal political principles. This attitude was rooted in his family's traditional dis-

41. See Réponse Confidentielle du Cabinet de Berlin au Précis des Communications Verbales faites par M. le Vicomte de Montmorency à la Conference du 20me Octobre, Verone, le 30 Octobre 1823, Wellesley, *Despatches of Wellington,* 1:499; Bernstorff to Ancillon, 30 October 1822, ZSA Me, AAI, Rep. 1, Nr. 44; Schroeder, *Metternich's Diplomacy,* pp. 213–216; Nichols, *Congress of Verona,* p. 94; and Memoir on the Observations of the French Minister respecting Spain, 30 October 1832, Wellesley, *Despatches of Wellington,* 1:499–501.

42. As Wellington noted, "The two German Courts are sincerely desirous of maintaining peace, and in reality dread war, and are determined to avoid it, if possible. They regret to be obliged to hold any language to Spain on this occasion, but they cannot separate themselves from the Emperor of Russia." Memorandum on the State of the Spanish Question, 12 November 1822, Wellesley, *Despatches of Wellington,* 1:519–523.

43. Nichols, *Congress of Verona,* pp. 112–119; and Schroeder, *Metternich's Diplomacy,* p. 219. A draft of the document is contained in ZSA Me, AAI, Rep. 6, Nr. 395.

44. Treitschke, *History of Germany,* 4:27.

45. Bernstorff to Schepeler, 22 November 1822, ZSA Me, AAI, Rep. 6, Nr. 395.

taste for political instability and popular rule and was also an outgrowth
of his noticeable conservatism after 1814. Yet, as was often the case with
many of the pronouncements of the period, ideological considerations
were only a secondary factor in determining state policy and should
not be interpreted as an expression of direct Prussian interest in crushing
the revolution in Spain. As has been shown, throughout the entire course
of the congress of Verona, Bernstorff worked to avoid armed intervention
by the powers. His dispatch was primarily a pro forma expression of
antirevolutionary sentiment. It was designed to maintain amicable relations with Russia and was only secondarily an example of his own political
feelings and of certain particular concerns of Frederick William III.
Spain was not vital to Prussian interests, but the eastern alliance was.
The true meaning of the dispatch was understood by Bernstorff's
contemporaries.[46]

Although French intervention in Spain was supposed to take place
under the auspices of the European alliance, France soon made it clear
that it was acting independently.[47] The veil of continental unanimity
failed to cover the fact that the era of the congresses had passed. Britain,
as expected, disassociated itself from the decision at Verona in the strongest
possible manner. The coalition of five great powers, willing to meet
periodically to settle the current problems of Europe, was disintegrating.
The powers' desire to cooperate to avoid major conflict was still very
great, but, to be successful, the highly structured system of congresses and
conferences required an extremely strong consensus on a wide variety of
issues. That consensus, which arose out of the powers' reaction to the
diplomacy of the eighteenth century, the French Revolution, and to more
than two decades of war, could not survive at full strength indefinitely.
As the memory of recent events weakened, the major powers' disparate
interests and divergent political and social systems became more significant determinants of state policy. The confluence of individual state
interests with a more general European interest became less natural and
valid and, as a result, it was recognized that the method for solving international disputes needed to be more flexible and less ritualistic. Some
writers have drawn a sharp distinction between the congress system and
the Concert of Europe.[48] This is a useful distinction as long as it takes

46. See for example, Wellington to Canning, 22 November 1822, Wellesley,
*Despatches of Wellington,* 1:566.
    47. Nichols, *Congress of Verona,* pp. 229–236.
    48. For example, see ibid., pp. 317–326.

into account the European powers' continued commitment to cooperation at the international level, which lasted until the outbreak of the Crimean War. To be sure, the era of the congresses was a period when this commitment was particularly accentuated. Its demise was the sign of a significant structural change in the international system and of an alteration in the relationship of national interests to European concerns, but it did not bring about a fundamental shift in the attitudes that governed European affairs during these years.

## THE VIENNA MINISTERIAL CONFERENCE

The Carlsbad Decrees ensured Austrian and, to a much lesser extent, Prussian hegemony in Germany. But many of the institutional arrangements and procedures of the *Bund* had not been established, and there was still considerable uncertainty about how the Confederation was to operate as a political body. For this reason, Bernstorff and other representatives of the seventeen members of the Select Council met in November of 1819 in Vienna to determine the final shape of the federal institutions for Germany. Hardenberg's instructions to Bernstorff stated that Prussia's first concern was to create a strong federal military system that would bolster Prussia's security as a European power. Bernstorff was to work for an increase in the strength and unity of the Confederation, particularly with regard to the organization of the federal army and the establishment of a reliable system of federal fortresses in the west.

Prussia was less interested in other questions. Hardenberg told Bernstorff to proceed cautiously on commercial and customs affairs to be sure that the conference's decisions did not interfere with the policies of the individual states such as Prussia's newly enacted customs regulations. Hardenberg felt that Article XIII of the federal constitution should be interpreted in a broad manner. Representative institutions could be based on modernized old estates or on newly constituted assemblies. His only requirement was that they not be constituted "on the basis of an undifferentiated mass of people, but rather be established according to the different classes into which the population is divided according to clear and historically delineated characteristics, for example, nobility, bourgeoisie, peasantry."[49] Bernstorff was to work for a stronger federation for defense,

49. Hardenberg to Bernstorff, 10 November 1819, ZSA Me, AAI, Rep. 6, Nr. 344.

but to block such a development in other areas. This combination proved impossible to achieve.

In accordance with his instructions, Bernstorff pressed as hard as possible to achieve Prussia's goal of a strong federal military structure.[50] For Prussia, this involved a defensive alliance with Austria and the German Confederation and the extension of federal protection to Prussia's territories in the east, which lay outside the Confederation's borders. Should such a defensive alliance prove impossible to achieve, then Berlin at least wanted a clear definition of what comprised a federal war. By the middle of January, however, it was clear that Prussia would be unable to establish the strong military system it desired.[51] For example, the conference ultimately decided that a declaration of war by the Confederation would require a two-thirds vote of approval by the Diet. An offensive war involving any of the German powers who possessed nonfederal territories and who were acting as European powers was excluded from consideration by the *Bund*. However, if the nonfederal territories of a German state were attacked by a foreign power, then the Select Council could decide by a majority vote that the Confederation was endangered. In that case, the Diet could proceed with its usual vote on a declaration of war. Given the undue proportion of votes allotted to the smaller states within the Confederation, Berlin did not see this complicated procedure as a secure arrangement. Prussian attempts to strengthen the fortifications along the Rhine were only partially successful, and a final decision on the organization of the federal army was deferred to a later date.[52]

The key issue with regard to internal affairs and institutions of the member states was the status and interpretation of Article XIII. Bernstorff joined the Bavarian representative in resisting all attempts to place restrictions on this article. He did not want the Confederation to come into conflict with the existing constitutional arrangements of the member states, and, as he clearly expected Prussia to adopt a constitution in the near future, he wanted to ensure complete freedom of action for his own government in constitutional affairs.[53] The decision of the conference was

50. Bernstorff to Frederick William, 7 December 1819, ZSA Me, AAI, Rep. 6, Nr. 344.

51. Bernstorff to Frederick William, 21 January 1829, ibid.

52. Bernstorff to Frederick William, 21 January, 12 March, 18 March, 30 April, and 31 May 1820; Bernstorff to Metternich, 18 May 1820; and Metternich to Bernstorff, 19 May 1820, ibid. Also see Treitschke, *History of Germany,* 3:320–323.

53. Bernstorff to Frederick William, 12, 18, and 25 December 1820, ZSA Me,

that the Diet should ensure the implementation of Article XIII in all of the member states and that each member of the Confederation should be able to request a federal guarantee of its constitutional arrangements. It was originally stipulated that constitutions could be altered "only in accordance with the methods specified by these constitutions." However, Bernstorff felt that the term "constitution" was so vague and broad that it could be interpreted as including remnants of old *ständische* institutions, which in effect would grant power to provincial groups in Prussia. Hardenberg also emphasized that complete control over the determination of the nature of the constitution must rest with the King alone. On the basis of these objections, Bernstorff had the wording of Article LVI, which dealt with this matter, changed to read that "representative constitutions, existing in recognized efficiency [in *anerkannter Wirksamkeit bestehende*]" could be changed only through constitutional methods.[54] To emphasize the monarchical nature of political institutions in Germany, the next article, Article LVII, read: "The entire state authority must be centered in the supreme head of the state, and it is only in the exercise of certain definite rights that by a representative constitution the sovereign can be found to accept the cooperation of the estates."[55]

With the exception of customs affairs, which will be discussed later, the proceedings at the conference went fairly smoothly until the end of the discussions. At that point, Metternich proposed that the results of the meeting be incorporated into a supplementary federal act. Württemberg, however, refused to sanction any such action without the European powers' prior approval of all the articles of the final act.[56] William, the King of Württemberg, was related to Alexander of Russia. This protest was the first concrete evidence of his attempt to construct a third unit of German power made up of the smaller states, supported by a major European state, and opposed to the domination of Austria and Prussia. Bernstorff was furious over this policy, which he felt threatened the en-

---

AAI, Rep. 6, Nr. 344; and Franz Dobmann, *Georg Friedrich Freiherr von Zentner als Bayerischer Staatsmann in den Jahren 1799–1821*, pp. 171–191.

54. Bernstorff to Hardenberg, 25 December 1819, and 8 January 1820, ZSA Me, AAI, Rep. 6, Nr. 344; Bernstorff to Hardenberg, 20 March 1820, ZSA Me, AAI, Rep. 1, Nr. 31; and Treitschke, *History of Germany*, 3:325.

55. Treitschke, *History of Germany*, 3:325.

56. Bernstorff to Frederick William, 6 and 26 March 1820, ZSA Me, AAI, Rep. 6, Nr. 345.

tire political structure of Germany.[57] In the end, he and Metternich managed to pressure William into backing down and announcing his willingness to agree to the final act.[58] On this note of discord, the Vienna conference ended.

Its results were affirmation of the status quo. Prussia's efforts to create
a more dynamic military structure in Germany had failed. The ultraconservatives' attempts to restrict or destroy existing constitutional arrangements were also not successful. Even Metternich abandoned Gentz's
emphasis on a narrow interpretation of Article XIII and unenthusiastically
supported the constitutional decisions of the conference. The German
Confederation remained a loose association of states with a minimum of
federal regulations and institutions. Some of the wording of the articles
of the final act had an unusually narrow and reactionary cast. For example, parliamentary institutions were described as having their origins
in the French Revolution and, therefore, being inherently "un-German."
As Hajo Holborn has pointed out, although no "historical justification
for such an association" existed, it unfortunately became a part of the
German political tradition.[59]

Two related problems still unresolved at the end of the conference
were settled in the next three years: the controversy over Württemberg
and the so-called Trias plan, and the determination of the final structure
of the federal army. The idea of the Trias—the creation of a separate
coalition of minor powers within the German Confederation—was primarily the concept of Karl August Freiherr von Wangenheim, Württemberg's envoy to the federal Diet.[60] In 1818, he tried to ensure that the troops
of the minor powers serving in the federal army would be grouped in
their own corps and would not fall under direct Austrian or Prussian
command. He was especially interested in erecting a military structure for
Germany that would ensure the neutrality of the smaller states in the
event of an Austro-Prussian conflict. Austria, at this time, was able to
use the smaller powers' fear of Prussian domination to block Berlin's
demands for a large and effective federal army. Metternich mistrusted
Prussian influence in Germany and was concerned about the liberal nature

---

57. Bernstorff to Frederick William, 27 March 1820, ibid.
58. Bernstorff to Frederick William, 22 April and 15 May 1820, ibid.
59. Hajo Holborn, *A History of Modern Germany, 1648–1840*, p. 467.
60. Curt Albrecht, *Die Triaspolitik des Frhr. K. Aug. von Wangenheim.*

of Prussia's military forces.[61] In 1819, Wangenheim lobbied for multi-national garrisons for the federal fortresses to reduce the dependence of the smaller states on Austria and Prussia. It was largely due to his efforts and to Metternich's support that Württemberg and the smaller German states succeeded in delaying most military issues at the Vienna conference.[62]

After negotiations that lasted until the middle of 1822, the Diet finally determined the structure of the federal army. The forces of particularism in Germany had triumphed. On paper, the federal army was assigned a troop strength of 300,000 men. Austria contributed three army corps of approximately 95,000 men; Prussia sent three corps of approximately 80,000 men. The smaller states supplied 120,000 men organized into four corps. The seventh corps was entirely made up of Bavarian troops, the eighth was made up of the forces of the other south German states, and the ninth corps of the forces of Hanover and the minor north German states. The tenth corps was a conglomerate made up of troops from Saxony, the Thuringian states, Electoral Hesse, Nassau, and Luxemburg. It was further stipulated that no state that had a full corps could combine the troops of another state with its own. The supreme commander of the federal army was to be chosen by the Diet.[63] This arrangement could not possibly produce an effective fighting force. In reality, Prussia still bore the prime responsibility for the defense of Germany, yet it exerted little influence within the federal military structure and could not depend on the federal military for substantive assistance in the event of war. The restructuring of this federal military system became a repetitive theme in Prussian policy for the next four decades.

Wangenheim also opposed Austria and Prussia in other areas of German affairs. He championed the cause of the constitutional governments in the south, opposed Prussia's new customs law, and encouraged William to tolerate the writings of those who attacked the hegemony of Austria and Prussia. In addition, William protested against the contents of the Troppau protocol and the Verona circular and was highly critical of the central commission of inquiry in Mainz.[64] As a result of these activities,

61. Albrecht, *Die Triaspolitik*, pp. 11, 17.
62. Ibid., pp. 67, 57–92.
63. Treitschke, *History of Germany*, 4:47–48.
64. Bernstorff to Schöler, 27 January 1823, ZSA Me, AAI, Rep. 1, Nr. 3210; and Treitschke, *History of Germany*, 3:507, and 4:73.

Bernstorff recommended that the eastern powers act decisively to force Württemberg to abandon its opposition to Austria and Prussia and to pressure William into replacing Wangenheim.[65] In view of the turbulent nature of the recent discussions in the federal Diet, it also was decided that the federal envoys of the various states were to be recalled and tighter controls established over the proceedings of the *Bundestag*. In the spring of 1823, thanks primarily to Bernstorff's initiative, the ministers of Austria, Prussia, and Russia were withdrawn from Stuttgart, and even France sent her envoy on a prolonged leave of absence.[66] This pressure surprised William; when he recovered, he recalled Wangenheim from Frankfurt and imposed stricter press censorship within Württemberg. Other envoys to the federal Diet were also replaced. When the *Bundestag* reconvened, its members were strictly bound to the instructions of their individual governments, and the vitality of the Diet, never very strong in the first place, suffered as a result.

Bernstorff's action proved that Prussia was willing to move decisively when its interests were directly involved. Berlin could not tolerate an attempt to create an independent power bloc that was tied to foreign interests and an even slightly independent *Bundestag* threatened the position of Prussia and Austria. As a result, Wangenheim and his plan were crushed by the two German great powers. Bernstorff never proposed interfering with the constitutional affairs of Württemberg. On the contrary, he opposed all attempts by Metternich, Gentz, and Blittersdorff of Baden to use the Württemberg controversy as an excuse for mounting an attack on representative institutions throughout Germany.[67] Bernstorff's attack on Württemberg was based on the security interests of the Prussian state, not on political ideology.

Berlin did not play an important role in European affairs from 1820 to 1823. On most of the important issues of the day, Prussia supported

---

65. Bernstorff to Küster, 24 January, 14 and 22 March 1823, ZSA Me, AAI, Rep. 1, Nr. 3210; and Zichy to Metternich, 25 February and 16 March 1823, HHSA, Stk., Preussen, Karton 116.

66. Bernstorff to Alopeus, 28 March 1823; Frederick William to William, 27 April 1823; Bernstorff to Küster, 27 April 1823; Bernstorff to Frederick William, 17 April 1823; and Bernstorff to Schöler, 22 April 1823, ZSA Me, AAI, Rep. 1, Nr. 3210; and Zichy to Metternich, 23 April 1823, HHSA, Stk., Preussen, Karton 116.

67. Treitschke, *History of Germany,* 4:78.

either the Russian or the Austrian position, and, as these two powers drifted farther away from Great Britain, Prussia followed. Metternich exerted a strong, but not predominant, influence on Prussian policy during this period. When it would not cost Prussia anything, Berlin did not hesitate to support Austrian policy. But when Metternich's views conflicted with Prussia's fiscal or military interests or with Russo-Prussian relations, Berlin followed an independent course.

As we have seen, Bernstorff was not an uncritical observer of Metternich's diplomacy. Early on, before the meeting at Troppau, he noted that Metternich was attempting to manage the European powers and European political systems in a manner analogous to his control over the German Confederation. Bernstorff considered this an unwise and impossible approach.[68] Thus, calling Prussia a typical, though obviously the weakest, member of the Concert of Europe is more useful than calling it a satellite of Austria.[69] Prussian leaders approached diplomacy with a European attitude, but, like the Austrians, they kept a firm grasp on their own interests. Like the other powers, Prussia was willing to meet formally or informally to discuss international problems. When the vital interests of the other powers were involved, Prussia readily gave way. Maintaining the support of Austria and Russia was clearly in Prussia's interest. The fate of Naples, Spain, Sardinia, and Greece was basically unimportant to Berlin. On the other hand, when more specific state interests came into conflict with the interests of others, these generally took precedence over European considerations. Prussia did not hesitate to act if its vital interests were threatened. When Württemberg posed a danger to Prussia's position, Bernstorff took the lead in demonstrating that small powers were not to exert a decisive influence within the European system and would not be allowed to fundamentally alter the powers' relationship to Germany. Prussia was not blindly subservient to Metternich. Prussia's state interests, the nature of the international system, and the character of the diplomatic crises of this period determined Prussian foreign policy.

68. Bernstorff to Frederick William, 21 October 1821, ZSA Me, AAI, Rep. 6, Nr. 376. For a similar observation, see Ivan Scott, "Counter Revolutionary Diplomacy and the Demise of Anglo-Austrian Cooperation, 1820–1823," p. 477.

69. For an excellent discussion of the basic principles of the Concert of Europe, see Gordon A. Craig, "The System of Alliances and the Balance of Power," p. 267. Also see Elrod, "Concert of Europe," pp. 259–261.

## THE ADMINISTRATION OF PRUSSIAN
## FOREIGN POLICY

Bernstorff began his official duties as Minister of Foreign Affairs on 1 January 1819. The date is symbolic: Bernstorff not only started a new career, but, more important, opened a new chapter in the history of the Ministry of Foreign Affairs in Prussia. He established the ministry at its famous location, Wilhelmstrasse Nr. 76, where it remained until 1945, and in many ways, he can be seen as the first modern foreign minister of Prussia.[70] Over a period of more than a century, the administration of Prussian foreign policy had become primarily concentrated in the hands of one minister and one department. This growth of a specialized ministry and of a responsible head paralleled other administrative developments in Prussia during the eighteenth and early nineteenth centuries. By 1802, Count Christian von Haugwitz had succeeded in setting aside the collegiate principle in the formulation of policy. He became the ministry's chief official and the King's primary advisor for external affairs. As part of the administrative innovations of the era of reform, the *Ministerium der auswärtigen Angelegenheiten* was created. Hardenberg inherited the fairly well-defined responsibilities established by Haugwitz, and, until 1818, he combined the duties of foreign minister with those of Chancellor. As a result, the lines of responsibility between Hardenberg's advisors and the ministry were often unclear. With Bernstorff's appointment, the position of a separate minister responsible for the administration of foreign affairs was reestablished. His long tenure in office (nearly fourteen years) strengthened the independence and identity of the ministry.[71]

70. While the Bernstorffs were attempting to locate a suitable permanent residence in Berlin, Count Alopeus, the Russian minister, offered to sell his spacious house on the Wilhelmstrasse to the King to serve as the new home for the minister and his staff. The building was purchased by the monarchy for 80,000 taler. Bernstorff and his family occupied one wing of the building; the remainder was used for the offices and reception rooms of the ministry. Prince Anton Radziwill lived next door. From 1820, Bernstorff's unofficial life primarily involved the Radziwills, Gneisenau, and Clausewitz, who had been appointed head of the War College in May 1818. Gräfin Elise von Bernstorff, *Aus ihren Aufzeichnungen,* 1:259–261.

71. See Reinhold Koser, "Die Gründung des Auswärtigen Amtes durch König Friedrich Wilhelm I. im Jahre 1728"; Peter Baumgart, "Zur Gründungsgeschichte des Auswärtigen Amtes in Preussen, 1713–1728"; Gustav Roloff, "Die Neuorganization des Ministeriums Auswärtigen von 1798–1802"; and Heinz Sasse, "Zur Geschichte des Auswärtigen Amts."

Of course, Bernstorff did not assume substantial control over the formulation of Prussian foreign policy immediately after his appointment. Although he was granted the right to report directly to the King and was excused from attending the meetings of the *Staatsministerium,* in reality he was treated only slightly differently than the other ministers who served under Hardenberg's "Chancellor-system."[72] Hardenberg retained control over the formulation of high policy, and, as we have seen, Bernstorff turned to him frequently for instructions. Apparently, the two men worked together satisfactorily. After Hardenberg's death, the Chancellor's responsibilities were divided between Bernstorff (foreign affairs) and Lottum (the *Staatsministerium* and domestic affairs in general). Bernstorff held the dual title of *Geheimer Staats-und Kabinettsminister, Kabinettsminister* indicating his special relationship to the King. From that point on, Bernstorff bore the primary responsibility for the external relations of the state. The *Staatsministerium* did not concern itself with diplomatic affairs, and Lottum demonstrated no desire to interfere in foreign policy.[73]

Even after Hardenberg's death, Bernstorff was not the sole formulator of foreign policy in Prussia. The King retained a strong interest in foreign affairs, and his desires shaped the major contours of Prussia's policy. However, he took Bernstorff's advice on most matters. When he disagreed with the policies of his foreign minister, it was usually due to the opposition of others rather than to his own initiative. Wittgenstein, for example, exercised a sporadic, but sometimes decisive, influence on the King.[74] His arguments were often counteracted by his pragmatic and talented adjutant, General von Witzleben, head of the military cabinet, as well as by Bernstorff. Witzleben was not intent on acquiring personal power, nor was he trying to increase the control of the military over foreign

72. Werner Frauendienst, "Das preussischer Staatsministerium in vorkonstitutioneller Zeit," p. 154; and Otto Hintze, "Das preussische Staatsministerium im 19. Jahrhundert, p. 567.

73. For a detailed discussion of the changes in government immediately after Hardenberg's death, see Hans Branig, "Die oberste Staatsverwaltung in Preussen zur Zeit des Todes von Hardenberg." Also see Hintze, "Das preussische Staatsministerium," pp. 561, 568; Ernst Klein, "Funktion und Bedeutung des preussischen Staatsministeriums," p. 209; and Heinrich Otto Meisner, "Zur neueren Geschichte des preussischen Kabinetts."

74. The best study of Wittgenstein will be, when published, Hans Branig, "Fürst Wittgenstein."

policy. He was an intelligent, capable, and creative officer with wide interests who did not hesitate to comment on political affairs. Because the King respected his judgment, he exerted an important influence on domestic and foreign affairs.[75] Depending on the nature of the crisis or of the particular negotiation that was being conducted, other ministers, court officials, princes, and military figures contributed on an ad hoc basis to the formulation of the government's foreign policy. Nevertheless, despite certain notable exceptions, Bernstorff and his ministry retained predominant responsibility for policy and its execution.

Since 1810, the staff of the ministry had been officially divided into two divisions: a political section, and an administrative/commercial section. Under Hardenberg, a separate official had administered the latter, but, until 1825, Bernstorff chose to supervise the entire department by himself. This proved to be a difficult task. Between 1818 and 1823, he attended seven major conferences and congresses, as well as a number of lesser meetings. He was away from Berlin a great deal of the time, and the burden of travel, the conduct of policy, and the administration of the ministry became very taxing. In the fall of 1824, Bernstorff, complaining of poor health, submitted his resignation to the King.[76] This appears to have been a device to pressure the parsimonious monarch into appointing another high-level official to administer the second division of the department. Frederick William refused to approve Bernstorff's resignation, but did agree to lighten his work load.[77] By December, Bernstorff had decided on Moritz Haubold von Schönberg, the *Regierungspräsident* of Merseberg, for the second position in the ministry. Under this arrangement, Bernstorff was the chief of the entire ministry and directly supervised the political section. Schönberg took over responsibility for the day-to-day conduct of administrative and commercial affairs when they did not involve matters of high politics.[78] This remained the organization of the department until 1831.

The responsibilities of the ministry in Berlin were substantial. In 1828, Prussia maintained diplomatic envoys to twenty-four major capitals. Some

---

75. There is no scholarly study of Witzleben. The only published account dealing with his career, written by a contemporary, is Wilhelm Dorow, *Job von Witzleben*.

76. Bernstorff to Frederick William, 24 September 1824, ZSA Me, Geheimes Civil Cabinet, Rep. 2.2.1., Nr. 12909.

77. Frederick William to Bernstorff, 2 October 1824, ibid.

78. Bernstorff to Frederick William, 24 December 1824; Frederick William to Bernstorff, 12 January 1825; and Frederick William to Schönberg, 17 June 1825, ibid.

positions, particularly those in Germany, combined representation to several states. For example, the minister to Saxony was accredited to twelve of the smaller German states, and the minister to Hamburg similarly conducted relations with Brunswick, Bremen, Lippe-Detmold, Lippe-Schaumburg, the two Mecklenburgs, Hanover, and Oldenburg.[79] In addition, the ministry maintained consular officials in 111 cities such as Alexandria, Canton, Rio de Janeiro, Odessa, and Malaga. In the United States, the Prussian government had consular officials in Baltimore, Boston, Charleston, New Orleans, New York, and Philadelphia. Some twenty-one countries maintained representatives in Berlin, and eleven foreign governments maintained over fifty consular officials in twelve major cities.[80] Thus, the ministry in Berlin had to handle a very substantial body of diplomatic correspondence and other business. Finally, the ministry also had important responsibilities in the area of censorship; the supervision of the publication of *Allgemeine Preussische Staatszeitung*, the official government newspaper; and the administration of the affairs of the principality of Neuchatel in Switzerland.

The mechanics of Prussian foreign policy involved difficulties common to the ministries of other countries. The movement of dispatches from Berlin to other capitals was very slow because of poor transportation and the small number of reliable couriers. Dispatches sent by less secure means were usually opened by foreign governments, and couriers were constantly subject to bribes. It took four to seven days for a dispatch to reach Vienna and between nine and twenty days to reach St. Petersburg. It took even longer for an envoy to proceed to a new assignment or to accompany the ruler to which he was accredited on various journeys. The business of diplomacy was also slowed by the mundane fact that it was all handwritten. The burden of work in the ministry in Berlin seems most comparable to that of London. It would contrast sharply with the more leisurely schedule of Paris or the extensive and evidently very corrupt staffing of the ministry in St. Petersburg. Prussian officials may also be compared to the more dedicated of Metternich's assistants within the foreign department of the Austrian *Staatskanzlei*.[81]

---

79. Britain had twenty missions in 1816 (thirty-seven by 1860). See S. T. Bindoff, "The Unreformed Diplomatic Service, 1812–60," p. 143.

80. *Handbuch über den Königlichen Preussischen Hof und Staat 1828*, pp. 126–137.

81. For the British foreign office under Canning and Palmerston, see Harold Temperley, *The Foreign Policy of Canning, 1822–1827*, pp. 258–296; and Charles

In 1828, the ministry was staffed by thirty-eight officials who appear to have had little free time. There was always a mountain of paperwork at the Wilhelmstrasse.[82] Bernstorff personally drafted a large number of his own diplomatic papers, but he also relied on several senior officials in the ministry to compose dispatches, instructions, *Denkschriften,* and other communications. He would usually revise these extensively before sending them on to a senior clerk who would supervise the preparation of the final, handsomely written document. This involved a laborious process of copying and recopying. Most dispatches and other documents contained numerous enclosures, for example, extracts from other pertinent papers, copies of dispatches to or from other envoys, and of correspondence from foreign governments to their envoys in Berlin. If the document was to be sent to several legations simultaneously, the copying process was terribly time-consuming for the small staff. Although French and German were used interchangeably by the ministry, matters involving the German state system were generally conducted in German and those involving European politics in French.

Two subordinate officials within the ministry were of special importance: Johann Peter Friedrich Ancillon and Johann Albert Friedrich Eichhorn. Because these two men were of very different political persuasions, they can be seen as a symbol of the split personality that Prussian foreign policy had during the years 1818–1832. Ancillon (1767–1837) descended from a French Huguenot family that had immigrated to Berlin

---

K. Webster, *The Foreign Policy of Palmerston, 1830–1841,* 1:55–75. For Russia, see Grimsted, *Foreign Ministers of Alexander I,* pp. 3–31. The operations of the French foreign ministry are discussed in Henry Contamine, *Diplomatie et Diplomates sous la Restauration, 1814–1830,* pp. 133–149; and Emmanuel de Levis Mirepoix, *Le Ministère des Affaires Étrangères,* pp. 33–81. For an excellent study of the Austrian *Staatskanzlei,* see Josef Karl Mayr, *Geschichte der österreichischen Staatskanzlei im Zeitalter des Fürsten Metternich.* Established working hours for all members of the ministry in Berlin did not exist. In 1821, however, Bernstorff had ordered that the subalterns work from 9 o'clock to 2 o'clock and from 4 o'clock to 7 o'clock daily. Senior councillors on the other hand, were only required to report in daily at the ministry to accomplish their work as necessary. See Sasse, "Zur Geschichte des Auswärtigen Amts," pp. 113–114.

82. At approximately the same time, France employed fifty-five officials, Russia approximately three hundred, and Britain thirty-six. See Levis Mirepoix, *Le Ministère des Affaires Étrangères,* p. 73; Grimsted, *Foreign Ministers of Alexander I,* p. 26; and Temperley, *Foreign Policy of Canning,* p. 259. For Prussia, see *Handbuch . . . 1828.*

at the end of the seventeenth century.[83] He studied theology in Geneva and became the pastor for the French Protestant community in Berlin. He was also a conservative historian and political writer and was elected to the Prussian Academy of Sciences in 1805. Later he became the tutor of Crown Prince Frederick William. In 1814, he entered the foreign ministry. In many ways, however, throughout his career he remained more of a court official than a professional civil servant. A strong supporter of absolutism, he was highly critical of any genuinely reformist programs. Early in his career, he was strongly inclined toward Alexander of Russia; subsequently he became a disciple of Metternich, although not to the extent that Wittgenstein was. He believed firmly in the European alliance and, like most Prussian leaders, saw the necessity for the maintenance of peace in Europe. He was pedantic and petulant and could not draft a concise dispatch or *Denkschrift*. All his papers are long-winded and redundant. Bernstorff was constantly slashing paragraphs from his drafts and eliminating whole pages. From 1818 to 1823, Ancillon played a significant role within the department, contributed several important papers, and was responsible for diplomatic correspondence in Bernstorff's absence. After 1825, when Prussian policy began to be colored by a more progressive outlook, his importance declined rapidly. In 1827, he complained that he was being entirely ignored by Bernstorff and had nothing to do. After 1831, when an ultraconservative campaign began to erode Bernstorff's authority, his influence again began to increase. An opposite oscillation of influence can be found in the career of his colleague Eichhorn.

Eichhorn (1779–1856) is a good example of the many middle-level Prussian officials who played an important role in implementing the programs of the government during the era of reform and then continued to have strong reformist tendencies after 1819. After studying law at the University of Göttingen and acquiring an early allegiance to the goals of the reform movement, Eichhorn held a series of significant positions within the Prussian state. He worked on the organization of the *Berliner*

83. There is no comprehensive study of Ancillon, although much useful information is contained in Paul Haake, *Johann Peter Friedrich Ancillon und Kronprinz Friedrich Wilhelm IV von Preussen.* His most influential published works, which were widely read, are *Tableau des révolutions du Systeme Politique de l'Europe depuis la fin du quinzième Siecle,* 4 vols. (Berlin, 1803–1805); *Über Souveränität und Staatsverfassungen* (Berlin, 1815); and *Zur Vermittlung der Extreme in den Meinungen,* 2 vols. (Berlin, 1828–1831).

*Landwehr,* served on Blücher's staff in Silesia, and was a key administrator in Stein's *Zentralverwaltung.* He wrote an important paper extolling the mission of the *Zentralverwaltung* in Germany as well as an extensive document justifying Prussia's claim to Saxony.[84] In 1816, he joined the foreign ministry, but he continued to be involved in domestic affairs, especially with regard to the implementation of a constitution. By 1819, he was viewed as one of the most dangerous revolutionaries within the Prussian government, and Wittgenstein tried repeatedly to get Hardenberg to dismiss him from the ministry.[85] Rose also hoped that Bernstorff would remove Eichhorn from office. But the two men appear to have been very compatible from the start, and, by 1820, it was clear that Bernstorff had great respect for Eichhorn's work. Eichhorn in turn seems to have had considerable admiration for his chief.[86] He was energetic, perceptive, and forthright, and he was loyal to Bernstorff throughout his ministry. After 1825, when Eichhorn became deeply involved in the negotiation of the *Zollverein* treaties, he was the most influential subordinate official within the ministry. If Bernstorff attempted to hold back Ancillon's advancement, he constantly pushed Eichhorn's career. By 1830, he was Bernstorff's closest collaborator on all matters of German policy, a role that was made official in 1831 when he was made director of the second section of the ministry, with special added responsibilities for German affairs. Bernstorff's fall from power in 1832 severely crippled Eichhorn's political influence until 1840.[87]

In addition to these two men, the ministry employed eight other *Vortragende Räthe.* These councillors were split between the two divisions of the ministry without any special distinctions between the two. They

---

84. See Peter Graf von Kielmannsegg, *Stein und die Zentralverwaltung 1813/ 1814;* and Karl Griewank, *Der Wiener Kongress und die Europäischen Restauration 1814 / 15,* p. 196.

85. Wittgenstein to Hardenberg, 4 and 7 December 1821; Hans Branig, ed., *Briefwechsel des Fürsten Karl August von Hardenberg mit dem Fürsten Wilhelm Ludwig von Sayn-Wittgenstein, 1806–1822,* pp. 287–289. Eichhorn's friendship with Clausewitz is another indication of his progressive political views even after 1815; see Paret, *Clausewitz,* pp. 212, 316.

86. Bernstorff to Hardenberg, n.d. (January 1820), ZSA Me, AAI, Rep. 1, Nr. 31; and Rose to Castlereagh, 3 August 1819, PRO F.O. 64/119.

87. Unfortunately, there is no study of Eichhorn. However, he is mentioned prominently in many of the standard and specialized works covering this period. Treitschke describes him in lively terms in *History of Germany,* 3:289–292. Also see *Neue Deutsche Biographie,* s.v. "Eichhorn, Johann Albrecht Friedrich."

were assigned much of the work concerning the preliminary drafting of documents, background research, analysis of treaties, and commercial activities. They were supported by a number of subaltern officials—senior clerks, copyists, journalists, archivists, translators, cryptographers, and accountants. The organization of the ministry remained quite uncomplicated, less specialized than in France or Austria, but each official had clearly defined duties. Specialists with long experience and considerable professional ability were developed in journalism, archival work, and cryptography, in addition to the expected concentrations of legal, commercial, financial, and German and European affairs. A distinct and important system of ranks existed within the ministry ranging from *Wirklicher Geheimer Rath,* down to *Wirklicher Geheimer Legationsrath, Geheimer Legationsrath, Wirklicher Legationsrath, Legationsrath, Geheimer Hofrath, Hofrath, Geheimer Expedient Secretair,* and *Geheimer Secretair.*

The Prussian state as a whole felt constrained by its financial problems, and so did the foreign ministry. Bernstorff was constantly urged to economize, and, in fact, the staff of the ministry had declined by six positions since 1818.[88] In 1821, in answer to complaints from the treasury, Bernstorff told Hardenberg that he understood the need for economy, but that reducing spending was a difficult task due to the added cost occasioned by the congresses and conferences of that time.[89] Salaries for officials in the ministry remained almost constant during the second quarter of the nineteenth century. The accompanying table gives a comparison between 1828 and 1845.[90] In contrast to these salary levels, Bernstorff paid his

|                           | 1828            | 1845            |
|---------------------------|-----------------|-----------------|
| Chief                     | 18,000 talers   | 18,000 talers   |
| Director of Second Division | 4,500–5,000   | 4,500           |
| *Vortragende Räthe*       | 2,000–2,800     | 2,000–3,000     |
| Subalterns                | 700–1,400       | 600–1,800       |

88. *Handbuch über den Königlichen Preussischen Hof und Staat 1818,* pp. 62–63.
89. Bernstorff to Hardenberg, 6 June 1821, ZSA Me, AAI, Rep. 1, Nr. 31.
90. See list of salaries in Prussian Ministry of Foreign Affairs given to the British minister to Berlin, in Brook-Taylor to Dudley, 24 March 1828, PRO F.O. 44/154; and financial report of the foreign ministry for 1845 in ZSA Me, Geheimes Civil Cabinet, Rep. 2.2.1., Nr. 24585. The cost of living rose significantly during this twenty-year period. See John R. Gillis, *The Prussian Bureaucracy in Crisis, 1840–1860,* p. 58.

gardener, servants, and coachman 180 talers a year each.[91] Relatively minor raises in pay (for example, a 100-taler increase on a salary of 2,400) had to be carefully justified at least in a pro forma way to the King.[92]

Prussian envoys to foreign courts were paid at a much higher level, but Prussia had few diplomats of great wealth serving as ministers. Throughout these years, their salaries also held steady. The ministers to Paris, London, and St. Petersburg were all paid 25,000 talers, 10,000 of which was intended to cover the expenses of maintaining a household, entertainment, and travel. A post of moderate importance, such as Stockholm, carried a salary of 11,000 talers. Emissaries to the more substantial German states were generally paid the same amount, although the envoy to Weimar only received 3,500 talers. These salary levels did not allow for a luxurious life-style. For example, Heinrich von Bülow, Humboldt's son-in-law and a man of modest means, became the minister to London in 1827. He was a frugal individual who personally tallied every expense he incurred, no matter how minor, in an account book. Despite this care, he still found it difficult to make his salary cover the necessary expenses of being a minister, and he complained to Bernstorff on numerous occasions.[93]

It was rare for a ministry official to be assigned to a foreign diplomatic post; those positions were reserved for aristocrats of considerable prestige. As a result, there was little direct contact between the personnel of the diplomatic service and that of the ministry. Military figures occupied a significant, but not inordinate, number of diplomatic positions during these years; in 1828, seven of the twenty ministers were officers in the army. However, only two were generals, and only one, General von Schöler, who was one of Prussia's most capable diplomats, was assigned to a major post (St. Petersburg). By 1831, only four ministers were in the military. However, officers rather than civilians were usually employed in special diplomatic missions (for example, Müffling's mission to Constantinople in 1829, which we will discuss later).

91. Bernstorff, *Aufzeichnungen,* 1:270.

92. See, for example, Bernstorff to Frederick William, 8 October 1831, ZSA Me, Geheimes Civil Cabinet, Rep. 2.2.1., Nr. 12909.

93. For this correspondence and for his account book, see the *Nachlass* of Heinrich von Bülow, Tegel Privatarchiv, West Berlin. Bernstorff tried to be sympathetic to Bülow's problem and did secure a single extraordinary payment of 400 talers to help cover moving costs and high rents in London. See Bernstorff to Bülow, 6 December 1827 and 17 October 1828, and Bernstorff to Legations Kasse, 6 December 1827, Heinrich von Bülow *Nachlass,* Tegel Privatarchiv.

Under Bernstorff, the Prussian foreign ministry worked reasonably well. With the important exception of relations with Austria, its control over the foreign relations of the Prussian state appears to have been relatively complete. Correspondence between Metternich and other officials outside the ministry constantly circumvented the formal foreign policy apparatus of the state. This practice was especially undesirable because Prussian ministers to Vienna quickly came under Metternich's influence and sometimes failed to represent Berlin's interests in a professional and loyal manner. This was true of Prince Hatzfeld in the 1820s and of Freiherr von Maltzahn, who succeeded him. Despite these exceptions, the ministry succeeded in achieving an identity of its own. By 1830, it was one of the most dynamic departments in government. Its structure and procedures had matured since the era of reform, and its basic organization remained relatively unchanged until the 1880s.[94] As an institution it appears to have adequately met the international needs of the Prussian state.

94. Lamar Cecil, *The German Diplomatic Service, 1871-1914*, pp. 3-20; and Paul Gordon Lauren, *Diplomats and Bureaucrats*, pp. 19-23.

✠ ✠ ✠ ✠ ✠ ✠ ✠ ✠ ✠ ✠ ✠ ✠ ✠ ✠

# Prussia's
# Customs Policy

When the federal Diet met in August 1824 and unanimously approved the continuation of the provisional press law adopted five years earlier at Carlsbad, it was clear that the forces of reaction were in firm control of Germany.[1] The policy of reaction seemed equally secure in Prussia. In retrospect, however, we can see that the most dogmatic and vigorous phase of the German reaction was over. In the next five years, press censorship was less rigidly enforced, and Frederick William became more tolerant toward former members of the reform movement.[2] However, it took some time before changes in attitude resulted in the adoption of more adventurous policies by the government. Despite the slowness of this transition, a process of regeneration did begin in the period from 1824 to 1830. Its development is not readily apparent in the purely political activities of the government, but it can be seen as an outgrowth of Prussia's financial and economic policies. As the political component of these policies gradually took shape, developed force, and combined with latent reformist attitudes held over from the earlier period, new activity and energy was generated in Prussia's German policy. The early negotiations that helped to create the German customs union, the *Zollverein* were central to this entire development.

1. Heinrich von Treitschke, *History of Germany in the Nineteenth Century,* 4: 98.
2. Ibid., pp. 111, 210, 246; L. F. Ilse, *Geschichte der deutschen Bundesversammlung,* 2:319; and Friedrich Kapp, "Die preussische Pressegesetzgebung unter Friedrich Wilhelm III, 1815–1840," pp. 207–208.

The founding of the *Zollverein* belongs to the pantheon of historic events leading to the unification of Germany. Interpretations of its early stages have often been distorted by the knowledge of its later contribution to the political as well as economic consolidation of the German states. Prussia's part in the evolution of the *Zollverein* has been particularly subject to this kind of misinterpretation. Referring to the period after 1819, Golo Mann has written, "Even during these years of peace Prussia's tariff policy was consciously directed toward the economic domination of Germany."[3] In his *Deutsche Geschichte im Neunzehnten Jahrhundert*, Franz Schnabel wrote, "From the beginning the Prussian government strove for the customs unification of Germany under Prussian leadership," and W. O. Henderson, author of the standard study in English of the *Zollverein*, has written:

> Through all these confusions the Prussian Civil Servants held their course steadily. They produced no genius for the hero-worshippers to admire, but their greatest representatives—men like Maassen, Motz, Eichhorn, Kühne, Delbrück, Philipsborn and Pommer-Esche—were men of ability, character and courage. By their tenacity of purpose they served not only Prussia but—sometimes without knowing it—a greater Fatherland. . . . The Zollverein is the contribution of the Prussian Civil Service to the founding of the German Empire.[4]

There is a strong element of truth in these statements, but they ascribe to the period 1818–1834 a continuity of purpose, a consciousness of national economic concerns, and a degree of Prussian initiative that in fact did not always exist. Moreover, this interpretation tends to ignore or subordinate the important, sometimes dominant, role played by the south German states in the formation of the customs union. What is most interesting about this period is not the steady, unfaltering nature of Prussia's customs policy, but rather the slow, hesitant, almost painful development of a comprehensive economic policy for Germany by Prussian officials. As Wolfram Fischer has stated:

> It should not be forgotten, . . . that the foundations of the German customs system were laid by Prussia not in order to assume leadership in

3. Golo Mann, *The History of Germany since 1789*, p. 56.
4. Franz Schnabel, *Deutsche Geschichte im Neunzehnten Jahrhundert*, 2:300; and W. O. Henderson, *The Zollverein*, pp. 342–343.

German affairs but to make her own law applicable. The trend towards an all-German union was fostered far more and much earlier by the middle states and by the spirit of the age, represented by the national and liberal movements.[5]

In time, however, the Prussian government did integrate its customs policy with an imprecise desire to exert greater leadership in the political affairs of Germany, and this makes an analysis of Prussia's customs policies crucial for an understanding of her German policy in the 1820s.

The Prussian tariff law of 26 May 1818 is the proper starting point for an analysis of Prussian economic policy during the 1820s. Although the Prussian reformers expressed a strong interest in rationalizing Prussia's and Germany's archaic customs system, the main stimulus for this law came from the financial need of the Prussian state and the depressed condition of the Prussian economy.[6] Many Prussian officials, schooled in the doctrines of Adam Smith, believed that the existing customs system exacerbated Prussia's economic and financial problems. Legitimate internal trade was hampered by over fifty-seven different arrangements in the old provinces alone, and the complexity of the tariff laws encouraged smuggling and made administration costly and inefficient. Prussia would have to compensate for the wide distribution of her territories through more efficient administrative practices.[7] In addition, after the demise of the Continental System, low import duties by Frankfurt am Main, Hamburg, and Bremen caused Prussia to be flooded with cheap English goods.[8]

With these problems in mind, Hans von Bülow submitted a detailed proposal for the reform of Prussia's customs policy in 1817. To eliminate internal barriers to trade, he urged that import duties be collected only at the exterior frontier. He also argued for a simple schedule of moderate

5. Wolfram Fischer, "The German Zollverein," p. 85.

6. Arnold Price, *The Evolution of the Zollverein*, p. 61. This is by far the best treatment of the founding of the German *Zollverein*.

7. Prussia "contained no less than thirteen enclaves, . . . its frontiers were 8,000 kilometers in length, and touched twenty-eight different states." John A. R. Marriot and C. G. Robertson, *The Evolution of Prussia*, p. 290.

8. Hermann Oncken, "Zur Einführung," Hermann Oncken and F. E. M. Saemisch eds., *Vorgeschichte und Begründung des deutschen Zollvereins 1815–1834*, 1:xxi; Henderson, *Zollverein*, pp. 22–23; and Michael Doeberl, "Bayern und die wirtschaftliche Einigung Deutschlands," 29:2:6.

import fees and transit charges to provide some protection for embattled domestic manufacturing. The new schedule would make smuggling unprofitable, encourage the transit trade, and would not provoke retaliation from Prussia's European neighbors.[9] Bülow's draft reflected the government's concern for domestic manufacturers as well as its desire for increased revenues from customs duties. Because customs duties and excise taxes were the main source of revenue for the state, in a period of financial stringency, commercial policy was often evaluated more from a fiscal standpoint than from the perspective of the home economy.[10] Bülow also advocated the simultaneous reform of Prussia's internal tax administration, but, when his proposal went to the tax commission of the *Staatsrat,* this aspect of his program met with widespread opposition. Consequently, the tax commission approved of Bülow's customs reforms, but postponed consideration of the taxation issue. Bülow was furious. He argued that the tax and customs proposals were both essential to overall financial reform. Unable to carry his point, he resigned as Minister of Finance during a ministerial crisis and became the head of the newly created Ministry of Commerce.[11] The new law, drafted in its final form by Maassen, was issued on 26 May 1818.[12]

In a period when high tariffs prevailed throughout much of Europe, Prussia's duties were low, and her system rational. Clapham wrote that

9. Bülow to Frederick William, 14 January 1817, Oncken and Saemisch, *Vorgeschichte und Begründung,* 1:35–45.

10. Oncken, "Zur Einführung," pp. *xix–xxi;* Fischer, "German Zollverein," p. 67; Wilhelm Treue, *Wirtschaftzustände, und Wirtschaftpolitik in Preussen, 1815–1825,* p. 140; and Gustav Schmoller, *Das Preussische Handels- und Zollgesetz vom 26. Mai 1818.*

11. Oncken and Saemisch, *Vorgeschichte und Begründung,* 1:4–6, 46–61, 61–88, 69–71.

12. Two schedules of tariffs were introduced: one for the eastern provinces, and one for the western. In 1821, one common schedule was adopted for the entire kingdom. Three kinds of duties were levied: an import duty, a consumption duty (for items imported and consumed in Prussia), and a transit duty. For manufactured goods, the first two duties were usually about 10 percent of the value of the product; they were somewhat higher for colonial products. Transit duties were levied solely according to weight. For the text of the law, see Gesetz über den Zoll und Verbrauchsteuer von ausländischen Waren und über den Verkehr zwischen den Provinzen des preussischen Staats, 26 May 1818, ibid., pp. 71–78; also see Henderson, *Zollverein,* for a convenient summary.

Prussia had "immeasurably the wisest and most scientific tariff then existing among the great powers."[13] Although we view this law as the first goal in the creation of the *Zollverein*, it must be strongly emphasized that this step was not in the minds of the Prussian officials at the time. As Hermann Oncken has noted: "The Prussian customs law was not only a product of the autonomous Prussian bureaucracy, it occurred without any regard for the remaining German states, or for the German Confederation; it was an act of Prussian state power, concerning which the national community remained unconsulted."[14]

## THE ENCLAVE NEGOTIATIONS

The new customs law went into effect on 1 January 1819. The government was immediately faced with the problem of how to treat the numerous enclaves, such as the principality of Schwarzburg-Sonderhausen and the three duchies of Anhalt-Koethen, Anhalt-Bernburg, and Anhalt-Dessau, which were located entirely or partly inside Prussian territory.[15] Prussia's policy toward these tiny enclaves is important and illuminating because it demonstrates the lack of any comprehensive or single-minded campaign on the part of Prussia to establish a German customs union in the years 1819–1828.

The commerce and finance ministries initially recommended to Hardenberg that import and consumption duties be collected at the Prussian frontier on all goods headed for the Anhalts. They would be compensated for the consumption duties collected, but they had to adopt the Prussian schedule of consumption taxes so that no loopholes would be left in Prussia's internal system of taxation. With such an arrangement, Prussia would save at least 34,000 talers in administrative costs and would take in an additional 37,000 talers from import and consumption duties.[16] The

13. J. H. Clapham, *Economic Development of France and Germany, 1815–1914*, p. 97.

14. Oncken, "Zur Einführung," p. *xxiii.*

15. For an excellent description of Prussia's customs relations with the enclaves, see Price, *Evolution of the Zollverein*, pp. 130–158.

16. The commerce and finance ministries to Hardenberg, 27 June 1818, Oncken and Saemisch, *Vorgeschichte und Begründung*, 1:83–85.

foreign ministry was instructed to negotiate treaties along this line with the Anhalts and with Schwarzburg-Sonderhausen. However, ministry officials were hesitant to approach the enclaves. Because they believed that the small German states would object to any attempt to subordinate their interests to those of Prussia, Bernstorff's department took no action.[17] The Ministry of Finance, unconcerned with the foreign ministry's misgivings ordered that the enclaves should be treated as Prussian territory for the purposes of the new law.[18] It was expected that this would facilitate the smooth implementation and comprehensive application of the new regulations and might possibly force the enclaves to come to some kind of agreement with Prussia.[19] Thus, the finance ministry disregarded the political consequences of Prussia's customs policy and moved ahead without any prior agreements with either the enclaves or the foreign ministry.

The enclaves promptly and vigorously protested to the government in Berlin.[20] Frederick William was furious about the finance ministry's shabby treatment of the duchies and the lack of preparations for handling the problem of the enclaves in general.[21] Bernstorff, who was charged with the duty of replying to the Anhalts, defended the legality of the Prussian action, but added that discussions on the matter would eliminate all difficulties caused by the new Prussian law.[22] However, the duchies were unwilling to negotiate. Instead, they protested directly to Frederick William, but to no avail. Bernstorff continued to maintain that the Prussian procedure was both necessary and just.

During this same period, the Prussian government also paid little attention to the commercial interests of other German states. For example, Nassau expressed a desire for a commercial agreement with Prussia, and Bernstorff even suggested to Bülow and Klewitz that it might be in Prussia's interest to consider such a proposition. But the two ministers argued that the agreement would be financially and commercially detrimental to Prussia, and the matter was dropped. The attempts of Weimar

17. Hoffman to Klewitz, 20 November 1818, ibid., pp. 88–89.

18. Finanzamt to the Regierung in Erfurt, 14 December 1818, ibid., p. 89.

19. Klewitz to Frederick William, 28 January 1819, ibid., pp. 91–94; and Price, *Evolution of the Zollverein,* p. 135.

20. The three Anhalt governments to the Prussian Ministry of Foreign Affairs, 29 January 1819, Oncken and Saemisch, *Vorgeschichte und Begründung,* 1:94–97.

21. Frederick William to Klewitz, 8 February 1819, ibid., pp. 97–98.

22. Bernstorff to the three Anhalt governments, 11 March 1819, ibid., pp. 98–101.

and Bavaria to establish better commercial relations with Berlin met with a similar rebuff.[23]

Schwarzburg-Sonderhausen's notes on the operation of the Prussian law received no reply from Bernstorff whatsoever; the principality's complaints were considered only when Weise, the Chancellor of this small state, arrived in Berlin on the initiative of his own Prince.[24] On 25 October 1819, the two governments concluded a customs accession treaty that provided for freedom of trade between Prussia and Schwarzburg-Sonderhausen and allowed Prussia to levy import and consumption duties at the frontier on goods bound for the principality.[25] The principality was to be compensated for its loss of revenue from consumption duties; the amount of compensation was to be proportional to the ratio of Schwarzburg-Sonderhausen's population to the population of Prussia's eastern provinces. No compensation was granted for the loss of import duties. Even though the treaty was financially severe to the smaller state, officials in the Ministry of Finance still criticized it as being too favorable to Schwarzburg-Sonderhausen.[26] The treaty is significant for two reasons: First, it served as a model for all other enclave treaties; and, second, it demonstrated the narrowly fiscal concerns of the Prussian government. It should be noted that there was no provision for the adhesion of a third party nor for modifying the terms of the agreement. Indeed, Berlin adopted an unusually restricted approach to commercial matters and demonstrated a remarkable disregard for the impression that this miserly policy might create in Germany. The assertion that, in 1819, Prussia was already striving for the economic domination of Germany is not borne out by the terms of the Schwarzburg-Sonderhausen treaty. In fact, Prussia was almost totally preoccupied with her acute domestic financial and economic problems.

In the course of the next twelve years, the remaining enclaves were included in the Prussian system on a similar basis. The agreements that proved most difficult to achieve and that are most interesting to analyze are those with the three Anhalts. Time and again, Bernstorff endeavored

---

23. Walter Menn, *Zur Vorgeschichte des deutschen Zollvereins*, pp. 40–42; Irmgard Kamlah, *Karl Georg Maassen und die preussische Finanzreform von 1816–1822*, pp. 32–33; and Price, *Evolution of the Zollverein*, p. 138.

24. Prince Günther of Schwarzburg-Sonderhausen to Frederick William, 24 July 1819, Oncken and Saemisch, *Vorgeschichte und Begründung*, 1:106–107.

25. For its text, see ibid., pp. 116–123.

26. Heinrich von Treitschke, "Die Anfänge des deutschen Zollvereins," p. 429.

to get negotiations started with these three states, but the foreign ministry's only accomplishment was a minor settlement with Anhalt-Bernburg that approved the inclusion of a small enclave of the duchies within the Prussian system.[27] The duchies' disinclination to make any accommodation to Prussian interests, especially with regard to acknowledging the extensive smuggling that was being carried on from their territory, was matched by the Ministry of Finance's reluctance to be flexible on the matter of compensation for the duties collected since 1819. In all these discussions, the Ministry of Finance resisted any agreement detrimental to Prussia's financial interests, while the foreign ministry advocated a more moderate policy that took political and commercial factors into consideration.[28] Frustrated by the fruitless course of the Anhalt negotiations, Bernstorff issued a directive to Prussia's diplomatic missions in Germany, stating that, while Prussia was ready to admit other states into her customs system, Prussia would not take the first step. This position was restated in 1825 and, as Eichhorn explained, was justified because of the sensitivity of the various dynasties to any Prussian initiatives in this area. "Such proposals could be misinterpreted as demands," he said, "for the change of their domestic institutions and as threats to their sovereignty."[29]

In the summer of 1825, Friedrich von Motz succeeded Klewitz as Minister of Finance. Energetic and in favor of reform, the new minister was determined to take decisive action to break the resistance of the Anhalt governments.[30] He urged the strictest possible enforcement of customs laws affecting goods passing to the Anhalts and called for the suspension of freedom of transit on the Elbe in contravention of the Elbe Ship Transit Treaty of December 1821.[31] Bernstorff, Heinrich von Bülow, and Eichhorn resisted the use of such threatening measures and, despite Motz's objections, successfully concluded a customs accession treaty with Anhalt-Bernburg.[32] However, the recalcitrant Anhalt-Dessau and Anhalt-Koethen were now subjected to the full retaliation of Motz and his min-

27. Price, *Evolution of the Zollverein,* p. 149.

28. Treitschke, "Die Anfänge des deutschen Zollvereins," p. 455.

29. Ibid., p. 458.

30. Hermann von Petersdorff, *Friedrich von Motz, eine Biographie,* 2:102.

31. Motz to Bernstorff, 24 July 1825, Oncken and Saemisch, *Vorgeschichte und Begründung,* 1:233.

32. Petersdorff, *Motz,* 2:90–92; Oncken and Saemisch, *Vorgeschichte und Begründung,* 1:238–239; and Motz to Bernstorff, 24 October 1825, ibid., 1:237–238.

istry. In early 1827, the Elbe was closed above and below Koethen and Dessau to traffic destined for the two duchies.[33] They immediately protested to the other German states and to the federal Diet. Metternich tried to mediate the controversy by removing it from consideration by the Diet. He also told the Austrian consul-general in Leipzig to try to force Duke Ferdinand of Anhalt-Koethen into some kind of accommodation with Prussia.[34] (Sometimes, Austro-Prussian dualism worked in Prussia's favor.) Talks did not begin until January 1828, and it took six months of hard negotiating before agreements similar to the Anhalt-Bernburg and Schwarzburg-Sonderhausen customs accession treaties were signed. With these agreements "cette affaire ennuyante," as Bernstorff used to call the Anhalt dispute, came to an end.[35]

Although these three small states had a combined population of less than 123,000, the negotiations between them and Prussia are important for a number of reasons. They demonstrate the confusion that existed within the Prussian government during the early years of customs negotiations. Disagreement between the government departments and indecisiveness in the foreign ministry indicate that this was a period of transition during which Prussian ministers had no clear concept of what Prussia's commercial policy in Germany should be. The Ministry of Finance consistently took a narrow, fiscal point of view toward the negotiations. The foreign ministry, on the other hand, adopted a more flexible position. Bernstorff remained fairly sympathetic to the smaller German courts, but had difficulty in defining the relationship of a small state to a large one in terms of sovereignty. He was consistently forced to choose between the concepts of power and legality, between efficiency and amity. He believed that small states such as the Anhalts, should be able to appreciate that joining the Prussian system could be mutually advantageous, and should therefore be willing to voluntarily modify their strict definition of sovereign rights. An inordinate use of power to force them into this

---

33. Treitschke, "Die Anfänge des deutschen Zollvereins," p. 456.

34. Die 2. köthensche Klage am Bundestag, 22 March 1827, Oncken and Saemisch, *Vorgeschichte und Begründung,* 1:270–271; Metternich to Zichy, 3 April 1827; Köthensche Vergleichsvorschlag, 26 May 1827; Eichhorn to Metternich, 31 May 1827, ibid., pp. 270–276.

35. See ibid., pp. 276–293; and especially the Prussian Ministry of Foreign Affairs to Motz (drafted by Eichhorn), 7 July 1827, ibid., pp. 282–283. Also see Treitschke, *History of Germany,* 4:281.

realization was both unnecessary and unwise. However, his approach was frustrated because the finance ministry's policies reduced the really advantageous nature of the relationship. While Bernstorff, Bülow, Hoffmann, and Eichhorn were more accommodating to the duchies for political reasons, they did not envision the building of a larger, Prussian-dominated economic community in Germany. The enclave negotiations do not provide any evidence of higher political-economic aims on the part of foreign ministry officials. On the other hand, they do mark the debut of Motz as a government minister and of Berlin's willingness to adopt harsh measures to coerce other states into joining the Prussian system. To that extent his methods were the first indication of a new energy that slowly permeated other aspects of Prussian policy and in turn merged with the changing viewpoint of the foreign ministry to create a new, more dynamic Prussian German policy.

## SOUTH GERMAN EFFORTS AT CUSTOMS REFORM

Prussia's customs reform represents only one line of development that led eventually to the German customs union of 1834. The south German states—especially Bavaria, Württemberg, Baden, and Hesse-Darmstadt—and public pressures, first mobilized and given direction by Frederick List's German Commercial and Industrial League, represented other forces that helped to establish a more rational system of customs administration in Germany. The German Commercial and Industrial League, which represented some seventy merchants and manufacturers from central and southern Germany, was founded in Frankfurt in the spring of 1819. Among other things, its program called for the economic unification of Germany as a first step toward the establishment of free trade in Europe.[36] It tried to arouse public opinion in order to pressure the various German governments into action. Southern Germany, in particular, was flooded with leaflets, pamphlets, and newspaper articles setting forth its proposals. This agitation had considerable impact, especially in Bavaria and Baden, where the parliaments began to urge the establishment of free trade and

---

36. Emmanuel N. Roussakis, *Friedrich List, the Zollverein, and the Uniting of Europe*, pp. 36–37.

customs unification.[37] At the Vienna ministerial conference, these two states and others officially endorsed the idea of free trade in Germany, and proposals were made for the creation of a common customs system within the Confederation.[38]

However, these plans came to nothing because neither of the major German powers was interested in them. Although Metternich thought it was politically advantageous to make some concessions to the demands for more liberal trade arrangements in Germany, Francis refused to authorize such a policy. Austrian involvement in any German economic system might disrupt the unity of the multinational Habsburg empire. Francis chose to uphold Austrian imperial interests in return for sacrificing some of Austria's leadership in German affairs.[39] Prussia also rejected the south German proposals for free trade.

Faced with the opposition of Berlin and Vienna, the league suggested the idea of a regional south German customs union to the King of Bavaria. This approach was gradually supported by Bavaria, Württemberg, and other central German states that wished to oppose the Prussian system.[40] These states met in a number of conferences in an attempt to create a new customs system. These meetings failed to accomplish their primary objective, but, by 1828, they had led to a separate agreement by Bavaria and Württemberg. On 18 January, a treaty was signed creating a *Zollverein* between these two states, the first true customs union in Germany.[41]

In 1822, Bernstorff asked Hans von Bülow and Klewitz to examine how Prussian interests would be affected by the conclusion of a customs

---

37. Doeberl, "Bayern und die wirtschaftliche Einigung Deutschlands," pp. 10–11.

38. Ibid., p. 12; and Price, *Evolution of the Zollverein*, pp. 53–59.

39. Adolf Beer, "Oesterreich und die deutsche Handelseinigungsbestrebungen in den Jahren 1817–1820," p. 277.

40. Roussakis, *Friedrich List*, pp. 41–44.

41. Ibid., pp. 44–45; Price, *Evolution of the Zollverein*, pp. 78–105; Henderson, *Zollverein*, pp. 57–63; Menn, *Zur Vorgeschichte des deutschen Zollvereins*, pp. 72–152; and Doeberl, "Bayern und die wirtschaftliche Einigung Deutschlands," pp. 18–30. The treaty dissolved the customs line between Bavaria and Württemberg and established Bavarian procedures and laws as the standard for the union's administration. Bavaria and Württemberg would retain control over their own administrations, but a representative from each state would survey the customs operations of the other. Each year, plenipotentiaries of the two members would meet to review and, if necessary, change the laws of the union. The division of revenues would be proportional to the populations of the two states.

agreement in the south.[42] Klewitz expressed a continued interest in Electoral Hesse as a key to uniting the western and eastern portions of Prussia, but he foresaw no adverse affects for Prussia if a regional customs union were created.[43] In 1824, the Ministry of Finance drew up a policy paper on the same question. It concluded that, "as has already been stated in a note to the foreign ministry of 27 June 1822, such a union of states . . . is of no worry, whatsoever, to Prussia."[44] To be sure, not all Prussian officials were this disinterested; Otterstedt, the Prussian minister to Darmstadt, was particularly concerned about the inactivity of Prussia's customs policy. He reported that the public and the lower house of the Darmstadt parliament were strongly in favor of freedom of trade in Germany and that, as a result, they were hostile toward Prussia. He wrote:

> Prussia can retain that importance among the great powers which it once possessed after the great deeds of the years 1813–1815 only through public opinion. At that time, all of Germany was united in its support of Prussia. Since that time, however, and especially since the introduction of the tariff system in 1818, the enemies of Prussia have tried to place everything, especially the related customs system, in an odious light, and to let Prussia in general appear as the hindrance to the achievement of positive arrangements.

Regardless of the other factors that determined the nature of Prussia's policy, Otterstedt believed that for political reasons Prussia should re-evaluate its approach to commercial affairs in Germany.[45]

After reading this report, the King asked Bernstorff to have the *Staatsministerium* render an opinion on the south German situation.[46] The foreign minister reported back that Otterstedt's account exaggerated the seriousness of the problem. He added that the foreign ministry had clearly stated that Prussia would not oppose south German attempts at customs unification. He did not believe that the south Germans were

---

42. Bernstorff to Bülow and Klewitz, 8 June 1822, in Oncken and Saemisch, *Vorgeschichte und Begründung,* 2:45.

43. Klewitz to Bülow, 27 June 1822, ibid., pp. 46–49.

44. Denkschrift des preussischen Finanzministeriums über die Frage, wie sich Preussen bei den Bemühungen mehrerer süddeutscher Staaten, sich zu einem gemeinschaftlicher Zoll- und Handelssystem zu vereinigen, gegen seine deutsche Nachbarstaaten zu verhalten hat, 28 December 1824, ibid., pp. 77–98.

45. Otterstedt to Frederick William, 3 March 1824, ibid., pp. 59–63.

46. Frederick William to Bernstorff, 13 March 1824, ibid., pp. 63–64.

hostile toward Prussia, but he admitted that the situation would be improved if "all tariff barriers between Prussia and southern Germany were dropped." He then explained that the obstacle to such an innovation

> lies primarily in the political fragmentation of single states and in the jealousy with which they guard their independence in consequence of which they fear any agreement made unavoidable by common pressures, on a customs system as a reduction of their sovereign rights. For this reason, the foreign ministry has avoided approaching the south German governments with offers of accommodation and prefers to wait until they feel a greater need for such an understanding and until the time when practical suggestions will get a better hearing and their eventual realization more satisfactorily prepared.[47]

These statements by Klewitz and Bernstorff demonstrate Prussia's passive attitude toward efforts to create a customs union in Germany. Berlin did not view the south German efforts as a threat to Prussia's overall plans for Germany because such plans were nonexistent in any active sense. No attempt was made to exploit these negotiations to further Prussia's interests in Germany. Prussia only expressed a strong interest in Electoral Hesse because it was strategically located and opposed the Prussian customs system more strongly than any other German state.

This inactivity in Prussian policy began to disappear after 1825. The reasons for this change in policy are not clear. Possibly as the high point of the German reaction passed, former members of the reform movement such as Motz and Eichhorn felt it was safe to quietly reassert reform ideas and attitudes. At the same time, more dissatisfaction was openly voiced over Prussia's close relations with Austria, and there was a strong desire to see more dynamism and confidence expressed in Berlin's foreign policy.[48] Motz's efficient handling of Prussian finances was an even more direct influence on Prussian policy, especially in the commercial area.

Prussian tax reforms in 1819 and 1820 had strengthened the government's financial position, but Klewitz was still unable to make the collec-

---

47. Bernstorff to Frederick William, 13 July 1824 (drafted by Heinrich von Bülow), ibid., pp. 67–74.

48. Clanwilliam to Canning, 15 June 1824, PRO F.O. 64/140; Seymour to Canning 19 June, 20 June, and 31 October 1824, PRO F.O. 30/24; and Clanwilliam to Canning, 13 April 1826, PRO F.O. 64/146.

tion of revenues significantly more efficient. Unable to balance the budget, he resigned on 4 December 1824.[49] The King selected Motz as his successor primarily because Witzleben had recommended him and because he approved of Motz's plan to improve efficiency by concentrating all power over financial affairs in the hands of the Minister of Finance. Motz was an excellent representative of the gifted, efficiency-oriented, often liberal *Oberpräsidenten* of Prussia. He did not actively belong to any faction, although his early writings placed him close to the camp of the reformers.[50]

Motz concentrated his efforts in three areas. First, he improved the administration of the crown domains, collecting 700,000 talers more in revenues in 1827 than in 1824.[51] Second, by 1826 he had consolidated the commerce ministry (Bülow had died) and the *General Controlle* (which became a section of the Ministry of Finance) under his authority, thus expanding his control over the formulation of Prussia's financial policies.[52] Finally, he increased the efficiency and certainty of tax collection throughout Prussia.[53] Continued government economies also helped to reduce the expenditures of the state. As a result, Motz was able to announce surpluses of 1,000,000 talers in 1826 and 4,400,000 talers in 1828.[54] These surplus revenues allowed him to authorize expenditures that would have been considered frivolous earlier in the decade.[55] By 1828, it was clear that, at least for the moment, the period of Prussia's extreme financial need was past.

---

49. Kamlah, *Maassen*, pp. 38–61; Bernard Brockhage, *Zur Entwicklung des preussischdeutschen Kapitalexports*, p. 118; and Petersdorff, *Motz*, 1:222.

50. Petersdorff, *Motz*, 1:152, 156, 168, 227; 2:3. He was closely identified with Witzleben, with whom he had discussed financial and administrative affairs as early as 1818. In 1817, he wrote an important *Denkschrift* on the desirability of uniting the eastern and western portions of the Prussian state. He opposed provincial assemblies for financial reasons, but he was also critical of the Carlsbad Decrees. In addition to Petersdorff, see Heinrich von Treitschke, "Aus den Papieren des Staatsministers von Motz."

51. Petersdorff, *Motz*, 2:47, 58.

52. Ibid., p. 21.

53. Ibid., p. 67; and Treitschke, "Die Anfänge des deutschen Zollvereins," p. 413.

54. Henderson, *Zollverein*, p. 54; and Petersdorff, *Motz*, 2:84. For more detailed information, see the financial reports of the government for this period in ZSA Me, Geheimes Civil Cabinet, Rep. 2.2.1., Nrs. 24584 and 24741.

55. Petersdorff, *Motz*, 2:82; and Wolfram Fischer, "Das Verhältnis von Staat und Wirtschaft in Deutschland am Beginn der Industrialisierung," p. 353.

## THE PRUSSIAN–HESSE-DARMSTADT
## CUSTOMS TREATY

As can be seen from an examination of the negotiations leading to the establishment of the Prussian–Hesse-Darmstadt Customs Union Treaty of 1828, Prussia's new-found financial stability had an immediate effect on her customs policy for Germany. In 1824, Hesse-Darmstadt was suffering from a severe economic and commercial depression. The leading minister, Freiherr du Thil, had hoped to solve some of Hesse's problems by joining the projected South German Customs Union. When the negotiations for this union proved unsuccessful, his eyes turned to Prussia.[56] In June 1825, the Darmstadt government inquired whether Prussia was interested in a customs arrangement with the two Hesses.[57] The foreign ministry replied that, although Prussia was naturally interested in better commercial relations, it was skeptical of their willingness to enter the Prussian system. Berlin would wait for more definite evidence that the two states were about to rearrange their commercial relations with Prussia, and it advised Darmstadt to consult with Kassel on the matter.[58] As suspected, Electoral Hesse was not interested in joining the Prussian system. Du Thil then inquired whether Darmstadt alone could reach an agreement with Prussia. When Motz and Schuckmann were consulted, however, they told Bernstorff that the advantages of such an agreement to Prussia were slight. As a result, the foreign ministry declined Darmstadt's offer.[59] Thus, Motz's entry into the Cabinet had an effect on the nature of Prussia's enclave policy and immensely improved Prussia's financial position, but it did not immediately alter Berlin's customs policy toward the other German states.

After this unsuccessful initiative, Hesse-Darmstadt again looked to southern Germany. However, efforts to join the Bavarian-Württemberg *Zollverein,* preliminarily agreed to on 12 April 1827, were aborted. Therefore, du Thil once again turned back to Prussia. He told Maltzan, the

---

56. Christian Eckert, "Zur Vorgeschichte des deutschen Zollvereins," pp. 513–523.

57. Maltzan to Bernstorff, 23 June 1825, Oncken and Saemisch, *Vorgeschichte und Begründung,* 2:100–102.

58. The Prussian Ministry of Foreign Affairs to Maltzan, 6 August 1825 (drafted by Bülow), ibid., pp. 104–105.

59. Schuckmann and Motz to the Prussian Ministry of Foreign Affairs, 25 March 1826, ibid., pp. 111–112; and the Prussian Ministry of Foreign Affairs to Maltzan, 16 April 1826, ibid., p. 112.

Prussian minister, that Darmstadt was seriously interested in better commercial relations, and he proposed two alternatives.

1. Complete entry into the Prussian customs system
2. A more restricted commercial treaty calling for mutual reductions in tariffs

Hofmann, du Thil's negotiator, was ready to come to Berlin to discuss these matters in detail.[60] Du Thil also noted: "I do not hide the fact that once we are bound in a commercial way to a great power, we will also be bound in the political sense." Thus, the political motif of these negotiations was noticeable from the start.[61]

Eichhorn immediately consulted the Ministry of Finance, asking Maassen on 9 September 1827 whether there were any specific reasons why Berlin should not enter into discussions with Darmstadt. He added that the foreign ministry "can only wish that one be as receptive as possible to the offer of the Grand Duchy of Hesse and not reject out of hand the establishment of relations that could develop closer connections between both governments."[62] This appears to be the first occasion where the government in Berlin (the foreign ministry, actually) began to focus on the political advantages of customs agreements. Despite Eichhorn's argument, Maassen only slightly modified his ministry's traditional position. As he wrote to the foreign ministry, he could only recommend du Thil's second alternative, especially as Darmstadt was largely isolated from Prussia.[63] He had earlier told the King that a customs union with Darmstadt was undesirable because of the high ratio of border to market area, low tax revenues, and an inefficient tax system.[64] However, because Maltzan and Otterstedt recommended it, Eichhorn authorized Maltzan to tell du Thil to send a negotiator to Berlin to begin serious discussions; he did not rule out the possibility of implementing du Thil's first alternative.[65] Motz also realized the possible political value of the Darmstadt negotiations.[66] But

60. Entwurf einer Verbalnote du Thils an Maltzan, August 1827, ibid., 2:117–120.
61. Eckert, "Zur Vorgeschichte des deutschen Zollvereins," p. 528.
62. Eichhorn to Maassen, 7 September 1827, Oncken and Saemisch, *Vorgeschichte und Begründung,* pp. 129–130.
63. Maassen to the Prussian Ministry of Foreign Affairs, 9 September 1827, ibid., pp. 133–134.
64. Treitschke, "Die Anfänge des deutschen Zollvereins," p. 506.
65. The Prussian Ministry of Foreign Affairs to Maltzan, 13 September 1827, Oncken and Saemisch, *Vorgeschichte und Begründung,* 2:134–135.
66. Ibid., 1:14.

the Ministry of Foreign Affairs was evidently worried that the hard-driving Minister of Finance would, for financial reasons, make the negotiations unduly difficult. For that reason the ministry wrote directly to Motz that

> this ministry must note . . . that it has new occasion to believe that from the political standpoint it considers the impending negotiations very desirable, and for that very reason earnestly wishes that demands will not be presented to Hesse that it either cannot in any way accede to, or that would place in the future relationship the seed of eventual dissolution and that would sooner or later force it into an accommodation with the south German governments.[67]

Hofmann arrived in Berlin in December 1827 to begin the negotiations. He met first with Bernstorff, who wholeheartedly endorsed the discussions, and then with Motz, who immediately declared that Prussia was more interested in Darmstadt's joining the Prussian customs system than in concluding a conventional commercial treaty. He also discussed the financial advantages of such an arrangement for Hesse.[68] He had dropped the finance ministry's narrowly fiscal viewpoint and instead adopted a broad economic and political approach that envisaged eventual connections not only with Hesse-Darmstadt, but also with Hesse-Kassel, Saxony, and even Bavaria, Württemberg and Baden.[69] The foreign ministry's new energy combined with the finance ministry's more comprehensive, flexible outlook resulted in a more effective and active policy for Prussia.

The actual negotiations were based mainly on Hofmann's detailed drafts, which reflected his long experience at the south German conferences. Motz and Maassen still endeavored to drive a hard financial bargain. At one point, this prompted Eichhorn to restate the importance of granting a financially and economically advantageous settlement to Hesse in order to "gain a greater *political* influence over the grand duchy and to make this state more dependent upon Prussia's system."[70] On 14

67. The Prussian Ministry of Foreign Affairs to Motz, 12 October 1827 (drafted by Michaelis), ibid., p. 38.

68. Aus dem Tagebuch Hofmanns, 2 January 1828, ibid., pp. 158–163.

69. Motz to the Prussian Ministry of Foreign Affairs, 4 January 1828, ibid., pp. 156–157.

70. The Prussian Ministry of Foreign Affairs to the Prussian finance ministry, January 1828, ibid., pp. 167–168.

February 1828, an agreement was signed. Darmstadt adopted the Prussian tariff schedules and shared in the customs revenues according to the ratio of her population to that of Prussia's western provinces. Hesse-Darmstadt was to model her customs administration after Prussia's, but could retain control over her own officials. Secret clauses gave Prussia additional power over Prussian and Hessian commercial relations with other states.[71]

The overall purpose of the Hesse treaty, above and beyond its purely technical aims, was best expressed by Bernstorff. In a report to the King, he wrote:

> A preliminary appraisal of the situation shows that financially and economically the advantages that will result from the prospective connection will be more on the side of the Grand Duchy of Hesse than on the side of Prussia. If, in the meantime, the example of the grand duchy of Hesse may cause other south German and north German states to follow a similar course, then, from our standpoint, our indirect tax and commercial system will gain in size and significance.
>
> However, even apart from this advantage, when viewed from the political side, the situation is to that extent of great value for Prussia, because such a union will arouse the interest of the smaller states in such arrangements and will place Prussia in a position to establish its influence over the same in the most equitable manner.[72]

Bernstorff was finally content. Now Prussia could project a progressive, reciprocal, and mutually advantageous customs policy to other states. The treaty would counteract particularistic fears and make the use of economic sanctions to further Prussian commercial interests unnecessary. This policy was primarily made possible by Motz's new flexibility and foresight. His position was in turn determined largely by Prussia's budgetary surplus; it is hard to believe that Motz would have accepted a financially disadvantageous agreement with Darmstadt if Prussia's financial situation had been as pressing as it was in the first half of the decade.

German and European reactions to the treaty were predominantly adverse. The mayor of Frankfurt am Main, Johann Thomas, was par-

71. For the full text, see Der Preussische-Hessische Zollvereins-vertrag vom 14. Februar 1828, ibid., pp. 196–197. The secret articles are contained in Geheimen Zusatzvertrag vom 14. Februar 1828, ibid., pp. 207–211.

72. Bernstorff to Frederick William, 24 January 1828, ibid., pp. 186–187.

ticularly alarmed and condemned the idea of customs uniformity.[73] Count
Münster of Hanover wrote that the expansion of the Prussian customs
system threatened the independence of those who participated; and
Freiherr von Marschall, the leading minister of Nassau, believed that the
new agreement endangered a number of states in Germany and completely altered Prussia's relationship to the German Confederation and to
Europe. The Netherlands, Baden, Bavaria, and France were all suspicious
of the Prussian-Hessian treaty.[74]

Austria's attitude was the most interesting. Metternich fully appreciated
the importance of the Prussian–Hesse-Darmstadt agreement. As he wrote
to Trauttmannsdorff:

> The course of the Prussian court in all German affairs has assumed in
> the last months a completely false direction, which I attribute to the
> agitation (*Umtriebe*) of a faction known only too well to me. Thus the
> recently concluded commercial and customs treaty engenders the most
> distressing and certainly proper concern of all the German governments.
> Now, everything on the part of Prussia will be directed toward entan-
> gling in its net the remaining states—the northern as well as the southern
> courts—an undertaking that in the course of time will probably succeed.

Despite these dangers, Metternich was not willing to disrupt Prussian-
Austrian relations. He told Trauttmannsdorff, "I request you to maintain
an absolute silence on customs developments. The point will eventually
arrive when we will have to assert ourselves, but that time has not come,
and I especially do not want our higher political relationships with the
court of Prussia to be spoiled by a bit of true political rubbish."[75] In other

---

73. Petersdorff, *Motz,* 2:159.

74. Ibid., p. 168, 158; Oncken, "Zur Einführung," 1:*lxiv;* Otterstedt to
Frederick William, 20 March 1828, Oncken and Saemisch, *Vorgeschichte und
Begründung,* 2:263–265; Waldburg-Truchsess to Bernstorff, 20 April 1828, idem,
*Vorgeschichte und Begründung,* 2:276–277; Bemerkungen über den Zollvertrag der
Krone Preussen mit dem Grossherzogtum Hessens, Bay GSA, MA III 2606 Preussen;
and Alleye de Cyprey to de la Ferronays, 29 February 1828, Anton Chroust, ed.,
*Gesandtschaftsberichte aus München 1814–1848: Abteilung I. Die Berichte der
französischen Gesandten,* 19:117.

75. Metternich to Trauttmannsdorff, 18 March 1828, HHSA, Stk., Preussen Karton
128.

words, Metternich, did not wish to endanger Austria's relationship to Prussia at a time when Vienna was becoming isolated in Europe as a result of the eastern question. Austria's European problems gave Prussia the opportunity to move with greater freedom within the German state system.

The greatest overt concern by Austrian officials was expressed at the federal Diet where the Austrian representative, Freiherr von Münch-Bellinghausen, stated that the expansion of the Prussian customs system was the work of the liberal, Prussian faction in Berlin who wanted to roll back Austrian influence in Germany.[76] The Austrian military envoy in Frankfurt, General von Langenau, immediately thought of the advantages he believed Austria had enjoyed and might now lose because of the separation of Prussia's eastern and western provinces. "Shall not," he wrote, "the fact that Prussia is divided in two halves have its importance in a war between Austria and Prussia! There would be no small result from 100,000 troops affiliated to Austria properly placed."[77] Metternich chose to try to hinder the further expansion of the Prussian system by instructing Münch on 24 March 1828 to attempt to block additional states from joining the Prussian-Hessian union and to encourage the creation of other customs associations as a hindrance to Prussian expansion. He felt that Münch's strategic location in Frankfurt gave him unique opportunities to come into contact with the various German states, but he cautioned him that he should not appear to openly oppose the policy of Berlin.[78]

Clearly, the Prussian–Hesse-Darmstadt treaty created new uncertainties in Germany. Under the apparent tranquility of federal dualism, anxiety over Prussia's policy was developing. The unanimity of 1824, as demonstrated in the renewal of the Carlsbad Decrees, seemed to be in doubt for the first time. A tense atmosphere prominent enough to be noted by foreign diplomats was beginning to develop in the politics of the Confederation.[79]

---

76. Albert Branchart, *Öesterreich und die Anfänge des preussisch-deutschen Zollvereins*, p. 10.

77. Petersdorff, *Motz*, 2:164.

78. Branchart, *Öesterreich und die Anfänge*, p. 57.

79. Millebanke to Dudley, 14 March 1828, PRO F.O. 30/28; also see Oncken and Saemisch, *Vorgeschichte und Begründung*, 2:247–248.

## THE CENTRAL GERMAN COMMERCIAL
## UNION

Motz, Eichhorn, and Bernstorff were unable to realize their hope that
the Prussian–Hesse-Darmstadt *Zollverein* would expand to include at
least Electoral Hesse and Nassau.[80] Influenced by Bavaria, Saxony,
Hanover, and Austria, the government in Kassel declined Darmstadt's offer
to enter the new customs union.[81] Efforts by Bavaria and Württemberg to
expand their customs union were equally unsuccessful. It soon developed that, rather than join either the Prussian-Hessian system or the
Bavarian-Württemberg system, a number of states preferred to erect their
own loosely organized and totally independent commercial association.
Nassau, Frankfurt, Saxony, Electoral Hesse, and other smaller principalities began to discuss the foundation of a customs community that would
encourage free trade and act as a sort of negative union to protect the
smaller states from the two other systems. The negotiations lasted six
months. The resulting agreements created a very incomplete commercial
unit in which anti-Prussian interests were mixed with a desire for freer
trade. Austria played some part in the negotiations, but the importance of
its role has often been exaggerated.[82] The final treaty establishing this
Central German Commercial Union was signed on 24 September 1828 by
Saxony, Hanover, Electoral Hesse, Weimar, Nassau, and several other
smaller states such as Saxe-Coburg-Gotha, Saxe-Meinigen, and the Reuss
principalities. By its provisions, member states agreed not to join another
customs union before the end of 1834. Efforts were also made to ensure
that trade between members and foreign nations flowed smoothly and to
reserve the right to raise duties and dues on the commerce of nonmember
states such as Prussia.

---

80. In February, Bernstorff had told the King that "the admittance of contiguous
German states, if requested under acceptable conditions, should remain open; it is
even already understood that Electoral Hesse and Nassau should be invited to join."
Bernstorff to Frederick William, 21 February 1828 (drafted by Eichhorn), Oncken
and Saemisch, *Vorgeschichte und Begründung,* 2:215–218.

81. Schminke to du Thil, 15 March 1828, ibid., p. 248; Wittgenstein to du Thil,
19 March 1828, ibid., p. 250; Maltzan to Frederick William, 28 March 1828, ibid.,
pp. 261–262; and especially Otterstedt to Frederick William, 30 March 1828, ibid.,
pp. 263–265.

82. Branchart, *Öesterreich und die Anfänge,* p. 111.

In contrast to the passive attitude Prussia had adopted earlier in the decade, Berlin reacted to the creation of this union with obvious disappointment. Motz was immediately hostile to the new association and proposed reprisals against its members, even suggesting the construction of a rail line and new roads to isolate them.[83] To Bernstorff, he wrote that the commercial union, ostensibly created to implement Article XIX of the federal constitution, was in fact aimed at the paralysis of the most important aspects of Prussia's internal development. He argued that Berlin ought to use every available means to counter the influence of the new coalition.[84] He also took this as an occasion to condemn Austria's policy in Germany.

> I cannot judge to what extent we can count on friendly relations with Austria; however, this much appears to be clear, that Austria wants to give the too hastily organized German Confederation the character of the former League of German Princes and wants to take over within it the role of Frederick the Great, but wishes, as long as we will permit it, to leave us in a subordinate position. . . . From all reports it can certainly be concluded that the Central German Commercial Union, obviously directed only against Prussia, could never have come to pass, if Austria had not encouraged the negotiations.[85]

Motz was wrong to blame Austria entirely for the Central German Commercial Union; the persistence of particularistic feelings in Germany and a genuine fear of Prussia's customs policy, not the policies of Vienna, had led to the creation of the union.

The foreign ministry disagreed with Motz's proposals and interpretations. Bernstorff felt that the idea of reprisals did not take political factors into consideration, and he resented Motz's circumvention of the foreign ministry on some commercial matters.[86] Bernstorff and Eichhorn were also critical of the new association, but they had a better understanding of the fears and apprehensions that had resulted in its formation. In an

---

83. Schuckmann and Motz to the Prussian Ministry of Foreign Affairs, Oncken and Saemisch, *Vorgeschichte und Begründung,* 3:33–35.

84. Motz to Bernstorff, 26 June 1828, ibid., pp. 45–47.

85. Motz to Bernstorff, 8 November 1828, ibid., pp. 64–65. Motz was angry at Austria because he believed that Metternich had blocked his attempt to make an agreement with Brunswick. See Motz to Bernstorff, 24 June 1828, ibid., pp. 47–48.

86. Ompteda to Bremer, 20 June 1828, ibid., pp. 42–43.

important circular dispatch to Prussia's envoys in Germany, Eichhorn analyzed the genesis and nature of the commercial union. He pointed out that Prussia was in favor of measures that improved trade and communications and emphasized that Berlin had no political designs on other states in Germany. However, the Prussian government could not enter into any kind of agreement with a large group of states such as those in the Central German Commercial Union because it was still the foreign ministry's policy to deal only with individual governments. Prussia was not following a policy of divide and conquer, he said. Its approach simply reflected the reality that customs negotiations conducted on a multilateral basis were impossibly complex. He also noted that, while there was no definite indication of hostility to Prussia in the Frankfurt agreement, any demands or efforts by the union to implement a "reciprocal relationship" postulated on Prussia's abandonment of her customs system would be firmly opposed. If the union persisted in trying to force through such a program, "it should consider what an association of states that brings together only six million people, and that is made up mainly of agrarian countries, could gain from growing conflict with a monarchy of twelve million inhabitants, which possesses all the important roads that unite the interior and connect it with foreign areas, which has rich and large cities and in which all branches of industry are booming, and whether as a result of such conflict interior communications would be stifled not stimulated, and commerce restricted not increased."[87] Eichhorn was trying, somewhat disingenuously, to disarm the worst suspicions of the other German states and to introduce a moderate amount of coercive pressure to keep the Central German Commercial Union from promulgating measures disadvantageous to Prussia.

Bernstorff and Eichhorn were also concerned about the role Austria had played in the creation of the commercial union. In a note to the Prussian embassy in Vienna, they expressed the hope that the actions of various Austrian diplomats in Germany reflected their own personal interpretations of Austrian interests, not the official policy of the Hofburg.[88] However, despite these misgivings, the foreign ministry did not want to resort

87. The Prussian Ministry of Foreign Affairs to the Prussian envoys in Vienna, Munich, Karlsruhe, Darmstadt, and Dresden, 14 August 1828 (drafted by Eichhorn), ibid., pp. 48–54.

88. The Prussian Ministry of Foreign Affairs to Brockhausen, August 1828 (drafted by Eichhorn), ibid., pp. 54–55.

to hostile measures that would further alienate other German states who had until now been friendly to Prussia. Above all, they argued that Prussia should not begin a policy of massive retaliation aimed at the general structure of the commercial union, but rather should pursue a selective policy that adopted measures of reprisal only in response to specific hostile acts aimed at Prussia.[89] In the course of the next year, most of Motz's diplomatic and journalistic attacks were moderated by Bernstorff and the King, but he was both active and successful in the areas of road construction and the manipulation of commercial routes and duties. As the anti-Prussian nature of the central union became more apparent, he won over Bernstorff and Eichhorn. At the same time, Motz moderated his own more adventurous, extreme position of 1828, thus making accommodation between the two ministries easier.

Until 1828, concern for improving its internal network of highways primarily governed Prussia's road construction program. However, after the beginning of that year road building came to be used as a weapon in the commercial battle with neighboring states.[90] Motz's revision of road financing gave Prussia the ability to conduct a far-reaching *Strassenkrieg*. At the end of 1827, Motz made the funding of construction independent of income from transit dues, and a certain amount of the state's general fund was set aside each year for roads.[91] For 1829, out of the overall budgetary surplus of 3,680,000 talers, 1,360,000 was projected for road construction. Financial solvency which allowed Prussia to embark on an ambitious program of road building also allowed it to offer attractive financial inducements to various states in an effort to disrupt the operation of the central union.[92]

The first victim of Motz's anticommercial union campaign was Nassau. In the course of 1828, transit trade was rerouted around the state and Prussia lowered its transit duties to entice foreign trade into using Prussian roads. These measures resulted in a fifty percent decline in Nassau's transit trade. Marschall complained bitterly that Nassau "was being

89. The Prussian Ministry of Foreign Affairs to Bülow, 26 September 1828 (drafted by Eichhorn), ibid., pp. 62–63; the Prussian Ministry of Foreign Affairs to Motz, 13 December 1828 (drafted by Eichhorn), ibid., p. 67.

90. Paul Thimme, *Strassenbau und Strassenpolitik in Deutschland zur zeit der Gründung des Zollvereins, 1825–35,* p. 35.

91. Ibid., pp. 36–37.

92. Ibid., p. 53.

treated like an island." Saxony was another major target. The construction of the road from Weissenfels to Zeitz was intended to isolate Leipzig and to divert traffic through Halle.[93] Finally, with Bernstorff's assistance, Motz was able to negotiate the construction of a north-south road from Hamburg, through Danish Lauenburg, and on to Magdeburg and Erfurt. This route isolated the commercial union, especially Hanover, from the trade between Hamburg and southern Germany.[94]

These routes were not only used to the detriment of the commercial union. They were also employed to make better connections with the Bavarian-Württemberg customs union, with which Prussia was beginning to have better relations. The rise of the commercial union made the other two systems pull closer together. For some time, Bavaria and Württemburg had been trying to improve their lines of communication with maritime regions. Negotiations with Switzerland had recently collapsed, and, since relations with the commercial union were uncertain, the southern union began to look toward Prussia. Berlin also saw an agreement with Bavaria and Württemberg as a way of delivering a decisive blow against the central union that would at the same time open up a new market for Prussian goods.[95]

This confluence of interests did lead to a commercial treaty between the two customs unions, which will be discussed shortly. It also resulted in a road agreement with two of the smaller members of the Central German Commercial Union. Saxe-Coburg-Gotha and Saxe-Meinigen wanted to construct a road uniting their territories. Because the proposed road passed through Prussian territory, Motz and the foreign ministry realized that this plan could be turned to Prussia's advantage. Motz proposed that the two states modify their plans to accommodate the construction of a north-south road uniting Prussia and Bavaria. He offered loans and outright grants to aid in the construction of their segments of the proposed road system. The duchies agreed to this proposal. No transit duties were to be collected on these highways, and, in the secret articles of the settlement, the duchies further agreed to join the Bavarian or the Prussian system after 1834.[96] For the first time, Motz had broken through

93. Ibid., pp. 38–39.
94. Ibid., pp. 51–53.
95. Ibid., p. 41.
96. Petersdorff, *Motz*, 2:271–277; Roussakis, *Friedrich List*, pp. 66–67; and Thimme, *Strassenbau und Strassenpolitik*, pp. 44–47.

the coalition of German states comprising the commercial union. The precedent of the two duchies was followed by the Reuss principalities, which concluded a similar road agreement with Berlin later in the year.[97] A final addition to Prussia's position vis-à-vis the commercial union was the successful negotiation of a tentative settlement with the Netherlands concerning navigation and commerce on the Rhine. Holland agreed to relax her monopoly of the Rhine trade in return for other considerations. Through Motz's efforts, Prussia had successfully erected a communications network that united its separate provinces, brought it into close contact with other parts of Germany, and also bypassed the commercial union.

## THE COMMERCIAL TREATY OF 1829

The gradual wearing down of the Central German Commercial Union was aided by the signing of the Prussian-Hessian and Bavarian-Württemberg Commercial Treaty on 27 May 1829. This agreement represents the last major phase of the *Zollverein* negotiations prior to the outbreak of the July Revolution. While it did not create a true customs union between the four states, it did establish a pattern of close cooperation between the two systems. It also demonstrated the degree to which political considerations had penetrated commercial negotiations.

As we have seen, for example, with Prussia's road building campaign, the two customs unions had begun to work together. King Ludwig of Bavaria's intermittent desire to establish a closer political relationship with Prussia eventually resulted in a private Bavarian initiative to explore the possibilities of a commercial agreement between Munich and Berlin.[98] Freiherr Johann Friedrich von Cotta, influential publisher of the *Augsburger Allgemeine Zeitung,* was selected for the mission. In late 1828 and the spring of 1829, he made three trips to Berlin to discuss commercial matters. During the initial discussions, Cotta received a favorable impression of the Prussian government and of its efficient and progressive policies. He was struck by Prussia's financial and economic improvements, the quality of its

97. Thimme, *Strassenbau und Strassenpolitik,* pp. 48–49.
98. For a brief summary of the stages of Ludwig's policy during this period, see Otto Westphal, "System und Wandlungen der auswärtigen Politik Bayerns in den ersten Jahren Ludwigs I," pp. 355–356.

public education, and the size and strength of its armed forces. Above all, he was impressed by the dynamic spirit that animated Prussia's German policy. He had good reasons for these feelings; Prussian officials told him these commercial discussions meant the beginning of a "new era for Germany." He wrote that

> the conviction that Prussia stands and falls with Germany may be seen as the leading concept of this feeling, and so as the Prussian government continues to try to increase the inner strength of their state, so they also wish to develop this in Germany and the first means to that end would be: the lifting of the multifarious tariff barriers that have restricted in such a damaging way the commercial and manufacturing capability of Germany.[99]

Although Motz did much to create this impression of Prussian policy, the classic statement of this outlook is contained in a letter from Witzleben to Cotta, written on 30 November 1828, in which he wrote that, because of Prussia's position in Germany and her commitment to the "free moral and intellectual development" of man, Prussia had been called to be the protector of Germany. This attitude was not based on an allegiance to Prussia, but rather on an "interest in the common fatherland and all its inhabitants." Witzleben emphasized that the King was firmly opposed to the expansion of Prussia's territory in Germany. Frederick William believed that "the strength of the state is based upon justice and public opinion." On the other hand, Prussia was primarily responsible for the military defense of Germany, and it was also apparent that, if other states, such as Bavaria and Württemberg, "with their sovereignty unimpaired," joined with Prussia in closer relationship, then the foundation for a new and beneficial union would be created.[100]

Witzleben's statement contains nearly all the major themes that would characterize Prussia's German policy for the next four years. The coupling of military strength and nonaggressive behavior is already clear. The concern for projecting a just and progressive image of Prussia in order to make the reconciliation of conflicting interests among the individual states

---

99. Bericht des Buchhandlers Geh. Rats Freiherrn Joh. Friedrich von Cotta, October 1828, Doeberl, "Bayern und die wirtschaftliche Einigung Deutschlands," pp. 73–75.

100. Ibid., p. 80.

and Prussia more possible is also indicated. Prussia would not actually take over Germany; its interests and those of the German states would simply become one. In this way, a new functional and moral basis for German unity would be created.

Although this appeal was consciously designed to make Berlin's policy attractive and unthreatening to Cotta, there is no reason to doubt Witzleben's sincerity. He based his proposal to a certain extent on a realistic appreciation of the particularist concerns of the German states, but he nevertheless pointed toward an ideal construct of what a confederated Germany under Prussian leadership would be like. It is a further statement of ideas from the reform era, already mentioned in a more restricted sense, by Bernstorff and Eichhorn. Witzleben now placed commercial policy more firmly within the framework of an overall approach to the German problem. Hermann Oncken has cited Witzleben's statement as one of the rare occasions in German history when alongside the tension there existed a harmony between the ideas of Weimar and Potsdam.[101]

Indeed, Witzleben's ideas reflected a fairly common synthesis of intellectual beliefs that was characteristic of a significant group of Prussian officials and soldiers. This synthesis was made up of a desire for a more rational organization of human affairs and for a sense of justice (derived from the European Enlightenment); a belief in the importance of moral forces in the shaping of society and in the validity and importance of the individualistic and unique aspects of human development (both of which found their origins in German idealism and early Romanticism); and a profound sense of realism born of lengthy government service in a professional state bureaucracy or military establishment and of an understanding of the major historical events that had dominated the age. Clausewitz, for example, achieved a high degree of precision in using this synthesis to analyze human experience.[102] Most of his contemporaries did not have the same intellectual drive and toughness and did not mature to the same degree. Their conceptions remained more cloudy, their logic less rigorous, and their insights less profound. But these individuals remain valuable representatives of an interesting and rich intellectual tradition that was present in Prussia during the first half of the Restoration.

---

101. Oncken, "Zur Einführung," p. *lxxiii*. For a similar assessment of Witzleben, see Luxburg to Ludwig, 19 January 1829, Bay GSA MA III, Nr. 2607 Preussen.
102. See Peter Paret, *Clausewitz and the State*.

The official negotiations for the Bavarian commercial treaty began on 26 March 1829; Motz, Schönberg, and Eichhorn represented Prussia. The finance minister took a hard line in the technical negotiations, while, true to form, the foreign ministry was much more accommodating to the interests of Bavaria and Württemberg.[103] But Motz soon eased his stand, and the negotiations were completed in two months. The treaty contained a number of provisions that aimed at improving trade between the two customs unions, and it called for the establishment of compatible administrative systems and annual conferences "for the support and expansion of this treaty."[104] The economic importance of the treaty cannot be denied, but the fact that, in the course of ten years, a near reversal in priorities had taken place was of greater significance. The political reasons for the agreement were mentioned more often than the financial or economic ones. Motz's memorandum to Eichhorn on the advantages of an agreement with Bavaria listed "political importance in relation to our position in Germany," as the first reason for such an agreement.[105] As the foreign ministry wrote to the Prussian envoy in Munich:

> This treaty has bound Bavaria and Württemberg closer to Prussia; finally Germany will obtain a coherence and comprise a whole. All influential statesmen of different opinions and views evaluate this commercial treaty as an encouraging beginning, as the cornerstone to a system that will have the most beneficial consequences for the independence, security, and prosperity of all the German states.[106]

Two other documents of this period discussed similar themes. One is Motz's *Memoire* on the treaty, written in June 1829. In this wide-ranging

103. Doeberl, "Bayern und die wirtschaftliche Einigung Deutschlands," p. 43.

104. Henderson, *Zollverein*, p. 60. For the documents on these negotiations see Doeberl, "Bayern und die wirtschaftliche Einigung Deutschlands," pp. 60–111; and Oncken and Saemisch, *Vorgeschichte und Begründung*, Vol. 3.

105. Motz to Eichhorn, 23 February 1829, Oncken and Saemisch, *Vorgeschichte und Begründung*, 3:462–463.

106. Petersdorff, *Motz*, 2:260. Foreign reactions to the treaty revealed a clear perception of the agreement's consequences. The French chargé d'affairs in Munich called the treaty "one of the most important events after the religious reformation" for "Prussia is about to include in a vast system, formed by this alliance of North and South, all the states lying between them and this Power will exercise over its associates a preponderance which will surpass anything that hitherto existed and anything that it is possible to imagine." Henderson, *Zollverein*, p. 100n.

paper, he systematically examined the commercial, financial, political, and military importance of the agreement. After describing the increased economic power of the new organization, he briefly described its financial advantages to Prussia. He then discussed the political significance of the agreement at length in a section entitled "Political unity—necessary consequence of the commercial." Finally, he noted that Prussia's connection with southern Germany would be important militarily; Prussia's Rhine province would be protected against France, as well as from the highly unlikely prospect of war with Austria. From the beginning of the discussions with Bavaria and Württemberg, there had been numerous rumors that a military alliance would be negotiated. None evolved in connection with the commercial treaty, but Motz's emphasis on its military advantages echoed concerns he had as early as 1817. It also demonstrates that Prussia was still obsessed with its own defense and that the creation of a military alliance between Berlin and the south continued to be an important objective. Motz concluded his *Memoire* with the following statement.

> Enough! the unending importance of a close connection of Prussia with Bavaria, Württemberg (Baden), and the Grand Duchy of Hesse is proven. . . .
> And only in this connection, erected on the basis of similar interests and a natural foundation, will again a really confederated, internally and externally truly free, Germany arise and be prosperous.
> The wise providence of the Almighty will protect and preserve it![107]

This paper shows the change that had occurred in Prussia's German policy in a period of six years. Nothing like it could have been written by a Prussian Minister of Finance in the first half of the decade. The *Memoire* clearly sets forth the new sense of energy and confidence that characterized the outlook of many officials in Berlin. It was also Motz's last major statement of his views, and indeed it has been called his political testament. He died one year later at the age of fifty-four.

The other document is the circular dispatch sent out by the foreign ministry in August 1829. Its carefully qualified statements contrast markedly with the robust nature of Motz's paper, but they also indicate

---

107. *Memoire* by Motz, June 1829, Oncken and Saemisch, *Vorgeschichte und Begründung,* 3:525–541.

a fundamental change in Prussian policy. The dispatch emphasized that the political component of the commercial treaty was limited; the initiative for the treaty came from Bavaria and Württemberg, not Prussia. It described the mutual advantage in the agreement and examined the many drawbacks of the Central German Commercial Union. It then argued with those smaller states that feared that joining the larger Prussian or Bavarian systems meant a loss in sovereignty.

> In fact it is almost ridiculous for one or the other of the small German states to believe it will lose some of its independence if it joins the Prussian-Hessian or Bavarian-Württemberg customs unions. On the contrary, in its isolation alone will it feel its lack of independence, which is a consequence of its small area and the poverty of its resources; this feeling will only be decreased by a formal entry into the larger union, and instead of losing, it will gain in independence.[108]

Aware of the hostility that was developing in Germany and abroad toward Prussia, the foreign ministry directed its envoys to describe the agreement in the least alarming manner possible. By deemphasizing the political side of the negotiations, it hoped to disarm those who were critical or fearful of Prussia. At the same time, it wanted to attract new members by extolling the real advantages of the new arrangement. By proposing a subtle change in the definition of sovereignty—that the economic and material well-being of a small state was more important than its political and dynastic sovereignty, narrowly defined, it hoped to prepare the ground for the further expansion of the Prussian system. Thus, the foreign and the finance ministries were both committed to the idea of economic unification, and both had a strong but still imprecise interest in uniting Germany under the aegis of Prussia. The position of leadership that Prussia had thereby assumed was potentially of great importance, for up to this point the evolution of partial economic unity in Germany had taken place entirely independent of Austria. As economic and commercial activities became increasingly significant in Germany in succeeding decades, this was a relationship that directly involved Prussia in the most advanced developments of the region.

108. The Prussian Ministry of Foreign Affairs to the Prussian envoys in Vienna, Paris, London, St. Petersburg, Brussels, Copenhagen, Stockholm, Dresden, Karlsruhe, and Hamburg, 18 August 1829, ibid., pp. 555–559.

It is tempting to seize on the statements made by Prussian leaders in the late 1820s to prove that they intended from the beginning to have Prussia lead Germany economically. But, in fact, Prussian policy evolved very slowly in this direction. For example, it is incorrect to state that, from 1819 on, Prussian bureaucrats and diplomats were striving for the economic unification of Germany; at that time, Prussian officials were primarily concerned with the smooth operation of the 1818 law. Throughout the next ten years, Prussia demonstrated little initiative in customs affairs; the few initiatives Prussia did make nearly always resulted in failure. Schwarzburg-Sonderhausen, Hesse-Darmstadt, Bavaria, and Württemberg had all approached Prussia. On the other hand, the enclave negotiations, in which Prussia eventually took the offensive, were long and drawn out, and Motz's invitations in 1828 were a total failure. Prussia's only success was in road building. Prussia's most effective initiative was simply to set a good example: Hesse-Darmstadt was deeply impressed by the operation of Prussia's customs system, and Bavaria and Württemberg were unable to match the efficiency of the Prussian system in their own *Zollverein.* Forty-four percent of Bavarian and Württemberg revenues were absorbed by administrative costs, whereas Prussia consumed only 14 to 15 percent, and revenue per head was nine and a half groschen in the two southern states as compared with twenty-four groschen per head in Prussia. These facts impressed Bavarian officials.[109] The excellence of the system's operation, not the predetermined intentions of Prussian officials, contributed to the economic unification of Germany.

Nevertheless, Prussian policy began to project new energy as the state acquired greater stability. The concept of peaceful dualism remained. The foreign ministry was reluctant to precipitate any break with Austria, but the changes in Prussia's policy toward Germany made dualism irrelevant to some extent. This new sense of independence was the result of a regeneration of creativity among Prussian officials as political and financial conditions improved and the French Revolution receded into the less immediate reaches of the minds of the Prussian leaders. Prussia's commercial policy became more successful in Germany only when Prussia felt secure enough to abandon its fiscal inflexibility and concentrate on the political side of customs affairs. Still, this regeneration was limited in scope.

---

109. Treitschke, *History of Germany,* 4:186; and Price, *Evolution of the Zollverein,* p. 121.

No calls for political reform were made in Germany and Prussia; this absence reflected both the transformation of the Prussian reformers and the reality of what was actually possible in Prussia and Germany in 1829. But the *Zollverein* movement carried a hidden political dynamic; it was a force for change. Politically, it altered the power relationships in Germany, and it bore some relation to the interests of the middle classes and of the more liberal states of Germany. If it were given additional room to operate, Prussia's customs policy had the potential to become part of a larger, quietly reformist approach to German affairs.

*Chapter 5*

✠✠✠✠✠✠✠✠✠✠✠✠✠

# Latin America
# and the
# Eastern Question

Was the European alliance still viable? Toward the end of 1826, struck by the decline in the vitality of the alliance, Bernstorff admitted that it had been clear to all the powers that

a system engendered by the force of extraordinary circumstances, calculated upon the necessities of the moment, [and] made up of different components, could find no guarantee in its inherent nature for its survival, but rather would find contained within itself the seeds of its dissolution. And so it should not appear strange that in particular some special and unilateral interests soon predominated, often over the interests of the whole, and that the true and great purpose of the alliance increasingly was lost from view. The operation of the alliance was also significantly weakened by trying to give it an injudicious direction or by trying to ascribe to its purpose a false or exaggerated application of its principles.

However, he came to the conclusion that the basic treaty arrangements and fundamental spirit of European politics were still intertwined with the system. Although, from

year to year it means more to stand on one's own feet, . . . there is no reason to voluntarily relinquish existing rights and still unlost advantages. We believe that duty and interest unite in bidding us to continue to belong to an alliance to which we owe freedom, honor, and power, until it has disintegrated in its outer form and disappeared into its final shadowy existence.[1]

This passage holds the key to an explanation of Prussian foreign policy in the second half of the 1820s. For Bernstorff, the decline of the Grand Alliance was unfortunate but predictable. He still believed that the alliance could be an effective and desirable tool for maintaining tranquility in Europe, but he also recognized that, as the experience of the Napoleonic Wars receded into the background, it was nearly inevitable that the European states would redefine their national interests. Prussia reflected the developments of this period of transition; increased financial and economic stability gave Prussia greater confidence and increased ability "to stand on its own feet," as Bernstorff put it. Prussia's definition of its national interests became more precise. The extent to which Prussia would defer to the interests of others, even on relatively unimportant issues, declined, and the imagination that was applied to its own European policy increased. But Prussia still operated in a European environment whose characteristics worked against any drastic reordering of external policy, and Prussia remained committed to the concept of the Concert of Europe in its broadest sense. In other words, the twin elements of continuity and change are constants of Prussia's foreign relations during this period. Prussia's policy toward Latin America and the eastern question are the most important examples of this duality in Berlin's approach to European affairs.

## PRUSSIA'S POLICY TOWARD LATIN AMERICA

In the beginning of the decade, Austrian and Prussian attitudes toward Latin America were based on several considerations. Neither Austria nor Prussia wanted political developments in the New World to disturb the tranquility of Europe. They desired to avoid any conflict between Spain and Portugal over Latin America and to block any armed intervention mounted by the powers to reestablish the principle of legitimacy in the former colonies. Austria and Prussia supported England's efforts to achieve some sort of reconciliation between the new Latin American re-

1. Bernstorff to Schöler, 27 November 1826, ZSA Me, Rep. 81, Petersburg I, Nr. 109.

publics and Spain. But, in deference to the doctrine of legitimacy, which was the theoretical basis for their policy toward Naples, Sardinia, and Spain, they refused to recognize the sovereignty of the republics until Spain had done so.[2]

This policy remained essentially unchanged until the middle of the decade. However, as early as 1818, Humboldt recognized that the eastern powers' attitude toward Latin America imposed special disadvantages on Prussia. In an interesting *Denkschrift* on the necessity of commercial connections with Latin America, he wrote, "It is apparent that between Russia, Austria, and Prussia, only the last named has to make a sacrifice when it refrains from intercourse with the American state," because neither Austria nor Russia carried on any significant overseas trade. With all due respect to Spain, Humboldt felt that the time had come for Prussia to establish commercial relations with the new republics.[3] The conflict, noted by Humboldt, between Prussia's economic interests and her political position vis-à-vis Latin America took several years to resolve. In the meantime, the Hanseatic cities led the rest of Germany in establishing unofficial commercial relations with the rebels in Latin America.[4]

Although Prussia's policy was still unchanged in 1823, Bernstorff was probably beginning to reevaluate it. Responding to an inquiry from France, he stated that Prussia was not prepared to recognize the new republics even if they were accorded full recognition by Great Britain.[5] However, he realized that

in view of the natural and not unjustifiable jealousy that France feels in being unable to hinder the commercial advantages enjoyed by England, perhaps the moment is not far off when no European government that gives attention to and protects the interests of its subjects involved in

2. See William S. Robertson, "Metternich's Attitude toward Revolution in Latin America"; also see Manfred Kossok's excellent work, *Im Schatten der Heiligen Allianz,* pp. 48–137. Russia pursued a slightly different policy toward Latin America; see William S. Roberston, "Russia and the Emancipation of Spanish America, 1816–1826"; and Kossok, *Im Schatten der Heiligen Allianz,* pp. 67–70.

3. "Über Friedenschlüsse mit den Barbaresken und die Anknüpfung von Verbindungen mit den südamerikanischen Kolonien (1818?)," Albert Leitzmann, Bruno Gebhardt, and Wilhelm Richter, eds., *Wilhelm von Humboldts Gesammelte Schriften,* 12:216–225.

4. Kossok, *Im Schatten der Heiligen Allianz,* pp. 30–47, 138–159.

5. Ibid., p. 115.

commerce and overseas trade will be able indifferently or inactively to allow England the undivided enjoyment of mastering new, important, and expanded commercial relations.[6]

During this same period, manufacturing groups in Prussia expressed their strong interest in the Spanish-American market. By 1823, the Prussian *Seehandlung* had dispatched two commercial agents to South America. However, neither mission signified a change in Prussia's official policy of nonrecognition.[7]

When Great Britain finally recognized Argentina, Colombia, and Mexico on 1 January 1825, Prussian manufacturers feared they would be shut out of the South American market. At this time, the Prussian embassy in London issued a passport to Manuel E. Gorotiza, an agent of the Mexican government, to go to Berlin to negotiate the official recognition of his country by Prussia. While traveling through the Rhineland, he met with directors of the *Rheinisch-Westindische Kompagnie,* who told him that many Prussian merchants had great interest in expanded trade with Latin America. They provided Gorotiza with letters of introduction to leading officials in Berlin and indicated that they would encourage the government to establish relations with Mexico. In Berlin, Gorotiza met first with Hans von Bülow, who then arranged for a meeting with Bernstorff. Gorotiza stated that the further expansion of Prussian trade could not take place without an exchange of consuls. Bernstorff told the Mexican agent that Prussia could not depart from the policy of the eastern alliance. Thus, although the meeting with Bernstorff was cordial, Gorotiza failed in his objective. Discouraged, he concluded that commercial interests in Prussia did not have sufficient influence to force the government to recognize Mexico.[8] However, Gorotiza had underestimated both Prussia's interest in trade with Latin America and the pressure that commercial and manufacturing groups could put on the government.

On 18 August 1825, the board of directors of the *Rheinisch-Westindische Kompagnie* sent a petition to Bernstorff requesting that Prussia send a commercial agent to Mexico, in order to comply with the new trade regu-

6. Bernstorff to Frederick William, 19 November 1823, ZSA Me, AAI, Rep. 1, Nr. 2990.

7. Kossok, *Im Schatten der Heiligen Allianz,* pp. 134–135.

8. Jaime E. Rodriguez O., *The Emergence of Spanish America, Vincente Rocafuerte and Spanish Americanism, 1808–1832,* pp. 143–145.

lations established by the Mexican Congress: "In recognizing the great importance of this commerce for Prussia, one need only to note that yearly consumption in Mexico is estimated at 150,000 units of Silesian linen, with a value of approximately two million Prussian talers and 100,000 units of Silesian cloth worth approximately one million Prussian talers." The board added that, if Prussia were excluded from the Mexican market for political reasons, then English and Dutch manufacturers would waste no time in taking over Prussia's share of the market. Therefore, they demanded that "a Mexican commercial agent be immediately admitted to Prussia and that a Prussian commercial agent be named in Mexico."[9]

Similar demands came from manufacturers in Breslau and from Vincke, the *Oberpräsident* of Westphalia. Even Schuckmann, the Minister of the Interior, sent Bernstorff a paper that urged him to give his closest attention to the question of trade with Latin America. As a result of these various pressures, Bernstorff instructed Maltzahn to make contact with Mexico's representative in London to discuss the formal regulation of commercial relations between the two countries. Bernstorff made it clear to Maltzahn that economic necessity, not political sympathy, had necessitated this move.

> Only since the commencement of direct commercial connections with South America and chiefly Mexico have our linen mills in all parts of the country improved and risen to an unrecognized prosperity. The maintenance of this industry and several others, which depend chiefly on the undisturbed trade with America, is of the greatest importance for Prussia, because the discontinuation of the carrying trade with Spain, Portugal, the Netherlands, and Russia ended these sources of markets from which otherwise a hundred thousand of his Majesty's subjects have gotten their income.

Bernstorff went on to say that, since England, France, and the Netherlands had already opened up trade routes to America, and Russia and Austria had no important trade interests there, only Prussia was forced to make major sacrifices for the sake of the principle of legitimacy. In consequence, it was now Prussia's responsibility to reconcile its long-standing principles with these special interests wherever possible. However, he added that this action, which had been brought about by the Mexican gov-

---

9. Ibid., pp. 149–150.

ernment's new regulations and England's recognition of the new republics, did not mean a disavowal of the rights of the Spanish throne or of the principle of legitimacy. Bernstorff had no doubt "that commercial relations quite properly could be kept separate from political relations without the slightest damage to the latter."[10]

When the initial discussions with Mexican diplomats in London and The Hague were unproductive, Bernstorff sent Gottlob Kunth, a prominent member of the reform movement and a strong believer in liberal economic theory, to Aachen, where he met with Gorotiza and concluded the so-called convention of Aachen. The agreement incorporated reciprocal commercial and most-favored-nation clauses for the two states.[11] Kunth reported that "my only remaining wish is that . . . this first official step will soon have such results that the condition of uncertainty, so detrimental to our trade, will end, and that, to use an expression of Minister vom Stein, the cabinet will not disappoint any longer the beginning of a new era in America."[12] Later negotiations in London between Maltzahn and the Mexican diplomat Sebastian Camacho expanded the convention of Aachen into the Mexican-Prussian official declaration of 20 January 1827. Prussia exchanged consuls with Mexico immediately thereafter. However, the agreement ran into opposition in the Mexican Congress, and it was not finally ratified until 8 February 1831.[13] Prussia attempted to arrange a similar agreement with Colombia, but the negotiations broke down when the Colombian representative stated that he could only agree to a conventional commercial treaty that included Prussia's full recognition of Colombia's independence. This was further than Bernstorff was prepared to go. Thus, Kunth's hopes for a "new era" in American trade were not immediately realized.

Bernstorff's middle path to the solution of the Latin American problem is characteristic of Prussian foreign policy in the later 1820s. Consciously or unconsciously, and in his own particularly reserved and cautious manner, Bernstorff expressed the interests of economic groups in Prussia; to some extent, he also expressed the ideas of representatives of the reform movement. It is no accident that Kunth, Vincke, and even Bernstorff echoed

    10. Kossok, *Im Schatten der Heiligen Allianz*, pp. 168–169.

    11. Canning to Strangford, 17 March 1826, Charles K. Webster, *Britain and the Independence of Latin America, 1812–1830*, 2:304; Rodriguez O., *Emergence of Spanish America*, p. 151; and Kossok, *Im Schatten der Heiligen Allianz*, p. 171.

    12. Kossok, *Im Schatten der Heiligen Allianz*, pp. 171–172.

    13. Rodriguez O., *Emergence of Spanish America*, pp. 152–153.

the words of Stein and Humboldt. As in the case of Prussia's customs policy, ideas and attitudes connected with the reform era were once again percolating to the surface and were slowly transforming some aspects of Prussian policy. As Bernstorff pointed out in 1826, Prussia's relations with Latin America also demonstrate that particular state interests were beginning to predominate over the common principles of the European community. However, Bernstorff made no clean break with the policy of legitimacy and continued to refuse to recognize the independence of the Latin American countries until Spain had done so.

## THE EASTERN QUESTION

Bernstorff's greatest problems in European affairs during this period were caused by the Greek struggle for independence and the resulting strains that conflict placed on the eastern alliance. The crisis of 1821–1822 had been temporarily settled by an agreement between Russia and the Ottoman Empire over the evacuation of the principalities. However, the Greek question remained unresolved, and the situation in Greece became more unstable during the next three years. In an attempt to settle the problem, Alexander I convened an ambassadorial conference in St. Petersburg in June 1824. The Tsar proposed that Greece be divided into three semiautonomous principalities that would be governed in a manner similar to Wallachia and Moldavia. Both the Greeks and the Turks refused to consider such an arrangement, and Austria and Great Britain did nothing to support Russia's efforts.[14]

Meanwhile, the unity of the Greek movement for independence disintegrated, and the country found itself in a state of civil war. In addition, the Sultan had called in the efficient military and naval units of Mohammed Ali to quell the revolution. In February 1825, the Egyptian army, after having subdued a Greek revolt on Crete, landed in the Morea and inflicted a series of defeats on the disorganized and feuding Greek forces.[15] With the Egyptian invasion underway, a second meeting took place in St. Petersburg, this time without the participation of Great Britain. The only

14. M. S. Anderson, *The Eastern Question*, p. 62; and C. W. Crawley, *The Question of Greek Independence*, pp. 35–36.

15. Anderson, *Eastern Question*, pp. 55–63; Crawley, *Question of Greek Independence*, pp. 30–41; and Douglas Dakin, *The Greek Struggle for Independence, 1821–1833*, pp. 103–106, 120–141.

result of this meeting was a proposal by the powers to attempt mediation with the Porte. Metternich, suspicious of Russian initiatives, objected strongly to any measures that would aid the Greeks. The Russian government was frustrated with its lack of success in solving the Greek problem within the framework of the European alliance. In August, Nesselrode announced that "it will be quite useless to become involved in new discussions with Russia's allies over the affairs of Turkey." From this point on, he said, "Russia will follow her own views exclusively and will be governed by her own interests."[16]

Of all the powers, Prussia had responded most favorably to Russia's proposals. But Bernstorff hoped that any Russian action would receive the sanction of the European alliance, and he continued to work for a peaceful solution of the Greek problem. He realized that Austria and Russia had reached a serious impasse following the second St. Petersburg conference.[17] As he reported to Frederick William in June 1825, "Austria wants war under no condition and at no price! Russia wants the preservation and pacification of Greece under any condition and at any price, hence even with the danger of war!" He continued:

> In view of this tension that has interceded between two courts equally friendly with Your Majesty, in the composition of a new instruction for your chargé d'affaires in Petersburg, I believe it is my duty to exercise the greatest caution and discretion in order to avoid on both sides any offense, any occasion for irritation and any suspicion or reproach because of partiality. . . . It seems advisable to me, therefore, to make the attempt to mediate between the opposing views of both courts . . . to the extent that the inner, in fact, almost insolvable difficulties of the matter can possibly permit.[18]

This report defined the basic position that Prussia would assume toward the eastern question and its accompanying complications for the next five years.

---

16. Anderson, *Eastern Question,* p. 63.

17. See Karl Ringhoffer, *Ein Dezenium preussischer Orientpolitik zur Zeit des Zaren Nikolaus (1821–1830),* p. 37, an excellent study that contains an appendix with an extensive collection of diplomatic documents for the entire decade.

18. Bernstorff to Frederick William, 15 June 1825, ibid., pp. 252–254. For further details, see Bernstorff's two instructions to Küster, dated 27 June 1825, ZSA Me, Rep. 81, Petersburg I, Nr. 107.

The eastern alliance, already threatened by the disagreement between Russia and Austria, was further weakened toward the end of 1825 by the death of Alexander I and the establishment of close relations between Russia and Great Britain. The Egyptian army's continued success had aroused increased sympathy for the Greeks in Great Britain. Partly because of popular pressure, but also because of the desires to prevent a Russo-Turkish war and to disrupt the unity of the eastern alliance, Canning announced his willingness to mediate between the Greeks and the Porte and to cooperate with Alexander's similar efforts, if the Tsar so desired.[19] Discussions between Canning and Lieven, the Russian ambassador, made the prospect of some sort of Anglo-Russian agreement likely.[20] Meanwhile, on 1 December 1825, Alexander died. His successor, Nicholas I, assumed the throne amid the confusion of the Decembrist revolt, which only reinforced his already strong dislike of revolutionary movements.[21] Although legitimist in outlook, Nicholas was far less committed to the Concert of Europe than Alexander had been. His attitude toward the Greek crisis was ambivalent: While he condemned the revolutionary activity of the Greeks, his profound Orthodox faith made his concern for the welfare of Christians in the Ottoman Empire even greater than his predecessor's.[22]

However, Nicholas's assumption of the imperial throne did nothing to damage the rapprochement between Britain and Russia. In the spring of 1826, Wellington left for St. Petersburg to discuss a common Anglo-Russian policy toward Turkey. The result of this mission was the protocol of 4 April 1826, which stipulated that both powers were ready to mediate between the Turks and the Greeks toward the goal of making Greece an autonomous dependency within the Ottoman Empire. The agreement would remain in effect if Russia went to war, and both powers had the right to intervene "jointly or separately" between the Turks and Greeks. Finally, Austria, Prussia, and France were to be invited to participate in the mediatory efforts on the Greek question.[23]

19. Anderson, *Eastern Question*, p. 64; and Harold Temperley, *The Foreign Policy of Canning, 1822–1827*, pp. 338–348.

20. Temperley, *Foreign Policy of Canning*, pp. 348–353.

21. Nicholas V. Riasanovsky, *Nicholas and Official Nationality in Russia, 1825–1855*, p. 33.

22. Ibid., pp. 238–239n.

23. The documents concerning Wellington's mission are in Arthur Wellesley,

The protocol represented a considerable achievement for Russia, and Canning felt that Wellington had given in too much. However, Wellington felt that war between Russia and Turkey was imminent and had therefore negotiated under a good deal of pressure. On 17 March 1826, the Russian government had sent a sharply worded ultimatum to the Porte demanding the reestablishment of the status quo in the principalities in accordance with the existing treaties, as well as the settlement of all outstanding issues between the two states. Turkey was given six months in which to reply, after which hostilities would begin. Wellington's negotiations with the Russians took place during this waiting period. The Sultan finally submitted to this ultimatum in May, and, in October, discussions between Russia and the Ottoman Empire resulted in the signing of the convention of Akkermann. This agreement was a victory for Russia: The Porte agreed to Russian demands concerning the administration of the principalities, outstanding border disputes, and the interdiction of the Russian grain trade.[24]

The protocol of 4 April 1826 was the first concrete evidence of the disintegration of the eastern alliance. Metternich disapproved of Russian policy throughout 1826 and tried several times to enlist Prussia's support against Britain and the Tsarist Empire. These attempts failed because Bernstorff was critical of Metternich's position and refused to cooperate.[25] However, although Bernstorff was unwilling to adopt a policy in opposition to Russia, he was also against formally allying Berlin with the policies of London and St. Petersburg. When the British and Russian representatives in Berlin officially presented the contents of the 4 April protocol to Bernstorff in August, he received the note with great satisfaction and said that he was happy to see that "the course now adopted by the British government is that which has been for the last three or four years recom-

---

First Duke of Wellington, *Despatches, Correspondence and Memoranda of Field Marshal Arthur, Duke of Wellington,* Vol. 3. Also see Anderson, *Eastern Question,* p. 65; Temperley, *Foreign Policy of Canning,* pp. 248–255; and Crawley, *Question of Greek Independence,* pp. 59–62.

24. Crawley, *Question of Greek Independence,* pp. 65–66; and Dakin, *Greek Struggle for Independence,* pp. 180–181.

25. Bernstorff to Frederick William, 13 January 1826, Ringhoffer, *Ein Dezenium preussischer Orientpolitik,* pp. 258–260; Clanwilliam to Canning, 2 May 1826, PRO F. O. 64/146; and Zichy to Metternich, 8 and 11 April 1826, HHSA, Stk., Preussen Karton 122.

mended by the continental allies, and by none more frequently and more earnestly (it must be confessed) than by Prussia."[26]

But this expression of approval did not mean that Bernstorff was willing to let Prussia become a party to the agreement. He was not convinced by Nesselrode's assurance that Russia was still firmly committed to the eastern alliance, and he knew that Austria would have nothing to do with the protocol agreement.[27] Bernstorff therefore decided that Prussia should declare its full approval of the contents of the Anglo-Russian protocol, but should add that it would not formally adhere to such an agreement without the full participation of all five powers, that is, without Austria's support. This policy was adopted to avoid completely isolating Austria and seriously damaging the eastern alliance.[28] Bernstorff assumed this position despite worsening relations with Metternich who, according to Elise von Bernstorff, was at this time carrying out an intrigue to try to have her husband replaced by Hatzfeld as Prussian foreign minister.[29] Schöler and Bülow were critical of Bernstorff's position. For example, Bülow argued that it would indeed be preferable if Austria would participate in efforts to maintain peace in the East, but, if Vienna refused, then it was better for Prussia to be aligned with France and Russia, rather than be condemned to passivity by having to wait for Austria. Prussia's active participation with the other powers would finally force Austria to join the common effort in the East. Within the Prussian government, Motz, Eichhorn, and Witzleben were generally considered to be pro-Russian, not because they necessarily favored Russia, but because they wanted Prussia to have a more flexible position within the European system.[30] Ancillon, Duke Charles, and Wittgenstein, as might be expected, were strongly pro-Austrian.

The court at St. Petersburg also criticized Bernstorff for being subservient to Metternich. However, there is no evidence that Metternich had influenced Bernstorff's policy on the April protocol. In fact, there is considerable evidence that at this very time Bernstorff was disappointed over major aspects of Metternich's policy and was taking active steps to

---

26. Temple to Canning, 31 August 1826, PRO F.O. 64/147.

27. Bernstorff to Schöler, 27 November 1826, ZSA Me, Rep. 81, Petersburg I, Nr. 109.

28. Bernstorff to Frederick William, 21 December 1826, Ringhoffer, *Ein Dezenium preussischer Orientpolitik,* pp. 268–271.

29. Gräfin Elise von Bernstorff, *Aus ihren Aufzeichnungen,* 2:58.

30. Ibid., pp. 67, 90.

counteract Austrian influence in Berlin. Although he had gone to great effort to try to convince Vienna to join the Anglo-Russian-French attempt to settle the Greek question, by April of 1827 he had few illusions that Metternich was sincerely willing to cooperate.[31] Bernstorff also systematically excluded Ancillon, who was highly critical of the 4 April protocol and a strong advocate of Austria's policy, from conducting important business in the Ministry of Foreign Affairs. When Ancillon complained that he no longer had any responsibilities in the ministry, Bernstorff replied that Ancillon would have to reconcile himself to the reduced nature of his assigned duties in view of the "incompatibility" of their political outlooks.[32]

Bernstorff also attempted to make the independent nature of his policy clear to Russia. As he wrote to Küster, the Prussian chargé d'affaires, in St. Petersburg:

> It is completely in error for one to suspect us of making any promise with the court of Austria, or to have made our participation in the negotiated treaty dependent upon this court in order to please it. If we connect our participation with the condition of unanimity of the allies, we base this upon higher and more general motives, and do so without asking ourselves in which way to bring about this unanimity or from which side opposition to it should be anticipated.[33]

In other words, Bernstorff remained a defender of what might be called the general interests of Europe, mainly because no direct Prussian interests were involved in the eastern question. He wanted a joint, five-power solution to the Greek crisis, wished to avoid the isolation of Austria, and hoped that the eastern alliance would continue to survive, even though he realized it had lost most of its vitality.[34] He was reluctant to abandon a

31. See Bernstorff to Albrecht, reply to the Cabinet Order of 13 March 1827, Ringhoffer, *Ein Dezenium preussischer Orientpolitik,* p. 279; and Heinrich von Treitschke, *History of Germany in the Nineteenth Century,* 4:590.

32. Zichy to Metternich, 23 June 1826, HHSA, Stk., Preussen, Karton 122; Ancillon to Bernstorff, 20 April, 4 May, 21 May, and 6 June 1827, and one undated letter; Bernstorff to Ancillon, 23 April, 27 April, 7 May, and 31 May 1827; and Frederick William to Ancillon, 19 May 1827, RA Stintenburg 5128/50. Also see Seymour to Aberdeen, 9 September 1829, PRO F. O. 64/159.

33. Ringhoffer, *Ein Dezenium preussischer Orientpolitik,* p. 76.

34. See Bernstorff to Werther, 11 February 1827 (copy), ZSA Me, Rep. 81, Petersburg I, Nr. 112.

political system that was now experiencing some difficulties because he still found the concept of a European community attractive and because he believed that the preservation of unity among the great powers was in the best interest of Prussia.

On 6 July 1827, Britain, France, and Russia concluded the Treaty of London. Prussia and Austria declined to take part. Bernstorff believed that, unless the treaty included all five powers, it would create "a schism in the alliance."[35] The terms of the treaty were basically the same as those of the 4 April 1826 protocol. France had not wanted to sign the agreement without Prussia, but finally did so in order "to keep England and Russia in check, just as England had signed the protocol in order to restrain Russia."[36]

Shortly thereafter, in an effort to impose an armistice on the Turks, British and French naval forces in the Mediterranean began to cut off supplies to the Egyptian army in Greece. A full-scale blockade of the area began in early September. On 12 September, a British squadron located a large Turkish-Egyptian fleet in the harbor of Navarino; on 20 October 1828, British, French, and Russian naval forces attempted to enter the harbor. The Egyptian-Turkish fleet was completely destroyed as a result of the battle that followed.

To Europe and Prussia, the battle of Navarino was a turning point in the eastern question: It converted the Greek crisis into a major armed conflict between the powers, primarily Russia and the Ottoman Empire. As war became nearly inevitable in the East, Bernstorff began to draw closer to France, Russia, and Britain. He had not abandoned Prussia's middle stance, but in a circular dispatch to all Prussian embassies in Europe he indicated that "although our court neither cooperated in bringing about the London treaty nor acceded to that treaty after it had been drawn up, its principles and aims are approved by us without reserve."[37]

## FROM NAVARINO TO ADRIANOPLE

The defeat of the Turkish-Egyptian fleet at Navarino led to a break in relations between the members of the Triple Alliance and the Ottoman

---

35. Bernstorff to Maltzahn, 18 June 1827, ZSA Me, Rep. 81, Wien I, Nr. 139.
36. Crawley, *Question of Greek Independence*, p. 7.
37. Treitschke, *History of Germany*, 4:591.

Empire. In November, the Sultan repudiated the convention of Akkermann and declared a holy war against the Russians. In February, he closed the straits to foreign ships. As pressure for war against Turkey increased in Russia, St. Petersburg tried to force Britain and France to join the conflict. Because Nicholas had never been a supporter of the revolution in Greece, the question of Greek independence declined in importance; Turkey's failure to honor the convention of Akkermann became the prime issue. By the end of April, the Russian army had begun military operations against the Turks.

France was willing to support the Tsar's operations against Turkey, but Britain and Austria were critical of his plans. The Duke of Wellington, who had succeeded Canning in 1827, was disturbed over the results of the battle of Navarino and suspicious of Russia's intentions in the Near East. He therefore declined to pressure the Porte to accept reasonable terms and refused to assist Russia against Turkey. Austria viewed Navarino as a disaster. Metternich feared Russian expansion in the Balkans and the general instability in Europe caused by the policies of St. Petersburg; Francis even considered mobilizing 100,000 troops to aid the Turks if necessary.[38] Metternich's first diplomatic counteroffensive aimed at capturing Prussia's active support for a policy directed against Russia. In a long *Denkschrift* to Bernstorff, Metternich explained how Europe was divided into two coalitions—France, Britain, and Russia on the one hand, and Austria and Prussia, on the other. He urged Prussia to join Austria in calling for the reestablishment of order in Greece and for the obstruction of military action against Turkey by the Triple Alliance.[39]

For Bernstorff, the battle of Navarino, which had occurred without a declaration of war, was the beginning of a new period of barbarism (he may have recalled the British attack on Copenhagen). In spite of this, he declined Metternich's proposal. On 9 December 1827, he wrote to Maltzahn in Vienna:

> A common initiative by Prussia and Austria, as appears attractive to Prince von Metternich since circumstance and the fear of standing completely isolated have forced him so vigorously upon us, is to us as difficult

38. Metternich to Apponyi, 13 November 1827, Clemens Lothar Wenzel Fürst von Metternich-Winneburg, *Aus Metternichs nachgelassenen Papieren*, 4:395–398; and Anderson, *Eastern Question*, pp. 67–68.

39. Ringhoffer, *Ein Dezenium preussischer Orientpolitik*, pp. 85–86.

as it is questionable, even if our whole position and the nature of our relations with the other powers does not prohibit an active intervention in the course of events, which are no longer so restricted. We will speak, when the opportunity exists, peacefully and conciliatorily; however, we would lose our carefully chosen and daily ever more obviously correct position if we oppose the complaints and propositions of the three powers, as expressed in the Treaty of London, which we have in their eyes no right to do, and which would, without doubt, work against their hoped-for success.[40]

Bernstorff and Frederick William were willing to try to achieve some sort of reconciliation between Austria and Russia and to work for a peaceful solution of the eastern question.[41] Bernstorff even drafted an article for the *Allgemeine Preussische Staatszeitung* that explained the mediatory role Prussia was attempting to play in the crisis. He told the King that, although it was difficult for the public to understand such a complicated affair, he felt strongly that the people should be kept informed of the government's activities.[42] He also redoubled his efforts to reconstitute a five-power approach to the eastern question, but he met with no success.[43] At the end of April, the Russian army crossed the river Pruth, and war began between the Tsarist and Ottoman empires. Apparently, none of the powers took Prussia's efforts at mediation very seriously. Bernstorff's activities are not particularly important in this chapter of European diplomatic history, but they do reveal his continued allegiance to the European alliance.

The Russian military campaign against Turkey in 1828 was not very successful. Slowed down by a poor supply system and dysentery, the Russian army found it difficult to make progress against the Turkish forces. Anglo-French support of Russia's operations was less than

40. Bernstorff to Maltzahn, 9 December 1827, ZSA Me, Rep. 81, Wien I, Nr. 139.

41. Bernstorff to Albrecht, 26 December 1827, and Bernstorff to Frederick William, 20 January 1828, Ringhoffer, *Ein Dezenium preussischer Orientpolitik,* pp. 312–313, 320–321.

42. Bernstorff to Frederick William, 4 and 8 January 1828, ZSA Me, Rep. 92, Witzleben, Nr. 109.

43. Ringhoffer, *Ein Dezenium preussischer Orientpolitik,* pp. 104, 106–115, and 330–356; Bernstorff to Maltzahn, 25 February 1828, ZSA Me, Rep. 81, Wien I, Nr. 140; and Trauttmannsdorff to Metternich, 23 February and 2 March 1828, HHSA, Stk., Preussen, Karton 128.

wholehearted. Metternich, pleased by the paucity of Russian military achievements in the 1828 campaign, hoped to exploit the dissension that was developing between the members of the Triple Alliance. Austria had placed 60,000 troops along its border in Galicia, but they were scattered in small units. Maltzahn stated that they posed no military threat to Russia, but were merely there to strengthen Austria's diplomatic position.[44]

In the fall of 1828, Metternich proposed a general conference of the powers on the eastern question in which France, England, Austria, and Prussia would mediate between Russia and the Porte. Nicholas, who correctly perceived that Metternich's intention was to disrupt the Triple Alliance, angrily rejected the idea. As Bernstorff wrote to Maltzahn, "They are convinced in St. Petersburg that the Viennese government is incessantly striving to incite the English government against Russia, to rupture the Triple Alliance, to create a decided ascendancy of English policy also in France, and in that way to bring about a new combination by which Russia will be isolated and forced to conclude peace with the Porte under unsatisfactory conditions."[45]

Bernstorff also opposed Metternich's plan. He felt that the isolation of Russia would be dangerous to Europe, just as two years before he had argued against the isolation of Austria. In addition to expressing his disapproval to Austria, he worked against Metternich's plan in Paris and London, especially after he found out that Metternich was informing other diplomats that Prussia had already agreed to Austria's proposal. He told Brook-Taylor, the British envoy in Berlin, "that there was a want of frankness and sincerity in the conduct of the Austrian government which must naturally give rise to suspicions of their intentions."[46] He instructed Bülow in London and Werther in Paris to correct the false impression that Metternich was creating and to clearly state Prussia's opposition to Metternich's policy.[47] In a letter to Metternich, he wrote that Vienna's efforts to isolate Russia were creating extreme suspicion in St. Petersburg and were aggravating the tensions that already existed between the two empires. He noted that the Tsar was worried about the disposition of Austrian troops along the Polish frontier.[48] Metternich rejected these

44. Ringhoffer, *Ein Dezenium preussischer Orientpolitik,* pp. 135–136.
45. Bernstorff to Maltzahn, 22 December 1828, ZSA Me, Rep. 81, Wien I, Nr. 140.
46. Brook-Taylor to Aberdeen, 21 December 1828, PRO F. O. 64/154.
47. Bernstorff to Werther, 24 December 1828, and Bernstorff to Bülow, 25 December 1828, Ringhoffer, *Ein Dezenium preussischer Orientpolitik,* p. 390.
48. Bernstorff to Metternich, 3 January 1829, ZSA Me, AAI, Rep. 1, Nr. 2259.

criticisms and placed all the blame for the present crisis on Russia.[49] He also said that he wanted to see documentary proof for Bernstorff's assertion that he was trying to form a coalition of Austria, France, Britain, and Prussia against Russia.[50] Bernstorff dismissed Metternich's reply as pure deception; even without a direct written request of this nature, the whole thrust of Austrian policy has obviously been pointed in this direction, and Metternich had been improperly associating Berlin with this policy in foreign capitals. Bernstorff said that he was well informed about Metternich's statements to the governments in Paris and London.[51] While working against Metternich's plan, Bernstorff also attempted to assuage Russian suspicions of Austria. He wrote to Schöler in February 1829 that one should view Metternich's actions as being opportunistic rather than systematically hostile to Russia's interests.[52] Bernstorff was correct. While Metternich was willing to try to make the most of circumstances favorable to Austria, he did not desire any open conflict with Russia.

No sooner had Bernstorff rejected Austrian attempts to isolate Russia than he had to ward off a Russian offer of a defensive alliance with Prussia. In January, Alopeus, the Russian minister, unofficially contacted Bernstorff about such an agreement. If a formal alliance was impossible, Alopeus then proposed a more informal arrangement in which Russia, to counter Austrian troop movements, would pull its units out of Poland and Prussia would supply temporary replacements. Although Bernstorff rejected both of these proposals, Alopeus's offer stimulated a half-year's dispute within the Prussian government involving those who supported a formal alliance with Russia.[53]

Witzleben argued forcefully for an agreement with St. Petersburg. Prussia, which, he said, had been merely following the policy of Austria, needed to assert itself in European politics; the Russian alliance would be the first step toward shedding Austrian domination. Bernstorff denied that Prussia had been following the dictates of Vienna. Through careful diplomacy Prussia had attained an independent position within Europe,

49. Metternich to Bernstorff, 10 and 23 January 1829, ibid. Also Metternich to Trauttmansdorff, 11 January 1829, HHSA, Stk., Preussen, Karton 132.

50. Metternich to Bernstorff, 23 January 1829, ZSA Me, AAI, Rep. 1, Nr. 2259.

51. Bernstorff to Metternich, 1 February 1829, and Bernstorff to Frederick William, 29 February 1829, ZSA Me, AAI, Rep. 1, Nr. 2259.

52. Bernstorff to Schöler, 19 February 1829, ZSA Me, Rep. 81, Petersburg I, Nr. 117.

53. Brook-Taylor to Aberdeen, 10 January 1829, PRO F. O. 64/158.

and it retained complete liberty of action. A Russian agreement would make Berlin dependent on St. Petersburg and might well have a negative effect on Prussia's position in Germany. Witzleben continued to argue for a Russian alliance until June of the same year; with Frederick William's support, Bernstorff withstood the pressure and succeeded in maintaining Prussia's neutral position.[54] As he told Witzleben, "If it is really true that the fundamental strength of a state lies in the complete independence of its own will and conduct, this is doubly true in application to the present situation for the position of Prussia."[55] Prussia should be friendly to Russia, but should avoid any binding obligations. However, he did not deny that Austria's weakened position had been created in part by a policy of contradiction, duplicity, and deceit.[56]

While Prussia continued to maintain a neutral stance (although favorable to Russia) on the eastern question, it also continued to express its desire for the reestablishment of peace in the Near East. In May 1829, Nicholas and his family were to meet with Frederick William, who was Nicholas's father-in-law. The meeting was to serve diplomatic as well as dynastic purposes, as Prussia had again expressed a willingness to mediate between Russia and Turkey.[57] Originally, Nesselrode had politely declined Prussia's offer, explaining that Russia would prefer to wait until it had achieved tangible success in the battlefield. However, Russia's military position was not strong. The campaign of 1828 had been costly in men and materiel, and the 1829 campaign promised to be more of the same. Nicholas had claimed all along to have only limited objectives in the war, and now, realizing the cost of the conflict, he decided that the time had come for a peace initiative. Nesselrode now asked Bernstorff if Prussia could induce the Sultan to begin negotiations with St. Petersburg. Bernstorff told Frederick William that Prussia's opportunity to fulfill its duty as a member of the Grand Alliance, to do its part to resolve a highly dangerous situation in Europe, had come at last.[58]

Unfortunately, Frederick William became ill in May and was unable to make the trip to the Polish border, where he and Nicholas were to have

54. Brook-Taylor to Aberdeen, 4 February 1829, ibid.; and Trauttmannsdorff to Metternich, 31 January 1829, HHSA, Stk., Preussen, Karton 131.
55. Bernstorff to Witzleben 8 June 1829, ZSA Me, Rep. 92, Witzleben, Nr. 109.
56. Ibid.; and Seymour to Aberdeen, 10 June 1829, PRO F.O. 64/158.
57. Ringhoffer, *Ein Dezenium preussischer Orientpolitik*, pp. 161–162.
58. Ibid., pp. 174–176.

met. After receiving the news of his father-in-law's sickness, Nicholas decided to go on to Berlin. To everyone's surprise, he suddenly appeared in the Prussian capital on 6 June 1829. The two monarchs quickly agreed that Prussia should undertake a peace mission to Turkey, and a Prussian officer, Lieutenant General von Müffling, was chosen for the task. Bernstorff instructed Müffling to tell the Porte that Russia did not intend to conquer new territory or to threaten the independence of the Ottoman Empire. Müffling was to say that the Tsar was prepared to end the war if the Sultan was ready to negotiate a peace; if the Sultan preferred not to commence peace negotiations, then Russia would continue the conflict.[59] Bernstorff emphasized that Müffling was only empowered to transmit Russia's conditions and to arrange for direct negotiations between the two powers; he was not in a position to mediate between them or to join with the envoys of the other powers in negotiating with the Sultan. In addition to emphasizing the independent nature of his mission, Müffling was to make it clear that none of his instructions were in conflict with the common wishes of the European powers.[60]

Müffling arrived in Constantinople in August. The terms he presented to the Sultan were adherence to the convention of Akkermann, free navigation of the Dardanelles and the Bosporus, an indemnity, and the ceding of some disputed territories on the Black Sea. The Reis-Effendi agreed to the first two demands, but he balked at the last two and refused to send a plenipotentiary to meet with the Russians. Müffling recommended that the Russian commander, Field Marshal Diebitsch, drop the demand for an indemnity, but Diebitsch refused.

Meanwhile, French and English envoys had persuaded the Sultan to begin talks with the Russians. The Porte sent two plenipotiaries, escorted by Müffling's assistant, von Küster, to Adrianople.[61] However, by this time, Diebitsch had overwhelmed the Turkish forces and brought his troops within forty miles of Constantinople. His army was sick and

---

59. Theodore Schiemann, *Geschichte Russlands unter Kaiser Nikolaus I*, 2:318; and Friedrich Carl Ferdinand Freiherr von Müffling, *Aus Meinem Leben*, pp. 292–371.

60. Draft of Bernstorff's undated instruction for Müffling, Schiemann, *Geschichte Russlands*, 2:465–467. Also see Bernstorff to Royer, 18 June 1829; Bernstorff to Nesselrode, 22 June 1829; and Bernstorff to Bülow, Werther, and Maltzahn, 5 July 1829, ZSA Me, AAI, Rep. 1, Nr. 3095.

61. Crawley, *Question of Greek Independence*, p. 163.

overextended, but the Turks were impressed with the speed of his advance. Diebitsch's campaign, rather than the efforts of Müffling, the French, or the British, finally convinced the Porte to start negotiating.[62] The resulting Treaty of Adrianople was signed on 14 September 1829. Russia received an indemnity, some additional territory (mainly in Asia), and an agreement on its rights in the principalities and the straits. It also provided for an autonomous Greek state as specified in an earlier Anglo-Russian-French protocol of 22 March 1829.[63]

Although Müffling's trip played only a small part in ending the conflict, it was an appropriate conclusion to Bernstorff's efforts. With few deviations and great perseverance, he insisted that Prussia might offer to mediate the crisis, but must not compromise its neutrality. This policy was compatible with the King's normal inclinations, but Bernstorff was the only one of the King's advisors who held this position. Witzleben, Motz, and Eichhorn were pro-Russian; Ancillon, Wittgenstein, and Duke Charles were supporters of Austria. Only Bernstorff held a middle ground, and his view finally prevailed.

France had followed Prussia's actions during this crisis with special interest. Since 1828, some French leaders had been speculating about the advantages of a Franco-Russian-Prussian alignment in Europe. There was a widespread feeling in Paris that France and Prussia were in a similar position—both found themselves in an unsatisfactory situation following the Congress of Vienna, and both were increasingly dissatisfied with Metternich's influence in Europe. A paper prepared in the French foreign office stated that the period of Prussia's passivity in Europe, which had been imposed by the unsatisfactory outcome of the Congress of Vienna, was over. It predicted the reemergence of an independent and energetic policy as traditionally personified by Frederick the Great. French observers were also increasingly impressed by Prussia's military strength and fiscal stability.[64]

Bernstorff, Witzleben, and other officers were inclined toward better relations with France. When Nicholas and Frederick William agreed to

---

62. Anderson, *Eastern Question*, p. 72.

63. Ibid., pp. 73–74.

64. Karl Hammer, *Die Französische Diplomatie der Restauration und Deutschland 1814–1830*, pp. 134, 141.

sponsor Müffling's mission to Constantinople, the French minister in Berlin reported that Bernstorff exclaimed, "The peace of Europe is assured so long as Prussia, France and Russia want it: A tacit and positive agreement between the three courts will suffice to impose peace in Europe against those who would want to disturb it." The French minister interpreted Bernstorff's statement as being tantamount to a proclamation of a Franco-Russian-Prussian alliance that could revise the Vienna settlement.[65] However, this was a total misinterpretation of Bernstorff's intentions; he was speaking only of the eastern question. There is no evidence that he intended to alter the territorial status quo. The French minister obtained an audience with Nicholas and overzealously presented the idea of a Franco-Russian-Prussian alliance. The Tsar turned the proposal down. The French diplomat was disappointed further when he later received a negative response from Bernstorff as well.

Nevertheless, the idea of a constellation of powers in Europe that would be more favorable to French interests died hard. The new ministry of Polignac, which took office in the fall, desired a dramatic success to ensure its tenure in office. Polignac therefore produced a paper that has come to be called Polignac's *Grand Projet*. The proposal, which restated ideas mentioned earlier by Chateaubriand and General Richemont, called for the dismemberment of the Ottoman Empire and the reordering of territorial arrangements in Europe. France would receive the left bank of the Rhine, and Prussia would be consolidated and compensated for this loss by territorial acquisitions in central Germany.[66] The French, convinced that Prussia was gaining ascendancy in Germany, felt that Prussia's willing participation in these plans was crucial to the success of the entire project. As one French diplomatic instruction noted:

> Prussia has succeeded in merging with several states . . . and in attracting other states and in placing itself at the head of commercial interests of a considerable part of Germany, and in creating interests and relations which tend to exclude not only the commercial, but even the political influence of the other powers. . . . Austria has declined and Prussia in proportion has risen.[67]

65. Ibid., p. 143.
66. Guillaume de Bertier de Sauvigny, *Metternich et la France après le Congrès de Vienne,* 3:1310–1311; and Hammer, *Die Französische Diplomatie,* p. 159.
67. Ibid., p. 166.

As a result of France's diplomatic probe, the Tsar asked Berlin whether Prussia would consider ceding part of the Rhineland to France in return for other considerations. Bernstorff firmly rejected any such arrangement. As he told Schöler:

> His Majesty has not held back his firm conviction that only in the unconditional preservation of territorial arrangements as have resulted from the period of Europe's rebirth, lies a guarantee for the tranquility and peace of this continent. Therefore duty and inclination unite in His Majesty's unshakeable decision never to detach pieces of territory whose safety and prosperity have been bought by sacrifice, whose efficacy is apparent already to a great degree, with whom we feel bound by a bond of love and trust that is stronger than all the treaties, and that draws closer every day and whose loss His Majesty believes he could not replace even in the sense of the most important material advantages.[68]

Bernstorff's pronouncement on the French plan ended all talk of a Franco-Russian-Prussian alliance. Nevertheless, the fact that France viewed Prussia as a potentially desirable ally shows that Prussia had moved into a position of greater flexibility in Europe during the late 1820s.

Bernstorff had presented three reasons for turning down the idea of any exchange of territory: First, peace in Europe depended on the sanctity of the territorial arrangements established at Vienna; second, the sacrifice in war and the bonds of affection that bound the Rhineland to the monarchy should not be betrayed; and third, the economic strength of the Rhineland could not easily be replaced. These three themes—the maintenance of the European peace, national pride, and economic interests—comprise the major components of Prussian policy at the end of the decade. Economic interest and a concern for the tranquility of Europe had been present throughout the decade, but the expressions of pride in Prussia, the reference to the War of Liberation, and to emotional feelings for a people were signs of a new element or at least of a new style in Prussian policy. After all, exchanges of territories without regard for the feelings of their inhabitants had been a standard practice for a long time. Bernstorff's assertion that, after only fifteen years, Prussia was bound to

68. Bernstorff to Schöler, 31 December 1829, ZSA Me, Rep. 81, Petersburg I, Nr. 117.

the Rhineland by feelings that were stronger than any treaty expressed a political ideal rather than a political reality.

After the signing of the Treaty of Adrianople, several European states expected the creation of a new constellation of powers in Europe. As a result, Metternich immediately made an attempt to enlist Berlin's aid in reconstructing the old alliance. He told Maltzahn that, if Prussia and Austria adopted a common policy, the resurrection of the alliance was a certainty. Bernstorff replied to Metternich's offer in a friendly but skeptical manner. He had no illusions about Metternich's policies and viewed the rebirth of the eastern alliance at this time as a virtual impossibility.[69]

Bernstorff also declined an English request to participate in a territorial guarantee of Greece by explaining that

> our position and our relations at the present moment leave nothing to be desired, and we have, since Prussia's lucky star, or I would like to say fortunate instinct, kept us out of [the Treaty of London], which has become an inexhaustible source of misunderstanding, embarrassment, and confusion of the worst possible sort, found out in the most gratifying way, that true strength lies only in freedom, and higher virtue only in unconditional independence.[70]

The last clause of Bernstorff's statement described, in an exaggerated way, his concept of what Prussia's policy should be. In a striking contrast to his earlier dispatches, he no longer emphasized solidarity, harmony, and passivity. However, Prussia's European policy could not be as dynamic as its policy in Germany. Prussia's powers were still limited, and the basic characteristics of the international environment remained unchanged. Therefore, caution and a sense of discipline were still paramount. Despite these constraints, a greater sense of firmness, assertiveness, and independence characterized Prussia's European policy by the end of 1829. The basic goals of Bernstorff's diplomacy had remained unchanged since

---

69. Ringhoffer, *Ein Dezenium preussischer Orientpolitik,* pp. 224–225; Bernstorff to Maltzahn, 20 October 1829, ZSA Me, Rep. 81, Wien I, Nr. 141. Also see Seymour to Aberdeen, 30 October 1829, PRO F.O. 64/159; Werner to Metternich, 22 October 1829, HHSA, Stk., Preussen, Karton 131; and Bernstorff to Bülow, 5 December 1829, Ringhoffer, *Ein Dezenium preussischer Orientpolitik,* p. 424.

70. Ringhoffer, *Ein Dezenium preussischer Orientpolitik,* p. 425.

the time he took office, but the manner in which he achieved these goals had undergone modification. When the crisis of the 1830s struck Europe and Germany, Prussia was prepared and willing to play an important and constructive role in European affairs.

# Chapter 6

✠✠✠✠✠✠✠✠✠✠✠✠✠✠✠

# The European Crisis
# 1830–1831

The Concert of Europe was severely tested in the early 1830s when revolutions and popular uprisings broke out in much of Europe. In France, the July Revolution threatened to resurrect the popular passions and military energies of the French Revolution and the Napoleonic era. The revolution in Belgium seemed to provide France with a unique opportunity to overthrow the Vienna settlement regarding the Netherlands, to expand its territorial holdings, and to export revolutionary doctrine to another part of Europe. Scattered revolts in Germany and Italy further complicated the European scene and increased the anxiety of the eastern powers. Finally, the Polish Insurrection disrupted the stability of Eastern Europe and eventually tied down a substantial portion of the Russian army. Despite these threats, the Concert of Europe operated effectively to settle the Belgium question, and the peace of Europe was maintained. Each of the powers demonstrated great self-restraint in areas that were crucial to the interests of another power.

In examining Prussia's role in the diplomacy of this period, certain questions are of special interest. For example, did Frederick William and his government favor intervention in Belgian affairs, as is usually asserted? What was Prussia's contribution to the Concert of Europe's success? Did a split between the eastern and western powers develop during this time, and, if so, when and for what reasons? Finally, how did Bernstorff deal with the many international issues that confronted Berlin?

## THE JULY REVOLUTION

On 3 August 1830, Frederick William was returning from Teplitz when a royal courier brought him the first word of the revolution in France.[1] That evening, he held a conference with Witzleben, Wittgenstein, and Jordan, the Prussian minister to Saxony, at Jordan's country home near Pillnitz. According to Droysen, who in 1874 presented the first detailed examination of Prussian policy during this period, Witzleben argued that "Prussia not intervene [in French affairs], since the *Landwehr* could not be called up for such a campaign." Wittgenstein, on the other hand, urged immediate action to save "the greatly endangered cause of legitimacy." The King told Wittgenstein that he had insufficient manpower for such an action. Frederick William decided that, although he would resist French aggression, he would not interfere in any way in French internal affairs.[2] When the King returned to Berlin, Crown Prince Frederick William and Duke Charles joined Wittgenstein in pressing for a counter-revolutionary campaign against France.[3] The Ministry of Foreign Affairs supported Witzleben's arguments for the maintenance of peace. Ancillon was temporarily in charge of the ministry (Bernstorff had suffered a severe attack of gout in late July and, on 1 August, had gone to Nenndorf to take the waters).[4] Ancillon recommended against intervention and instead argued that Prussia should concentrate on creating unity among the powers. It was most important to demonstrate that the Grand Alliance was strong; this fact alone, if realized in France, should be sufficient to guarantee peace for all of Europe.[5] Nevertheless, the first official directive,

1. The initial report on the revolution was submitted by Nagler from Frankfurt. See Nagler to Frederick William, 31 July 1830, ZSA Me, AAI, Rep. 1, Nr. 1377; and Gneomar Ernst von Natzmer, *Unter den Hohenzollern*, 1:240.

2. Johann Gustav Droysen, "Zur Geschichte der preussischen Politik in den Jahren 1830–1832," p. 9; Heinrich von Treitschke, *History of Germany in the Nineteenth Century*, 5:43; and Natzmer, *Unter den Hohenzollern*, 1:240. Also see Peter Paret, *Clausewitz and the State*, pp. 396–399.

3. Natzmer, *Unter den Hohenzollern*, 1:240–241; and Clausewitz to Gneisenau on 20 August 1830, G. H. Pertz and Hans Delbrück, *Das Leben des Feldmarshalls Grafen Neithardt von Gneisenau*, 5:608–611; and Paret, *Clausewitz*, p. 396n1.

4. Gräfin Elise von Bernstorff, *Aufzeichnungen*, 2:176; and Luxburg to Ludwig, 23 July and 1 August 1830, Bay. GSA, MA III, Nr. 2608.

5. Ancillion to Frederick William, n.d. (but written before 14 August 1830), ZSA Me, AAI, Rep. 1, Nr. 1377.

written by Ancillon, was not reassuring to the French. It authorized Werther, the Prussian minister, to move the Prussian legation from Paris after consulting with the envoys of the other major powers.[6] Fortunately, the other ministers advised Werther to await instructions, and he remained in the French capital.[7] Despite his apparent approval of this communication, Frederick William was determined to do nothing to threaten the peace of Europe. The fall maneuvers of the Prussian army in the vicinity of Coblenz were cancelled, and the British minister in Berlin was told that the King wished to avoid irritating France.[8] Later Frederick William wrote to his daughter, Charlotte, the Empress of Russia, that

> the events in Paris [have created] such a shocking [situation], that the fate of Europe and especially Germany, together with the Netherlands, hangs once again in the balance, as it did between the years 1789 and 1814. . . . To provoke France means to enter into a dangerous game, and yet sooner or later war can be counted upon with certainty, for there will surely be an opportunity for [France] . . . to seize Belgium and the left bank of the Rhine. There can be no doubt that this can never be permitted by us; and at that time I will count with certainty upon the protection and support of your country.[9]

Ancillon communicated the King's anxious but pacific attitude to Prussia's representatives in St. Petersburg, London, and Vienna on 14 August 1830. He discussed how Prussia's geographical position made it essential that it precisely determine its relations with the other powers; he also noted that Prussian policy was particularly dependent on the attitude of Great Britain. Finally, to help stabilize the situation in France, he said that the

6. Ancillon to Werther, 7 August 1830, ibid. Kurt Hoffmann in *Preussen und die Julimonarchie, 1830–1834,* p. 20; and Karl Hillebrand, *Geschichte Frankreichs (1830–1871),* 1:22n, incorrectly credit Bernstorff as the author of this dispatch. In reality, Bernstorff disapproved of this document when he saw it on his return to Berlin; see Brook-Taylor to Aberdeen, 6 September 1830, PRO F.O. 64/163. For the French reaction, see Eugène Vicomte de Guichen, *La Révolution de Juillet 1830 et l'Europe,* pp. 129–130.

7. Treitschke, *History of Germany,* 5:44.

8. Brook-Taylor to Aberdeen, 8 August 1830, PRO F.O. 64/163. Also see Chad to Aberdeen, 9 August 1830, PRO F.O. 30/31; and Mortier to Jourdan, 15 August 1830, A.M.A.E., C. P. Prusse, Vol. 274.

9. Frederick William to Charlotte, 16 August 1830, Paul Bailleu, "Aus dem letzten Jahrzehnt Friedrich Wilhelms III," p. 152.

King urged the earliest possible recognition of the Duke of Orleans by all
the powers, although that recognition would be dependent on the new
King's making a binding declaration to honor all international commitments made by France since 1815.[10]

Bernstorff returned to Berlin on the evening of 18 August and approved
the essential features of the government's policy toward France. The
Bavarian minister, Luxburg, who met with him shortly afterwards, reported that Bernstorff was calmly evaluating relations with the new
regime and felt strongly that Prussia should refrain from any intervention.[11] Bernstorff emphasized to Mortier, the French chargé d'affaires, that
Prussia wanted continued peace with France, was ready to recognize the
new political order in France, and hoped to influence the other powers to
do the same.[12] Bernstorff, out of concern for the disruptive influence that
French émigrés might have in Prussia, refused to allow the Bishop of
Nancy, who had fled France in the wake of the revolution, to reside in the
Rhineland.[13] To the King, Bernstorff stressed that Prussia's recognition of
Louis Philippe must be determined solely by the reality of the new political configuration in France; the violation of certain dynastic principles
or the usurpation of specific rights was an irrelevant issue. He believed
that Austria, Great Britain, and probably Russia would support the joint
recognition of the new ruler, and he thought that Louis Philippe should
acknowledge the validity of the territorial status quo in Europe. However,
he was against making the powers' recognition of Louis Philippe directly
conditional on such an acknowledgement, because it would place the new
French government in an uncomfortable position and might force it to
make a counterdeclaration that would not agree with the aims or the
interests of the other powers.[14]

In the meantime, reports from France seemed to justify the wisdom of
a moderate and amicable policy toward the new regime. On 5 August,

10. Ancillon to Bülow, Maltzahn, and Galen, 14 August 1830, ZSA Me, AAI,
Rep. 1, Nr. 1377.

11. Luxburg to Ludwig, 23 August 1830, Bay. GSA, MA III, Nr. 2608.

12. Mortier to Molé, 22 August 1830, A.M.A.E., C.P. Prusse, Vol. 274.

13. See Schuckmann to Bernstorff, 17 August 1830; Ingersleben to Bernstorff, 17
August 1830; Ingersleben to Schuckmann, 12 August 1830; Bernstorff to Schuck-
mann, 24 August 1830; and Bernstorff to Werther, 24 August 1830, ZSA Me, AAI,
Rep. 1, Nr. 1377.

14. Bernstorff to Frederick William, 24 and 30 August 1830, ibid.

Werther wrote that "all monarchists urgently desire that the four powers should show themselves friendly to the new crown; otherwise the republic, anarchy, will ensue." Count Molé the new French Minister of Foreign Affairs, wrote to Werther on 12 August that "we must save France, and I may add Europe, from a great convulsion. In this struggle the tricolor has been unfurled. But now that it has once more become the banner of France, this glorious flag can only be regarded as an emblem of moderation and defense, of a judicious conservatism, and of peace."[15] Louis Philippe sent a special emissary, General Lobau, to Berlin to gain formal recognition. In a personal letter to Frederick William, the French King explained that he regretted the political difficulties experienced by the senior branch of his family. Circumstances alone had forced him to assume the throne, and he could assure the King of Prussia that he wished to maintain the peace of Europe at all costs.[16] Bernstorff in turn told Lobau that he considered the "consolidation of the constitutional monarchy in France the sole guarantee of tranquility and repose in Europe."[17]

Prussia's desire for peace was matched by the other major powers. In England, public opinion strongly supported the new French regime. Whigs and Radicals in Parliament sympathized with the July Revolution, seeing in it a parallel to their own efforts at reform. Although the Tory government, under the Duke of Wellington, was more critical, its attitude did not delay early recognition of the new monarchy, which occurred on 27 August 1830.[18] Metternich and Nesselrode were both convinced that neither Austria or Russia ought to provoke war with France. Shortly after hearing of the revolution in Paris, they met in Carlsbad and drew up the so-called *Chiffon de Carlsbad*.[19] This informal diplomatic note stated that Austria and Russia would not interfere in French internal affairs, al-

15. Treitschke, *History of Germany*, 5:44–45; and Hoffmann, *Preussen und die Julimonarchie*, p. 20.

16. Louis Philippe to Frederick William, 19 August 1830, ZSA Me, AAI, Rep. 1, Nr. 1377.

17. Mortier to Molé, 25 August 1830, A.M.A.E., C.P. Prusse, Vol. 274.

18. Memorandum on the revolution in France, 14 August 1830, Arthur Wellesley, First Duke of Wellington, *Despatches, Correspondence and Memoranda of Field Marshal Arthur, Duke of Wellington, K.G.*, 7:162–169; and Sir Charles Webster, *The Foreign Policy of Palmerston, 1830–1841*, 1:95. Also see William to Louis Philippe, 27 August 1830 (copy), ZSA Me, AAI, Rep. 1, Nr. 1377.

19. Clemens Lothar Wenzel Fürst von Metternich-Winneburg, *Aus Metternichs nachgelassenen Papieren;* 5:9–12.

though they would repel any attack or threat to the internal peace of the European states.[20] Metternich was eager to convene a ministerial conference of the powers in either Berlin or Vienna to coordinate policy toward France and to prepare for revolutionary activity elsewhere in Europe. Not wanting Austria to assume a position of dominance among the eastern powers, Nesselrode opposed such a meeting and indicated that Nicholas was against intervention in the politics of other nations.[21] In reality, however, Nicholas did want such a meeting. He dispatched Count Orloff to consult with the Austrians, but, because Great Britain opposed the idea of a conference, and Bernstorff and Frederick William considered it unwise, Metternich had to abandon this approach.[22] On 8 September 1830, Francis formally recognized the new French King.[23] Although Metternich intensely disliked the new regime, he acquiesced in what, to him, was violation of the principle of legitimacy. As Srbik has noted, considerations of *Realpolitik* forced Metternich to compromise his fidelity to strict conservative doctrine.[24]

Despite his initially bellicose attitude toward the July Revolution, even Nicholas assumed a pacific stance toward France.[25] In a letter to his brother, Grand Duke Constantine, Commander-in-Chief of the Polish Army, he wrote that "Orleans will never be anything but an infamous usurper." Nevertheless, he indicated that he would not interfere in French affairs; "our opposition will be moral," he told his brother, unless revolutionary France tried to recover its former frontiers. In preparation for such a possibility, Constantine was asked to submit his ideas on the mobiliza-

20. The full text of the *Chiffon de Carlsbad* is given in Ernst Molden, *Die Orientpolitik des Fürsten Metternich, 1829–1833,* p. 119.

21. Ibid., p. 8.

22. Alopeus to Bernstorff, 28 August 1830, and Aberdeen to Cowley, 29 August 1830 (copy), ZSA Me, AAI, Rep. 1, Nr. 1377; Brook-Taylor to Aberdeen, 21 and 27 August 1830, PRO F.O. 64/163.

23. Metternich to Apponyi (draft), 26 August 1830 (copy), ZSA, Me, AAI, Rep. 1, Nr. 1377. The letter of recognition from Francis to Louis Phillippe, as well as Metternich's circular dispatch to the diplomatic missions of Austria are in Metternich, *Papieren,* 5:30–31.

24. Heinrich Ritter von Srbik, *Metternich,* 1:651.

25. Russia's reaction to the July Revolution is described in F. de Martens, *Recueil des Traités et Conventions conclus par la Russie avec les Puissances étrangères,* 15:101–125; and Theodore Schiemann, *Geschichte Russlands unter Kaiser Nicholaus I* 3:13–15.

tion of the Polish army, and, shortly afterwards, Nicholas sent Field Marshal Diebitsch to Berlin to discuss military and political matters.[26] The Tsar did not recognize Louis Philippe until 30 September 1830, some time after Austria and Prussia had already accepted the new political order in France.[27]

The actual recognition of Louis Philippe by Frederick William required the constant urging of Bernstorff. On 30 August, Bernstorff recommended that the King unilaterally recognize the new monarch without further delay; he argued that this step was in the interest of all the powers, but added that, if the King preferred, common action with England, Russia, and Austria was also possible.[28] This option was removed later in the day, when Bernstorff learned that Britain had already recognized Louis Philippe.[29] He then drafted two letters for Frederick William to send to the French monarchy. These were discussed at a conference of the King's advisors on 1 September, but no action was taken. Bernstorff was told that the King needed more time to evaluate the revolution that had just broken out in Belgium and was instructed to ask General Lobau to postpone his departure for Paris by four or five days.[30] On 2 September, Bernstorff forwarded the Tsar's request that the powers follow a united policy toward France to the King, noting that such a policy was no longer

26. Nicholas to Constantine, 18 August 1830, *Russkoe Istorischeskoe Obshchestvo Sbornik,* 132:35–38.

27. The Tsar recognized Louis Philippe primarily because of Nesselrode's consistent efforts. But Nicholas could not bring himself to address the French King with the usual salutation "Monsieur mon frère"; he simply wrote "Sire" on his letters of recognition to Louis Philippe. See Martens, *Recueil des Traités* 15:123; Schiemann, *Geschichte Russlands,* 3:26; and Nicholas to Constantine, 29 August 1830, *Sbornik,* 132:44–46.

28. Bernstorff to Frederick William, 30 August 1830, ZSA Me, AAI, Rep. 1, Nr. 1377.

29. Aberdeen's note to Brook-Taylor of 27 August 1830 arrived at the Prussian foreign ministry on 30 August, after Bernstorff had composed his note to Frederick William. See ZSA Me, AAI, Rep. 1, Nr. 1377. Later that same day, Bernstorff told Mortier that Berlin had decided to recognize Louis Philippe, not to outstrip England, but rather because Prussia did not wish to see war break out along the Rhine frontier. See Mortier to Molé, 30 August 1830, A.M.A.E., C.P. Prusse, Vol. 274.

30. See Bernstorff's drafts of the letters of recognition, originally dated for signature in the month of August, and Albrecht to Bernstorff, 2 September 1830, ZSA Me, AAI, Rep. 1, Nr. 1377.

possible. In any case, it seemed advisable to him to establish friendly relations with France before Diebitsch's mission aroused suspicions in Paris
and before events in Belgium led to additional tensions in Europe.[31] Duke
Charles, who opposed Bernstorff's recommendations, argued that Prussia
should recognize Louis Philippe only in common with the other eastern
powers; Frederick William's letters of recognition should be sent to St.
Petersburg and Vienna for review, and actual recognition should be tied
to France's agreement to uphold the existing treaties and territorial
arrangements.[32]

The King was clearly resistant to Bernstorff's proposals. On 5 September,
he wrote to Bernstorff that he still had reservations about recognizing
Louis Philippe, and, on 6 September, Witzleben told Bernstorff that the
King remained unconvinced by Bernstorff's arguments.[33] Finally, on the
evening of 7 September, the King met with the princes of the royal family,
Duke Charles, Wittgenstein, Lottum, and Bernstorff to discuss recognition.[34] Despite the unfavorable composition of the meeting, Bernstorff's
view prevailed. The next day, he drafted the final version of the King's
letters of recognition. They were presented to General Lobau on 9 September. Bernstorff had written two letters. The *Lettre Formelle* stated that it
was not the King's duty to judge the circumstances that had elevated Louis
Philippe to the throne. He wished the French King complete success in
restoring prosperity and tranquility to France and applauded his desire to
maintain peace between France and the others powers of Europe. He
urged him to honor all the treaties that served as the basis for Europe's
territorial arrangements. In the second letter, the *Lettre Confidentielle,*
Bernstorff emphasized Frederick William's concern that revolutionary
activity in France would spill over into neighboring provinces (for example, the Rhineland) and his desire that Louis Philippe control the

31. Alopeus to Bernstorff, 2 September 1830, and Bernstorff to Frederick William,
2 and 3 September 1830, ibid.

32. Duke Charles to Frederick William (1830), ZSA Me, Haus Archiv, Frederick
William III, Rep. 49, B. VI, 33.

33. Frederick William to Bernstorff, 5 September 1830, and Witzleben to Bernstorff, 6 September 1830, ZSA Me, AAI, Rep. 1, 1377. Bernstorff was openly disappointed by the King's hesitancy; the British minister reported "that he complained
bitterly of the conduct of Prince Metternich as being the probable cause of the
indecision of His Prussian Majesty." Brook-Taylor to Aberdeen, PRO F.O. 64/163.

34. Albrecht to Bernstorff, 5 September 1830, ZSA Me, AAI, Rep. 1, Nr. 1377.

"turbulent spirit" inside France.[35] Of the letters of recognition sent by the eastern powers to Louis Philippe, Prussia's was the most conciliatory.[36]

Bernstorff briefly explained Frederick William's decision in two dispatches to Prussia's diplomatic representatives and informed Alopeus that circumstances and the pressure of time made a joint declaration of recognition by the eastern powers impossible.[37] Bernstorff's most important statement on Prussian policy toward France is contained in a *Denkschrift* written in the middle of September that presents several major themes that characterized Prussian policy for the next year and a half.[38] In this paper, he wrote that the existence of a new government was an "accomplished fact," and for the moment it had saved France from a "terribly menacing anarchy." What policy should be adopted toward the new regime? This question could be analyzed, he said, from the standpoint of general European concerns or in terms of Prussia's specific interests and situation. Bernstorff argued that no treaty guaranteed the right to intervene in French affairs. Of course, by international law and tradition, states had the right to intervene if their security were threatened by the new political arrangements in France. However, he doubted that intervention would really increase the security of neighboring states.

Bernstorff went on to describe Europe as an area that had been slowly restored to order and prosperity after twenty-five years of destruction and disorder. Echoing his father, he said, "It is indisputable that the first duty of governments toward their subjects is the maintenance of peace so long as it is somehow compatible with honor and security. Even the most successful war inflicts a tremendous toll on the welfare of the people, but a war with France had special dangers and risks. "In case of foreign attack, the French nation would be aroused to a fanatical resistance, and

---

35. Frederick William to Louis Philippe, 9 September 1830 (2), *Lettre Formelle* and *Lettre Confidentielle,* ibid.

36. In fact, Metternich complained that the Prussian response was too moderate in tone and was not sufficiently condemnatory of the events in Paris. Bernstorff defended himself against this criticism in Bernstorff to Frederick William, 23 September 1830, ibid.

37. Bernstorff to Maltzahn and Bülow, 10 September 1830, ibid.; Bernstorff to Arnim, 17 September 1830, ZSA Me, Rep. 23.13, Nr. 242 (Darmstadt); and Bernstorff to Alopeus, 22 September 1830, ZSA Me, AAI, Rep. 1, Nr. 1377.

38. Sent to Maltzahn in Vienna on 30 September 1830; see ZSA Me, AAI, Rep. 81, Wien I, Nr. 142.

in that all parties would unite into a single mass, would generate a colossal energy that would not be an easy task for even the mightiest states to overcome." An attempt should be made to avoid such a hazardous enterprise, and moreover, at the present time, the French government was offering its hand in an effort to maintain peace. Bernstorff admitted that the new government was insecure and might not last long, but it was peacefully inclined, monarchically constituted, and in the best position to act in a way that was favorable to Europe. Therefore, it would be unwise to hasten its demise. Caution dictated that the European powers adopt the most practical and secure path. They should tolerate the lesser of two evils in the hope that something better will prevail; most especially, they should do nothing to overthrow, weaken, or restrict the new French government.

But what about the concept of legitimacy? Could the monarchs of Europe abandon this principle in France without danger to themselves? This was a serious concern, for "the surest legal basis, the most valid, deeply rooted principle of all governmental authority lies indisputably in legitimacy and where traditional attachment is joined with a respect preserved over generations, legitimacy is also the first moral guarantee of the same." On two separate occasions between 1813 and 1815, the powers had been able to restore the Bourbons to the throne. This was accomplished only because the allies were able to conduct a national war based on a desire for freedom and independence. Should they now risk the welfare of their peoples a third time in such a dangerous enterprise? What would be the purpose of the powers' intervention—the reestablishment of a ruling house that France justly or unjustly, but nevertheless with an almost overwhelming majority, has rejected? Under the present circumstances, such an attempt would lead to "unsolvable complications." Bernstorff believed that the concept of legitimacy stood in complete opposition to the national feelings of France "and to a certain extent has become a mere abstraction."

He also noted that the campaigns of 1813, 1814, and 1815 were unique. The allies fought them successfully partly because they were able to mobilize the kind of energy that had created the initial successes of the French revolutionary armies and because they were united in a strong alliance. Now the situation was different. The Grand Alliance was weak and disunited. One need only to look at England, who played such a key role in the campaigns against Napoleon. Beset by financial difficulties, political instability, and military unpreparedness, England would never participate in a campaign against the revolution in France. Obviously, these relationships would change, if France attacked its neighbors. Then the right, interest, and duty of the European powers to conduct a defensive war against France would be clearly evident; means and force, not present in a war of aggression, would then be available to them. "Only the obvious necessity to defend one's own possessions and directly endangered independence would arouse the moral energy of the people to the extent needed for such a struggle."

Despite the peaceful assurances of the new French government, Bernstorff continued, war was not only possible, but probable. Therefore, the powers should use this opportunity to strengthen their alliance. In the meantime, doing nothing to provoke war would preserve the blessings of peace for their peoples and gain time for their military operations. For all these reasons, the recognition of Louis Philippe was absolutely necessary. Joint recognition by the eastern powers would be unwise, because England had already recognized the new regime. If the eastern powers took joint action, it would clearly demonstrate that England was no longer a member of the alliance. For the sake of the Grand Alliance, each of the powers should follow Great Britain's example.

Finally, Bernstorff briefly addressed himself to Prussia's particular situation. Any hesitation in the recognition of Louis Philippe would damage Prussia's future relations with France. This would make the settlement of future difficulties more complicated and increase the chances of drifting into conflict. Thus, it was especially urgent that Prussia recognize the new King. "It is the recognition of a historical fact, the existence and effect of which cannot be denied."

This *Denkschrift* contained a number of ideas central to Bernstorff's approach to European affairs. His ideas on policy toward France were influenced first and foremost by his analysis of European politics during the revolutionary and Napoleonic eras. Beyond an appreciation of the dynamic of revolution first revealed in 1789 and the years thereafter, he was impressed by the changes that had taken place in European warfare. He understood the energies that the French revolutionary armies had harnessed, and he appreciated the added strength that the reformed Prussian army had developed by adopting some French concepts as well as through innovations of its own. Above all, he was struck by the dependence of the state's military power on the psychological outlook of its people; the energies of the revolutionary period could be mobilized in a defensive war, but not in one of aggression for a cause of dubious validity.

Prussia was more sensitive than the other eastern powers to public opinion. Russia, Austria, France, and England all maintained professional standing armies on the model of the eighteenth century.[39] Only Prussia had an army theoretically based on universal conscription in which a popular militia played an important role. As Clausewitz pointed out in 1819, because Prussia did not have the resources necessary to support a standing army of comparable size, only the existence of the *Landwehr* enabled Prussia to maintain the military strength of a great power. Yet, Clausewitz viewed the *Landwehr* only as a defensive weapon. His argument that the *Landwehr's* reliability should not be a major concern to the monarchy was postulated on the belief that revolution in Prussia was much less likely than foreign invasion, as well as on the assumption or hope that Prussia would continue to be a reasonably progressive state, attentive to some of the needs of its inhabitants.[40] It was not by accident, therefore, that Witzleben's first recorded reaction to the July Revolution was that "Prussia not intervene, since the *Landwehr* could not be called up for such a campaign." One must remember that the capability of the Prussian government to shape public opinion was severely limited; it operated primarily in a negative sense, that is, by restricting public access to certain information. Because there was little chance of justifying a war of aggression, Bernstorff argued for a pacific policy toward France.

In addition, Bernstorff felt that the success of the allies' campaigns

---

39. The Russian army had no system of universal military service and lacked an adequate reserve system. The term of service for a Russian enlisted man varied from fifteen to twenty-five years. See John Shelton Curtiss, *The Russian Army under Nicholas I, 1825–1855*, pp. 110–111. The Austrian *Landwehr* was gradually abandoned after the Napoleonic Wars and was "completely shelved" in 1831. See Gunther E. Rothenburg, "The Austrian Army in the Age of Metternich," p. 159. The British army also reverted to eighteenth-century models after 1815. See Michael Howard, *Studies in War and Peace*, pp. 50–64. France returned to the idea of a small professional army, abolishing the reserve in 1824 "to insulate the army against outside political influence." The period of service for French enlisted men increased from six to eight years. Douglas Porch, *Army and Revolution;* pp. 6–7; and B. H. Liddell Hart, "Armed Forces and the Art of War," p. 312.

40. Published in Karl Schwartz, *Leben des Generals Carl von Clausewitz*, 2:288–293; and Carl von Clausewitz, *Politische Schriften und Briefe*, pp. 142–153. See also Paret, *Clausewitz*, pp. 292–298.

against Napoleon only came about because the powers coordinated their efforts in an alliance in which England played an important role. At all costs, therefore, the alliance of the four powers must be maintained both as a deterrent and as a mechanism for defeating France if war broke out. This meant that England must not be isolated from the eastern powers.[41] Actually, Bernstorff felt that France's inclusion in the system was the best hope for peace, and no one in Prussia worked harder than Bernstorff to maintain peace with France.

Although few European statesmen defined the interests of their countries in peace as precisely as Bernstorff did, a European consensus for peace did exist. No major leader, with the possible exception of Nicholas, contemplated the prospect of war with France with any enthusiasm. For political reasons alone, there was practically no chance of Great Britain's going to war against France; this stance was reinforced by a lack of financial resources and military weakness. Austria, Russia, and Prussia were also financially strapped and militarily unprepared for a major campaign.

## THE REVOLT IN BELGIUM

On 25 August 1830, revolution broke out in Brussels. The initial details of the uprising were relayed to Berlin by Waldburg-Truchsess, Prussian minister to The Hague.[42] Frederick William's premonition that France would attempt to seize Belgium and the Rhineland now seemed to be coming true. Nevertheless, the King was still committed to maintaining the peace of Europe. On first hearing of the revolution, he told General Krauseneck that he would resist a French attack, but would not interfere in the affairs of other states.[43] The King of the Netherlands, however, was hoping for aid from his relative and neighbor, and, on 28 August, asked

41. Bernstorff to Bülow, 3 September 1830, ZSA Me, AAI, Rep. 1, Nr. 1377.
42. Waldburg-Truchsess to Frederick William, 27 August 1830, in H. T. Colenbrander, ed., *Gedenkstukken der Algemeene Geschiednis van Nederland van 1795 tot 1840*, 44:1–3. The best study of the Belgian Revolution is Robert Demoulin, *La Révolution de 1830;* the diplomatic events surrounding the birth of the Belgian state are described in Fl. de Lannoy, *Histoire Diplomatique de l'Indépendance Belge.*
43. [Major von Felgermann], *General W. I. von Krauseneck*, p. 159.

Frederick William for military support. Specifically, if the Dutch forces were unable to maintain his rights in Belgium, he requested that Prussian troops be sent from the Rhineland in conformity with existing treaties governing the security of the Netherlands.[44]

Frederick William met with Bernstorff, Lottum, Witzleben, and Krauseneck on the evening of 1 September to consider William's request. Bernstorff indicated from the outset that Prussia had no specific treaty obligations to the Netherlands; William could only be referring to the general European commitment to the kingdom of the Netherlands. Therefore, they decided to tell William that Prussia's strength in the Rhineland was insufficient to allow Prussia to assist the Dutch forces. However, to be prepared for any eventuality, the Seventh Army Corps, presently stationed in the Rhineland, would be reinforced by the Fourth Corps. In addition, Bernstorff was instructed to notify the French government in advance of these troop movements to reduce any suspicion of hostility on Prussia's part.[45] Thus, from the first, neither the King nor his chief advisors felt a strong desire to intervene in Belgian affairs. The reports of the French chargé d'affaires also confirm that Prussia never seriously contemplated military action.[46] This initial inclination to maintain peace was reinforced by the policies of Great Britain and France, as well as by unrest in the Rhineland. The British government did not intend to forcefully intervene on behalf of the Netherlands and had indicated that it would support Prussian intervention only if it were adopted in concert with the other powers.[47] Without Britain's support, Prussia would not move.

The wisdom of Prussia's pacific policy was further confirmed when scattered rioting occurred in the Rhineland, especially in Cologne and Aachen. In Aachen, workers, inspired by the revolutionary example of a

44. William to Frederick William, 28 August 1830, in Colenbrander, *Gedenk-stukken,* 44:3–4.

45. See Bernstorff's notes for the protocol of the meeting of 1 September 1830, ZSA Me, AAI, Rep. 1, Nr. 1793.

46. Mortier to Molé, 1, 4, 6, and 12 September 1830, A.M.A.E., C.P. Prusse, Vol. 274.

47. [Felgermann], *Krauseneck,* p. 160; and Aberdeen to Wellington, 31 August 1830, Colenbrander, *Gedenkstukken,* 40:7. As a matter of fact, it later developed that Bernstorff did not want to intervene in Belgium even if Britain decided to unilaterally. See Brook-Taylor to Aberdeen, 6 October 1830, PRO F.O. 64/163.

nearby community in Belgium, and disgruntled because of an incident involving wages at a local textile mill, took to the streets.[48] The uprising in Cologne was more political; some demonstrators openly called for revolution and affiliation with France.[49] Although the rioting in the Rhineland was not of major proportions, General Borstell, commander of the Seventh Corps, was forced to dispatch troops to quell the unrest, and Frederick William became worried that the spirit of revolution might spread to the entire province.[50] Prussia, now more than ever, clearly needed to avoid foreign entanglements and to keep its army in the Rhineland.

The French government was equally concerned with the effect of the Belgian Revolution on its relations with the other powers, especially Prussia. The revolution created a serious dilemma for Louis Philippe and Molé. They could not disapprove of the Belgian uprising because the French public was enthusiastic over the Belgians' success and viewed the revolution as a sequel to their own. Moreover, the revolution promised to destroy the United Netherlands set up by the allies to restrict France. On the other hand, overt support of the Belgian revolutionaries would endanger France's relations with all the great powers and immediately open up the prospect of a European war, for which France was unprepared. In addition, the outbreak of hostilities could easily recreate a revolutionary dynamic and push the country toward a more radical domestic political system. Therefore, Molé moved to assure the powers that the French government was not responsible for the outbreak of the Belgian revolt and would give no material support to the rebels.[51] Then, to simultaneously

48. Eberhard Kliewer, *Die Julirevolution und das Rheinland*, p. 21.

49. Ibid., pp. 31–37. A small demonstration precipitated by the arrest of some journeymen tailors also occurred in Berlin in front of the royal palace. Order was immediately restored and no recurrence was experienced. See Bernstorff to all Prussian legations, 25 September 1830, ZSA Me, AAI, Rep. 1, Nr. 26.

50. Witzleben to Bernstorff, 4 September 1830, ZSA Me, AAI, Rep. 1, Nr. 26; Leopold von Gerlach to Waldburg-Truchsess, 2 September 1830, Colenbrander, *Gedenkstukken*, 44:4–6; Bernstorff to Maltzahn, 6 September 1830, ZSA Me, AAI, Rep. 1, Nr. 26; and Brook-Taylor to Aberdeen, 4 September 1830, PRO F.O. 64/163.

51. Lannoy, L'Indépendance Belge, p. 15; and Molé to La Moussaye, 29 August 1830, Colenbrander, *Gedenkstukken*, 42:3. Also see Stuart to Aberdeen, 31 August 1830, Colenbrander, *Gedenkstukken*, 40:5–6.

satisfy the demands of the French public and preserve peace, he expounded the principle of nonintervention to various diplomats. For example, on 29 August 1830, in a letter to La Moussaye, the French representative in Brussels, he wrote: "France and its government do not intend to interfere directly or indirectly in the domestic affairs of other states so long as this principle is respected by all the cabinets."[52] He told the Russian minister, Pozzo di Borgo, "that it behooves no power to aid another against its rebellious subjects . . . and I assert that this doctrine is inseparable from the stability of the throne of Louis Philippe I."[53] Molé was most afraid that Prussia would intervene in the Netherlands. In a private interview with Werther on 31 August, he said, "The entry of Prussian troops into Belgian territory, in that they will approach our frontier, will on our part necessitate the occupation of all of the opposing border, at no point to engage in hostilities or to seize territory, but to render the situation between Prussia and France perfectly equal."[54]

Bernstorff was critical of the French position. He told Mortier that he could never accept Molé's pretensions, "which speak of a French right to intervene in the affairs of Belgium if the King of the Netherlands requires the military assistance of another power."[55] Nevertheless, France's attitude caused Frederick William and his advisors to be very cautious about intervening in Belgian affairs. When Frederick William finally replied to William's request for military aid, the Prussian King never mentioned the possibility of assisting Dutch forces inside Belgium. Rather, he indicated that Prussia and its allies could be depended on to neutralize France and that he was directing part of his forces to the Rhine for that purpose. He went on to emphasize that Prussia's relations with France were delicate and filled with grave danger and that the situation called for unusual "prudence and circumspection."[56] The orders given to the military forces in the Rhineland reflected Prussia's cautious attitude. The King instructed General von Nostiz, Chief of Staff of the Fourth Corps, to avoid any complications that might lead to war and ordered his

52. Molé to La Moussaye, 29 August 1830, Colenbrander, *Gedenkstukken*, 42:3.
53. Guichen, *La Révolution de Juillet 1830*, p. 170.
54. Werther to Frederick William, 1 September 1830, Hillebrand, *Geschichte Frankreichs*, 1:144 n.
55. Lannoy, *L'Indépendance Belge*, p. 18.
56. Frederick William to William (drafted by Bernstorff), 9 September 1830, ZSA Me, AAI, Rep. 1, Nr. 1793.

brother, Prince William, to make sure that no Prussian soldier crossed the border into neighboring countries.[57]

As the situation in the Netherlands worsened, William was forced to contemplate the administrative separation of Belgium from the northern Netherlands. On 13 September, he convened the States-General to discuss plans for altering the constitution; simultaneously he asked the powers to approve any constitutional changes that he and the States-General might make.[58] Bernstorff told Frederick William that, considering France's instability, the situation in the Netherlands should be brought under control as soon as possible. The administrative division of the Netherlands was desirable, he believed, because it would preserve William's rights, enable the country to continue to serve as a defensive bastion against France, and gain the support of all the powers, including England. Such a solution would be preferable to continued friction between the Dutch and Belgian peoples. He added that, although France was not a signatory of the relevant treaties and should not be involved in the discussions concerning the structure of the Netherlands, keeping the French government fully informed would help to secure France's support for the settlement of the Belgian problem.[59]

Bernstorff's efforts to avoid any conflagration over Belgium encountered momentary difficulty when either imprecision on his part, or misinterpretation by Werther and Bülow, led to reports in France and Great Britain that the Prussian troops in the Rhineland were preparing to enter the Netherlands. According to the French historian D'Haussonville, toward the end of September, Molé asked Werther, "Is it true that you have an army corps assembled on the Dutch frontier and intend to intervene in the affairs of Belgium?" Werther replied, "Yes, indeed." "But that is war," said Molé. "What do you mean—war?" answered Werther, "Your army is completely disorganized, you could not assemble four regiments."[60] It

57. Werner Gronemann, *Die Haltung Preussen in der belgischen Frage, 1830–32,* p. 5.

58. See the reports of Waldburg-Truchsess to Frederick William for 5, 6, 7, and 9 September 1830 in Colenbrander, *Gedenkstukken,* 44:6–12; and Gronemann, *Die Haltung Preussens in der belgischen Frage,* p. 5.

59. Bernstorff to Frederick William, 17 September 1830, ZSA Me, AAI, Rep. 1, Nr. 1793. Also see Bernstorff to Waldburg-Truchsess, 24 September 1830, ZSA Me, AAI, Rep. 1, Nr. 1793.

60. M. O. D'Haussonville, *Histoire de la Politique Exterieure du Gouvernement Français; 1830–1840,* 1:21.

seems doubtful that Werther could have spoken exactly those words in view of his prior reports and Bernstorff's earlier instructions, but there is no question that the interview took place. Possibly, Prussia's representatives abroad were confused about the object of Prussian troop movements. For example, Bülow wrote on 23 September that his understanding was that Prussia had promised to help the King of the Netherlands; Bernstorff told Bülow by return dispatch that this assertion was entirely incorrect. Bernstorff reminded Bülow that Prussia had no obligation to William and that he had already told Bülow that the troops had been sent to the Rhineland to strengthen its security, not to intervene in Belgian affairs.[61] Perhaps Frederick William's statement that William could count on Prussia to "neutralize France" had been misconstrued by Werther and Bülow.

In the meantime, William's attempt to retake Brussels by military force had failed miserably, and the Belgian provisional government had proclaimed its independence. Any hope of an administrative separation of the country was gone; the Belgians were lost to the King of the Netherlands. Bernstorff had no doubt about the consequences of the changed situation. He wrote to Bülow that the strength of the insurrection would now be greatly increased, and it was likely William would ask the powers for assistance. Bülow was to ask the British government if it still thought peaceful negotiations and mediatory efforts could head off a conflict and if direct or indirect participation of the French in these discussions would be advisable to maintain good relations with France and preserve the peace. The English government must know that Prussia was as committed to peace as they and would do everything consistent with Prussia's treaty commitments to that end. However, if London decided on armed intervention, then Prussia would consult with England concerning common action.[62] After Bernstorff had talked in a similar vein to Chad, the British minister to Berlin, the English diplomat noted that Bernstorff's

> absolute disinclination to any movement on the part of Prussia which may be considered as an aggression by France is very marked, and the only measure which he has determined to recommend is a conference of the Five Powers including France.

61. Bernstorff to Bülow, 3 October 1830, ZSA Me, AAI, Rep. 1, Nr. 1377.
62. Bernstorff to Bülow, 3 October 1830, ibid.

But why I observed, admit France into this counsel? Because we can't keep her out was his reply.

"If she be excluded, she will look upon it as a hostile measure, if we admit her, we shall avoid this, and obtain her cooperation."[63]

Bernstorff's thinking coincided with the British government's. In fact, from the beginning of the Belgian crisis, the attitudes and decisions of the British and Prussian governments were strikingly similar.[64] Wellington quickly concluded that no treaty obliged Britain to assist William; in fact, no specific guarantee by the powers existed for the Netherlands at all. In addition, he and Aberdeen supported the idea of an administrative separation of the Low Countries, but opposed a more drastic division. They agreed that France should somehow be involved in the discussions concerning the future of the Dutch and Belgian territories; Wellington felt that the four allied powers should agree on a settlement among themselves and then inform Louis Philippe who he was sure would approve it.[65] Thus, when the Dutch expedition against Brussels failed, and the Dutch King called on France and the allies to assist him in reestablishing order in Belgium, the British were willing to participate.[66] Britain and France were able to quickly agree on the general idea of discussions on the Netherlands. In fact, as early as 1 October 1830, Molé had told Talleyrand to express France's strong desire to negotiate with the other powers on the Belgian question.[67]

After a talk with Werther in Paris, Lord Stuart reported that the

63. Chad to Palmerston, 7 October 1830, PRO F.O. 64/164.

64. In December of 1830 Palmerston wrote: "[Prussia and England] have common interests, which can hardly fail to lead them to pursue on great occasions a similar course. Interested as England must be in the maintenance of the Balance of Power in Europe, there is no state to which she can look with juster confidence than to Prussia for cooperation in her endeavors to preserve the Balance." Palmerston to Chad, 31 December 1830, PRO F.O. 64/164.

65. Wellington to Aberdeen, 3 September 1830, Colenbrander, *Gedenkstukken,* 40:14; Wellington to Aberdeen, 8 September 1830, ibid., p. 28; Aberdeen to Wellington, 9 September 1830, ibid.; Aberdeen to Bagot, 19 September 1830, ibid., pp. 52–54; and Wellington to Aberdeen, 10 September 1830, ibid., p. 29.

66. Aberdeen to Wellington, 29 September 1830, ibid., p. 79.

67. Molé to Talleyrand, 1 October 1830, ibid., 42:34. Also see Molé to Wellington, 3 October 1830, ibid., 40:87–88; Talleyrand to Molé, 4 October 1830, G. Pallain, ed., *Correspondance Diplomatique de Talleyrand,* pp. 14–15; and Stuart to Aberdeen, 8 October 1830, Colenbrander, *Gedenkstukken,* 40:97–99.

position of the Prussian government on "this important question" was "perfectly analogous" to that of His Majesty's government and that Werther would support efforts to begin discussions on Belgium. The Prussian diplomat had added, however, that should Louis Philippe "be disposed to encourage projects, equally incompatible with existing treaties and with the tranquility of other states, the military preparations in Germany are in a state of forwardness which will permit Prussia to bring a force of 260,000 men to the Rhine, within two months from the 1st of October."[68] This statement was an outright bluff; such a force would have meant total mobilization and the concentration of all Prussian troops in the West. This time, Werther accurately reflected the attitude of his government. Bernstorff continued to try to restrain any official French encouragement of the revolution in Belgium. He repeatedly told Mortier that Prussia and the other powers did not want war. However, he pointed out that the French government "is inclined to morally support the insurrections of peoples against governments wherever they occur. Foreign sovereigns will never be able to tolerate this because it concerns the stability of their states and the tranquility of Europe." He also continued to reject the validity of the French doctrine of non-intervention.[69]

Despite his criticism of France, he still remained opposed to the intervention of Prussian forces in the Netherlands.[70] He told the Dutch ambassador that Frederick William had no intention of sending troops into the Netherlands and, when the Dutch diplomat protested, added, "You do not mean we should bring about by a military movement toward your provinces a war with France as well as with four million Belgians, when we are the ones who will have to fight."[71] In a lengthy *Denkschrift* to Frederick William, Bernstorff went so far as to recommend that Prussia should decline to assist William individually or as part of an allied military effort because such forceful action would alienate France and further fuel radical activity. England could not support such a mea-

---

68. Stuart to Aberdeen, 8 October 1830, Colenbrander, *Gedenkstukken,* 40:97–99.

69. Mortier to Molé, 6 and 11 October 1830, A.M.A.E., C.P. Prusse, Vol. 274; and Lannoy, *L'Indépendance Belge,* p. 24.

70. Waldburg-Truchsess to Frederick William, 28 September 1830, Colenbrander, *Gedenkstukken,* 44:18–19; also Waldburg-Truchsess to Frederick William, 3 October 1830, ibid., p. 21.

71. Lannoy, *L'Indépendance Belge,* p. 24.

sure, and the peace of Europe would be endangered. The British government's policy would inevitably incline toward France. The best hope for the King of the Netherlands was for Prussia to work with the other powers for a negotiated settlement.[72] Frederick William accepted Bernstorff's advice and informed William that Prussia would do nothing without first consulting her allies and that Prussia preferred to take the path of conciliation and discussion.[73]

Simultaneously, Bernstorff received official word of the British and French proposals for a five-power conference to discuss the Belgian Revolution and the maintenance of the House of Orange's rule over the southern Netherlands. The question of the location of the conference was still unresolved: The British wanted London; the French, Paris. In fact, the French had requested that Prussia use its influence with the other powers to select Paris as the site of the conference. Werther favored Prussian support for the French proposal because it might strengthen the new government's position and cause the French people to view the conference in a more favorable light. However, Bernstorff, felt that the British would not modify their position and that Austria and Russia would dislike discussions in the French city. Therefore, he suggested to the King that Prussia merely call the powers' attention to the French proposal, clearly stating Prussia's willingness to agree to any site decided on by Britain and France.[74] The King agreed, and, on 20 October, Bernstorff wrote to Bülow that Prussia enthusiastically supported a conference of the five powers. Bernstorff felt that the first consideration of the conference was to arrange for a cease-fire between the Dutch and the Belgians. The question of the location of the meeting was entirely unimportant; he wanted the negotiations to open without delay.[75]

Shortly thereafter, Austria and Russia also agreed to participate. Met-

72. Bernstorff to Frederick William, 11 October 1830, ZSA Me, AAI, Rep. I, Nr. 1793. He also told Diebitsch to try to convince Nicholas that this approach was the only sensible one for Russia. See Bernstorff to Schöler, 17 October 1830, ZSA Me, Rep. 81, Petersburg I, Nr. 120.

73. Bernstorff to Perponcher, 15 October 1830, ZSA Me, AAI, Rep. I, Nr. 1793.

74. Bernstorff to Frederick William, 16 October 1830, ibid.; Mortier to Molé, 22 October 1830, A.M.A.E., C.P. Prusse, Vol. 274; and Chad to Palmerston, 17 October 1830, PRO F.O. 64/164.

75. Bernstorff to Bülow, 20 October 1830, ZSA Me, AAI, Rep. i, Nr. 1793; and Mortier to Molé, 30 October 1830, A.M.A.E., C.P. Prusse, Vol. 274.

ternich had taken relatively little interest in Belgian affairs. His major worry was that similar developments might take place in Italy, an area of far greater concern to Austria. At first, he favored Prussian and British intervention in Belgium. When he was forced to recognize the antipathy that existed between the Dutch and Belgian peoples, and it was clear that Prussia and England would not intervene, he supported the administrative separation of the two areas. Above all, he wanted the revolution brought under control, and he hoped that the Netherlands could continue to play its role in the defense of Europe.[76] After the Dutch failed to take Brussels, he denied William's request for aid and told Francis that "my feelings are that the cause of the Netherlands is entirely lost."[77] While refusing to accept the French principle of nonintervention, he still thought that France should be included in the discussions on the Netherlands. By 21 October, he had decided that Austria would participate in the conference and had sent instructions to Esterhazy and Wessenberg, Austria's diplomatic representatives in London.[78] Despite this willingness to work with the other powers to maintain the peace of Europe, the government in Vienna was very critical of the conciliatory policies of Berlin and London. As the British envoy to Vienna reported on 3 November 1830, "England and Prussia to-day are in deep disgrace here. Count Bernstorff is the butt of all the sarcasm and abuse which season the ministerial conversation. The English government is treated rather more tenderly; they content themselves with pitying remarks on her policy."[79]

Russia's national interest in Belgium was no greater than Austria's but, even more than Metternich, Nicholas viewed the Belgian Revolution as part of a subversive threat to all of Europe. In early October, Nicholas wrote: "It is not Belgium that I am thinking of fighting, it is the revolution in general, which by degrees, and more quickly than one thinks, is threatening us; are they to see us tremble before it as well?"[80] He was

76. Srbik, *Metternich*, 1:658–659; and Metternich to Wessenberg, 3 October 1830, Metternich, *Papieren*, 5:39–43.

77. Metternich to Francis, 11 October 1830, Metternich, *Papieren*, 5:43–44.

78. Metternich to Esterhazy, 21 October 1830 (two dispatches); and Metternich to Wessenberg, 21 October 1830, ibid., pp. 44–53.

79. Cowley to Aberdeen, 3 November 1830, in F. A. Wellesley, ed., *The Diary and Correspondence of Henry Wellesley, First Lord Cowley, 1790–1846*, pp. 184–186.

80. Martens, *Recueil des Traités*, 11:437.

eager for British and Prussian troops to crush the rebellion in the Netherlands and was more than willing to assist them. He told the British
government that he could immediately send an army of 60,000 men to
support his allies.[81] In Berlin, informal talks between Prussian officers,
Diebitsch, and his staff had included plans for joint Prussian-Russian
operations in Flanders and even a combined campaign aimed directly
toward Paris. Although some Prussian officers, especially the younger ones,
were for war, Frederick William opposed Diebitsch's mission from the
beginning, and Bernstorff and Witzleben did their utmost to neutralize
the Russian field marshal's bellicose proposals.[82] Nicholas ordered the
Polish army to be fully mobilized by 22 December and said he was prepared to march 150,000 men into Western Europe—a wildly unrealistic
figure—as soon as one French soldier set foot in Belgium.[83] However,
Nicholas found little actual support for his views among the other powers.
In answer to William's request for aid, he was forced to admit that, while
he was more than ready to send the necessary troops, he had to act in
conjunction with his allies. As armed intervention was not feasible,
Nicholas agreed to support efforts to settle the Belgian question by the
mediation of the great powers.[84]

Thus, by the first of November, all the powers had decided to participate in the conference, and the British had succeeded in having London
designated as the site of the discussions.[85] Bernstorff had reason to be
satisfied. While the Belgian Revolution had succeeded, France had not

81. Ibid., p. 438.

82. Gneisenau to Clausewitz, 5 November 1830, in Pertz and Delbrück, *Neithardt
von Gneisenau,* 5:615. For Bernstorff's reaction to Diebitsch's mission, see Bernstorff
to Maltzahn, 30 September 1830, ZSA Me, Rep. 81, Wien I, Nr. 142; Mortier to
Molé, 10 September 1830, A.M.A.E., C.P. Prusse, Vol. 274; Brook-Taylor to
Aberdeen, 10 September 1830, PRO F.O. 64/163; and Chad to Palmerston, 6
November 1830, PRO F.O. 64/164.

83. Theodore Schiemann, "Die Sendung des Feldmarschalls Diebitsch nach
Berlin," p. 18.

84. Nicholas to William, 25 October 1830, Nesselrode to Matuszewic, 31 October
1830, and Nesselrode to Gourieff, 31 October 1830, Colenbrander, *Gedenkstukken,*
44:410–416.

85. Stuart to Aberdeen, 31 October 1830, ibid., 40:156; Bernstorff to Schöler and
Maltzahn, 7 November 1830, ZSA Me, AAI, Rep. 1, Nr. 1793; and Webster, *Foreign
Policy of Palmerston,* 1:105–106.

intervened, war had not broken out, the European alliance had been resurrected, and the chance of a peaceful settlement of the Belgian problem had been increased.

In Prussia, leading government and military figures generally approved the government's policy. Boyen, for example, favored keeping France out of Belgium, but opposed a war of intervention to save the principle of legitimacy. However, he felt that Prussia should be prepared for war and that such preparation implied domestic reform. Mobilization meant loans, and, according to the law of 17 January 1820 concerning the state debt, additional loans could not be sought without the approval of the *Stände*. The time seemed right to resurrect the idea of implementing national representative institutions in Prussia.[86] General von Rochow, whose views were strongly conservative, was pessimistic about the prospects for peace and was convinced that Prussia's institutions permitted it to fight only a defensive war. "I hope," he wrote, "one realizes how constraining our institutions are, namely, how our military arrangements, our *Landwehr* system, is not appropriate for a European power. We have no constitution but a *Landwehr*, which is far worse, for as a consequence we can conduct only a people's war, a *Meinungskrieg*."[87] Gneisenau felt that the revolutionary turmoil in 1830 was worse than in 1790 and that England and Austria could not be counted on in a war against France. Prussia's only reliable allies were Bavaria, Darmstadt and—with an ironic touch—Russia, although Russian effectiveness was obviously hampered by distance.[88] Thus, Prussia's commercial allies were also its political allies. In November, Gneisenau discussed some of the points brought up by Boyen and Rochow. "After the costs of mobilization (for seven corps more than 20 million) have been covered, one will have to figure on the maintenance of the army for one year of war at 78 million. In other words, we would begin the war immediately with debts." Although Gneisenau did not mention the issue of national representative institutions, he did discuss the problem of public opinion. "The wishes of

86. Friedrich Meinecke, *Das Leben des Feldmarschalls Hermann von Boyen*, 2:437.
87. Rochow to Nagler, 18 October 1830, Ernst Kelchner and Karl Mendelsohn-Bartholdy, eds., *Preussen und Frankreich zur Zeit der Julirevolution*, p. 30.
88. Gneisenau to Brühl, 1 November 1830, H. von Sybel, "Gneisenau und sein Schwiegersohn, Graf Friedrich Wilhelm v. Brühl," p. 265; and Gneisenau to Clausewitz, 18 August 1830, Pertz and Delbrück, *Neithardt von Gneisenau*, 5:604.

the public are said to be for France and even for Belgium. War is not in favor with the public."[89]

In September, Clausewitz also agreed that a campaign to intervene in Belgium was unwise; later, in his most thoroughgoing examination of the problem of war in the West, Clausewitz maintained that the powers should remain on the defensive.[90] According to Clausewitz, the question of whether there was war or not rested entirely with France. The other powers were not only restricted from attacking by the moralistic judgment of public opinion, but also by the civil-military necessity of remaining on the defensive. It was necessary to mobilize the forces of public opinion behind the governments and against the enemy for the kind of war that he anticipated would have to be conducted, not just with *Cabinetsmitteln,* "but with the hearts of the people." In order to ensure this kind of support, the powers could never afford to give up a defensive posture.[91] Clausewitz was generalizing on the basis of Prussia's military institutions; these thoughts did not apply to the same degree for Russia and Austria. Austria used its forces in a successful antirevolutionary campaign in Italy, and Russia, with the exception of its Polish contingents, did likewise in Poland. Despite this analysis, Clausewitz, like Gneisenau and most others in and out of government, felt that war was practically unavoidable. The revolution would continue to spread to other areas; France's lust for territory would likewise increase. For this reason, in early November, Clausewitz felt that "one will have to pronounce it half a miracle if the peace should endure for still another year."[92]

By contrast, the influence of those who not only expected but advocated war was slight. Duke Charles, the princes, and a number of younger officers favored a more aggressive policy.[93] However, as Prince William

89. Gneisenau to Clausewitz, 22 November 1830, Pertz and Delbrück, *Neithardt von Gneisenau,* 5:624.

90. Clausewitz to Gneisenau, 21 October 1830, ibid., p. 609. A full discussion of Clausewitz's position is found in Paret, *Clausewitz,* p. 398.

91. Schwartz, *Carl von Clausewitz,* 2:414–416.

92. Clausewitz to Gneisenau, 13 November 1830, Pertz and Delbrück, *Neithardt von Gneisenau,* 5:618–619.

93. Gneisenau to Clausewitz, 22 November 1830, Pertz and Delbrück, *Neithardt von Gneisenau,* 5:623; E. von Conrady, *Leben und Wirken des Generals der Infantrie und Kommandirenden Generals des V. Armeekorps Carl von Grolman,* 3:116; and Heinrich von Brandt, *Aus dem Leben des Generals der Infanterie z. D. Dr. Heinrich von Brandt,* 2:36–37.

the younger complained, anyone in the army who spoke of war was immediately labeled in the Cabinet and the ministries as a traitor who was encroaching on the King's prerogatives.[94] Few officials or officers expressed much enthusiasm for the revolution. Major Willisen, an ardent supporter of the Belgians, was one exception.[95] However, nearly all military men agreed that the Prussian government was poorly led, especially in the area of military affairs. Clausewitz, Grolman, and Brandt all complained of a lack of leadership and central direction from Berlin. The government had no mobilization plans; important matters were not attended to or were resolved only after long delay; and vital information on military and political affairs was often lacking. The Minister of War, Hake; the Chief of the General Staff, Krauseneck; and sometimes Witzleben were the main targets of this criticism, although Witzleben was also complemented for his sound grasp of diplomatic and military matters.[96] Most prominent individuals in Prussia saw little alternative to the government's policy, although some agreed that preparations for the defense of the country should be pursued with greater vigor.

While the agreement of the powers was being obtained for a conference on Belgium, an additional complication occurred. Shortly after the outbreak of the revolution in Belgium, disturbances also occurred in Luxemburg. By October, revolutionaries sympathetic to Belgium had seized control of the duchy. Belgian revolutionaries claimed that Luxemburg belonged to the new Belgian state. This position was made official in early November when the Belgian National Congress formally laid claim to the duchy while continuing to recognize its affiliation with the German Confederation.[97] On 15 October 1830, the King of the Netherlands, asked the German Confederation for assistance in suppressing the rebellion in Luxemburg. The Confederation decided to take no action until it could get detailed information on the events in Luxemburg. The Prussian and

94. Meinecke, *Hermann von Boyen,* 2:459.

95. For Willisen's views, see his *Denkschrift,* "Ueber die niederländische Frage," 8 November 1830, ZSA Me, Rep. 92, Eichhorn, Nr. 4.

96. Brandt, *Heinrich von Brandt,* 2:34; Conrady, *Carl von Grolman,* 3:115–117; and Schwartz, *Carl von Clausewitz,* 2:303. For Gneisenau's very positive view of Witzleben, see Gneisenau to Clausewitz, 30 October 1830, Pertz and Delbrück, *Neithardt von Gneisenau,* 5:612–613.

97. Wolfgang von Franqué, *Luxemburg, die Belgische Revolution und die Mächte,* pp. 28–30.

Austrian representatives were delegated the task of getting the Confederation information on the Luxemburg problem.

Bernstorff felt that the situation in the grand duchy was extremely delicate. In a dispatch to Maltzahn, he analyzed the implications of this crisis for the politics of Europe.[98] There was no question that the events in Luxemburg threatened the security of Germany, and there was likewise no doubt that Germany had both the duty and the right to assist the Netherlands in this affair. The claims of the Belgian provisional government were absurd. William participated in the Confederation as the Grand Duke of Luxemburg, not as the King of the Netherlands. In other words, Luxemburg was a separate polity not integrated into the Kingdom of the Netherlands. Moverover, the grand duchy was to remain in the Confederation regardless of who its sovereign was. At the present time, the heirs of the House of Nassau happened to possess it as compensation for the loss of their lands in the Rhineland. French intervention in Luxemburg would be seen as a clear attack on the Confederation. Therefore, from all aspects, it was obvious that the Confederation had the duty and the right to suppress the rebellion in Luxemburg.

But what about European considerations? First and foremost, all the European states wanted to preserve peace, and Bernstorff argued that peace "must be the policy of the German Confederation, for that was the purpose of its creation and the entire nature of its institutions are confined to defensive arrangements." Therefore, any step that might contribute to war had to be considered carefully. Although there was certainly nothing to fear from the rebels in Luxemburg or Belgium, the involvement of France would create the prospect of war. Should the Confederation therefore shrink before any action in the grand duchy? No, Bernstorff answered, because the aggressor would be France. In that situation, the German Confederation would be able to muster a high level of enthusiasm because those under arms would be defending German honor and the German nationality. But he added that all peaceful means of solving the problem should be exhausted first and that any action by the Confederation should be coordinated with the conference of the powers in London. It would also be preferable not to use Austrian or Prussian troops in any operation in Luxemburg. As Prussia had already reinforced its army in the Rhineland and preferred to cause no additional

98. Bernstorff to Maltzahn, 1 November 1830, ZSA Me, Rep. 81, Wien I, Nr. 142.

alarm, it would be better, he said, to use the troops of the Seventh and Tenth Corps of the federal army to restore order in the grand duchy.[99]

France took an equivocal position on the Luxemburg question. The government recognized the Confederation's right to restore order in the area. However, it indicated that contingents of troops from the other German states should be combined with Prussian units in any action in the duchy to clearly demonstrate that it was an act of the *Bund* and not a unilateral Prussian decision. At the same time, Talleyrand was told to attempt to work with the Prussian and Austrian representatives to postpone any intervention by the Confederation.[100]

The representatives of the Diet had little enthusiasm for military involvement in Luxemburg. Afraid of creating tensions with France, they preferred to treat the Luxemburg problem more as a dynastic affair of the House of Nassau than as a concern of the Confederation.[101] When the Diet met on 18 November, Nagler and Münch nevertheless overcame the objections of the middle and smaller states and, in a stormy session, succeeded in having the Confederation recognize its duty to assist the House of Orange. No actual intervention was agreed upon, but the Diet instructed Prussia and Austria to attempt to solve the problem at the London conference in order to make any armed intervention by the *Bund* superfluous. Thus, the London conference was charged with another highly complicated task.[102]

On 4 November 1830, the London conference opened at the British Foreign Office. Britain, as the host power, presided over the meeting and was initially represented by Aberdeen; Palmerston took over later. The other powers were represented by their ministers in London: Talleyrand for France, Wessenberg and Esterhazy for Austria, Matuszewic for Russia, and Bülow for Prussia. Bernstorff's initial instruction to Bülow gave him great latitude. The first task of the conference should be the restoration of peace and stability in Belgium. It would obviously be necessary to create some kind of separate status for Belgium, and, as long as the new

99. Bernstorff to Maltzahn, 3 and 9 November 1830, ibid. Also see Chad to Palmerston, 6 November 1830, PRO F.O. 64/164.

100. Franqué, *Luxemburg,* p. 33; Werther to Frederick William, 10 November 1830, ibid., p. 247; and Maison to Talleyrand, 12 November 1830, Pallain, *Talleyrand,* p. 81.

101. Franqué, *Luxemburg,* p. 37.

102. Ibid., pp. 37–38.

arrangements did not make Belgium a client of France, any solution would be satisfactory to Prussia. If the new arrangements were to endure, it was also essential that France be involved in and approve of the settlement. Bernstorff added that special attention should be paid to the status of the Belgian fortresses, Luxemburg, and the districts of Venloo and Maastricht, which bordered on Prussia. Moreover, Belgium should continue to play its role as a *Bollwerk* of European security. Bernstorff concluded his instructions by noting that the unanimity of the powers in these arrangements was absolutely necessary.[103]

Although it is often stated that Bernstorff reluctantly agreed to the London conference, in fact he believed that it was probably the best way to solve the Belgian question.[104] He particularly realized the importance of England's participation in the conference and in the European community: "By the loss of England the position of the remaining allies would be worsened in an incalculable way, and the prevention of that is worth great sacrifice." Bernstorff knew that the outbreak of war would place Prussia in grave danger. England would not enter the conflict, Austria would probably become involved with Italy, and Russia, weakened by cholera, was far away. If war broke out with France, an uprising in Poland was likely, which would further neutralize Russia's ability to act in the West. The members of the German Confederation did not desire war with either France or Poland, and the attitude of the German public largely depended on the nature of the conflict itself and could not be predicted. In other words, Prussia would fight alone and with uncertain strength.[105] Therefore, Bernstorff was pleased when the conference began its work by successfully imposing an armistice on the Dutch and the Belgians.[106]

Prussia's commitment to peace was further demonstrated by the *Denk-*

103. Bernstorff to Bülow, 3 and 7 November 1830, ZSA Me, AAI, Rep. 1, Nr. 1793. He also urged that Russia approach the Belgian question in a similar manner. See Bernstorff to Schöler, 7 November 1830, ZSA Me, Rep. 81, Petersburg I, Nr. 120.

104. See, for instance, Charles Breunig, *The Age of Revolution and Reaction, 1789–1850*, p. 148.

105. Bernstorff to Werther, 9 November 1830, and Bernstorff's answers to questions posed by the King, Bernstorff note (n.d.), ZSA Me, AAI, Rep. 1. Nr. 23.

106. Protocols of conference held on 4 November 1830 and 17 November 1830 (2), *Papers Relative to the Affairs of Belgium*, pp. 275–281; Bernstorff to Schöler, 17 November 1830, ZSA Me, Rep. 81, Petersburg I, Nr. 120; and Bernstorff to Bülow, 23 November 1830, ZSA Me, AAI, Rep. 1, Nr. 1793.

*schrift* Diebitsch was given to take back to Russia. In it, Bernstorff wrote that, while Prussia was still committed to the eastern alliance, it also saw the necessity of the closest possible relations with France and especially England. He summarized Prussia's reasons for desiring peace, but added that, if France provoked war, Prussia would be ready to fight. However, he emphasized, the German people, who almost universally opposed such a war, would only fulfill their duty if they were convinced that all attempts to maintain the peace had been sincerely explored.[107] Thus, before the outbreak of the Polish Revolution, Prussia's position had been unequivocally stated to Russia, the power that perhaps was the least committed to peace. Clearly Prussia's first choice in the crisis year of 1830 was the avoidance of armed conflict.

On 3 December, Bernstorff, while suffering an attack of gout, learned of the revolt in Poland. He wrote, "We were shaken this morning by the news of the outbreak of the uprising in Warsaw. How many dismal observations may be made in connection with this essentially more disheartening than unexpected event."[108]

## THE POLISH INSURRECTION

The Polish Insurrection was precipitated by students, army officers, and cadets. In Warsaw, on 2 November 1830, a small group of conspirators attacked the Belvedere Palace, the residence of Grand Duke Constantine, Commander-in-chief of the Polish army. Constantine barely escaped from the palace and, with troops loyal to him, withdrew outside the city. The insurrection soon gained substantial support from the citizens of Warsaw as well as from Polish soldiers. High food prices caused by a poor harvest and a financial scandal involving the municipal administration of Warsaw had made the lower classes disgruntled. The Prussian consul in Warsaw reported "that the revolution, once begun, has become fully national."[109]

---

107. See "Mémoire sur la position de la grande alliance relativement à la France et à l'Europe," 24 November 1830, ZSA Me, AAI, Rep. 1, Nr. 23.

108. Bernstorff to Schöler, 3 December 1830, ZSA Me, Rep. 81, Petersburg I, Nr. 120.

109. Schmidt to Bernstorff, 5 December 1830, Stanislaw Smolka, ed., *Korespondencya Lubeckiego z ministrami sekretarzami stanu Ignacym Sobolewskim i Stefanem Grabowski,* 4:389.

As it turned out, he was exaggerating; in reality, the support of the middle classes and the peasantry for the rebellion was less than total. After a period of confusion, during which efforts to negotiate a peaceful settlement between the Tsar and the insurrectionists proved unsuccessful, the Polish Diet deposed Nicholas I as King of Poland and set to work constructing a new government. When Nicholas learned of his deposition, he ordered the Russian army into Poland.[110]

The Polish Insurrection was greeted with considerable interest and enthusiasm in much of Western Europe. Many Frenchmen felt a revolutionary kinship with the Poles and assumed that the revolt had paralyzed Nicholas's plan for a counterrevolutionary campaign against France.[111] In England, there was a similar, but more subdued, interest; the energies of the public and Parliament were primarily directed toward the struggle over the Reform Bill.[112] Within Germany, considerable sympathy for the Poles existed even among government officials, and a wave of enthusiasm for the revolutionaries swept the country much as Philhellenism had in the 1820s.[113]

Bernstorff and most of the King's chief advisors did not share this attitude. They viewed the revolution as a serious threat to the security of the Prussian state. They feared the influence of the Polish Insurrection on the formerly Polish provinces that were now part of Prussia and viewed the emergence of an independent Polish state as a threat to Prussia's position in Europe.[114] For Frederick William, the revolt was another in a series of

110. See R. F. Leslie, *Polish Politics and the Revolution of November 1830;* and Schiemann, *Geschichte Russlands,* 3:31–165. For the international repercussions of the revolution, see Jan Andrzej Betley, *Belgium and Poland in International Relations, 1830–1831;* and Charles Morley, "The European Significance of the November Uprising," pp. 410–412.

111. Thaddäus Jungfer, *Die Beziehungen der Julimonarchie zum Königreich Polen in den Jahren 1830/31,* pp. 9–27.

112. Webster, *Foreign Policy of Palmerston,* 1:183.

113. J. Müller, *Die Polen in der öffentlichen Meinung Deutschlands, 1830–1832,* pp. 28–79; and Treitschke, *History of Germany,* 5:249.

114. Müller, *Die Polen,* p. 20; Treitschke, *History of Germany,* 5:248, 74. Palmerston concisely summarized Prussia's attitude toward the Polish crisis in a letter to Chad dated 3 May 1831. It is reprinted in Betley, *Belgium and Poland,* pp. 274–277. Clausewitz examined the Polish situation in his paper entitled "Die Verhältnisse Europa's seit der Theilung Polens," reprinted in Schwartz, *Carl von Clausewitz,* 2:401–408. Also see Gneisenau to Gibsone, 24 April 1831, Pertz and Delbrück, *Neithardt von Gneisenau,* 5:668.

disquieting events. After first hearing of the events in Warsaw, he wrote to his daughter, "God, what a new horrible misfortune! I am completely depressed by it and am not in a state to add another word to these lines except may God inspire our dear Nicholas to take the quickest and most effective measures to control this new calamity. Also we may not delay, for certainly Posen will not lag behind, and the strongest measures here as well may not be suspended for long."[115] Later in the month, he again wrote to his daughter, "I have never experienced a worse and more complicated political situation in Europe, and how many bad situations have I already experienced!"[116]

The King's first response to the Polish Insurrection was to mobilize the regular units of the First, Second, Fifth, and Sixth Army Corps, including the artillery of the Fifth Army Corps, and to station these forces in the grand duchy of Posen under Gneisenau's command. Substantial portions of the first levy of the *Landwehr* were to be called up, and the fortresses of Posen, Glogau, Cobel, and Thorn were to be provisioned.[117] When these precautionary measures were communicated to the powers, it was emphasized that the King was primarily concerned over the security of his Polish provinces. Although the provisional government of Poland announced its formal intention to "religiously respect the borders of all the states of His Majesty the King of Prussia," Frederick William was not reassured.[118]

Bernstorff was not as shocked as the King by the events in Poland. He had not only felt that a revolution there was probable, he also knew that Nicholas intended to take energetic and prompt action to quell the revolt without making any concessions to the rebels. He was confident that the Tsar could quickly reestablish control.[119] Unlike the Belgian crisis, Bern-

---

115. Frederick William to Charlotte, 3 December 1830, Bailleu, "Aus dem letzten Jahrzehnt Friedrich Wilhelms III," p. 153.

116. Frederick William to Charlotte, 21 December 1830, ibid., p. 154.

117. Hake to Bernstorff, 7 December 1830, ZSA Me, AAI, Rep. 1, Nr. 2333; and Gneisenau to Clausewitz, 4 December 1830, Pertz and Delbrück, *Neithardt von Gneisenau,* 5:630–631.

118. Schmidt to Bernstorff, 5 December 1830, Smolka, *Korrespondencya Lubeckiego,* 4:390.

119. Circulare für die Königs Missionen im Auslande mit ausnahme der Petersburg u. Copenhagen, 9 December 1830, ZSA Me, AAI, Rep. 1, Nr. 2333; also Bernstorff to Schöler, 12 December 1830, ZSA Me, Rep. 81, Petersburg I, Nr. 120; Alopeus to Bernstorff, 18 December 1830, and Bernstorff to Maltzahn, 13 December 1830, both ZSA Me, AAI, Rep. 1, Nr. 2333; and Betley, *Belgium and Poland,* p. 101.

storff displayed no interest in ending the Polish conflict through negotiations. For example, in January, he refused a request from Generals Kniacsewicz and Chlopicki that Prussia mediate between the Tsar and the provisional government, replying that the Poles would have to settle their differences with Nicholas themselves.[120] In general, the Prussian government's attitude was uncompromisingly disapproving of the revolt. When the Polish government announced Nicholas's deposition, Prussia, in contrast to Austria, withdrew its consul from Warsaw and, at the request of Alopeus, confiscated the assets of the Bank of Warsaw in Berlin and placed the funds at his disposal.[121]

On 7 February, Russian forces under Diebitsch's command crossed over into Polish territory, and the Polish Diet declared a state of war. With some 79,000 men, Diebitsch slowly moved toward Warsaw, where on February 23–25 he encountered the main body of the Polish army. In the battle of Grochów, the Russian army defeated the Polish forces on the plains east of Praga, the bridgehead over the Vistula that leads into Warsaw. However, because his losses were so heavy, Diebitsch chose not to follow this victory with a rapid advance on the city. He was short of supplies, and his troops were beginning to be ravaged by cholera, which had been spreading slowly westward across Russia and into Poland. Diebitsch's position was further complicated by some minor successes on the part of the Polish army under General Skrzynecki and by the outbreak of another insurrection in Lithuania in April.

Nicholas ordered his commander to move his army northward near the borders of East and West Prussia, where it could easily gather food and other supplies. From there, it was to move across the Vistula to approach Warsaw from the west. Diebitsch won an important victory in the north at Ostroleka, but once again he did not pursue the defeated Polish forces as they retreated in disorder back to Warsaw. As it became clear that a rapid victory over the Polish forces was not in sight, military observers in

---

120. Jordan to Bernstorff, 12 January 1831, and Bernstorff to Wittgenstein, 15 January 1831, ZSA Me, AAI, Rep. 1, Nr. 2333; and Ancillon to Schöler, 19 January 1831, ZSA Me, Rep. 81, Petersburg I, Nr. 124. Frederick William completely agreed with Bernstorff's position; see Wittgenstein to Bernstorff, 15 January 1831, ZSA Me, AAI, Rep. 1, Nr. 2333.

121. Alfred Stern, *Geschichte Europas seit den Verträgen von 1815 bis zum Frankfurter Frieden von 1871*, 4:144–145; Martens, *Recueil des Traités*, 8:172–173; and Treitschke, *History of Germany*, 5:74.

Russia and Prussia became critical of Diebitsch's handling of the campaign. Diebitsch died of cholera on 10 June 1831 and was succeeded by Field Marshal Paskevich.

Prussia did not attempt to be impartial toward the war in Poland. As Bernstorff later told a French emissary, Prussia was an ally of Russia, not a neutral. In a talk with the British minister to Berlin, he said with exaggeration, "With rebellion triumphant in Poland we should tremble even for our monarchy."[122] He continued to reject the argument that Prussia should undertake mediation between the two warring parties for humanitarian reasons.[123] Although Bernstorff's pro-Russian attitude was fully shared by other leaders in Berlin, there is no evidence that the King or the government seriously considered intervening in the Polish war.[124] Frederick William was willing to give the Russians indirect support. He instructed Theodore von Schön, *Oberpräsident* of the provinces of Prussia, to allow the Russian army to buy supplies in East and West Prussia and to have access to goods in the Prussian military magazines. Prussian authorities were "to be helpful to the Imperial officials in every possible way."[125] Treasury officials in Danzig, Königsberg, Marienwerder, and Gumbinnen were ordered to extend credit up to 30,000 talers to Russian officials for the purpose of buying supplies.[126] In addition, Frederick William ordered the confiscation of all property belonging to any Pole residing in Posen who crossed into Poland to fight in the rebel army. To hinder the flow of supplies to the Poles and to keep the cholera from spreading westward, Gneisenau's army of observation attempted to seal off the border between Congress Poland and the grand duchy of Posen.[127] Despite the Prussian

---

122. Webster, *Foreign Policy of Palmerston,* 1:188.

123. For example, see the request of Freiherr von Maltzahn, Hereditary Marshal of Silesia, to Bernstorff, 7 March 1831, and Bernstorff to Maltzahn, 12 March 1831, ZSA Me, AAI, Rep. 1, Nr. 2333.

124. Frederick William to Nicholas, April 1831, ZSA Me, AAI, Rep. 1, Nr. 2333; and Pertz and Delbrück, *Neithardt von Gneisenau,* 5:648–654.

125. Frederick William to Schön, 13 May 1831, ZSA Me, Geheimes Civil Cabinet, Rep. 2.2.1, Nr. 13311.

126. Schön to Lottum, 18 May 1831, Lottum to Maassen, 22 May 1831, Schön to Lottum, 22 May 1831, and Lottum to Königliche Regierungen in Königsberg, Danzig, Gumbinnen, Marienwerder, 22 May 1831, ibid.

127. See "Décret de roi Frederic-Guillaume III, contre les Polonais du Grand Duché de Posen, qui combattent dans les rangs de l'armée polonaise, 26 April 1831," Leonard Chodzko, *Recueil des Traités, Conventions, et Acts diplomatiques concernant la Pologne, 1762–1862,* pp. 813–814.

cordon, several thousand Poles from Posen crossed into Congress Poland to join in the fight against Russia, and Russian officials were allowed to break the quarantine in order to procure supplies in Prussia.[128] The citizens of Königsberg protested to the king that making an exception for the Russians increased the danger of cholera.[129] Although Frederick William refused to allow the Russian army to cross the Vistula near Thorn in Prussian territory, the Poles charged that Prussian authorities provided materials and that at least one engineer assisted in the building of a bridge across the river near Zlotorya.[130]

Although Frederick William and Bernstorff were interested in the earliest possible end to the Polish conflict, they also wished to avoid any direct involvement in the military operations in Poland. For example, in June, when Nicholas was evidently discouraged by the course of the war, Count Orloff, on a special mission for the Tsar, indirectly presented a vague plan for another partition of Poland to Gneisenau. Prussia and Austria were to receive additional territory in return for prompt military action in support of Russia in Poland. Orloff's later presentation to Bernstorff in Berlin was evidently more vague and so confusing that Bernstorff indicated to Gneisenau that Prussia had no desire whatsoever for additional Polish territory and had no interest in working with Austria to solve the Polish problem. He still believed that Nicholas desired no interference in Russian-Polish affairs. Gneisenau had also advised strongly against the project.[131]

The revolutionary situation in Poland did not stimulate the foreign ministry to produce the kind of policy papers that had explained Prussian policy toward France and Belgium. However, available evi-

---

128. Müller, *Die Polen*, p. 63; and Leslie, *Polish Politics*, p. 223.

129. See "Adresse des magistrats de la Ville de Koenigsberg au roi de Prusse Frederic-Guillaume III en se plaignant, au nom de la Prusse Orientale, des vexations, des exigences des Russe, et du Choler qu'ils ont importé dans le pays," Chodzko, *Recueil*, pp. 833–834.

130. Schiemann, *Geschichte Russlands*, 3:111; Martens, *Recueil des Traités*, 8:173; and Skrzynecki to Frederick William III, 19 June 1831, Chodzko, *Recueil*, pp. 825–826.

131. See Gneisenau to Bernstorff, 21 June 1831, ZSA Me, AAI, Rep. 1, Nr. 2333. For Bernstorff's views on Orloff's offer, see Bernstorff to Gneisenau, 23 June 1831, ibid. The suggestion by Webster that Bernstorff was in favor of accepting the Russian proposal is incorrect, and his chronology is badly confused. See Webster, *Foreign Policy of Palmerston*, 1:187–188.

dence indicates the Prussian policy of benevolent neutrality was determined by the same factors that had created its policy toward the West. Frederick William was inherently cautious, and the foreign ministry was aware of the influence that involvement in Polish affairs might have on the strength of Prussia's position vis-à-vis France and Belgium.[132] Moreover, there is some evidence that the government was sensitive to the pro-Polish feeling of public opinion. Flahaut, the French emissary who went to Berlin in July 1831, was convinced that Prussia would not intervene in Poland because of this factor.[133] Friedrich von Gagern wrote to his son on 9 September 1831 that "no one knows what is going on in Berlin. The King supports the Russians, and the nation supports the Poles."[134] The government also went to some effort to refute Polish charges of violations of neutrality by Prussia. For example, in a letter to Frederick William, General Skrzynecki complained that the Prussian government was assisting the Russians in a variety of ways.[135] Because Berlin did not recognize the Polish government, it did not accept the letter. However, when it was subsequently published in a Warsaw newspaper and was reprinted in several newspapers throughout Germany, the foreign ministry felt the need to respond. A formal rebuttal was published in the *Preussische Staatszeitung*.[136] In addition, Clausewitz wrote an anonymous letter, which appeared in the *Zeitung des Grossherzogtums Posen*, attempting to explain and minimize aspects of the government's assistance to Russia.[137] Frederick William personally praised Clausewitz's defense of Prussian policy.[138] As Flahaut reported to Sebastiani, "It is remarkable to see public opinion forcing one of the major governments to go into explanations concerning a government that it does not recognize."[139] In addition, the high cost of military operations undoubtedly made deeper involvement in Poland unattractive.[140]

132. Betley, *Belgium and Poland,* pp. 59, 68, and 158.

133. Ibid., pp. 176, 177, 179.

134. Friedrich von Gagern, *Das Leben des Generals Friedrich von Gagern,* 2:128.

135. Chodzko, *Recueil,* pp. 825–826.

136. Betley, *Belgium and Poland,* p. 179.

137. This letter and its implications are discussed in detail in Peter Paret, "An Anonymous Letter by Clausewitz on the Polish Insurrection of 1830–1831." See also the section in the same author's *Clausewitz and the State,* pp. 410–430.

138. Schwartz, *Carl von Clausewitz,* 2:384.

139. Betley, *Belgium and Poland,* p. 179n.

140. Ibid., p. 227.

Prussia's policy toward Poland was naturally influenced by the attitudes of the other powers. The French government once again found itself in a difficult position; many citizens, especially in Paris, supported the Poles enthusiastically. Lafayette declared that France was honor-bound to help resurrect a fully independent Poland.[141] Demonstrations occurred before the Russian embassy with the crowd shouting "Long live Poland, down with the Russians!"[142] The government's first response was to restrain Prussia from intervening; Werther was informed that, if Prussia participated in the conflict, France would be forced to move into the Rhineland.[143] In Berlin, Chad reported that Flahaut had told Bernstorff "that if Prussia aided Russia by force of arms to put down the Poles, the French government would make war upon Prussia upon that account, and would be backed in so doing by every honest man in France."[144] The government also attempted to gain some diplomatic assistance for the Poles through representations in London, Berlin, and Vienna. The French hoped that Russia would be forced to reestablish the constitutional order in Poland that had been instituted in 1815. Although Metternich indicated that a friendly Poland might make a better neighbor than a jealous Russia, these attempts did not result in any action favorable to the Poles. In August, Périer told the Chamber of Deputies that the recognition of Polish independence was impossible. It would lead to war with the strongest European power and would not save Poland. Thus, although Louis Philippe and some French officials made statements sympathetic to the Poles, there was never any question of direct French interference in Poland. The French diplomatic offensive on behalf of the Poles was restricted to trying to preserve the status of Congress Poland as it had existed prior to the revolution.[145]

Despite a good deal of public sympathy for the Poles in Great Britain, both Palmerston and Grey wanted the Russians to put down the revolution as soon as possible. The Polish conflict lessened the eastern powers' ability to act as a possible block to any French expansionist aims in Belgium. Palmerston hoped that the Russians would be moderate, but he made it clear that Britain would not mediate alone, or with France, be-

141. Jungfer, *Die Beziehungen der Julimonarchie*, p. 31.

142. *Ibid.*, p. 227.

143. Betley, *Belgium and Poland in International Relations*, pp. 140–141.

144. Chad to Palmerston, 20 July 1831, PRO F.O. 64/173.

145. Jungfer, *Die Beziehungen der Julimonarchie*, pp. 31–65.

tween the Poles and Russians. On 19 April 1831, he told Heytesbury, the British minister to St. Petersburg, to assure Nesselrode that the government in London was most anxious to keep on good terms with Russia. He added that Britain wished to see the Polish struggle end, "but, however, we do not intrude our advice nor offer our mediation much as we have been pressed by several to do so." However, Palmerston did inform Berlin that, if Prussia intervened in the Polish conflict and France retaliated by attacking the Rhineland, Britain would not be able to come to Prussia's aid.[146] He also halfheartedly and unsuccessfully attempted to get Prussia and Austria to mediate between the two parties; subsequently, he appealed to Nicholas to be lenient toward the defeated Poles and to preserve the special status of Poland that was established after the Congress of Vienna. On the whole, British policy toward the Polish question, much like that of France, was marked by restraint and noninterference.[147]

Metternich reacted predictably to the first word of revolution in Poland; the revolt in Warsaw was a severe blow to the eastern monarchies and was a further example, he said, of the insidious spread of the concept of revolution. However, despite his ideological distaste for the Polish revolutionaries, the Austrian Chancellor viewed the insurrection in a different light than the leaders of Prussia. An independent Poland might endanger Austria's hold on Galicia, but might also be a better neighbor than the Russian Empire. Unreserved support for Russia seemed to conflict with the state of Austro-Russian relations, which were still strained in the wake of the Greek crisis. Finally, after March 1831, when revolutionary unrest broke out in Italy, Austria feared French intervention in the Italian peninsula and did not wish to provoke French public opinion on the subject of Poland. Austria never rendered aid to Russia that was comparable to Prussia's and was lenient in the internment of Polish troops, many of which subsequently returned to service in Poland. The Austrian consul remained in Warsaw, and, although Metternich refused to play any role in mediating between the Russians and the Poles, he was more willing than either Bernstorff or Ancillon to discuss the subject of mediation openly with French and British representatives.[148] In conclusion, British

146. See Palmerston to Chad, 3 May 1831, PRO F.O. 64/166.

147. British policy toward the Polish crisis is described in Webster, *Foreign Policy of Palmerston*, 1:181–199.

148. Betley, *Belgium and Poland*, p. 91; Srbik, *Metternich*, 1:653–657; D'Haussonville, *Histoire de la Politique du Gouvernement Français*, 1:29; and Jungfer, *Die Beziehungen der Julimonarchie*, p. 55.

and French attitudes toward Prussian involvement in Poland and the lukewarm position of Austria reinforced Prussia's disinclination to directly intervene in Polish affairs.

Warsaw finally fell to Russian forces on 8 September 1831. Ancillon wrote that the defeat of the Polish insurgents by the legitimate ruler constituted an important lesson to the forces of revolution throughout Europe. Moreover, the resolution of the Polish question would increase the influence of the eastern powers in the settlement of the Belgian crisis.[149] However, two matters involving Poland continued to demand the attention of the government in Berlin after the end of the conflict. One concerned Russian policies toward the defeated Polish army; the other dealt with the new political arrangements for Poland in the wake of the insurrection. With the end of the war, thousands of refugees poured into Prussia, and units of the Polish army under the command of General Rybiński were interned inside Prussia's borders. Bernstorff instructed Witzleben to follow the relatively lenient internment measures taken by the Austrian government. He had also stipulated that any attempts by Russian officials to reclaim interned Poles as deserters under the terms of the extradition convention between the two countries should be referred to the Ministry of Foreign Affairs.[150] In general, the foreign ministry took the position that the convention only covered the extradition of criminals and deserters in the usual legal sense; it did not apply to political offenses. It was possible that some criminals or assassins might be among the Polish refugees, but, said Bernstorff, their names and the specific nature of their crimes would have to be indicated by the Russian government.[151] As the country became flooded with Polish officers who had been banished forever from the Russian Empire, Prussian authorities in Berlin urged Nicholas to develop more lenient amnesty stipulations.[152]

Prussia's position on the question of Poland's future political status was clear. The government did not support the French and British argument that, according to the Vienna treaty, Nicholas was obligated to restore Poland's constitution as well as its autonomous status. Bernstorff and

149. Ancillon to Schöler, 17 September and 6 October 1831, ZSA Me, Rep. 81, Petersburg I, Nr. 124.

150. Bernstorff to Witzleben, 19 May 1831, ZSA Me, AAI, Rep. 1, Nr. 2333; and Bernstorff to Witzleben, 5 October 1831, ZSA Me, Rep. 92, Witzleben, Nr. 112.

151. Bernstorff to Witzleben, 7 July 1831, ZSA Me, AAI, Rep. 1, Nr. 2333.

152. Ancillon to Schöler, 10 November 1831, ZSA Me, Rep. 81, Petersburg I, Nr. 124.

Ancillon argued that the Poles had forfeited their constitutional rights by revolting and that the wording of the Treaty of Vienna was very vague and only obligated Russia to establish "national institutions" for Poland. Because Alexander I had given Poland its special status, Nicholas had the power to take it away.[153] The nature of the new political arrangements for Poland remained a European problem of moderate concern for some time, but the end of the Polish Revolution stabilized the political situation inside the Russian Empire and allowed Nicholas to pay closer attention to Belgium.

Prussia's policy toward the Polish Insurrection had several consequences. Berlin's benevolent support of Russia seriously damaged Prussia's moderately progressive image in Germany and Western Europe. It contrasted sharply with Berlin's prudent and tolerant attitude toward political change elsewhere in Europe. In Poland, Prussia clearly and unequivocally supported the cause of autocracy. Yet Prussia's Polish policy, like the approach to problems in the West, was in reality tied to the security interests of the state, not to ideological considerations. Bernstorff had no particular prejudices against the Poles. Once they were defeated, he insisted on observing accepted legal procedures in the treatment of soldiers and refugees and displayed no special favoritism toward St. Petersburg. While the fighting continued, however, the government feared the strategic and especially political consequences of a Polish victory or of a protracted conflict. The desire to end the war as soon as possible determined Berlin's policy of indirect aid to Russia.

153. Ancillon to Schöler, 20 October 1831, and Ancillon to Bülow, 5 December 1831 (copy), ZSA Me, Rep. 81, Petersburg I, Nr. 124; Chad to Palmerston, 3 October 1831, PRO F.O. 64/174.

*Chapter 7*

✠✠✠✠✠✠✠✠✠✠✠✠✠✠

# The Belgian Settlement

The Belgian National Congress met on 10 November and eight days later proclaimed the independence of the Belgian people. It voted to exclude members of the House of Orange from any future position of leadership and declared that the treaties of 1814 and 1815 were no longer applicable. However, the Congress indicated that Luxemburg's relationship to the German Confederation would not be altered.[1] Shortly thereafter, on 1 December 1830, Lafitte's government announced that the French army would be increased by 80,000 men. Because of these two developments, the powers became increasingly concerned that France would attempt to annex the newly proclaimed Belgian state. As a consequence, Palmerston took the lead in recognizing the new arrangements in Belgium.

In December, the five-power conference in London began to discuss the question of Belgian independence. The effects of the Polish Revolution on the eastern powers' freedom to act aided the work of the conference. The insurrection ended whatever plans Nicholas might have had for a counterrevolutionary crusade in the West and preoccupied the strongest of the eastern powers with affairs in Eastern Europe, just when the conference was attempting to resolve the Belgian issue. Russia's distraction strengthened the position of Great Britain and France. The Polish Revolution also reinforced Bernstorff's reasons for following a policy aimed at the preservation of peace. During the month of December, he held out no hope to William that Prussia would consider any independent action in support of the Dutch, and he felt that it was essential

---

1. Fl. de Lannoy, *Histoire Diplomatique de l'Indépendance Belge,* p. 73.

to keep France and Great Britain engaged in the peaceful solution of the Belgian problem.[2]

## THE LONDON CONFERENCE

As the London conference turned its attention to a permanent settlement for the Netherlands, Bernstorff, in an instruction dated 17 December, outlined his position on the future of Belgium. He wanted to give Bülow the "freest possible hand" in the negotiations and did not want to burden him with a large number of detailed guidelines. However, he did want to call Bülow's attention to several considerations. It was now clear that a member of the House of Orange had little chance to be chosen as the King of Belgium. The other candidates mentioned—Archduke Charles of Austria, the Duke of Reichstadt, and the Duke of Leuchtenburg—had obvious drawbacks. Bernstorff felt that the same principle used in the case of Greece should be applied to Belgium: Namely, no candidate for the throne should come from the courts participating in the discussions in London. He told Bülow, "In this connection Prussia has no special wishes or interests; we will agree to any suggestion that promises to solve the present difficulties without causing new ones."

Prussia was interested in the effect an independent Belgium would have on the security of the Prussian state. Therefore, constitutional arrangements, as well as questions involving the fortresses and the delineation of borders, would be of the greatest importance: He added that Prussia was also interested in future close relations, especially of a commercial nature, between Holland and Belgium. Finally, there was the question of how to enforce the decisions of the conference, especially if Belgium should refuse to abide by them. In that case, he indicated that Prussia would be prepared to act in concert with France to ensure compliance. In answer to reports in England that Prussia, Russia, and Austria were forming some sort of separate combination, he said accurately that "any rumor to this effect is completely without substance."[3]

2. Bernstorff to Waldburg-Truchsess, 12 December 1830, and Bernstorff to Bülow, 17 December 1830, ZSA Me, AAI, Rep. 1, Nr. 1793; Bernstorff to Schöler, 15 December 1830, ZSA Me, Rep. 81, Petersburg I, Nr. 120.
3. Bernstorff to Bülow, 17 December 1830, ZSA Me, AAI, Rep. 1, Nr. 1793. However, Russia and, to a certain extent, Austria were less committed to retaining

On 18 December, Palmerston, following Talleyrand's suggestion, proposed that the conference recognize Belgium's independence. Although Palmerston and Talleyrand had the same goal, the two statesmen were pursuing different aims. The French representative was attempting to dismantle the barrier state erected on France's northern border; Palmerston, on the other hand, hoped to preserve the European role of the Low Countries and to keep France out of Belgium by recognizing the accomplished fact of Belgian independence.[4] The representatives of the eastern powers objected to the word "independence"; they preferred the word "separation." Moreover, in Bülow's support, they argued that the recognition of Belgian independence should depend on William's approval and on the stipulation that the treaties of 1814 would be upheld.[5] The divergent views of the five powers were combined in the important protocol of 20 December. From the start, the question of independence was integrally connected with the European function of the Low Countries. The most important section of the protocol stated:

> United to Holland, and forming an integral part of the kingdom of the Netherlands, Belgium had to fullfill its part of the European duties of that kingdom, and of the obligations which the Treaties had caused it to contract towards the other Powers. Its separation from Holland cannot liberate it from that part of its duties and obligations.
>
> The Conference will consequently proceed to discuss such new arrangements, as may be most proper for combining the future independence of Belgium with the stipulations of Treaties, with the interests and security of other Powers, and with the preservation of the balance of Europe.[6]

---

England in the Grand Alliance. See, for example, Nesselrode to Alopeus, 4 December 1830 (O.S.) (copy), ZSA Me, AAI, Rep. 1, Nr. 23; and Bernstorff's critique of Metternich's views on Russian intervention in the west, Bernstorff to Albrecht, 10 December 1830, ZSA Me, AAI, Rep. 1, Nr. 1377.

4. Charles K. Webster, *The Foreign Policy of Palmerston, 1830–1841*, 1:121; Lannoy, *L'Indépendance Belge*, p. 83; and Talleyrand to Sebastiani, 17 and 20 December 1830, G. Pallain, ed., *Correspondance Diplomatique de Talleyrand*, pp. 139–142.

5. Lannoy, *L'Indépendance Belge*, pp. 84–85; and Werner Gronemann, *Die Haltung Preussen in der belgischen Frage, 1830–1832*, p. 29.

6. Protocol of the conference held on 20 December 1830, *Papers Relative to the Affairs of Belgium*, pp. 289–290.

Berlin received the protocol with some misgivings. Ancillon, who was deputizing for Bernstorff, criticized it because it recognized the reality of Belgian independence without William's sanction. Nevertheless, he defended it to The Hague as the best obtainable settlement under the circumstances.[7] The protocol of 20 December was the first major territorial revision of the Vienna settlement. It was especially distasteful to the eastern powers because it recognized a violation of legitimacy by popular action. However, the eastern powers had little choice. As Wessenberg wrote Metternich on 24 December 1830:

> This very painful decision was unavoidable in order for us, or better said, in order to keep England, in the alliance. We could not risk the opposite approach in view of the circumstance that France would arm itself from head to toe and, burning with impatience, cross over its borders. I am aware of the painful and regrettable nature of the action in which we are participating. Nevertheless, we have been spared war, we have hindered the unification of Belgium with France, and we have set constraints upon the spread of jacobinism.[8]

Once the fact of Belgian independence was recognized, the conference had to determine security arrangements that would preserve European interests in the Low Countries. Out of these discussions came the protocol of 20 January, which proclaimed the permanent neutrality of the Belgian state. The issue of Belgian neutrality has been exhaustively investigated. There is no question that Talleyrand's claims that he originated the idea of neutrality are false. The concept of Belgian neutrality emerged in November 1830, when Bülow, Esterhazy, and Matuszewic, realizing that the separation of Belgium from Hollond was inevitable, sought to guarantee the security of the new state against French encroachment; in so doing, they independently came up with the essence of the idea of neutral status for Belgium.[9]

---

7. Ancillon to Waldburg-Truchsess, 5 January 1831, H. T. Colenbrander, ed., *Gedenkstukken der Algemeene Geschiednis van Nederland van 1795 tot 1840,* 44:35–37; and Gronemann, *Die Haltung Preussens in der belgischen Frage,* p. 30.

8. Alfred Ritter von Arneth, *Johann Freiherr von Wessenberg* 2:103–104.

9. On Belgian neutrality, see William E. Lingelbach, "Belgian Neutrality," pp. 56–57; Karl Hampe, *Das belgische Bollwerk,* pp. 40–48; Lannoy, *L'Indépendance*

In early January, Palmerston's concern for Belgium intensified when Talleyrand suggested that France acquire Luxemburg and the Belgian towns of Philippeville and Marienburg. Talleyrand also proposed that perhaps the King of Saxony should receive Belgium, Prussia in turn would acquire Saxony, and France would get the left bank of the Rhine. (This resurrected Polignac's plan of 1829.) At the same time, Sebastiani expressed a strong interest in acquiring Belgium and proposed a treaty of alliance with Prussia, probably in preparation for additional territorial rearrangements. Prussia declined the offer, and Palmerston told Talleyrand that his proposals were impossible—no one would consent to them. To Granville he said, "I do not like all this; it looks as if France was unchanged in her system of encroachment, and it diminishes the confidence in her sincerity and good faith which her conduct up to this time had inspired."[10] Wary of France, Palmerston adopted the idea of neutrality for Belgium propounded by the representatives of the eastern powers, refined the concept still further, and presented it to the conference. As Bülow reported on 15 January 1831:

> Always occupied with this question, the Secretary of State consulted me a few days ago upon the advantages of a perpetual neutrality of Belgium after the fashion of that agreed upon at Vienna in favor of the Swiss in the declaration of March 20, 1815. . . .
> The plan to assure the independence of Belgium by a guarantee of the Five Powers was made the subject of my very humble report . . . of November 23, last year. This project received the complete approval of Lord Palmerston from the first day of his entry into the ministry. He has never lost sight of this object, and has made it entirely his own.[11]

When the conference met on 20 January, Talleyrand actually fought against the proposal establishing Belgian neutrality. At first, he argued that Luxemburg should be neutralized as well and, if this was not

---

*Belge,* p. 129; and F. de Martens, *Recueil des Traités et Conventions Conclus par la Russie avec les Puissances Etrangères.*

10. Bülow to Frederick William, 5 January 1831, Wolfgang von Franqué, *Luxemburg, die Belgische Revolution, und die Mächte,* pp. 260–261; Lannoy, *L'Indépendance Belge,* pp. 93–96; and Palmerston to Granville, 7 January 1831, Henry Lytton Bulwer, *The Life of Henry John Temple, Viscount Palmerston,* 2:27–29.

11. Lingelbach, "Belgian Neutrality," p. 56.

possible, that Philippeville and Marienburg should be ceded to France as compensation. In a very long session, Palmerston and Bülow rejected Talleyrand's demands, and the neutrality of Belgium was agreed to by the conference.[12] This concept and a number of other important stipulations were spelled out in the protocol of 20 January, which, together with the protocol of 20 December 1830, forms the foundation of the Belgian settlement. The protocol defined the limits of Holland on the basis of its territory in 1790. Belgium was to consist of the other territories granted to the Kingdom of the Netherlands in the treaties of 1815, with the exception of the grand duchy of Luxemburg, which was to remain a possession of the House of Nassau and a member of the German Confederation. The Conference anticipated that some territorial exchanges would be necessary in order to obtain contiguity of possession. Finally, the protocol declared that "Belgium shall form a perpetually neutral state," guaranteed by the five powers.[13]

For the most part, officials at the foreign ministry in Berlin were satisfied with the neutralization of Belgium. Ancillon and Eichhorn felt that the new arrangement would help to keep Belgium separate from France and would hinder France's use of Belgium as a possible base of attack. Still, both men wondered whether, in the long run, a "moral barrier" would be sufficient against France.[14] Although Bernstorff was sick during most of December and all of January and did not actively direct Prussian policy during this period, he approved of the major decisions made at London. He told General von Müffling that the peaceful settlement of the Belgian question was the key to the continued tranquility of Europe. With this in mind, the results of the London conference should not be judged in absolute terms, but rather in relation to the "immeasurable difficulties" of trying to peacefully accommodate highly heterogeneous wishes, interests, and aims.[15]

12. Palmerston to Granville, 21 January 1831, Bulwer, *Viscount Palmerston,* 2:29–31; and Bülow to Frederick William, 22 January 1831, Franqué, *Luxemburg,* pp. 261–264.

13. Protocol of the conference held on 20 January 1830 in *Papers Relative to the Affairs of Belgium,* pp. 298–300.

14. Kurt Hoffman, *Preussen und die Julimonarchie, 1830–1834,* p. 46; Eichhorn to Frederick William, 15 February 1831, and Eichhorn to Bülow, 15 February 1831, ZSA Me, AAI, Rep. 1, Nr. 1794.

15. Bernstorff to Müffling, 1 February 1831, ZSA Me, Rep. 92, Müffling, Nr. B. 2.

## THE TREATY OF 15 NOVEMBER

For Prussia, the last months of 1830 and the first months of 1831 were filled with considerable uneasiness concerning French intentions. Officials were worried about the increase in French armaments and were bothered by the indications in Paris and London that France was intent on acquiring additional territory in Western Europe. The confusing and contradictory reports, received at the end of 1830, that France was attempting to make arrangements with some of the south German states to remain neutral in the event of war, were equally unnerving.[16] The French government also no longer unconditionally recognized the rights of the German Confederation to suppress the revolution in Luxemburg. Sebastiani indicated that if the Confederation took action in the grand duchy, he hoped that it would not apply to the duchy of Beulen, which France was interested in separating from Luxemburg. Talleyrand even indicated that France would prefer to see no federal intervention in Luxemburg whatsoever.[17]

The anxiety of Prussia and the other powers increased still further when the Belgian National Congress decided to consider the Duke de Nemours, Louis Philippe's second son, as a possible candidate for the Belgian throne.[18] In London, Palmerston and the representatives of the three eastern powers quickly stated their opposition to the election of Nemours or of any other prince directly connected with the powers.[19] Palmerston told Talleyrand that the election of the Duke de Nemours would be looked on as the equivalent to the union of Belgium with France. He added, "The acceptance of the crown for Nemours would produce a general war in Europe."[20]

In Berlin, Bernstorff, Gneisenau, Hake, Krauseneck, Witzleben, and Clausewitz met at the order of the King to consider what action should

16. Hoffmann, *Preussen und die Julimonarchie,* pp. 45–57; and Ancillon to Werther, 17 February 1831 (copy), ZSA Me, Rep. 81, Petersburg I, Nr. 124.

17. Franqué, *Luxemburg,* pp. 44–45.

18. Mortier to Sebastiani, 15 February 1831, A.M.A.E., C.P. Prusse, Vol. 275; and Chad to Palmerston, 6 February 1831, PRO F.O. 64/167.

19. Protocol of the conference held on 7 February in *Papers Relative to the Affairs of Belgium,* p. 312.

20. Palmerston to Granville, 1 February 1831, Bulwer, *Viscount Palmerston,* 2:35–36; and Webster, *Foreign Policy of Palmerston,* 1:130.

be taken in the event of armed conflict in Europe. Bernstorff indicated from the outset that he still had considerable hope that peace could be preserved. However, the possible election of the Duke de Nemours, French public opinion, and the increases in the French army were certainly major causes for worry. Those at the meeting recognized that Prussia might not be fully prepared for war, especially in the Rhineland. Troop strength there was so weak that the fortresses could barely be manned; the French and Belgians could easily penetrate far into the province. It was therefore decided to place the fortresses of Luxemburg and Saarlouis at full wartime strength. For the districts on the left bank of the Rhine, the first levy of the *Landwehr* infantry, cavalry, artillery, and pioneers was to be called up. Additional line regiments of the Seventh, Eighth, and Ninth Army Corps would be placed at full strength, together with the entire Seventh and Eighth Artillery Brigades. The French government was to be told of the nature and purpose of Prussia's actions, and Hake took special care not to implement these decisions until France had been fully informed.[21] Bernstorff told Werther that, given the uncertain situation in the Rhineland and France's increased troop strength, Prussia planned to augment its forces in the Rhine province. The maintenance of peace, however, was still the foremost goal of the Prussian government. Alexander von Humboldt was chosen to carry this note to Paris to emphasize Frederick William's pacific inclinations.[22] Prussia's representatives at Karlsruhe and Frankfurt, as well as military authorities in the Rhineland, were also directed to announce the purpose of the partial mobilization. The foreign ministry drafted articles emphasizing Prussia's desire for peace and the defensive nature of the military measures taken; these were placed in Rhenish newspapers.[23] Among the major figures in the Prussian

21. Protocol of 7 February 1831 meeting of Gneisenau, Bernstorff, Hake, Krauseneck, Witzleben, and Clausewitz; and Hake to Bernstorff, 17 February 1831, ZSA Me, AAI, Rep. 1, Nr. 29.

22. Bernstorff to Werther, 18 February 1831 (drafted by Eichhorn), ibid.; and Gneisenau to W. von Scharnhorst, 22 February 1831, Albert Pick, "Briefe des Feldmarschalls Grafen Neithardt v. Gneisenau an seinen Schwiegersohn Wilhelm v. Scharnhorst," p. 236.

23. Witzleben to Bernstorff, 22 February 1831, Bernstorff to Otterstedt, 11 March 1831, Otterstedt to Bernstorff, 22 March 1831, Bernstorff to Witzleben, 18 February 1831 (draft of newspaper article enclosed, drafted by Varnhagen von Ense, and revised by Bernstorff), ZSA Me, AAI, Rep. 1, Nr. 29.

government, only Duke Charles, who advocated a war of all the German
princes against France to restore Charles X, was eager to fight.[24]

The seriousness of the European crisis was confirmed when the Belgian
national Congress elected the Duke de Nemours King on 3 February.
In addition, the outbreak of revolution in Modena, Parma, Bologna, and
the Papal States in early February presented the possibility that France
and Austria would become embroiled in additional difficulties. However,
on 7 February, just as war seemed imminent, the intensity of the crisis
was greatly eased when Louis Philippe declined the Belgian throne on
his son's behalf.[25] The King of the French had been more concerned with
preventing the Duke of Leuchtenburg, a Bonapartist, from becoming
the King of Belgium than in actually placing his son on the throne. On
24 February, the Belgian National Congress proclaimed a regency under
President Surlet de Chokier.[26]

The situation in Europe improved still further when Lafitte's government, which represented the "party of movement" in France, fell and was
replaced by a more moderate regime led by the very capable Casimir
Périer. Although Périer restated France's belief in the principle of nonintervention and inquired whether France might receive Beulen or
Landau, he wanted to avoid war and wished to work harmoniously with
the powers at the conference in London.[27] Most of the powers felt that
the new government greatly increased the chances of peace in Europe.
For the first time in months, Werther saw a glimmer of peace, and
Ancillon praised Périer for his intelligence, character, and commitment to
peace.[28]

---

24. See Herzog Carl v. Mecklenburg, Denkschrift betr. Kriegerische Zustände in
Europa, Volkssouveranität, Organization des deutschen Bundes, March 1831; also
Wittgenstein to Albrecht, 21 March 1831, ZSA Me, Geheimes Civil Cabinet, Rep.
2.2.1., Nr. 13070.

25. For Bernstorff's relief on receiving this news, see Mortier to Sebastiani, 19
February 1831, A.M.A.E., C.P. Prusse, Vol. 275.

26. Lannoy, L'Indépendance Belge, pp. 141–147.

27. Eugène Vicomte de Guichen, La Révolution de Juillet 1830 et l'Europe, pp.
336–338; David H. Pinckney, The French Revolution of 1830, p. 367; Lannoy,
L'Indépendance Belge, pp. 159–160; and Granville to Palmerston, 25 March 1831,
Bulwer, Viscount Palmerston, 2:57–60.

28. Lannoy, L'Indépendance Belge, p. 158; Guichen, La Révolution de Juillet
1830, p. 457; Karl Hillebrand, Geschichte Frankreichs 1830–1871, 1:207n; and
Ancillon to Schöler, 5 May 1831, ZSA Me, Rep. 81, Petersburg I, Nr. 124.

Three major issues dominated the affairs of Europe for the next several months: First, the question of disarmament brought forth by France; second, the selection of a monarch for Belgium; and third, the creation of a comprehensive settlement for the Belgian state. Shortly after taking office, Périer proposed that, if the other powers would carry out proportional reductions, France would reduce its army from 450,000 men to 250,000 men. The ensuing negotiations led to nothing, but they did serve to increase the Prussian government's confidence in France's peaceful intentions.[29]

The selection of a new monarch for Belgium proved to be relatively easy: Leopold of Saxe-Coburg was the only candidate acceptable to the powers and to the Belgians. If Belgium could not be ruled by a member of the House of Orange, Frederick William felt that Leopold was the candidate most acceptable to Prussia. Only Nicholas refused to recognize any candidate outside the House of Orange; the Prussian government formally disagreed with Russia's position.[30] On 4 June, the Belgian National Congress elected Leopold by a wide majority. However, there remained some doubt that Leopold would accept the crown.

The precise territorial configuration of the new Belgian state proved to be the most difficult issue to settle. Disagreement centered on the fate of Maastricht, Limburg, and Luxemburg, which were claimed by both Holland and Belgium. The Belgian representative in London was able to show that some portions of Limburg east of the Meuse had not belonged to Holland prior to 1790. According to the protocol of 20 January, these territories could be allotted to Belgium; thus, the Belgian government had bargaining power concerning the claims on Luxemburg. The German Confederation had found it almost impossible to act on the Luxemburg question.[31] The hesitation of the Confederation and Prussia's reluctance to press for any action that might offend France, together with the desire of all the powers to settle the Belgian question, resulted in the

---

29. Werner Näf, *Abrüstungsverhandlungen im Jahre 1831;* Hoffmann, *Preussen und die Julimonarchie,* pp. 58–62; and Ancillon to Schöler, 22 June 1831, Ancillon to Maltzahn, 16 June 1831 (copy), and Ancillon to Werther, 19 June 1831 (copy), ZSA Me, Rep. 81, Petersburg, I, Nr. 124.

30. Lannoy, *L'Indépendance Belge,* p. 126; Webster, *Foreign Policy of Palmerston,* 1:133; and Ancillon to Schöler, 21 May 1831, ZSA Me, Rep. 81, Petersburg I, Nr. 124.

31. Franqué, *Luxemburg,* pp. 71–84.

controversial protocol of 21 May. In this protocol, the conference stated that, in order to speed Belgium's acceptance of the separation agreement and Leopold's election as King, it would be useful for Belgium to acquire Luxemburg, though the grand duchy would remain part of the German Confederation. The conference proposed to open negotiations with the King of the Netherlands and the Confederation to affect the transfer of Luxemburg to Belgium in return for due compensation. The Confederation was asked to suspend all military operations against Luxemburg for the duration of the negotiations.[32]

In general terms, Bernstorff was not opposed to the transfer of Luxemburg in an effort to solve the Belgian problem. However, he felt that a Belgian Luxemburg could not remain inside the Confederation. He placed no great value on Luxemburg's military importance, and he told Mortier that Prussia was willing to relinquish the fortress. Ancillon had outlined similar considerations in an instruction to Bülow dated 19 May 1831. In other words, in the interest of facilitating a lasting settlement of the Belgian problem,[33] the ministry had modified its position on the Luxemburg question.

However, Metternich and the Kings of Bavaria and Württemberg strongly opposed this position.[34] Under pressure, Frederick William, who had not been informed of his ministry's policy, altered the position of his government. Together with Austria, Prussia declared that the London conference had exceeded its authority and had transgressed on the rights of the Confederation. Belgium could not become part of the German Confederation, and the fortress of Luxemburg must remain part of Germany's defensive system. Berlin did indicate that it would be willing to consider the partition of Luxemburg in exchange for the assignment of Limburg to Holland. The German part of Luxemburg containing the

---

32. Protocol of a conference held on 21 May 1831 in *Papers Relative to the Affairs of Belgium*, pp. 332–333.

33. Franqué, *Luxemburg*, pp. 113–114; and Mortier to Sebastiani, 31 May 1831, A.M.A.E., C.P. Prusse, Vol. 276. Also see Ancillon to Bülow, 19 May 1831, Franqué, *Luxemburg*, pp. 274–276. In his discussion of the Luxemburg question, Heinrich von Treitschke completely omits any mention of these events, perhaps because they did not demonstrate Prussia's resolve to settle the controversy "without any diminution of the federal domain," as he asserted. *History of Germany in the Nineteenth Century*, 5:284.

34. Metternich to Trauttmannsdorff, 27 May 1831, and Metternich to Esterhazy, 27 May 1831, Franqué, *Luxemburg*, pp. 279–281, 114–119.

fortress would remain under the rule of William and inside the Confederation, but the Walloon portion could conceivably go to Belgium. For
compensation, the Confederation should be given occupation rights in
Maastrict and the right to an additional fortress.[35]

Bülow was disappointed by the contents of Ancillon's new instructions.
First of all, he said the protocol of 21 May was faithful to his earlier instructions from Berlin. Second, while he admitted that it was possible that
the protocol had infringed on the interests of the German Confederation,
he argued that, in effect, the Confederation had already relinquished its responsibilities in the matter and had lost the respect of the powers because
of its inability to take coercive action in Luxemburg. Finally, as long as
the preservation of general peace and the maintenance of harmonious relations among the five great powers was a primary objective, the protocol of
21 May did not appear to him to be too great a sacrifice.[36] Bülow, of
course, was revealing the inherent difficulty of reconciling Prussia's
European interests with its responsibilities within the Confederation.[37]

By this time, Bülow's position in London had been further weakened by
a reorganization of duties within the Ministry of Foreign Affairs (discussed in detail in the next chapter). Bernstorff had informed Frederick
William of his desire to resign due to poor health. He remained foreign
minister, but the day-to-day administration of Prussia's European policy
was transferred to Ancillon, who became a Secretary of State within the
ministry, while Bernstorff concentrated most of his efforts on Prussia's
German policy. Bernstorff had aided Bülow throughout his career and
thought highly of him, but relations quickly deteriorated between Bülow
and Ancillon, who felt that the ambassador was too favorable to the
interests of the western powers.[38] In any case, the objections of Berlin and
Vienna forced the powers to defer the fate of Luxemburg and Maastrict.

35. Ibid., pp. 117–118.

36. Ancillon to Bülow, 7 June 1831, ZSA Me, Rep. 81, Petersburg I, Nr. 124;
and Bülow to Ancillon, 17 June 1831, Franqué, *Luxemburg,* pp. 296–300.

37. Franqué, *Luxemburg,* p. 118. This theme is also developed in Franz Richter;
*Das europäische Problem der preussischen Staatspolitik und die revolutionäre
Krisis von 1830 bis 1832.*

38. The disagreement between Bülow and Ancillon can best be traced in some
of Bülow's own papers contained in the private archive of Schloss Tegel in Berlin.
For example, see Bülow's "Estraits des rescrits de M. Ancillon constatant une
divergence d'opinion remarquable d'après l'ordre de dates du 26 Sept. 1831 jusqu'au
5 Dec. 1832.

But they were able to agree on eighteen articles that incorporated the essentials of the protocols of 20 December 1830 and 20 January 1831 as the basis for a definitive treaty.[39]

During the remainder of 1831, the major problems in the international affairs of Europe were nearly solved. But, as the international situation became less grave, the willingness of all five powers to work together also declined. Slowly, a noticeable division emerged between the three eastern states and the two liberal powers, Britain and France. However, in June 1831, this division was not quite so evident. Prussia had cooperated continually with Great Britain in London; Austria and Russia had also supported the work of the conference. These four powers had often successfully worked as a check on French ambitions, which, it must be admitted, were not pursued with much vigor. Despite the constant threat of war and close geographical proximity, relations between Prussia and France remained remarkably cordial.[40] However, Franco-Prussian relations worsened dramatically when the King of the Netherlands refused to accept the Eighteen Articles and invaded Belgium.

The Dutch operation, led by the Prince of Orange, was well planned and skillfully carried out. When the Belgian army crumbled under the Dutch attack, Leopold first called to the French and then to the conference in London for military aid. The French armies reacted with dispatch and quickly moved into Belgium and occupied Brussels. Because William had no desire to become engaged in a conflict with France, the Dutch troops retreated just as rapidly as they had advanced. Still William had proved that the Belgian state was a shaky affair. The Prussian government was critical of the French incursion into Belgium, and Werther demanded that Prussia be allowed to participate in the French operation; Sebastiani refused the request. In London, Bülow insisted that Leopold should have addressed his call for aid to the conference first and then perhaps to France, Prussia, and Great Britain jointly. He set to work to restrain France.[41] The French operations were subsequently sanctioned by the conference in its protocol of 6 August 1831. Out of deference to Prussia, the French army was not allowed to occupy either Maastricht or Venloo

---

39. See protocol of a conference held on 26 June 1831, in *Papers Relative to the Affairs of Belgium*, pp. 337–339.

40. Hoffman, *Preussen und die Julimonarchie*, pp. 45–66.

41. Ibid., p. 72; and Jan Andrzej Betley, *Belgium and Poland in International Relations, 1830–1831*, p. 198.

and was to leave as soon as an armistice was reestablished.[42] At the time, it was commonly assumed that the eastern powers had encouraged William to invade Belgium, but this was not the case. Berlin believed that William was wrong to refuse the Eighteen Articles and condemned the Dutch invasion as an imprudent violation of the armistice.[43] Duke Charles felt that Prussia was greatly endangered by the presence of the French army in Belgium and that the French forces should be ejected, but his view did not prevail.[44]

Berlin, however, was alarmed by the attitude of the French government. In early August, Sebastiani told Werther that France wished to prolong its occupation of Belgium and that, as compensation for evacuation, France wished to receive Philippeville, Marienburg, and the duchy of Beulen. In return, France would agree to leave Luxemburg in the German Confederation and to assign Maastricht to Holland.[45] Ancillon stated that Sebastiani's first point was not negotiable—France was already committed to withdrawing its troops from Belgium as a result of communications with the Prussian court and by virtue of the protocol of 6 August signed in London by Talleyrand. The other questions were entirely separate and were in no way related to the question of evacuation. In general terms, he indicated that Prussia was against ceding any territory to France, but would be willing to discuss the matter if Paris so desired. Prussia's position was that the basis of negotiation for the status of Luxemburg should not change and that Maastricht and Venloo should go to Holland.[46] Ulti-

---

42. Protocol of a conference held on 6 August 1831, in *Papers Relative to the Affairs of Belgium*, pp. 355–356.

43. Ancillon to Bülow, 26 July 1831 (copy), Ancillon to Bülow, 11 August 1831 (copy), Ancillon to Schöler, 13 August 1831, and Ancillon to Waldburg-Truchsess, 27 August 1831 (copy), ZSA Me, Rep. 81, Petersburg I, Nr. 124. Also see Frederick William to Charlotte, 4 August 1831, Paul Bailleu, "Aus dem letzten Jahrzehnt Friedrich Wilhelms III," p. 158.

44. Carl von Mecklenburg, "Über das Einrücken der Franzosen in Belgien und dessen Nachtheil für Preussen," 18 August 1831, ZSA Me, Geheimes Civil Cabinet, Rep. 2.2.1., Nr. 13210.

45. Hoffman, *Preussen und die Julimonarchie*, pp. 74–75. In London, Talleyrand once again proposed the partition of Belgium to Bülow; see Lannoy, *L'Indépendance Belge*, p. 217; and Franqué, *Luxemburg*, p. 137.

46. Ancillon to Werther, 26 August 1831 (copy), ZSA Me, Rep. 81, Petersburg I, Nr. 124.

mately, Palmerston's pressure and Périer's good sense secured the withdrawal of French troops from Belgium.[47]

The powers were now faced with drawing up a new agreement to replace the discredited Eighteen Articles. Palmerston suggested to Bülow that a partial transfer of Luxemburg to Belgium might be the best way to settle the Limburg problem. In an answer to Bülow's request for guidance, Bernstorff agreed that perhaps the Belgian question could be settled by moving forward on the status of Luxemburg. This would only be possible if William would be willing to exchange part of Luxemburg and if it did not damage the security of the Confederation. The *Bund* would also have to empower Austria and Prussia to negotiate on this question at London. In the end, William was willing to consider a territorial exchange involving Luxemburg, and the federal Diet provided the necessary authorization.[48] The result was the Twenty-four Articles, agreed to by the London conference on 14 October after lengthy and detailed negotiations. The articles specified that the eastern and largely German portion of Luxemburg containing the fortress was to be ruled by the House of Orange and would remain a member of the German Confederation. The western portion was to be transferred to Belgium. In return, Holland would receive all of Limburg on the right bank of the Meuse as well as Maastricht. Articles IX, X, and XI reasserted the importance of free navigation on the Scheldt and the Rhine and gave Belgium convenient commercial access to Germany through Maastricht. These articles satisfied important commercial interests of both Prussia and Great Britain. Additional articles restated the perpetual neutrality of Belgium and regulated the division of the state debt of the old United Netherlands.[49] Palmerston successfully applied pressure to the Belgian government to accept the twenty-four articles, and then through his efforts, these articles were converted into a formal treaty dated 15 November 1831

47. Ancillon to Schöler, 17 September 1831, Ancillon to Werther, 10 September 1831 (copy), and Ancillon to Bülow, 12 September 1831 (copy), ibid.

48. Franqué, *Luxemburg,* pp. 154–157; and protocol of a conference held on 24 September 1831, in *Papers Relative to the Affairs of Belgium,* p. 377, Annex A:378–379.

49. Lannoy, *L'Indépendance Belge,* pp. 226–253; and Annex A to protocol of a conference held on 14 October 1831, in *Papers Relative to the Affairs of Belgium,* pp. 414–420.

between the five powers and Belgium. He expressed his great satisfaction to Granville: "It is an immense thing done to have got Austria, Russia and Prussia to sign a formal treaty of friendship and guarantee with Leopold. Belgium is thus placed out of all danger and the sulky silence of the Dutch King becomes at once a matter of little or no importance to anybody but himself."[50] Palmerston's satisfaction, however, was rather short-lived.

## THE RATIFICATION CONTROVERSY

Bernstorff basically approved of the treaty's contents. While it did not fulfill all of Prussia's requirements, the essential ones were taken care of. Bernstorff particularly emphasized its favorable commercial arrangements.[51] Frederick William, hoping to secure a stable peace in Europe, was willing to ratify the agreement immediately.[52] Ancillon congratulated Bülow on his work at London and added that it was an honor for Prussia to be part of such an important diplomatic transaction.[53] He felt that, while the treaty was not perfect, it was as impartial and equitable as possible, and he urged William to ratify it.[54] Eichhorn, who was also in favor of ratification, argued that the treaty was favorable to Holland, compared to its territorial configuration in 1790.[55] Thus, the men who directed Prussian foreign policy were united in approving the treaty.

However, their attitude was not shared by the Dutch, Austrians, and Russians. William considered the treaty unacceptable.[56] Metternich was

50. Webster, *Foreign Policy of Palmerston*, 1:145.

51. Bernstorff to Nagler, 4 November 1831, Franqué, *Luxemburg*, pp. 326–329.

52. Ibid., p. 190; and Ancillon to Schöler, 1 December 1831, ZSA Me, Rep. 81, Petersburg I, Nr. 124.

53. Ancillon to Bülow, 24 October 1831 (copy), ZSA Me, Rep. 81, Petersburg I, Nr. 124.

54. Ancillon to Waldburg-Truchsess, 25 October 1831, and Ancillon to Bülow, 30 October and 26 November 1831, ibid. Also see Chad to Palmerston, 7 November 1831, PRO F.O. 64/175.

55. Memoire by Eichhorn, 25 October 1831, Colenbrander, *Gedenkstukken,* 44: 48–50.

56. Lannoy, *L'Indépendance Belge,* pp. 290–293; and Note Addressed to the Conference by the Plenipotentiaries of His Majesty the King of the Netherlands, 14 December 1831, Annex A to protocol of a conference held on 4 January 1832, *Papers Relative to the Affairs of Belgium,* pp. 437–440.

highly critical of Wessenberg's work and called "the treaty of 15 November the scandal of his life."[57] His disapproval was primarily based on the conversion of the Twenty-four Articles into the definitive treaty signed by the plenipotentiaries in London. Emperor Francis was also greatly dissatisfied with the document. "If I have to sign this treaty," he commented, "I will certainly do it in a way that no one can read my name. This treaty is a true scandal."[58] Metternich and Francis, dissatisfied with Prussia's policy, blamed the final outcome of the Belgian crisis on Berlin's unwillingness to play a more aggressive role.[59] In addition, the federal Diet decided that it could reach no decision on the treaty because William had sent no instructions to the Dutch representative. While Metternich approved of this attitude, Bernstorff regretted the Diet's passivity toward the work of the conference.[60]

Nicholas also opposed the treaty. In making a final appeal for the Tsar's support, William attacked the work of Lieven and Matuszewic, and Nicholas, accepting William's criticism, ordered that the Russian plenipotentiaries be censured.[61] He agreed not to ratify the treaty until William approved of it. Berlin was unhappy with the Tsar's attitude; Ancillon felt that Russia's support encouraged Holland to resist the action of the conference. Delay, he said, would gain nothing for Holland; it would only compromise her reputation in Europe and place additional strains on her friends. The solidarity of the powers should be maintained. Russia's position contradicted the entire work of the conference, and Prussia, he said, was interested in preventing the breakup of the meeting in London. He concluded that Russia should simply ratify the treaty.[62] Bülow joined

57. Franqué, *Luxemburg*, p. 190; Arneth, *Johann Freiherr von Wessenberg*, 2:130–136; and Clemens Lothar Wenzel, Fürst von Metternich-Winneburg, *Aus Metternichs nachgelassenen Papieren*, 5:214–221.

58. Franqué, *Luxemburg*, p. 190n.

59. Arneth, *Johann Freiherr von Wessenberg*, 2:130; and Auszug aus einem Bericht Mollerus des niederländischen Gesandten in Wien, Alfred Stern, *Geschichte Europas seit den Verträgen von 1815 bis zum Frankfurter Frieden von 1871*, 4:606–607.

60. Franqué, *Luxemburg*, p. 192.

61. Webster, *Foreign Policy of Palmerston*, 1:149–150; and Martens, *Recueil des Traités*, 11:462–463.

62. Ancillon to Bülow, 26 November 1831 (copy), ZSA Me, Rep. 81, Petersburg I, Nr. 124; Ancillon to Waldburg-Truchsess, 28 November 1831, Colenbrander, *Gedenkstukken*, 44:51–53. Also see Ancillon to Schöler, 18 and 28 December 1831,

Ancillon in criticizing Russia's position. In December, when the Dutch King formally expressed his opposition to the treaty to Frederick William, the Prussian King replied that he approved of the Twenty-four Articles because they represented the best hope for settling the Belgian problem.[63]

Nevertheless, neither Prussia nor Austria was willing to ratify the treaty until Russia agreed to do so. Bernstorff explained to Chad that he did not think that Russia's refusal was "final or absolute." Eichhorn emphasized to the British diplomat that Prussia still wanted to settle the Belgian question, "but that she could not ratify immediately without impairing her intimate relations with Austria and Russia."[64] Unfortunately, Ancillon also told Chad that nonratification by any of the parties nullified the treaty and that he considered the Tsar's refusal to be final.[65] Apparently, it was Ancillon's statement that especially infuriated Palmerston. The entire future of the treaty now seemed to be in doubt. In response to Berlin's refusal to ratify the treaty immediately, Palmerston sent a dispatch and a separate letter to Chad in Berlin. In the dispatch he noted that

> during the last fourteen months the Peace of Europe has been preserved by the union of the Five Great Powers. . . . Among the five powers represented in the Conference of London, there were none whose interests in the great Questions which have there been discussed were more nearly identified than Prussia and Great Britain; and the union which has subsisted between them has on that account been perhaps more intimate than that which has existed between any others of the Five. . . .
>
> But the Prussian Government must not disguise from themselves that that union which has hitherto produced such salutary effects, could not survive their refusal to ratify the treaty; and at this last stage of a long and laborious negotiation, when the object for which we have all been struggling is almost within our grasp, the defection of the Prussian government may frustrate all our past exertions, and throw the whole of Europe back into that confusion, from which it appeared to be on the point of escaping.[66]

---

ZSA Me, Rep. 81, Petersburg I, Nr. 124; and Ancillon to Maltitz, 25 December 1831, ZSA Me, AAI, Rep. 1, Nr. 1794.

63. William to Frederick William, 6 December 1831, and Frederick William to William, 24 December 1831, Colenbrander, *Gedenkstukken,* 44:53–57.

64. Chad to Palmerston, 18 and 11 December 1831, PRO F.O. 64/175.

65. Chad to Palmerston, 18 December 1831, ibid.

66. Palmerston to Chad, 30 December 1831, PRO F.O. 64/166.

He was even more outspoken in his private letter to Chad, who was to communicate its contents to the Prussian government as well. He accused the Prussians of bad faith, threatened them with an Anglo-French alliance, and demanded that Prussia join with France and Great Britain in ratifying the treaty by 31 January 1832. He wrote that

> I see nothing that can prevent a war except the ratification of the treaty. If Prussia refuses, one or other of the two things will be demonstrated: either that in spite of her pacific professions Prussia is panting for war, or else that she is not an independent agent and is dragged by Russia at her chariot wheels. You must insist upon having an immediate answer, yes or no, will Prussia ratify or not, and it should be given in a Prussian note in order that it may be produced, if it should become necessary to do so, if the Papers are laid before Parliament, which upon all occasions of unsuccessful negotiations [they] invariably are.

Palmerston closed by saying, "Tell M. Ancillon that we are beginning to regret that we did not take a more decided part in Polish Affairs before the capture of Warsaw, we might have done some good in Poland and have less trouble with the treaty."[67]

Bernstorff was nearly as frustrated by this controversy as Palmerston was. He told Chad, "We have made great sacrifices—sacrifices of our most intimate affections, nay, of our duties—for what? For the preservation of the solidarity of the five powers and to prevent war by keeping those five powers together, and now you call upon us to do an act that must necessarily destroy the solidarity for which we have made all those sacrifices."[68] Bernstorff told the King that Palmerston's argument was ridiculous. Prussia could wait to ratify the treaty in common with the other powers. While Palmerton's words were regrettable, he felt that they should not be taken too literally; they were probably just a crude attempt to force Prussia and Austria to ratify the treaty. He recommended that Frederick William remain true to his commitment to ratify, although he need not actually do so until the other powers had done likewise. It was essential, he said, to maintain the principle of solidarity among the great powers.[69]

---

67. Palmerston to Chad, 30 December 1831, in Betley, *Belgium and Poland,* pp. 286–288.

68. Chad to Palmerston, 7 January 1832, PRO F.O. 64/181.

69. Bernstorff to Frederick William, 6 January 1832, ZSA Me, AAI, Rep. 1, Nr. 1794.

Ancillon, in turn, wrote to Bülow that the King would not ratify the treaty because of his fidelity to the unity of the five powers. Palmerston's threat that Britain and France would form a dual alliance and implement the treaty on their own did not cause the King to change his mind. "The concert and the union of the five powers is the surest and also the only guarantee for the preservation of the peace."[70] As a result, France and Great Britain ratified the treaty alone on 31 January 1832.[71]

Whether because of Palmerston's threats, the urging of Prussia, or the realization that the Belgian settlement could not be changed substantially, Nicholas began to reconsider his position on ratification. He decided to send Count Orloff to The Hague to convince William that further resistance to the powers was useless. Berlin naturally supported this mission.[72] Orloff quickly concluded that William was merely being obstinate and advised the Tsar to ratify the treaty without further delay.[73] In London, the representatives of the eastern powers continued to delay ratification, although Bülow had already received preliminary authorization on 12 January, and Wessenberg had received his on 21 March, with permission to sign as soon as Bülow received final approval. After many discussions on the ratification issue in Berlin and London, with accompanying ill-feelings on both sides, Ancillon finally directed Bülow to ratify the treaty on 7 April. The actual signing by Prussia and Austria took place on 18 April. Russia did not ratify until 4 May.[74]

The dispute over the ratification of the treaty was unfortunate since it unnecessarily damaged the high degree of cooperation achieved by the powers at London. Prussia, in particular, was hurt by the controversy because it felt that it could not abandon a policy that was coordinated with its eastern allies, yet it still desired to have the treaty approved. In the end,

70. Ancillon to Bülow, 23 January 1832 (copy), ZSA Me, Rep. 81, Petersburg I, Nr. 127.

71. Lannoy, *L'Indépendance Belge*, pp. 296–297; also see protocol of a conference held on 31 January 1832, in *Papers Relative to the Affairs of Belgium*, pp. 464–465.

72. See Chad to Palmerston, 12 February 1832, PRO F.O. 64/181; Ancillon to Schöler, 15 February 1832, ZSA Me, Rep. 81, Petersburg I, Nr. 127; and Ancillon to Waldburg-Truchsess, 15 February 1832, Colenbrander, *Gedenkstukken*, 44:64–67.

73. Lannoy, *L'Indépendance Belge*, pp. 298–307.

74. Ancillon to Bülow, 7 April 1832 (copy), ZSA Me, Rep. 81, Petersburg I, Nr. 127; and Chad to Palmerston, 8 April 1832, PRO F.O. 64/182. Also see Lannoy, *L'Indépendance Belge*, pp. 307–312; and protocols of a conference held on 18 April and 4 May 1832, in *Papers Relative to the Affairs of Belgium*, pp. 466–468.

the impression was left that Prussia's position on the Belgian question was little different from that of Austria and Russia, when in fact Berlin had, as we have seen, worked very closely with Great Britain to solve the problem of the Netherlands and had, in contrast to St. Petersburg and Vienna, approved of the final settlement with few reservations. These distinctions were clouded at the time and have sometimes been lost sight of since, primarily because of the confusion and disagreement that surrounded the final ratification of the treaty.

The treaty of 12 November 1831 did not completely settle the Belgian question. It was supplemented by the Fortress Treaty of 14 December 1831 (signed by Austria, Great Britain, Russia, and Prussia), which called for the demolition of a series of fortifications along the French frontier. Belgium was to maintain all other defensive works in good repair, and the rights of the four courts concerning the defense of the region were to be recognized by the King of Belgium.[75] In addition to the Fortress Treaty, detailed agreements on the status of the Scheldt, on transit rights through Dutch territory for Belgium, and on the division of the national debt had to be worked out. These discussions and William's continued obstinacy caused long delays and great resentment. A comprehensive and universally recognized settlement was not finally established until 1839.

The Belgian settlement was one of the most important and enduring achievements of the Concert of Europe, and it marked the end of a period of intense diplomatic activity in Western Europe. Because armed conflict did not occur among the powers, there is a natural tendency to forget the very real tensions that existed at the time. In securing peace for Europe, the leadership exercised by Great Britain was of the greatest significance, particularly in the case of the Belgian negotiations. Still the participation of all the great powers was essential, and the constructive attitude of Prussia and France was especially important. In the first major crisis of the post-Napoleonic period that actually threatened to develop into a major European war, Bernstorff successfully guided Prussian policy on the basis of a careful calculation of Prussia's interests and capabilities; his judgments derived from his understanding of recent history and an acceptance of the balance of power, not from preconceived ideological notions. Above all, he wanted to preserve the peace. As he told Chad in November

---

75. The whole question of the Fortress treaty is discussed in detail in Hampe, *Das belgische Bollwerk;* and in Lannoy, *L'Indépendance Belge,* pp. 254–284.

of 1830, "War is not to be undertaken in these times lightly; it is no longer a question of a Fortress or of a province. He who draws the sword now risks every thing. Such immense masses must now be brought into the field, and the people must be so pressed—so impoverished, that the savings of twenty-years—the prosperity of twenty years—may be squandered in one campaign."[76] He was, of course, also concerned with containing revolution as much as possible. Radical revolution, and all the popular energies associated with it, was a threat to his class and opposed to his political philosophy, but above all it was equated with war, specifically with the expansion of French power. Therefore, he attempted to do nothing that would stimulate a move to the left in France, while at the same time trying to contain expansionist impulses on the part of Louis Philippe's government. In this delicate balancing act, Bernstorff expressed the sentiment of the King and of most of the Prussian government, but it was he, more than anyone else, who strove to create this proper sense of proportion.

Like most statesmen in Europe, Bernstorff also realized that the key to containing the power of France lay in the Grand Alliance, or preferably in a five-power configuration involving France. This conviction, as we have seen, was not created solely by the fear of revolution that swept Europe in 1830. It represented a long-term commitment on Bernstorff's part, a commitment that he clearly restated at the time of the eastern question. Fragmentation in the alliance could lead to diplomatic instability. The consequences of instability in the international system during the Napoleonic years in the case of Prussia and Denmark were very clear. For Prussia, the essential elements in a stable system were close relations with Great Britain and Russia. Perhaps because of his Danish experience, Bernstorff was especially impressed by Great Britain's importance to the European system. He repeatedly argued for a strong relationship with England because he believed that London could check the ambitions of Paris more effectively than the eastern powers could. However, Russia was also crucial to the security of Prussia, not only because of the status of Poland, but because Russia had repulsed Napoleon and had earlier played the key role in the survival of the Prussian state. This meant that Prussian policy not only had to encompass the attitude of Great Britain, but simultaneously had to cope with the interests and behavior of

76. Chad to Palmerston, 10 November 1830, PRO F.O. 64/164.

the most autocratic state in Europe. Just as Bernstorff had attempted to contain the revolutionary impulses of France, he also had to try to curb Nicholas's antirevolutionary zeal without alienating St. Petersburg. This was a difficult path to follow and ultimately led to the conflict with Great Britain over the ratification of the Belgian treaty.

Military arrangements and their connections with public opinion placed additional constraints on Prussian power. As we have seen, Prussia's military system allowed the state, despite its limited strength, to play a major role in European affairs. However, those same military institutions placed definite limitations on Prussia's activities as a great power, primarily because of the government's fear of public opinion. While public attitudes may not have had a decisive impact on the formulation of Austrian and Russian foreign policy during these years, this is not true for Prussia. As one foreign observer in Berlin noted in 1831, "This government stands very much in awe of Public Opinion, although it has no legal organ here, and Public Opinion would I think be decidedly against a war of principles, or in short, any war but one absolutely necessitated by foreign aggression."[77] Concern for public opinion restricted the number of options that the government felt was available to it.

Domestic political considerations and financial factors also placed additional limitations on foreign policy. Although careful administration and strict economy had restored Prussia to financial stability and had thereby given it greater confidence and independence, as Bernstorff pointed out, those gains could be quickly lost in a war of major proportions. A significant increase in indebtedness posed special problems for the Prussian monarchy and could conceivably force the crown to reform its political institutions or, at the very least, create considerable embarrassment to the King. As we have previously noted, the King's directive of 17 January 1820 provided that no additional loans could be subscribed without the consent of the representatives of the *Stände*. The government's natural reluctance to establish a national representative assembly placed very real limits on its ability to raise funds for the purpose of war. Even contemporaries understood how the government's desire to maintain an absolutist system worked against the pursuit of an aggressive foreign policy. For example, Chad discussed this problem in a report to Palmerston dated 28 November 1831. After observing in general how financial

---

77. Chad to Palmerston, 28 November 1831, PRO F.O. 64/175.

considerations had made Prussia support the cause of peace, and how an increase in taxes was not, for a variety of reasons, a real alternative at this time, he wrote:

> The King promised by a Royal order dated 17 January 1820 of which I enclose an extract, not to borrow any more money with the consent of the future states of the Kingdom.
>
> No states exist but Provincial assemblies, calculated only for provincial administration and it would be therefore necessary if a loan were required to give a representation to this Kingdom, a hazardous measure at any time, and more particularly hazardous now, when the ferment caused by the French explosion is but just subsiding. It would under any circumstances be a strong measure, and it is therefore one not likely to be adopted by the present King who is disposed upon all occasions to temporize, and to put off the Evil day; and his ministers mostly very old men, who leave much of the practical Duties of their Department to persons of talent acting under them, are also (with the exception of Count Bernstorff) inclined to a palliative system.[78]

What Chad meant by excepting Bernstorff will be discussed later, but what is important here is that in addition to all the other reasons already discussed that reinforced a policy of peace, the crown, because of its basic conservatism, was not willing to pay the political price necessary to prosecute a major war even in support of conservative doctrine. Thus, in addition to Bernstorff's sound understanding of the affairs of Europe and the basic timidity and pacifism of the King, the desire to maintain the domestic political status quo also contributed to the maintenance of peace.

A frequent weakness of studies that examine this period of European international relations is a failure to differentiate among the three eastern powers. To state that Prussia simply followed Austria's lead is obviously inaccurate. As a matter of fact, some people in Berlin argued that Austria was the least essential power to Prussia during the 1830–1831 crises, and this attitude became apparent in Prussia's German policy. Nor did Prussia follow the dictates of Russia. Over the years, the tyranny of the categories "liberal" and "conservative" has clouded and confused some of the most interesting aspects of international relations during this period and has blurred the distinctions between the powers' policies. The fact that Great

78. Ibid.

Britain and Prussia worked more closely together than any other two powers throughout most of the crisis has sometimes been forgotten, while, in anticipation of later developments, many accounts overemphasize the intimacy of the Anglo-French relationship. Bernstorff's policies, the proceedings in London, Palmerston's statements with regard to Prussia, and scores of documents demonstrate the high degree of cooperation that existed between London and Berlin during the entire period when the most crucial issues of European politics were being settled. Ideological considerations based on the differing political and social systems of the western and eastern powers were, of course, a significant factor in the international politics of the period, but a sharp division of the powers along ideological lines did not take shape until 1832, and it would be a mistake to overemphasize its importance prior to that time.

In addition to being miscategorized, Bernstorff's policies have also been criticized for not being forceful enough. Those who have made this argument have taken their cue from Bismarck who wrote, "It was only in Prussia that the military machine, cumbersome though it was, functioned with complete precision, and had Prussian policy been capable of forming its own resolutions, then it would have found the strength to prejudice the situation in 1830 in Germany and the Netherlands toward its views."[79] This evaluation confuses the Prussia of 1830 with the Prussia of the 1860s and postulates a leadership that possessed an entirely different set of political values. The central fact is that Prussia at this time was a state of only moderate strength, and its leadership, although aware of the potential of the nation-state, thought primarily in European terms—that also happened to represent the interest of the state. Power was to be used responsibly and morally. No one wanted to unleash the naked drive for territorial aggrandizement that had nearly destroyed the European states decades earlier. The reaction of the powers to France's attempt to exploit the Belgian crisis to her own advantage made this abundantly clear. Furthermore, Prussia was restricted in the use of its power, such as it was, by the renewed vitality of the Concert of Europe and, as a consequence, had to straddle East and West in the conduct of foreign relations. This did not allow Prussia much freedom to pursue initiatives of its own in an unrestricted manner, for wherever it turned, it was hemmed in by the fundamental ideological and geopolitical characteristics of the age. This

79. Otto von Bismarck, *Gedanken und Erinnerungen,* 1:276.

was what Clausewitz was getting at when he wrote in July 1831, "Among the five great powers, no minister of foreign affairs has as difficult a position as the Prussian."[80] The problems that accompanied Prussia's intermediate position were sometimes not recognized by the rest of Europe, particularly by Great Britain. In the end, this misapprehension, together with Prussia's policy toward Poland and her unwillingness to ratify the Belgian treaty without Russia, led in part to poorer relations with Great Britain and France. Likewise, the restricted position of Prussia made it seem to some as if Berlin were following a policy of weakness. In fact, Prussia probably made as positive a contribution to the affairs of Europe and to her position in Germany as was possible given its limited resources and even more limited room to maneuver. Bernstorff probably cooperated with Great Britain and France to the maximum degree possible, given the political realities and prejudices that existed in Berlin.

The deterioration in Prussia's relations with the West was deepened by a series of diplomatic crises after 1832, which are beyond the scope of this study. However, Prussia's position in Europe was also affected by its failure to respond to the changes in the political spectrum in Europe brought about by the revolutions of 1830 and the Reform Bill of 1832. A symptom of this failure became evident in May 1832 when Bernstorff was forced to resign as Minister of Foreign Affairs. He was replaced by Ancillon, and Eichhorn's influence within the ministry was severely restricted. But these changes in personnel were not primarily connected with Prussia's European policy; they were directly related to serious disagreements within the government over the nature of Prussia's German policy.

---

80. Karl Schwartz, *Leben des Generals Carl von Clausewitz*, 2:363.

*Chapter 8*

✠ ✠ ✠ ✠ ✠ ✠ ✠ ✠ ✠ ✠ ✠ ✠ ✠ ✠ ✠

# The German Revolutions
# of 1830

In 1830, popular uprisings and revolts occurred in a number of the German states. The objective of most of these movements was the introduction of some kind of constitutional government and the alleviation of social and economic distress, which was particularly pronounced in the fall of that year. If Prussia followed Metternich's advice and joined with Austria in suppressing the rebellions, it would be impossible for Berlin to project the progressive image in Germany that some members of the government desired. In all likelihood, it would be difficult to complete the *Zollverein* in the immediate future and to enhance Prussia's political influence inside the Confederation. On the other hand, the spread of political agitation could affect the stability of Germany, its military capability, and the domestic political situation in Prussia. Thus, Prussia could neither disregard nor repress these political movements; some middle path had to be found.

## BERNSTORFF'S POLICY TOWARD POLITICAL
## UNREST IN GERMANY

In the summer of 1830, an economic crisis caused by a poor harvest and some long-standing and bitter political disputes, usually caused by the ruler's irresponsible conduct or anachronistic practices, created an environment that was particularly susceptible to political upheaval in several German states. The revolutions in France and Belgium did not cause the revolts in Germany, but they did give greater confidence to those who were critical of the existing regimes and made the authorities feel more insecure. They increased the likelihood that a local incident could develop into a major political crisis. As a result of this dynamic, popular revolts in Brunswick, Electoral Hesse, Saxony, and Hanover led in time to the establishment of some form of constitutional government and the energy displayed by parliamentary bodies in southern Germany increased.

Conservative German statesmen, who naturally feared that revolution was about to sweep Germany, contemplated how to best suppress the new movements and control the spread of political activism. On 18 September 1830, without any prior consultation with Berlin, Münch-Bellinghausen told the federal envoys in Frankfurt that Austria advocated a commitment by the Diet to enable the Confederation to intervene militarily in the member states to quell revolutionary activity.[1] This approach was immediately opposed by Bavaria and Prussia.

In an instruction to Nagler, Bernstorff set forth his attitude toward the revolutionary disturbances in Germany. The Austrian government, he said, wanted to know how the power of the Confederation could be strengthened to counter the evil influences of political upheaval. Although this was important, Bernstorff said that he was even more interested in why these revolts occurred in the first place. The answer to that question, he argued, might provide guidance on how the Confederation should act. The actual violence in German communities had been committed by those who were out of work, were homeless, or had criminal tendencies. The central issue was why did sensible, dutiful citizens support these people? Why did they become infected with the spirit of revolution? Bernstorff contended that a detailed and comprehensive examination of this question showed that these people did not support revolutionary causes merely because of the influence of events in Paris or Brussels, as Austria argued. In reality, these events would have never affected those elements of society unless a serious discontent had already existed in certain parts of Germany, a dissatisfaction frequently caused by archaic governmental institutions, by "the blundering and injudicious administrative practices of individual officials and leaders," or even in a few cases by the regrettable behavior of the sovereign. On the basis of this analysis, Bernstorff believed that the *Bund* should approach the question of intervention in the internal affairs of the German states with great caution.

1. Viktor Bibl, *Metternich in neuer Beleuchtung,* p. 106.

Many governments might find it necessary to make political concessions to popular forces, and these should be tolerated unless they came into conflict with the legal arrangements of the Confederation. He indicated that the degree to which a government wished to satisfy certain desires of its subjects depended solely on that government's "evaluation of the domestic situation inside its country." If a government were forced to make concessions that brought it into conflict with the Confederation, then it could bring the matter before the Diet. The *Bund* should only take action if invited to do so by the state involved, and even then, Bernstorff emphasized, the moral impression of military action by the *Bund*, not the actual size of its forces, would have the greatest impact on political events.[2] Prussia was clearly not interested in a counterrevolutionary crusade throughout Germany, although Bernstorff did believe that all member states should be prepared to act in case of violent internal disorders.

The result of the negotiations at Frankfurt was a compromise. In a resolution on 21 October 1830, the Diet announced that the German states were to be prepared to assist their neighbors by military force; if requested by a member, a state could intervene directly without prior sanction by the Diet. The remaining laws of the Confederation were to be diligently enforced, especially those dealing with press censorship, and governments were asked to make a special effort to keep the Diet fully informed concerning domestic political disturbances. Prussia and Bavaria softened the repressive nature of the resolution by noting that certain governments had often created their own difficulties by their failure to establish representative assemblies as specified in Article XIII of the federal constitution and they had the resolution expressly state that governments should attempt to alleviate the legitimate grievances of their subjects.[3] Prussia's support of Bavaria in the call for the implementation of Article XIII created suspicion in the mind of at least one Austrian diplomat. Count Kaspar von Spiegel, Austria's minister to Munich, told Metternich that Ludwig and his foreign minister, Count Joseph Ludwig von Armansperg, both of whom strove to adhere as closely as possible to Berlin, were over-

2. Bernstorff to Nagler, 6 October 1830 (copy), enclosed in Bernstorff to Arnim, 6 October 1830, ZSA Me, Rep. 23.13 (Darmstadt), Nr. 242.

3. Heinrich von Treitschke, *History of Germany in the Nineteenth Century,* 5:258–259; and Ernst Rudolf Huber, *Deutsche Verfassungsgeschichte seit 1789,* 2:152.

joyed with Prussia's position "and think they see in it a glimpse of the political system whereby Prussia will be placed at the head of the movement of constitutional states in Germany."[4] This political idea, sensed by Spiegel in the fall of 1830, would be a central theme in German affairs for the next two years.

Bernstorff's nonbelligerent attitude toward revolutionary activity and his reluctance to involve Prussia in a repressive campaign were evident in the way he handled the numerous crises that developed in the medium- and smaller-sized states of Germany. When the Prince of Schwarzburg-Sonderhausen requested Prussian military assistance to maintain order inside his principality, Bernstorff refused, explaining that Prussia's military responsibilities were already extensive. The Prince was advised to take his case to the Confederation.[5] A similar request from Weimar was also rejected.[6] On the other hand, units of the Prussian army did assist in quelling demonstrations in the principalities of Reuss-Schleitz and Reuss-Ebersbach, and Prussian troops would be part of a reserve unit that could aid a mobile antirevolutionary force made up by the Confederation out of troops from Nassau, Bavaria, Baden, and Hesse-Darmstadt.[7] But the most interesting example of Prussia's policy toward revolution in Germany is the case of Brunswick.

Few German states were as vulnerable as Brunswick to the revolutionary impulse that swept Europe in 1830, and few demonstrate more conclusively Bernstorff's belief that domestic political tensions, not events in Paris and Belgium, were the prime causes of unrest in Germany. The source of Brunswick's difficulties stretched back for more than a decade. By 1830, the stupidity and obstinacy of the ruling prince, Duke Charles, had succeeded in antagonizing most of the population of the duchy, including the aristocratic officials of his own government. In early September, following a bread riot, there was a widespread call for the reconvening

---

4. Spiegel to Metternich, 15 October 1830, Anton Chroust, ed., *Gesandtschafts-berichte aus München, 1814–1848: Abteilung II*, 36:281.

5. Frederick William to the Prince of Schwarzburg-Sonderhausen, 6 October 1830 (drafted by Bernstorff), ZSA Me, AAI, Rep. 5, Nr. 604.

6. Bernstorff to Grosshzg. Sachsen-Weimar Staatsministerium, 15 October 1830, ibid.

7. Martin Kitchen, *A Military History of Germany*, p. 71; and Johann Gustav Droysen, "Zur Geschichte der preussischen Politik in den Jahren 1830–1832," pp. 42–43.

of the Estates, and, on 7 September, the ducal palace was attacked by demonstrators. Although Charles managed to escape, government troops stood by passively while the building was ransacked and subsequently burned. In most ways, the Brunswick uprising was not a modern liberal-democratic revolution, but rather an attempt by traditionally constituted classes to defend their rights against an irresponsible and immature ruler.[8]

With Charles out of the country, the Brunswick *Landtag* met on its own authority and decided to send emissaries to Berlin and Hanover to gain political support. It also asked William, Charles's brother, to take over the reins of government. Promised Berlin's support (William was a major in the Prussian guards), he arrived in Brunswick on 10 September.[9] The more liberal officials in the government told him that the uprising had not been a true political revolution, but was directed solely against Charles. The loyalty of the people to the Guelphs was still unbroken. Convinced by these arguments and seeing that order had already been reestablished, William decided to stay in Brunswick as the representative of his dynasty, although his legal position was as yet undefined.[10] On 20 September, he was empowered by his brother to act as his Governor-General in Brunswick and to exercise governmental authority. The *Landtag*, however, declared that Charles was incapable of ruling and invited William to assume full authority. On 28 September 1830, when William announced his assumption of the position of *Statthalter,* he referred to neither mandate, but based his authority on his rights as the heir to the throne. This act, although supported by the ministry in Brunswick, further complicated William's constitutional status.[11]

Meanwhile Charles appealed for the support of the powers. He soon discovered, however, that no help could be expected from London, the German Confederation, or Austria. Frederick William refused Charles's request that Prussian troops occupy the duchy and added that Charles

---

8. For the revolution in Brunswick and its causes, see Huber, *Deutsche Verfassungsgeschichte,* 2:46–62; Treitschke, *History of Germany,* 5:117–150; Otto Böse, *Karl II, Herzog zu Braunschweig und Lüneburg;* the same author's earlier dissertation, *Die Enthronung des Herzogs Karl II von Braunschweig;* and Margaret Kruse Wallenberger, "The Revolutions of the 1830s and the Rise of German Nationalism."

9. Huber, *Deutsche Verfassungsgeschichte,* 2:54; and Böse, *Karl II,* p. 139.

10. Böse, *Karl II,* pp. 138–142.

11. Huber, *Deutsche Verfassungsgeschichte,* 2:55.

alone was responsible for the loss of his state and must accept the consequences. As might be expected, Bernstorff was also opposed to Charles's demands.[12] Frustrated at every turn, Charles decided to reestablish his power on his own by armed might. In November, as the confused defender of legitimist principles, he made a pathetic attempt to reassert his authority. He received no support in the duchy, and the undertaking failed miserably. Its only result was to further discredit Charles in the eyes of the governments of Europe.

Berlin could not support Charles's cause if it really desired to see the introduction of sound, responsible government—an essential ingredient for political stability in Germany. Therefore, even before Charles attempted to regain power by force, the Prussian government had already concluded that William's position had to be legitimized. Seizing on a suggestion by Münster, Berlin proposed that the agnates of the Guelph house, with the permission of the *Bund,* reestablish "competent authority" in Brunswick. With the aid of Eichhorn and the Prussian foreign ministry, the agnates announced to the *Bund* on 10 March that, because of Charles's incapacity to rule, William was the legal ruler of Brunswick. To make this decision a political reality, Eichhorn drafted the patent of 20 April 1831, which was used by William to proclaim his formal assumption of ducal authority.[13] Thus, Prussia took positive steps to create a sensible political system in Brunswick, even though, in a way, it was acknowledging the illegal activities of the inhabitants of the duchy.

Austria soon opposed Prussia's efforts to have William recognized as the legitimate prince. Metternich disapproved of the agnates' decision, which belonged, he said, to "the most deplorable products of the present turbulent times." It was the work of liberals who wished to cripple the principle of legitimacy and had used the agnates as tools "to promote such outrageous crimes." Austria's task, he told Münch-Bellinghausen, was "to destroy this ploy spun from afar."[14] Metternich did not deny that Charles was incapable of ruling the country, but he did not wish to see an actual change in rulership brought about by popular action. He preferred a regency that would ignore the question of dynastic succession. In May, the federal Diet voted on the 10 March 1831 pronouncement of the

12. Böse, *Karl II,* pp. 143–170; and Bernstorff to Wittgenstein, 22 October 1829, GSA PKB, Rep. 192, Wittgenstein, VI, 6, 1–2.

13. See Treitschke's colorful, but prejudiced, account in his *History of Germany,* 5:141–142; and Böse, *Karl II,* pp. 199–200, 206–207.

14. Böse, *Karl II,* p. 205.

agnates. The competition for votes between Austria and Prussia was intense, and, in the end, after considerable confusion, Austria prevailed by a vote of nine to eight.[15] Subsequently, at the instigation of Münch-Bellinghausen and over Prussia's protest, the Diet also censured William for establishing his rule without federal sanction. This measure also passed by a vote of nine to eight. Rarely in the early history of the *Bund* had conflict between Austria and Prussia been so apparent as in the case of the Brunswick succession.[16] Metternich clearly attached great importance to the vote at Frankfurt. As he wrote to the Austrian president: "In case we end up in the minority, the most lamentable result will occur, namely, the *Bund* will have formally sanctioned by its decision a violation of the principle of legitimacy, whose *'inkorrektheit'* was absolutely clear."[17]

The Prussian government made several efforts to try to get the agnates' resolution reconsidered and laboriously built up a favorable majority inside the Diet. But political and legalistic complications prevented the matter from being brought to a vote, and William's status remained uncertain for more than a year. Finally, after lengthy negotiations, Prussia and Austria arrived at a suitable compromise in April 1832, and, on 12 July 1832, the Diet officially recognized William as a voting member of the Confederation. However, it passed over the issue of his accession to the throne, thus not introducing any legal recognition of a violation of legitimacy. Metternich's maneuvering could not hide the reality of the events in Brunswick: The new ruler, who had the support of the populace, was installed legally without any formal abdication. As Ernst Huber has written: "Brunswick was the only German state in the nineteenth century in which a popular uprising succeeded in expelling a prince by force and finally also removing him legally." Voluntary abdications took place in 1848 in Bavaria and Austria, but "the removal of a prince by revolution . . . only occurred in Brunswick. The overthrow of Duke Charles of Brunswick is therefore one of the constitutionally significant events in the constitutional era in Germany."[18] In October 1832, William issued a new representative constitution no longer based on the old Estates.

15. Ibid., p. 208; Treitschke, *History of Germany,* 5:143; Ancillon to Maltzahn, 12 May 1831, ZSA Me, Rep. 81, Wien I, Nr. 124; and Metternich to Trauttmanns-dorff, 8 May 1831, HHSA, Stk., Preussen, Karton 139.

16. See, for example, Ancillon to Schöler, 11 June 1831, ZSA Me, Rep. 81, Petersburg I, Nr. 124.

17. Böse, *Karl II,* p. 208.

18. Huber, *Deutsche Verfassungsgeschichte,* 2:56.

Prussia had not been passive in these developments. Berlin's policy toward Brunswick demonstrated that the foreign ministry was not interested in blindly supporting the concept of legitimacy. Legitimacy was a desirable principle, but was not absolute or universal. Where, as in France, Belgium, or Brunswick, it stood in opposition to the needs of the state and society, it became irrelevant. Charles's immature and disruptive rule was anathema to Bernstorff and Eichhorn; in their eyes, legitimate rule meant responsible rule. Metternich, perhaps because of the insecurity of the political system that he served, chose to define legitimacy more rigidly. He resisted Bernstorff's attempts to encourage orderly progress through sound government reestablished on a new basis that had been approved by the German community.

Although the political unrest in Electoral Hesse, Saxony, and Hanover did not directly involve Prussia, it demonstrates Bernstorff's continued reluctance to take repressive measures against constitutional movements. In Electoral Hesse, the Elector, William I, had promised that, after 1814, a constitution based on the old representative Estates, which had become defunct during the Napoleonic era, would be drawn up. However, in 1816, negotiations with the *Landtag* led to conflict with William I, and no constitution was granted. Although his successor, William II, who ascended the throne in 1821, carried out some administrative reforms, he also imposed an oppressive financial burden on his subjects. Furthermore, entry into the Central German Commercial Union in 1828 led Electoral Hesse into a bitter tariff war with Prussia. The trade of the country was crippled, and, by 1830, social and economic unrest was widespread. In addition, William had become involved with a certain Emilie Ortlöpp, to whom he gave the title Countess Reichenbach. For many people, this affair and the embarrassment it caused the Electress, Princess Augusta of Prussia, seemed to symbolize the ruler's corruption and incompetence. In the late summer of 1830, William traveled to Vienna in an attempt to have the electoral title granted to Countess Reichenbach. When he returned from this unsuccessful mission, he found that the revolutionary events in France, Belgium, and Brunswick had had effect. The population was greatly agitated and expressed its opposition to the Countess. On 15 September, William agreed to convene the representative Estates.

In the countryside, peasants stormed manor houses and burned feudal records; at Hanau, the customs house was destroyed by a mob—an act of violence brought on by the disastrous consequences of the tariff war with

Prussia. With difficulty, the electoral regime succeeded in reestablishing order throughout the state, making its request for federal troops unnecessary. In October, the Estates met and, under the leadership of Sylvester Jordan, drew up a remarkably modern and liberal constitution. It was accepted by the Elector and went into effect on 5 January 1831.

But, just as the political situation seemed stabilized, Countess Reichenbach once again became the center of controversy. The citizens of Kassel refused to allow her to reenter the city, and William transferred his court to Hanau. The new *Landtag* then demanded that he either abandon the Countess and return to Kassel, or lay down the reins of government. When William refused both alternatives, the *Landtag* made the Electoral Prince, Frederick William, co-regent and empowered him to run the country. Numerous complications involving the Elector's mistress, a new mistress of the co-regent, and repeated conflict with the representative assembly plagued electoral politics for most of the decade.[19]

Bernstorff's attitude toward the events in Hesse was consistent with his policy toward Brunswick. On 12 October 1830, he wrote to the Prussian minister in Kassel, "We deplore the necessity to recognize that the present excesses of the populace are the inevitable outcome of the past excesses of the ruler." He agreed that the Elector had been forced by his subjects to share political power with them, but he concluded that "these concessions have been made, and it is inconceivable they can be revoked without the disintegration of all remaining social relationships. The universal wish must be that the path now entered shall lead as speedily and quietly as possible to the goal of firm legal order."[20]

In the spring of 1831, the federal Diet began deliberations on the new electoral constitution. Metternich instructed Münch-Bellinghausen to block its guarantee by the *Bund* and to declare that Austria would not accept it as a legal constitution. When the Diet took up the matter in May 1831, Bavaria, Württemberg, and especially Prussia opposed Austria's position. The foreign ministry in Berlin advised Vienna that, by attacking the electoral constitution, it was missing an opportunity to establish better relations among the various states of Germany and that its attitude would lead to an undesirable division of opinion between the constitutional and

19. Treitschke, *History of Germany,* 5:150–170; Huber, *Deutsche Verfassungsgeschichte,* 2:62–76; and Wallenberger, "Revolutions of the 1830s," pp. 215–264.
20. Treitschke, *History of Germany,* 5:155.

the nonconstitutional states. Despite this admonition, Metternich did not change his policy, and the *Bundestag* took no action on the constitution. However, this had no consequences for the operation of the constitution inside the Electorate.[21] As in the case of Brunswick, Bernstorff was willing to accept the reality of a new political system in Hesse, and he wanted it to be joined promptly with the larger political community of Germany. Metternich, on the other hand, resorted to short-sighted, legalistic devices in his attempt to stave off the full recognition of more progressive forms of government in Germany. Even when his policies were successful, Metternich's victories had a negative and hollow tone and contributed nothing to the political growth of Germany.

Until 1830, Saxony had retained the political structure of a German state of the *ancien régime*. Frederick August III, a Catholic ruling a Protestant population, was closely aligned with Austria and relied entirely on the ultraconservative leader of the privy council, Count Einsiedel, for advice. The old *Landtag* was still in existence, but it was dominated by prelates, the high aristocracy, and the urban patriciate. When Frederick August died in 1827 and was succeeded by his seventy-two-year-old brother, Anton, many hoped that the new King would permit more responsive government; however, the old policies were continued. As a result, progressive members of the aristocracy and the bourgeoisie begin to agitate for reform. Demonstrations took place in Leipzig, Dresden, and other communities in September 1830. The goal of the agitation was to force the replacement of Anton by the younger and more progressive Prince Frederick August. What began as a movement with considerable support from the middle and lower classes was soon taken over by the senior bureaucracy under the leadership of Bernard August von Lindenau. The King capitulated before this moderate reformist group. He dismissed Einsiedel and named Frederick August as co-regent. The promulgation of the constitution of 4 September 1831 represented the victory of a reformist bureaucracy over the *altständische* forces in Saxony and gave the state political arrangements modeled on those of the south German states.[22]

Bernstorff was critical of the events in Saxony. He felt that the government had not demonstrated much vigor in the face of popular upheaval,

21. L. F. Ilse, *Die Politik der beiden Grossmächte und der Bundesversammlung in der kurhessische Verfassungsfrage vom 1830 bis 1860*, p. 15.

22. Treitschke, *History of Germany*, 5:170–183; Huber, *Deutsche Verfassungsgeschichte*, 2:76–83; and Wallenberger, "Revolutions of the 1830s," pp. 174–214.

and he believed that there was little justification for the revolt.[23] As he later told Jordan, "The rising in the duchy of Brunswick was the outcome of oppression, and that in Hesse finds its explanation in the accumulated errors and gross injustice committed by the government, but for the Saxon troubles there is hardly any excuse and still less a reason."[24] This attitude is curious in view of the archaic structure of the Saxon state and Bernstorff's usual desire to see government administration meet the needs of the public. Perhaps it can be partially explained by his lack of detailed knowledge about Saxon affairs. For several years prior to 1830, he had been intimately involved in the problems of Brunswick and Hesse, but had not concerned himself with Saxony. His attitude, however, also demonstrates a narrow approach to politics; he was concerned with the rule of law. In the case of Saxony in 1830, the King had not violated accepted political practices within the state, and thus, in Bernstorff's eyes, there was no legitimate cause for revolt. Although he disapproved of the Saxon uprising, Bernstorff still opposed any interference by neighboring states in Saxony's internal affairs.[25] Later, Bernstorff rejected Metternich's proposed intervention plan, noting that the government under Lindenau, not the people, had carried out the institutional changes in the state.[26] Thus, even in Saxony, where he felt the actions of the population were unwarranted, Bernstorff resisted any attempt to use coercive measures to suppress a constitutional movement. With Electoral Hesse and Saxony, this approach may have seemed all the more advantageous; the new regimes were favorably inclined toward Berlin and soon begin negotiations for entry into the *Zollverein*.

For the most part, political agitation in Hanover was subdued and did not attract substantial attention from Prussia. In the post-Napoleonic period, Hanover remained strongly dominated by the aristocracy. Led by the experienced Count Münster, they wished to continue the *altständische* system that had long prevailed in the state. Opposed to them was a more reform-oriented group composed of enlightened bureaucrats such as Rehberg and progressive conservatives such as Stüve. In the fall of 1830, scattered unrest occurred in the towns and countryside. Because Hanover

---

23. Bernstorff to Maltzahn, 28 October 1830, ZSA Me, Rep. 81, Wien I, Nr. 142.
24. Treitschke, *History of Germany*, 5:177.
25. Bernstorff to Jordan, 24 October 1830, ZSA Me, AAI, Rep. 5, Nr. 604.
26. Huber, *Deutsche Verfassungsgeschichte*, 2:84–92; and Treitschke, *History of Germany*, 5:177.

was ruled in absentia from London by King William IV of England, Münster was the target of these demonstrations. On 8 January 1831, a serious revolt led by lecturers, students, and townspeople resulted in a takeover of the town of Göttingen. Five days later, 7,000 troops retook the town without resistance, but the government felt that the uprisings were symptomatic of a groundswell of discontent that could threaten the entire state. As a result, William IV replaced Münster with the more moderate Ludwig von Ompteda. Long negotiations with the existing *Landtag* finally led to the promulgation of the constitution of 26 September 1833.[27]

Prussian involvement in Hanoverian affairs was never required, but when Maltzahn, the Prussian minister to Hanover, arrived in the capital after the fall of Münster to observe the proceedings of the *Landtag,* he noted that rumors were being spread that he had been sent to support the Hanoverian government and to arrange for military assistance should further unrest occur. Maltzahn corrected this false impression. Prussia was supportive of the Hanoverian government, but he made it clear that Berlin had no blind affection for the old and the traditional and did not wish to support "obviously faulty institutions." Maltzahn believed that it was in Prussia's "higher political interests" to support sensible progress; this was a role that would produce many dividends and "would necessarily make Prussia the moral leader of Germany."[28] Eichhorn, substituting for Bernstorff, naturally agreed with these sentiments and reiterated that Maltzahn must counter the incorrect view that Prussia "in any way opposed the natural development of the [state] in accordance with the true necessities of the times and the wise reform of internal institutions by other governments."[29] Thus, in Hanover, as in the other three states, Berlin made known its willingness to tolerate the introduction of representative institutions that were consistent with the principles of reform conservatism.

While Prussia's policy toward the revolutionary unrest in Germany in 1830 was a reflection of the moderate reformist political philosophy influential in Berlin, it also was determined by the requirements of the European crisis. Unity among the German states, particularly in southern

---

27. Huber, *Deutsche Verfassungsgeschichte,* 2:84–92; Treitschke, *History of Germany,* 5:183–203.

28. Maltzahn to Bernstorff, 15 May 1831, ZSA Me, AAI, Rep. 1, Nr. 1465.

29. Eichhorn to Maltzahn, 9 June 1831, ibid.

Germany, was needed to cope successfully with a French invasion. As we shall see, the suspicions that the constitutional states in the south had for Austria's conservative policies limited their willingness to collaborate with Vienna militarily. Counterrevolutionary policies by Prussia would arouse similar suspicions, and Prussia had much more at stake in western Germany than Austria did and, therefore, was more dependent on the participation of the other German armies. It has often been stated that the unrest in Germany in 1830 restricted Prussia's ability to act militarily in the European crisis. This may be so, but, as we have seen, Prussia had already decided not to intervene in the affairs of France and the Netherlands before any significant unrest had occurred in Germany. There may be more validity to the reverse of that assertion, namely, that preoccupation with the events in Europe encouraged Prussia to take a tolerant attitude toward political change in Germany. But this attitude was not purely the product of fear. Many officials in Berlin might have regretted the manner in which the new political arrangements were brought into being, but they recognized the need for innovation.

## TOWARD THE SIX ARTICLES

Although Metternich received little cooperation from Bernstorff in suppressing revolution or moderate reform in Germany, he did not give up. In September 1831, after nearly a year of discussions in Vienna between Metternich, Maltzahn, Bray (the Bavarian minister), and Blomberg (of Württemberg), and after Frederick William had agreed to future bilateral talks between Austria and Prussia on German affairs, the Austrian Chancellor formally proposed that Prussia and Austria take measures as they had done in 1819 to suppress the work of German liberals and French propagandists. In a dispatch to Trauttmannsdorff, he explained that the revolutionary unrest of the times was the product of destructive political developments in Germany over the last fifty years. Specifically, he mentioned the dissolution of traditional bonds between sovereign and subject, the effects of the Rhenish Confederation on Germany, the implementation of *landständische* constitutions, and the attempt of rulers to placate liberals in order to be popular—all made even worse by the moral sickness of the age. As a result, some German princes no longer retained full control over their states. These circumstances called for new and extraordinary action by the *Bund*.[30]

Bernstorff replied to this proposal in late September. He agreed that the situation in Germany was disturbing, but was adamant in stating that it would be improper for the two great German powers to impose counter-revolutionary measures on the other German states. This approach could be resented by the German states and could draw undesirable attention to Prussia and Austria from the European powers. Thus, unlike 1819, Bernstorff refused to participate in a counterrevolutionary crusade. His sense of judgment and toleration had returned. Not only did he refuse to endorse Metternich's suggestion, he took the opportunity to set forth a more progressive approach to the problems of unrest in Germany. The German governments (he used the word *Regierungen*) must develop a sense of trust in one another. This was the key to political stability in Germany, and this had been the goal of Prussian policy in customs and commercial affairs. Prussia was willing to discuss Austria's concerns, but it was essential to understand that the cause of the problem lay in the nature of the organization of Germany. It was not necessary to review the genesis of the *Bund;* the task at hand was to work with facts and real-life situations in order to confront the future in a practical manner. The German Confederation had an abundance of repressive laws, Bernstorff said, but some princes refused to enforce them. New coercive regulations or individual action to crush revolutionary activity would only have negative results. The proper approach was to create a voluntary desire to enforce existing statutes.[31]

Metternich's reply to Bernstorff took a characteristic form. After agreeing with everything Bernstorff said, he proceeded to hedge his position on nearly every significant point. For example, while he acknowledged that the laws of 1819 and 1820 were sufficient for the situation, he felt that it still might be advisable to supplement them with additional legislation. Furthermore, he emphasized that he certainly did not contemplate an attack on the constitutions of the member states, except, it should be noted, when they had become a battleground for political factions or exceeded their original authority. Noting Bernstorff's use of the word *Regierungen*

---

30. Metternich to Trauttmannsdorff, 5 September 1831, HHSA, Stk., Preussen, Karton 140, f. 81–86.

31. Bernstorff to Maltzahn, 26 September 1831, ZSA Me, Rep. 75A, Nr. 457.

instead of "princes" in his statement, Metternich went on to argue that a serious difference existed between the cabinets of the various states and their sovereigns—the governments tended not to comprehend the seriousness of the situation or, out of error, compromised with the forces of revolution. Austria advocated close and direct connections with the princes themselves and efforts to help them to regain their lost powers.[32] Here was a clear delineation of the contrasting approaches of the two men. Bernstorff was willing to work constructively with the present situation, deplorable though it might be, in an effort to keep the process of change under control and to maintain the authority of constituted government. (By "government," of course, he meant well-informed, elitist officials such as himself.) Metternich, on the other hand, had nothing to offer except an additional dose of restrictive measures, which attempted to freeze political life in Germany. He emphasized the concept of princely rule because the princes were easier for him to control and because rule based on such authority would be less susceptible to policies that attempted to respond to the perceived needs of the times.

With the positions of the two governments unresolved, discussions on the best way to suppress liberal tendencies in Germany continued in Vienna between Metternich and Maltzahn. As a result of these talks, Metternich ultimately proposed that a number of German princes meet with the representatives of Austria and Prussia to decide what action should be taken by the Confederation to quell revolutionary activity. Such a conference, he said, would remove these rulers from the undesirable influence of their own governments.[33] However, Bernstorff told Trauttmannsdorff that such a meeting was ill-advised. It would be preferable, he said, for Austria and Prussia to agree on what measures should be taken and then to negotiate these results individually with the various states. Trauttmannsdorff pointed out that a great difference of outlook existed between most of the princes of Germany and their governments and that the isolation of the princes from their own cabinets would enable the negotiations to proceed with greater ease. Bernstorff immediately attacked this concept. "I cannot hide the fact," he said, "that

32. Metternich to Trauttmannsdorff, 9 October 1831, HHSA, Stk., Preussen, Karton 140, f. 159-175.

33. Diary entry of 30 October 1831 in Grafen Anton Prokesch von Osten, *Aus den Tagebüchern, 1830–1834*, p. 107.

I view this method of negotiation as a highly dangerous game. The princes in this way will be separated from their normal advisors, they will be isolated, placed in a very equivocal (*schlüpfrige*) position, and may be easily embarrassed. . . . This method of direct intercourse with the princes appears to me, as I have said, extremely dangerous."[34] He also expressed to Arnim and Maltzahn his opposition to another meeting similar to Carlsbad. He opposed any forcible suspensions of constitutional arrangements because he felt that constitutional commitments made by the German sovereigns should be honored. The existing laws of the Confederation should be enforced, but any illegal activity by the *Bund* would invite foreign intervention and internal chaos.[35]

In a lengthy *Denkschrift,* Bernstorff offered Metternich some of his own ideas on how to create greater stability in Germany. Again focusing on the lack of unity among the German princes as a cause of unrest in Germany, he suggested an oblique and partial solution to the problem. To make the German princes more responsible and to educate the German public in the ways of federal politics, he proposed the full publication of the protocols and proceedings of the federal Diet immediately after the close of each session. Since 1829, Bernstorff had opposed keeping the discussions at Frankfurt a secret. He felt that secrecy encouraged the misinterpretation of the affairs of the Confederation and especially Prussia's role in them. However, his effort to abandon this policy had always been blocked by Münch-Bellinghausen. He again confronted Metternich's objections to the constitutional arrangements of the German states. Although Austria and Prussia might well have constituted these governments differently if they had been involved, he strongly believed that the two powers should do nothing illegal to disturb the operation of these new political systems. Finally, he indicated that the Prussian government, like that in Vienna, was concerned about the influence of foreign periodicals and over the misuse of the press inside Germany. In fact, Berlin was presently examining its censorship policies and would communicate its ideas to the Austrian government at a later date.[36]

Bernstorff's attempt to create more rational institutional arrangements

34. Trauttmannsdorff to Metternich, 24 October 1831, HHSA, Stk., Preussen, Karton 138.

35. Bernstorff to Arnim and Bernstorff to Maltzahn (copy), 1 November 1831, ZSA Me, Rep. 23.13 (Darmstadt), Nr. 242.

36. Bernstorff to Maltzahn, 6 November 1831, ZSA Me, Rep. 75A, Nr. 457.

in Germany was a logical extension of enlightened bureaucratic absolutism at home. Giving greater publicity to the proceedings at the Diet would obviously work to Prussia's advantage. Public knowledge of the Diet's operations might make that body more responsive to Germany's needs, but, in any case, publication of its proceedings would demonstrate that Prussia was not a blind supporter of reaction or opposed to constitutional government per se, but simply desired greater efficiency in the institutions of Germany. Bernstorff wanted educated Germans to become better informed about the politics of the Confederation. He was not afraid to expose the federal policies of Prussia to public scrutiny because he had a basic confidence in the beneficial nature of Prussia's approach to German affairs. Although the hope that Metternich would approve such a proposal was entirely unrealistic, there is no evidence that Bernstorff realized the futility of his suggestion. Perhaps he mistakenly expected the Kings of Bavaria and Württemberg to support this measure; perhaps his proposal was simply a gesture, or possibly he was just naïve.

Metternich was infuriated by Bernstorff's refusal to agree to his plan for a conference of princes. He even went so far as to threaten to give the left bank of the Rhine to France and to reconstitute Germany entirely.[37] In his attempt to get Ludwig and William to agree to the talks that Bernstorff opposed, Metternich described the threat of Prussian and south German liberals to princely rule in Germany.[38] This scare tactic met with some success, and, as a result, the two monarchs agreed to discussions in Vienna.[39] By December, Frederick William wanted closer relations with Austria, and Bernstorff finally agreed that, if Austria were willing to proceed on the basis of his own last proposal, Berlin would consent to direct discussions with the monarchs of Bavaria and Württemburg or their designated representatives.[40] Metternich edited out the objectionable

37. Diary entry of 29 October 1831 in Prokesch von Osten, *Aus den Tagebüchern,* p. 106. At Frankfurt, the British envoy reported on the same possibility. Cartwright to Palmerston, 22 October 1831, PRO F.O. 30/35.

38. Metternich to Wrede, 15 November 1831, Bibl, *Metternich in neuer Beleuchtung,* pp. 268–270; also Metternich to Spiegel, 15 November 1831, ibid., p. 267n; and Robert D. Billinger, Jr., "Metternich's Policy toward the South German States, 1830–1834," pp. 150–152.

39. Wrede to Metternich, 24 November 1831, Bibl, *Metternich in neuer Beleuchtung,* p. 276; and Billinger, "Metternich's Policy," pp. 156–157.

40. Metternich to Wrede, 1 December 1831, Bibl, *Metternich in neuer Beleuchtung,* pp. 281–282.

portions of Bernstorff's last proposal, the memorandum of 25 November, including the provisions for publication of the full proceedings of the *Bundestag.* This was evidently done with Maltzahn's complicity. The edited *Denkschrift* was then presented to the south Germans as Prussia's proposal.[41] Predictably, in January, Maltzahn reported that Metternich opposed the publication of the Diet's full proceedings and would agree only to printing its decisions. Because the south Germans supported Metternich, he said, the protocol signed on 2 January 1832 by Metternich, Maltzahn, and Bray accepted Metternich's version.[42]

Metternich attacked Bernstorff's proposal in a letter written later in 1832 to Wittgenstein. The only argument, he said, that Berlin could muster in its support was "that journalists would be better informed. . . . There is already too much written, criticized, and polemicized in Germany; why would we want to sacrifice the German political congress—and what else is the *Bundestag*—to these elements."[43] But Metternich also felt that wider publicity might lead to attacks on the federal envoys from the representative bodies of the German states.[44] Bernstorff continued to reject these criticisms, but, by March, encountering numerous difficulties with other aspects of his policies, he dropped the idea and reluctantly agreed to the results of the ministerial negotiations in Vienna.[45]

The final outcome of the discussions in Vienna—not an innovation in the procedures of the Diet, but rather a restatement of conservative principles in the Six Articles—was adopted by the *Bundestag* on 28 June 1832. By April 1832, Bernstorff had capitulated to the Austrians on all essential points. However, by that time his position in Berlin had been entirely undermined; in a matter of weeks, he would be forced to resign as Minister of Foreign Affairs.[46] As Treitschke has pointed out, Metternich's original intention of restricting or even doing away with the new con-

41. Ibid., p. 158; and diary entry for 30 December 1831, Prokesch von Osten, *Aus den Tagebüchern,* p. 124.

42. Maltzahn to Bernstorff, 7 January 1832, ZSA Me, Rep. 75A, Nr. 457.

43. Metternich to Wittgenstein, 25 March 1832, HHSA, Stk., Preussen, Karton 146.

44. Maltzahn to Bernstorff, 11 January 1832, ZSA Me, Rep. 75A, Nr. 457.

45. Bernstorff to Maltzahn, 21 February and 3 March 1832, ibid; and Bibl, *Metternich in neuer Beleuchtung,* p. 164.

46. Maltzahn to Bernstorff, 27 March 1832, and Bernstorff to Maltzahn, 19 April 1832, ZSA Me, Rep. 75A, Nr. 457.

stitutional arrangements in Germany had been frustrated, but the Six Articles were nevertheless a resurrection of the spirit of the Carlsbad Decrees, something Bernstorff had originally opposed.

The articles stated that the authority of the monarch and of the German Confederation was clearly superior to that of the representative assemblies in all respects, and they authorized the creation of a special committee of the federal Diet to examine any encroachment by legislative bodies on the Confederation's prerogatives. Even if these articles were innocuous and, in most cases, self-evident restatements of monarchical principles (to paraphrase Treitschke), they did inaugurate a period of conflict between monarch and legislature in several German states and of the reapplication of strict censorship to some of the most prestigous liberal publications of the times. The reaction that followed the Hambach Festival accentuated this move toward ultraconservatism.

Thus, political developments that might have led to a closer relationship between governments and the articulate elements in society had been blunted. The perception, indeed the reality, was that the age of the Carlsbad Decrees had returned. That this was in almost direct opposition to Bernstorff's intentions is demonstrated by an analysis of his most detailed response to the problems of political unrest in Germany—a document that not only discussed domestic upheaval and linked it to Prussia's international position, that not only laid down the major components of Prussia's German policy for the years 1830–1832, but also ultimately led to Bernstorff's fall from office.

## BERNSTORFF'S *Denkschrift* OF 29 JANUARY 1831

In a Cabinet Order dated 10 November 1830, Frederick William asked Bernstorff how internal peace could be maintained in Germany in the event of an unavoidable European war and, specifically, what Prussia should do to avoid the consequences of internal unrest in neighboring states. After some delay, Bernstorff sent his reply, drafted by Eichhorn, to the King. In this *Denkschrift,* he first reiterated his explanation of the causes of political unrest in Germany, which we have already examined.[47]

47. For a copy of this *Denkschrift,* see Bernstorff to Frederick William, 29

He then pointed out that this unrest was also brought about by the numerous tensions that were a natural result of the division of Germany into many political units and of the accompanying desire to create comprehensive, beneficial arrangements for the entire German community, a desire that had frequently been frustrated or only partially realized.

In view of all of this, the key to creating solid, popular support among the people for the governments of Germany in the event of war was the just handling of "the majority of those of education and property." It was essential that "this majority not remain neutral, but rather heartily agree with the policies of the government." This would only happen if they felt that the government was working for "the public welfare" in a way that was free of any partisan spirit. A war fought by the German states could not be a war of principles; only a war caused by the attack of the enemy would receive enough public support. Should an unavoidable conflict be forced on Germany, the allegiance of the people would depend on whether the German princes avoided creating mistrust among the people. Writers of talent and "sound convictions" should be won over to the state to the extent that their individual outlooks permitted. If they were given greater latitude in expressing their ideas, they could aid the task of government.

The establishment of common institutions for Germany—especially a comprehensive system of free trade and commerce—was also essential. The Duke of Saxe-Coburg-Gotha had said in an earlier paper that the *Bundestag* must turn its attention without delay to these kinds of matters. Bernstorff disagreed. It was possible that, within the confines of its present responsibilities, the *Bund* might be able to improve some of its federal functions, such as completing the organization of the federal army (obviously needed because of the European crisis), but, in general, it was unrealistic to expect the *Bund* to create new kinds of institutions for Germany. "The creation of a common system of customs and commerce for Germany," he said, "or any other kind of similar common and permanent institution is a problem whose solution the *Bund* will never be able to provide," unless it assumed a character dramatically different from the one it currently possessed. Unless one of the strongest federal states,

---

January 1831, GSA PKB, Rep. 192, Wittgenstein, VI, 3, 1.2.3.; it has also been published in C. Spielmann, "Regierungspräsident Karl von Ibell über die preussische Politik in den Jahren 1830 u. 1831," pp. 66–76.

namely, Prussia, could constitutionally exercise a greater influence in the *Bund* than it did, all attempts to establish institutions desirable for the common interest of Germany through the Confederation would be unsuccessful.

Fortunately, Bernstorff noted, Prussia had established, apart from the *Bund,* a means to create, by the mechanism of separate individual agreements, new conditions that would have been impossible to realize through the *Bund*. The possibilities of this path had been already demonstrated in the customs negotiations. The more the Prussian government obtained the trust of the other German governments, the more the German people would look to Berlin. It was Prussia's function to exert moral influence in Germany. This could be done "by steadfast adherence to justice and legality, through frankness and truth in all relations and by receptivity to all reforms that respond not to a haphazard clamor for new things, but to the intelligent recognition of the needs of the time." Bernstorff expected that the other German states, inspired by Prussia's example, would voluntarily imitate the Prussian model, thereby creating conditions that would maintain the peace and stability of Germany.

Ideally, the Confederation would undertake massive reform to increase German unity, thus enabling Prussia to exercise a stronger and more beneficial influence than was possible under the present system. But he did not believe that this goal could be achieved in the near future. Only with the passage of time and with the beneficial results of experience would the German governments no longer regard arrangements that were in the best interests of Germany as restrictions or reductions of their sovereignty. When they realized that such arrangements were in their own interests, then they would voluntarily move in that direction. Only then could the institutions of the Confederation be improved in accordance with the principles advocated by Prussia. It is clear that the King did not fully comprehend what Bernstorff was talking about. Perhaps his brief, bland, but approving answer to this important document partially misled Bernstorff into believing that this kind of approach was really possible.[48]

Bernstorff argued that Prussia should follow a policy of moderate reformism and should be especially attentive to the interests of those of education and property. A freer—though not totally free—press would enable individ-

48. Frederick William to Bernstorff, 22 March 1831, GSA PKB, Rep. 192, Wittgenstein, VI, 3, 1.2.3.

uals with sensible political views to express their ideas concerning the problems that faced the Prussian government and to counter unwarranted criticism of the state. No mention was made of representative institutions. Bernstorff's model was late eighteenth-century Denmark, which had successfully combined freedom of the press with an enlightened absolute monarchy. In addition to rallying the population behind the King so the state could fight with full energy if faced with a French attack, this approach also meant that Prussia could project a favorable image throughout Germany, which would increase its influence inside the Confederation.

There is only one rather insignificant mention of Austria in this lengthy document. The paper only deals with Prussia's leadership in Germany. Through a series of separate agreements, patterned on the customs negotiations, Prussia could take the lead in creating more rational institutions in Germany. The self-evident success of these arrangements, Bernstorff implied, would in time wear down the vigor with which the princes and governments of Germany defended their outdated forms of sovereignty. Eventually, a more unified whole under the leadership of Prussia would evolve. This new, more unified region would be better able to meet the needs of the German people and would more accurately reflect Prussia's true position within Germany. This *Denkschrift* was not anti-Austrian, but it is clear that the concept of Austro-Prussian dualism was largely irrelevant to its ideas.

Bernstorff's view of Germany's future development is admittedly vague as well as overly idealistic and rational. At first glance, it seems that such a scenario could have never succeeded. What would be the driving force behind this process? As Bernstorff envisioned it, practical benefits and moral energy would combine, developing momentum as it became more evident that the progressive interests of Prussia and Germany were the same. This is an uncertain process of development, but, on the other hand, change can take place as new conditions influence attitude. In the old Danish monarchy during the reform era of his father, Bernstorff had seen rational institutions created that were sensitive to the feelings and needs of a diverse population; these institutions had succeeded in binding Germans, Norwegians, and Danes together in a political and economic community. Only war had destroyed this federal monarchy. On the basis of his experience, it seemed entirely possible that similar institutions could link the various states of Germany into a more coherent and a more successful whole.

Judged by the standards of the Bismarckian era, Bernstorff's solution to the German question seems weak. But, today, we question the unity and coherence of Bismarck's German Empire, as well as its appropriateness for the European system. A more truly federal solution based on a strong, but not domineering, Prussia, brought together by functional needs, rather than national desires and military conquest, is an alternative that in retrospect deserves some attention.

Aside from speculative considerations, Bernstorff's *Denkschrift* has a more concrete meaning. First, it is not an unusual statement of how the German problem was viewed in the early 1830s. Second, in terms of domestic and German politics, it is an important example of reform conservatism in Prussia. Finally, it outlined the approach Berlin would follow with regard to the major aspects of Prussia's German policy: commercial and customs affairs, the question of the military organization of Germany, and the problem of the press and public opinion.

## THE ESTABLISHMENT OF THE *Zollverein*

In a way, the success of the customs negotiations in the late 1820s provided the inspiration for Bernstorff's entire *Denkschrift*. Berlin continued to assign a high priority to the conclusion of additional commercial agreements and still hoped for the creation of a *Zollverein* for all of Germany under Prussia's aegis. From 1830 to 1832, while the foreign ministry was deeply involved with the European crisis, it, together with the Ministry of Finance, continued to carry on a wide variety of discussions on commercial matters with a number of German states. As the British envoy to Frankfurt noted:

> The Prussian Government appears to be pressing forward its project for establishing one common System of Customs for the whole of Germany with incredible activity . . . No means are left untried to arrive at the result desired, which is the total Union of Germany in one commercial system; and Prussian agents are to be found everywhere actively engaged in furthering this project.[49]

Some of these discussions, such as the negotiations with Hesse-Kassel and Saxe-Weimar, were immediately successful; others became temporarily

49. Cartwright to Palmerston, 22 October 1831, PRO F.O. 30/35.

stalled because of political or technical difficulties. Still, Prussia's commercial policy in Germany continued to gain momentum. By 1833, one year after Bernstorff had left office, the initial treaties that formed the original *Zollverein* agreements had been concluded. On 1 January 1834, this new commercial system went into effect throughout most of Germany. The negotiations continued to demonstrate the same concerns that characterized Prussia's customs policy in the late 1820s. A brief analysis of the essential aspects of Prussia's activity in this area is necessary to understand the basic contours of Prussia's German policy, as well as the evolution of the *Zollverein*.

Although Motz, Bernstorff, and Eichhorn would have preferred that the Central German Commercial Union fade away into oblivion, it continued to exist despite its essentially negative character. However, its survival did not alter Prussia's position on multilateral negotiations. As Bernstorff reiterated to the government of Hanover, Berlin would only negotiate with single states, not with larger associations.[50] Thus, in early 1830, despite the great success of the south German and Prussian negotiations, the creation of a single, comprehensive customs system for Germany had reached a momentary impasse. However, the political upheavals in Germany immediately following the July Revolution brought about changes in the leadership of several German states and made governments more aware of the social and economic problems present in Germany. Some governments, in an effort to respond to the economic needs of their states, saw advantages in the more efficient and comprehensive approach to customs reform represented by the Prussian model. The government of Hesse-Kassel fell into this category. Its defection from the Central German Commercial Union signified a major victory for Prussia in the economic struggle that was being waged in Germany.

Until the July Revolution, for dynastic and economic reasons, the Elector of Hesse and his government had been one of Prussia's most adamant opponents. But, as we have seen, William's embarrassing private life and the tariff dispute with Prussia actually created some of the conditions that had caused the outbreaks of public violence within that state. However, as a result of the accession of the Electoral Prince as co-regent and the forma-

---

50. Bernstorff to the Hanoverian Kabinettsministerium, 31 October 1829, Hermann Oncken and F. E. M. Saemisch, eds., *Vorgeschichte und Begründung des deutschen Zollvereins, 1815–1834*, 3:130–135.

tion of a new government, many of those officials who were hostile toward Berlin were removed from power. One of the men who now formulated Kassel's economic policies was Gerhard Motz, Friedrich Motz's cousin.

In January, the Diet in Kassel urged that a representative be sent to Berlin to open discussions on customs affairs.[51] Due to the efforts of Gerhard Motz and his associates, the Elector finally agreed to send two emissaries to Berlin.[52] The discussions between Eichhorn, Kühne (representing Maassen), and the Hessian negotiators proceeded without incident and led to the signing of a treaty between Prussia, Hesse-Darmstadt, and Hesse-Kassel on 29 August 1831 (dated 25 August 1831).[53] Its stipulations were basically the same as the Prussian–Hesse-Darmstadt Treaty of 14 February 1828. Kassel agreed to join the customs union between Darmstadt and Prussia's western provinces on 1 January 1832. The importance of this agreement is obvious. It strengthened Prussia's economic position in Germany by economically uniting the western and eastern portions of the monarchy. Likewise, the Prussian *Zollverein* now stood astride the major trade routes of Germany, disrupting the communications of the Central German Commercial Union and making the establishment of a single customs union under Prussia's leadership nearly inevitable.

The only other state to conclude a formal customs agreement with Berlin during Bernstorff's ministry was Saxe-Weimar. Even before the July Revolution, the grand duchy had shown interest in joining the Prussian and south German associations; this interest became even more intense after the summer of 1830. Met with an initial rebuff by the foreign ministry in his efforts to begin negotiations on customs policy with Prussia, Grandduke Charles Frederick (whose daughter Augusta had just married Prince William of Prussia, the future Emperor), wrote directly to Frederick William and requested that the government in Berlin receive his minister, Freiherr von Gersdorff, and begin negotiations concerning Weimar's entry into the Prussian *Zollverein*.[54] This letter was enough to

51. Haenlein to Frederick William, 22 January 1831, ibid., p. 157.

52. Treitschke, *History of Germany,* 5:428; and William to Frederick William, 19 June 1831, in Oncken and Saemisch, *Vorgeschichte und Begründung,* 3:166–167.

53. See Vertrag zwischen Kurhessen und dem Preussisch-Hessischen Zollverein vom 25. August 1831, Oncken and Saemisch, *Vorgeschichte und Begründung,* 3:168–171.

54. Charles Frederick to Frederick William, 27 December 1830, ibid., pp. 156–157.

get the negotiations started between the two states.[55] As had been the case with Darmstadt, Bavaria, Württemberg, and Hesse-Kassel, Berlin had been approached by another German state with regard to affiliation with the Prussian system. By February, Gersdorff and Eichhorn had agreed on the wording of the treaty. Signed on 11 February 1831, the final document called for Weimar to join in a *Zollverein* with Prussia's eastern provinces on 1 January 1835.[56] Weimar had decided that its future lay with Prussia and that, in the final analysis, the Central German Commercial Union was inadequate to meet Germany's pressing economic needs.[57]

Perhaps no series of negotiations was as protracted and as frustrating for Bernstorff as those connected with the attempt to have Baden enter the Bavarian-Württemberg and, in time, the Prussian customs union. This difficulty was not caused primarily by disagreement over the details of the customs arrangements; it was the result of a festering territorial dispute between Baden and Bavaria. Motz had previously agreed to the Bavarian demand that Baden join its *Zollverein* with Württemberg before the southern union combined with the Prussian system. Bernstorff continued to honor this policy. However, Baden's adherence to the Bavarian system could not realistically take place until the dispute between the two states over Bavarian claims to the *Grafschaft* of Sponheim has been settled.

Sponheim had been acquired by Baden years earlier, but the Wittelsbachs still held a vague claim to the territory.[58] In return for relinquishing their title and as compensation for other territorial changes in the southwest, Ludwig wanted to receive a significant piece of territory. In recent years, Prussia had consistently supported Baden in this dispute. But because the conclusion of the commercial treaty with Bavaria and Württemberg and the entry of Baden into the larger association was so obviously desirable, Berlin and Württemberg agreed to mediate the dispute.[59] Bernstorff at-

55. Schönberg to Gersdorff, 31 January 1831, and Frederick William to Charles Frederick, 31 January 1831, ibid., pp. 157–161.

56. For the text of the treaty, see Vertrag zwischen Preussen und Sachsen-Weimar vom 11 Februar 1831, ibid., pp. 161–164.

57. Treitschke, *History of Germany*, 5:432.

58. The entire dispute is examined in great detail in Liselotte von Hoermann, *Der bayerische-badische Gebietsstreit 1825–1832.*

59. Prussia's mediatory efforts are described in Hoermann, *Der bayerische-badische Gebietsstreit,* pp. 141–218. The documents are contained in ZSA Me, AAI, Rep. 1, Nrs. 824–826.

tempted to personally negotiate a settlement; indeed, after painstaking discussions, he believed that he had drafted an agreement acceptable to both parties. However, the government of Baden was unwilling to take responsibility for the proposed settlement and instead indicated that it would abide by the decision of the Badenese Diet.[60] While the political turbulence of the period had worked in favor of the *Zollverein* in Hesse-Kassel, the momentary strength of parliamentary forces in Baden served as a block to further progress. On 5 October 1831, it voted to reject the preliminary agreement that had been arrived at with such difficulty in Berlin.[61] Bernstorff's efforts at mediation had now obviously failed, and his hopes of personally facilitating the future expansion of the *Zollverein* were disappointed.[62] The Sponheim question was never actually resolved. During the course of the century, as its historical relevancy disappeared, it simply faded from the political scene. Baden did not enter the Bavarian system and was not a member of the original *Zollverein* established in 1834,

Negotiations between Bavaria, Württemberg, Hesse-Darmstadt, and Prussia were resumed in the spring of 1832. One year later, on 22 March 1833, these four states agreed to consolidate their two systems. They were then joined by Saxony and the Thuringian states, which were the last to join the original union. This combination of separate agreements constituted the founding treaties of the German *Zollverein*. They stipulated that the new union would begin operation on 1 January 1834. No description of the opening of the *Zollverein* can match Treitschke's; it not only captures the spirit of the moment, but also associates it unabashedly with his belief in Prussia's mission to rule Germany. He wrote:

> Then came the momentous new year's eve of 1834, which announced even to the masses the dawning of a better day. On all the high roads of Central Germany, long strings of heavily laden freight wagons were waiting in front of the customs houses, surrounded by jubilating crowds. With the last stroke of twelve and the close of the old year, the toll gates were thrown wide. The traces tightened, and amid shouts of exhultation and the cracking of many whips the trains of goods moved forward

60. The foreign ministry of Baden to Otterstedt, 24 April 1831, Oncken and Saemisch, *Vorgeschichte und Begründung*, 3:624–625.

61. Second Chamber of the Diet of Baden to Leopold, 5 October 1831, ibid., pp. 638–640.

62. See Bernstorff to Frederick William, April 1832, ZSA Me, AAI, Rep. 1, Nr. 826.

across the enfranchised land. A new link, strong though inconspicuous, had been welded into the long chain of events leading the margravate of the Hohenzollerns onward towards the imperial crown. The eagle eye of the great king looked down from the clouds, and from a remote distance could already be heard the thunder of the guns of Königgrätz.[63]

Treitschke may have overly dramatized the *Zollverein's* debut, but he correctly focused attention on its political importance, which was recognized by contemporary observers and has been discussed by historians ever since.[64] For example, the French minister to Frankfurt wrote of Prussia's ambition to expand its political power in Germany and regretted the disadvantageous effects the *Zollverein* would have on French commerce.[65] This view was echoed by the Under-Secretary of the Board of Trade in London, Thomas Lack, who wrote: "Their Lordships observe with great regret the perserverence of the Prussian government, and the success which has attended its endeavors to establish and extend a system, the manifest object of which is that of combining commercial monopoly with political aggrandizement."[66]

Perhaps no power was as sensitive to the economic and political consequences of the *Zollverein* as Austria. Metternich's apprehensions, aroused when Hesse-Darmstadt joined the Prussian system in 1828, intensified as each year went by.[67] In 1829, Austria's minister to Karlsruhe wrote with reference to Bernstorff's attempt to mediate the Sponheim question:

> The goal that [the Prussian] government pursues with tenacity is clearly indicated; it seeks to win greater political influence in Germany by emphasizing its commercial interests and expanding these to the greatest extent possible; in this way it strides forward intelligently and indeed not without success, and it is especially intent not to prematurely arouse the jealousy of the weaker states."[68]

63. Treitschke, *History of Germany,* 5:461.

64. See, for example, Eugen Franz, "Ein Weg zum Reich."

65. Alleye de Cypray to the French foreign ministry, 30 March 1833, in Oncken and Saemisch, *Vorgeschichte und Begründung,* 3:714–716.

66. Thomas Lack to George Shee (Under-Secretary in the Foreign Office), 25 May 1833, ibid., p. 719.

67. For Metternich's most extensive, but quite restrained, discussion of the *Zollverein,* see Metternich to Francis, June 1833, Clemens Lothar Wenzel Fürst von Metternich-Winneburg, *Aus Metternichs nachgelassenen Papieren,* 4:502–519.

68. Buol to Metternich, 23 September 1829, Oncken and Saemisch, *Vorgeschichte und Begründung,* 3:576–578.

By October 1831, the British minister in Frankfurt noted that Austria "is jealous of the growing power of Prussia. She is annoyed at the success of the Prussian Commercial Union, which by drawing closer the ties of the Prussian Government with the other German states, must henceforth give it greater weight and political influence in the Confederation."[69]

How did Metternich react to this Prussian threat? Did he merely pursue negative measures, such as bolstering up the Central German Commercial Union, or did he also attempt to adjust Austrian policy to the economic needs of Germany? In reality, he did both. He worked diplomatically in numerous ways to hinder the growth of the Prussian system, although he never mounted a direct frontal assault against Prussian policy for fear of alienating Frederick William and thereby permanently damaging Austria's relationship with Prussia. He preferred an indirect approach for the elimination of the most dangerous aspects of Prussia's commercial policy. He also attempted to counter Prussia's program by bringing about changes in Austria's commercial policies. For example, on 21 January 1830, Metternich explained to Francis the dangers posed by Prussia's commercial successes in Germany in considerable detail. He urged Francis to consider sensible and moderate modifications in Austria's system of tariffs, which would allow Vienna to offer an alternative to the Prussian system.[70] The Emperor referred the matter to the *Hofkammer,* which quickly decided on February 1830 that any modification of Austria's system was impossible.[71] Although Metternich continued to press his case with the Emperor and Austria became involved in commercial discussions with Bavaria, Württemberg, and Hanover, the position of the central administration never changed. Thus, Metternich had nothing to offer the other states.[72] With his options reduced by the immobility of his own government, Metternich could only resort to negative, destructive devices in his efforts to block developments that were obviously not in Austria's interest.

Of course, Metternich was mainly worried about the political, rather

69. Cartwright to Palmerston, 22 October 1831, PRO F.O. 30/35.

70. Metternich to Francis, 21 January 1830, Oncken and Saemisch, *Vorgeschichte und Begründung,* 3:144–146.

71. Adolf Beer, *Die österreichische Handelspolitik im neunzehnten Jahrhundert,* pp. 61–62.

72. Ibid., pp. 62–70. See also Metternich to Francis, 11 June 1831, Oncken and Saemisch, *Vorgeschichte und Begründung,* 3:164–165; Metternich to Klebelsberg (President of the Hofkammer), 17 February 1832, ibid., pp. 225–226; and Klebelsberg to Metternich, 4 March 1832, ibid., pp. 237–241.

than commercial, implications of Prussia's customs policy. Indeed, in the *Memoire* by Motz and in Bernstorff's *Denkschrift* of 29 January 1831, it is obvious that the *Zollverein* was to be only the first step in a coordinated Prussian effort to expand its influence in Germany and restructure the German Confederation. The *Zollverein* was not intended to be an isolated act of state; it was a fully integrated part of Prussian policy. For example, Bernstorff pursued a peaceful European policy from 1830 to 1832 in part because of his concern for German public opinion. If Prussia seemed to be aggressive and counterrevolutionary toward France and Belgium, the constitutional states in Germany would have been reluctant to affiliate with the Prussian system. Likewise, his concern for the success of Prussia's customs policy led Bernstorff to adopt a tolerant attitude toward the constitutional movement within Germany. As the British minister to Frankfurt noted, Prussia's opposition to Austrian efforts to introduce additional repressive measures in Germany might have been designed to avoid alienating liberal opinion. But Prussia was also

> so wrapped up in her plan for embracing the whole of Germany in one Grand Commercial Union under her protection, from which system she flatters herself she shall derive immense advantages and political importance—she is very loath to involve herself openly in transactions which may have a detrimental influence on her grand project, and she is well aware that by taking too deep a part, or appearing too ostensibly as a Principal in any coercive measures against the constitutional States, or the Liberal System, she might bring upon her the hostility of the liberal leaders in the Chambers of those States with whom she wishes to form this close commercial connection.[73]

Prussia's desire to expand the *Zollverein* also had significant connections with the Prussian government's domestic political philosophy. Frederick Engels once wrote that the 26 May 1818 tariff law was the first official recognition of the bourgeoisie by the Prussian government, and Marxist historians have since emphasized that the *Zollverein* was an attempt by the ruling class to pacify the middle classes through economic concessions, while, at the same time, retaining all political power for themselves.[74]

---

73. Cartwright to Palmerston, 23 November 1831, PRO F.O. 30/35.
74. G. Vogler and K. Vetter, *Preussen, Von der Anfangen bis zur Reichsgründung,* p. 205; and Karl Obermann, *Deutschland vom 1815–1849,* p. 99.

This is a partial exaggeration. As Gustav Schmoller demonstrated, the 1818 tariff law was not exclusively a product of economic interest groups, although certainly manufacturers and merchants played an important part in its creation.[75] Likewise, the *Zollverein* was brought into being as the result of a complex number of factors. Still it is basically true that the foreign ministry viewed the economic unification of Germany as a means to pacify political discontent. In addition to strengthening Prussia economically, financially, and politically, its purpose was to create a sense of satisfaction and harmony among the population within the union. This view, expressed in 1828, was a central idea in Bernstorff's *Denkschrift* of 29 January 1831 and was mentioned by the ministry in routine correspondence.[76] As such, the domestic political approach embodied in the creation of the *Zollverein* can be viewed as a classic example of reform conservatism in practice.

The political side of these negotiations are also important for a proper evaluation of Bernstorff's role in the establishment of the customs union. It has been asserted that Bernstorff's only contribution to Prussia's customs policy was in giving Eichhorn complete latitude in that area.[77] Without a doubt, Motz, Eichhorn, and Maassen were most responsible for the success of these difficult transactions; Bernstorff, Witzleben, and others played a subsidiary role. But Bernstorff, in fact, made a number of significant contributions. He had insights into the essence of the German state system that Motz lacked and used this knowledge to soften Motz's approach, thereby making Prussia's policies more successful. Bernstorff also helped to integrate Prussia's commercial policy with its broadly defined German policy. Furthermore, Bernstorff did more than just give Eichhorn a free hand in commercial affairs. He purposely assigned these tasks to Eichhorn because he felt that they were of the greatest importance and he considered Eichhorn to be one of his most talented assistants. He also protected Eichhorn from the attacks of reactionaries and made his continued service

75. Gustav Schmoller, *Das preussische Handels- und Zollgesetz vom 26. Mai 1818.*

76. Prussian Ministry of Foreign Affairs to Brockhausen, 14 August 1828, Oncken and Saemisch, *Vorgeschichte und Begründung,* 3:54–55; and Eichhorn to Maassen, 24 July 1832, ibid., 3:680–684.

77. For example, see the comment of Hubatsch and Botzenhart, "the only great project of Prussian policy of that period, the founding of the German *Zollverein,* is not [Bernstorff's] work." In Heinrich Friedrich Karl Freiherr vom und zu Stein, *Briefe und Ämtliche Schriften,* 5:821n.

in government possible. Finally, as foreign minister, Bernstorff pursued policies that generally gained respect for Prussia from those governments and elements in society most essential for the success of the *Zollverein* negotiations.[78] Bernstorff did much to create a political environment that was conducive to the success of Prussia's commercial policies. Hermann von Petersdorff, who consistently underplayed the activities of the foreign ministry, is incorrect in his statement that only Motz aroused the slumbering foreign ministry to action.[79] Contemporary observers saw a much closer connection between Motz's ideas and those of the Wilhelmstrasse. As the Bavarian minister to Berlin reported shortly after Motz's death: "The concepts of M. de Motz have not been buried with him; they live and will always develop further and will bear fortunate fruits. Count Bernstorff and his ministry are the inheritors of his ideas."[80]

Because political aspects of the *Zollverein* are complicated, they have been the cause of considerable confusion among historians. For example, A. J. P. Taylor wrote, "The Prussian statesmen who made the *Zollverein* had not the slightest idea of its political consequences; they saw only the rambling, unworkable frontiers and desired to save money on their customs officers."[81] This is true for the early 1820s, but, by the 1830s, it is clear that Motz, Eichhorn, Witzleben, Bernstorff, and others had much more in mind than merely improving the efficiency of Prussia's customs system. During the years from 1828 to 1832, they had thought intensely about the political ramifications of the *Zollverein,* and their approach to German affairs was partly based on the political benefits they expected to accrue from the creation of a German customs union. Yet, if the *Zollverein* was so packed with political meaning, why in the years immediately following its creation was its contribution to the political unity of Germany so slight and its impact on the political aspects of Prussia's German policy equally insignificant? Obviously something must have happened in the 1830s to the relationship between the *Zollverein* and

---

78. For just one of many examples, see Arnim to Prussian Ministry of Foreign Affairs, 2 January 1831, ZSA Me, AAI, Rep. 1, Nr. 825.

79. Hermann von Petersdorff, *Friedrich von Motz, eine Biographie,* 2:108–128.

80. Luxburg to Ludwig, 5 July 1830, Bay. Gsa, MA III, Nr. 2608. Petersdorff used this same document in his study of Motz, but he omitted the last sentence with its reference to Bernstorff and the foreign ministry. See Petersdorff, *Motz,* 2:378.

81. A. J. P. Taylor, *The Course of German History,* pp. 62–63.

politics. Somehow the *Zollverein* was largely stripped of its political meaning, both for Prussia and for Germany. To find out how this came about we must now direct our attention to other aspects of Prussia's German policy.

*Chapter 9*

✠ ✠ ✠ ✠ ✠ ✠ ✠ ✠ ✠ ✠ ✠ ✠ ✠ ✠

# Prussia and the Federal Military System

In 1830, the threat of a European war caused Prussia's leaders to re-examine the German Confederation's military capability. During the middle and late 1820s, the military issue had not figured prominently in German affairs because there was no great prospect that the Confederation and Prussia would be involved in a war. However, the Belgian crisis and French military preparations made the military question once again a matter of prime concern. Bernstorff's papers and dispatches constantly discussed the need to mobilize Germany's full military potential. Concern for Germany's strength was also widespread among the conservatives. For example, in October 1830, Duke Charles suggested that Berlin under-take an energetic effort to reorganize the structure of the federal army. In view of Austria's disparate European interests, he did not consider the exclusion of Austria from this effort to be a disadvantage.[1] In November 1830, Rochow wrote that reliance on foreign powers was risky in the event of war; "therefore we are limited to ourselves and the German states, and we must direct affairs in such a way that we will be prepared for a life and death struggle."[2] The importance of the German states to Prussia's

1. Herzog Carl von Mecklenburg Denkschrift betr. kriegerische Zustände in Europa, Volkssouveränität, Organization des deutschen Bundes, ZSA Me, Geheimes Civil Cabinet, Rep. 2.2.1., Nr. 13070.

2. Rochow to Nagler, 6 November 1830, Ernst Kelchner and Karl Mendelsohn-Bartholdy, eds., *Preussen und Frankreich zur Zeit der Julirevolution*, p. 37.

security made it apparent that the confusing and untested structure of the federal army needed to be better organized. Attention centered on the south German states, which were the strongest militarily and which lay astride the probable route the French would take into Central Europe.

## GENERAL RUHLE VON LILIENSTERN'S MISSION

As laid down by the Diet in 1821 and 1822, the army of the Confederation was to be organized as one massive unit under the control of a supreme commander, presumably an Austrian. Like many others, Bernstorff felt that this form of military organization was unsatisfactory. On 8 October 1830, he wrote to the King that, because the prospects of rapidly creating strong military power in Germany through the mechanism of the Diet were poor, direct consultations with the major German courts would be more effective. "Prussia," he said, "as the state that would have to bear the greatest burden in the event of a federal war, is therefore called upon to seize the initiative in all areas where successful leadership will lead to greater preparedness and security; in addition, such action will create a general trust in Prussia so that one will depend upon her advice, her suggestions, and her beneficial influence."[3] He suggested that high-ranking officers should be sent to the major German courts to begin these discussions and to report on the strength of the armed forces of the German states. In this letter, in addition to connecting the military question with Prussia's larger goal of exerting moral influence in Germany, Bernstorff also adopted the model of the *Zollverein* negotiations as the best way to establish new military arrangements in Germany.

This suggestion coincided closely with the desires of the Bavarian government. On 22 October 1830, Ludwig decided to send Field Marshal Wrede to Berlin to discuss defensive measures along the Rhine frontier. Frederick William asked, however, that Wrede's mission be postponed. Diebitsch was already in Berlin, and Frederick William was afraid that the presence of another field marshal might cause suspicion in France. Ludwig was promised that a Prussian envoy would soon be sent to Munich and the other south German courts to discuss the defense of

3. Johann Gustav Droysen, "Zur Geschichte der preussischen Politik in den Jahren 1830–1832," p. 50.

Germany. It was emphasized that Prussia would only fight to protect the Confederation from a French attack and that it expected that such a war, if it came, would be a national war as in 1813.[4]

The Prussian reply was welcomed in Munich. Since August there had been numerous communications between the ministers and monarchs of the south German states aimed at establishing a neutrality agreement. These governments were afraid of being dragged into a European conflict in which they had no interest. Rather than being pawns of the two German powers and victimized in war, they sought strength in unity among themselves and in independence from the great powers. But their desire for such an arrangement was biased in Prussia's favor. Berlin's pacific policy during the first months of the European crisis and its more progressive political outlook made the south Germans feel that a community of interests existed between them and Prussia; although they had a common desire to avoid a war based on non-German, ideological considerations, they were willing to cooperate to prepare militarily for a French attack.[5] On the other hand, such a plan was prejudiced against Austria because of its extensive non-German interests, particularly in Italy, and because of the strongly conservative nature of its foreign policy, which could easily bring Austria into conflict with France's new policy of nonintervention. Thus, the south Germans were primarily concerned for their own independence, but began to look to Prussia for guidance.

Bernstorff was sympathetic to the south German outlook. In October, he wrote that a closer association of these states would cause them to follow common interests compatible with the "true interests of Prussia and Germany."[6] But, while the Prussian government wanted to create a more effective military organization for Germany, it did not wish to alienate Austria. On the contrary, a certain degree of cooperation by Austria in increasing the military strength of Germany was expected. Thus, the first official Prussian military mission was to Vienna where General von Röder began discussions with the Austrians in December 1830.

Röder's instruction, drafted by Eichhorn, stated that, in the event of

---

4. Hans Helmut Böck, *Karl Philipp Fürst von Wrede als politischer Berater König Ludwig I von Bayern (1825–1838)*, pp. 146–147.

5. Robert D. Billinger, Jr., "Metternich's Policy toward the South German States," pp. 60–62, 84–90.

6. Droysen, "Zur Geschichte der preussischen Politik," p. 52.

war, it would be highly desirable to bring the total military strength of the south German states into action. However, as relations between these states and Austria were strained, Prussia was taking the lead in this matter. Röder was to tell the Austrians that Prussia would come forward not just with her 80,000 man federal contingent, but would commit 200,000 troops to the campaign in the west. He was to ask the Austrians whether, in view of their obligations in Italy and Galicia, they would absolutely, under all conditions, honor their commitment to provide 95,000 men for the federal army. Regarding the disposition of federal troops, Röder was to indicate that Prussia and the Ninth and Tenth Federal Army Corps hold the right flank on the lower Rhine, Bavaria with the Seventh and Eighth Federal Army Corps and possibly a Prussian corps would hold the middle, and Austria would hold the left flank on the upper Rhine. Röder was also to discuss the question of a supreme commander for the German army. It was well known that Vienna hoped that an Austrian prince or general would be chosen by the Diet, but Eichhorn indicated that such a choice might cause numerous difficulties. If a supreme commander were to be chosen, he should come from the state providing the greatest number of troops and having the greatest interest in a federal war, and, as Eichhorn said, "that is Prussia."[7] Thus, Berlin was interested in involving the south German states more intimately in the defense of Germany, but it also wanted to establish its right to lead the military forces of the Confederation.

In Vienna, Röder met with Metternich and with the President of the *Hofkriegsrath,* Count Giulay. Both assured him that Austria would be able to meet her military obligations. They predicted that Austria would have 200,000 troops mobilized by the end of February, of which 100,000 would be assigned to the federal army. Röder nevertheless was skeptical of Austria's military strength, and because of Austria's responsibilities in Galicia and Italy, he doubted that it would be able to act effectively in other theaters. He questioned whether the artillery and cavalry were satisfactorily equipped for an immediate campaign and worried about Austria's financial resources. He felt that Austria would wait until the Poles had been defeated before making a firm commitment to a federal

7. A copy of the instruction to Röder dated 19 December 1830 is contained in Eichhorn's letter to Witzleben of 8 January 1831, ZSA Me, Rep. 92, Witzleben, Nr. 111.

army. In his first meetings with Metternich, he apparently did not get any definite answer on the question of a supreme commander or on the deployment and organization of federal troops.[8] He did report that Metternich had indicated in vague terms that if war, but not a federal war, occurred over Belgium, then Austria would assume a policy of armed neutrality. Thus, Austria's attitude toward the crisis in the Netherlands was similar to Prussia's and especially to the south Germans', who were concerned over a possible conflict that would involve Austria in Italy.[9]

As we have noted earlier, political unrest in Italy first occurred in Modena on 5 February 1831; Metternich received word of it five days later.[10] Was Metternich suggesting to Berlin that Austrian support on the Belgian question could only be bought by Prussian support of Austria in Italy, or was he saying that, because of its problems in Italy, Austria did not have the resources to assist Prussia in a conflict over Belgium? There is no available evidence that provides an answer to this question. Nor do we know how officials in Berlin reacted to Röder's report. Perhaps because of Austria's position on Belgium, Bernstorff and others found the idea of an independently constituted south German army more attractive. Regardless of what Austria did, such a force could assume a defensive position opposite France, even if only in a stance of armed neutrality, thus freeing Prussian troops to concentrate on Belgium. In any case, after the outbreak of revolution in Italy, Metternich began to view the Prussian proposals with a more critical eye, probably because he wanted to secure the defense of Austria's northern frontier in the event of war with France over Italy. Thus, by the middle of March, Röder was reporting that Metternich and other officials had some misgivings about the Prussian plan. No actual opposition was voiced, but they refused to commit themselves on the issue of a supreme commander (although they clearly favored Archduke Charles for the position), and they expressed vague doubts over Prussia's suggested deployment of the federal army.[11] But real opposition

8. Röder to Frederick William, 19 January 1831 with addenda (n.d.), and 5 February 1831, ZSA Me, AAI, Rep. 5, Nr. 592.

9. Röder to Frederick William, 11 February 1831, ibid. Bernstorff's guarded attitude toward such a conflict is reported in Chad to Palmerston, 5 April 1831, PRO F.O. 64/170; and Mortier to Sebastiani, 8 April 1831, A.M.A.E., C. P. Prusse, Vol. 276.

10. Droysen, "Zur Geschichte der preussischen Politik," p. 69.

11. Röder to Frederick William, 21 February 1831, ZSA Me, AAI, Rep. 5, Nr. 592.

surfaced after Prussia had sent another emissary, General August Rühle von Lilienstern, to the courts of southern Germany. Metternich now complained that he had not been informed of the mission beforehand, and he enunciated his own ideas for the defense of Germany based on a line established along the Danube.[12]

In his final report to Frederick William, Röder said Metternich was now opposed to creating a middle army out of the Seventh and Eighth Corps, fearing that the south German states, by having a separate command, would achieve "an independent political position for themselves." Langenau, who had replaced Giulay in the discussions with Röder, argued that Austria would have little influence over such a configuration and that, by the nature of things, it would fall under Prussian domination. The Austrians now favored just two army units—one north and one south—each dominated by one of the great German powers. Metternich also opposed any alteration in the plans for a supreme commander; the laws of the Confederation were quite clear on this issue, and, although he said that either an Austrian or a Prussian could be the commander, he clearly considered Archduke Charles the prime candidate. Evidently, Münch-Bellinghausen had informed him that the Archduke already had sufficient votes at the Diet to be elected. Röder concluded his final report by noting that there was considerable mistrust and suspicion of Prussia, not just because of the present situation, but because of a "wounded vanity stemming from the years of 1813 and 1814."[13] At the same time, Metternich announced that he now planned to begin military discussions with the south German courts. Thus, Metternich's opposition to Prussia's military proposals was initially influenced by Austrian defensive needs as a result of the Italian crisis. But, subsequently, his concern over the activities of the second Prussian military envoy, Rühle von Lilienstern, also became apparent. Rühle von Lilienstern's mission worried Metternich because it appeared to be related to Prussia's attempts to create a stronger relationship with the constitutional states and to develop additional opportunities for Prussian leadership in Germany.

The European situation worsened while Röder was in Vienna. The candidacy of the Duke de Nemours for the Belgian throne and the in-

---

12. Droysen, "Zur Geschichte der preussischen Politik," p. 71; and Röder to Frederick William, 17 March 1831, ZSA Me, AAI, Rep. 5, Nr. 592.

13. Röder to Frederick William, ZSA Me, AAI, Rep. 5, Nr. 592.

crease in the strength of the French army caused great alarm in Berlin. In addition, Bernstorff began to receive reports of an attempt by French diplomats in southern Germany to get Württemberg, Baden, and Bavaria to join an armed neutrality pact in the event of war.[14] Although the Bavarian government reiterated its desire to support Prussia, these reports from southern Germany were not encouraging. Neither was Röder's mission, which had as yet produced no tangible results. Under these circumstances, Bernstorff made plans to send Freiherr August Rühle von Lilienstern to the south German courts to present essentially the same points outlined in Röder's instruction. He was also instructed to invite representatives of the Bavarian military command and another officer representing the Eighth Federal Army Corps to come to Berlin where detailed discussions on defensive arrangements could begin. Bernstorff had already circulated Rühle's instruction to Krauseneck and Witzleben, who approved it.[15]

The choice of Rühle for such a mission was not without significance. He was one of the best and most broadly educated officers in the Prussian army. Service at the court of Weimar earlier in his career had brought him into close contact with the literature and philosophy of the age of Goethe. He had served on Stein's staff in the *Zentral Verwaltung* where he had been concerned especially with military arrangements for all of Germany. He was also a supporter of constitutional government in which representative institutions based on traditional elements of society would play a modest role in determining the political life of the nation. Thus, he was an officer whose political outlook was especially well suited for dealing with the south German states.[16]

On his arrival in Munich, Rühle found Ludwig favorably inclined to-

14. See, for example, Küster's reports of 18 January, 22 January, and 3 March 1831, to the Ministry of Foreign Affairs, Anton Chroust, ed., *Gesandtschaftsberichte aus München, 1814–1848, Abteilung III.,* 40:183–184. One should also consult the reports of the French minister to Bavaria, Rumigny, which are printed in the same series as part one, under the title *Die Berichte der französischen Gesandten,* 19:300–344; and Chad to Palmerston, 30 January 1831, PRO F.O. 64/167.

15. Bernstorff to Witzleben, 19 February 1831, and Witzleben to Bernstorff, 23 February 1831, ZSA Me, Rep. 92, Witzleben, Nr. 111. A copy of Rühle's instruction is contained in Eichhorn's letter to Witzleben dated 26 February 1831, ibid. For the Rühle mission and its subsequent impact, see Robert D. Billinger, Jr., "The War Scare of 1831 and Prussian–South German Plans for the End of Austrian Dominance in Germany."

16. On Rühle, see Erich Weniger, *Goethe und die Generale der Freiheitskriege,* pp.

ward Prussia. The King rejected the possibility of a Franco-Bavarian agreement or of Bavaria's remaining neutral in the event of a German war. He supported what he called Prussia's political system and its approach to German affairs, which at the federal level "was not merely conservative." On the other hand, Ludwig was very suspicious of Austria and Metternich. As Küster later reported, "Trust is lacking here in the moral strength of the Austrian monarchy as well as in the uprightness and loyalty of its policy."[17] After Rühle had explained the purpose of his mission, the King stated that he was opposed to a single large federal army and to the idea of an overall supreme commander, but did indicate that he was willing to let Prussia exert some sort of supervision over the combined operations of the German forces. The King also discussed the Sponheim affair and the negotiations concerning the *Zollverein*.[18] Ludwig expressed these same ideas even more strongly in a letter to Frederick William in which he wrote, "I know no north and no south Germany, only Germany. I am convinced that safety is only to be found in a firm connection with Prussia and it appears to me that Prussia and Bavaria are especially closely allied and shall stand and fall together."[19]

On 27 March, Rühle reported that the Bavarian position paper handed to him agreed with Prussia's tripartite plan for the federal army, and it concluded that the Seventh and Eighth Corps should be positioned on the middle Rhine. The Bavarians continued to oppose a supreme commander for the federal army, but had no objections to the two corps operating with the Prussian army under Gneisenau's command. Armansperg, the Bavarian foreign minister, also spoke enthusiastically about close relations with Prussia, and Rühle reported:

> The sure, wise, magnanimous, and prudent attitude that has characterized Prussia's recent policy and that has proven in every way to

---

160–167; Peter Paret, *Clausewitz and the State,* pp. 272–274; and *Allgemeine Deutsche Biographie,* s.v. "Rühle von Lilienstern, Johann Jakob Otto August." In 1815, Rühle drew up a paper concerning constitutional arrangements for the German states. It is contained in Franz Rühl, *Briefe und Aktenstücke zur Geschichte Preussens unter Friedrich Wilhelm III, 2:61–67.*

17. Küster to Ministerium der Auswärtigen Angelegenheiten, 15 March 1831, Chroust, *Gesandtschaftsberichte aus München, Abteilung III., 40:198–199.*

18. Rühle von Lilienstern and Küster to Frederick William, 7 March 1831, ibid., pp. 193–196.

19. Ludwig I to Frederick William III, 17 March 1831, ibid., pp. 196–197n.

be so beneficial has resulted in general in great respect, trust, and sympathy. All attention is turned in expectation that this policy devoid of foreign influence will strongly assert itself, will make the peace of Europe more secure, and will be a dependable support and point of reference for the smaller German states.

Here was clear evidence that Bernstorff's skilled handling of Prussia's European policy had enhanced its position of leadership in Germany and made its German policy more effective. Armansperg reiterated his interest in expanding and strengthening the *Zollverein* and felt that Prussia was well equipped to build on the glorious beginning of Frederick the Great and the *Fürstenbund*.

Rühle continued to report that there was strong opposition on the part of most Bavarians to any connection or subordination to Austria. In the last meeting of the Bavarian *Landtag,* one delegate said, "Better to die Bavarian, than to be wasted by the Empire" (*Besser bayerisch sterben, als kaiserlich verderben*). This, according to Rühle, expressed a general attitude. He added that Austria would probably oppose Prussia's ideas, and he had already heard that the Austrians were attempting to instigate the overthrow of Armansperg.[20] A later meeting with the foreign minister and Ludwig showed that both felt that the question of war or peace should not be left to the *Bund,* but should be decided by the courts of Prussia, Bavaria, Württemberg, and Baden. This would avoid the intrigues, ineffectiveness, confusion, and machinations of the *Bundestag.* It was agreed that, while the German states should fight with all their forces and stand together, it was also important that they do nothing to aggravate France or make themselves unpopular with their own people. Austria was not, however, to be entirely excluded from these arrangements.[21]

Rühle then traveled to Stuttgart where his proposals were received in a warm but more cautious manner than in Munich. He reported that Prussia was held in high esteem and that the political views of the two

20. Rühle von Lilienstern to Frederick William, 27 March 1831, ZSA Me, AAI, Rep. 5, Nr. 593. Rühle was reporting Armansperg's outlook accurately; see Armansperg to Ludwig, 27 March 1831, Bay. GSA, MA 24 076.
21. Rühle von Lilienstern to Frederick William, 28 March 1831, ZSA Me, AAI, Rep. 5, Nr. 593.

courts coincided closely.[22] He again noted that the armies and peoples of southern Germany opposed being put under the command of Austria in the event of war with France. Officials in Stuttgart also wanted the Seventh and Eighth Corps to be located on the middle Rhine. They favored establishing a defensive line, or route of retreat, along the Main, based on Mainz and Würzburg and convenient to Prussian support.[23]

Rühle's next destination was Karlsruhe, where his reception, as in Stuttgart, was less enthusiastic than in Munich. However, the government of Baden essentially agreed with the basic points of the Prussian proposal.[24] The same was true of officials in Hesse-Darmstadt, with whom Rühle met after leaving Karlsruhe. In Darmstadt, he became aware for the first time of Austria's opposition to Prussia's suggestions for reorganizing the federal army. Nevertheless, Rühle felt that Berlin should press forward with its plans and should counter Austrian lies. Anticipating Metternich's later line of attack, he told Bernstorff that Berlin should make it clear that Frederick William approved of these proposals.[25]

By the first week in May, Küster also reported that Metternich was trying to create mistrust in Ludwig's mind toward Prussia and to undermine the position of those Bavarian ministers who were favorable to Berlin. But although Metternich had Spiegel and Prince Alfred von Schönburg hard at work in Munich and Stuttgart trying to win Ludwig and William over to his views, their efforts could not allay these monarchs' suspicions of Austria. Rather than agreeing with Austria's outlook, they decided that Wrede should be the supreme commander of the combined south German army.[26] Thus, when Rühle returned for a final meeting

22. Rühle von Lilienstern to Frederick William, 5 April 1831, ibid.; and verbal note of the first meeting on 2 April 1831 of Rühle von Lilienstern with representatives of the Württemberg Ministry of War, Bay. GSA, MA 24 076.

23. Rühle von Lilienstern to Frederick William, 8 April 1831, ZSA Me, AAI, Rep. 5, Nr. 593; and Droysen, "Zur Geschichte der preussischen Politik," p. 65.

24. Rühle von Lilienstern to Frederick William, 17 and 18 April 1831, including enclosure by Jolly for the government of Baden, ZSA Me, AAI, Rep. 5, Nr. 593; and Armansperg to Ludwig, 15 April 1831, and Küster to Armansperg, 23 April 1831, Bay. GSA, MA 24 076.

25. Rühle von Lilienstern to Bernstorff, 19 and 21 April 1831, ZSA Me, AAI, Rep. 5, Nr. 593.

26. Küster's reports of 1 and 7 May 1831, Chroust, *Gesandtschaftsberichte aus München, Abteilung III.*, 40:205; Billinger, "Metternich's Policy," pp. 115–119; and Böck, *Karl Philipp Fürst von Wrede*, p. 148.

before going back to Berlin, he found that Ludwig and Armansperg were still in favor of the Prussian proposal.

Evaluating the reception he had gotten throughout southern Germany, Rühle told Frederick William that, within the cabinets, as well as among the different classes of people, it was felt that the closest possible relationship to Prussia was necessary for the independence of Germany and peace with France. They considered Austria to be too deeply involved in Italian, Polish, and Turkish affairs to support faithfully the true interests of Germany. Bavaria, he said, had little confidence in Austria's military power or political policies; Prince Metternich's contradictory, suspicious, and self-centered policy was alien to the south German states. Armansperg also argued that Bavaria was constrained by the same civil-military considerations as Prussia—the Bavarian people would only fight for the protection of their homeland, not to support some conservative cause. Prussia, whose forces were needed to ward off a French attack, could also, by its wise leadership, aid in the legal development of domestic political life in Germany. Thus, admirable institutions, a common interest in peace, and the foundation already laid in the *Zollverein* were important reasons for the desire for a close relationship between Bavaria and Prussia. Armansperg also agreed that Munich would support Berlin on the Brunswick matter and on a prompt settlement of the Sponheim affair.[27] Here, we find some appreciation in Bavaria of Prussia's approach to German affairs; at least one prominent south German minister felt that Prussia was indeed exerting moral leadership in Germany.

Droysen concluded that, by May, the conflict between Austria and Prussia for predominance in Germany was clear for all to see. On the one hand, there was the idea of the more narrow federation under the Prussian leadership that was based on the economic elements in the *Zollverein* and the political factors that emerged in the discussions over the federal military. On the other hand, there was the "older federal constitution under the presidency of Austria."[28] The reference to the configuration of political forces in Germany later in the century was obvious. Treitschke, however, severely criticized this view as an anticipation of nationalistic

---

27. Rühle von Lilienstern to Frederick William, 14 May 1831, ZSA Me, AAI, Rep. 5, Nr. 593. Also see Rumigny to Sebastiani, 19 April 1831, Chroust, *Gesandtschaftsberichte aus München, Abteilung I.,* 19:389–390.

28. Droysen, "Zur Geschichte der preussischen Politik," pp. 81–82.

aims on the part of Prussia that did not in fact exist to any significant degree in 1831. He argued that the question of the organization of the federal military, with only a few exceptions, involved purely technical military considerations, not important political issues.[29] In general, as the next stage of the negotiations shows, Droysen was closer to the truth. By June 1831, it was already clear that Rühle's mission and the ensuing negotiations were packed with political meaning and were of more than purely military interest. Many officials in the south who viewed Prussia as a reasonably progressive and wisely led state were obviously strongly inclined to follow Prussia's lead. Similarly, the southern states' dislike for Austria is already apparent. But did this mission in fact relate to the sort of national idea suggested by Droysen? There is no clear answer to this question. The southern Germans felt that Prussia represented Germany's interests and their own individual interests more satisfactorily than Austria did, but alliance with Prussia also implied greater independence and freedom to operate for the south Germans. They had no desire to relinquish their sovereignty to Prussia—quite the opposite. Nor was there any desire to exclude Austria completely from the Confederation or the proposed military arrangements. Both the south Germans and the Prussians agreed on this point. The whole idea seems more similar to traditional alliance politics within the German state system than it does to a more truly national tendency. The Prussian initiative threatened to destroy a balance of power inside Germany that had normally worked to Austria's advantage. This, of course, does not invalidate Droysen's emphasis on the political side of the negotiations.

An important element in this prospective alliance was the domestic political factor. The south German states were constitutional monarchies of sorts, and they did not view Prussia as being hostile to their internal political arrangements. Furthermore, Bernstorff had been convinced for a long time that the German governments would have to see the tangible advantages of a closer and more dependent relationship with Prussia before they would be willing to sacrifice any component of their sovereignty. This system of individual agreements provided just such an opportunity. Thus, in the long run, some Prussian officials—Rühle, Krauseneck, Witzleben, and Eichhorn, in addition to Bernstorff—were thinking in terms of

29. Heinrich von Treitschke, *History of Germany in the Nineteenth Century,* app. XXIV, 5:621–631.

a more dynamic German federation under Prussian leadership, but there seems to be no evidence that the south German governments were looking that far ahead.

Certainly these Prussian leaders saw the mission to the south German states as a great success. As Witzleben told Eichhorn:

> Above all, it appears necessary to nourish and strengthen the favorable attitude that has become manifest among the south German courts. They have demonstrated their trust in us; we must respond positively. The character of Prussian policy is rectitude and openness—and we must communicate in that way with our south German brothers. The true interests of Germany will also always be the wishes of Prussia, the former is not opposed to the latter and therefore can only be supported by us, and there can be no doubt that we can come to an understanding on this with Austria.[30]

Witzleben's description was unusually optimistic with regard to Austria. Already Gneisenau, Clausewitz, and others were becoming increasingly concerned over the effect of Rühle's mission on the attitude of the Austrians. For example, Gneisenau noted Vienna's strong opposition to the plan in May 1831, although at that time he felt that the Prussian initiative had produced "a very encouraging situation if we use it properly."[31] But, by June, he said, "We must . . . proceed with the greatest caution, in order not to make Austria suspicious."[32] Clausewitz was even more critical of Prussia's federal military policy. After corresponding with Krauseneck on the subject, he told his wife that the idea of Prussia's assuming leadership in Germany through the support of the constitutional states in the south was both unrealistic and dangerous. Prussia had neither the resources nor the talents to assume such a position, and, more importantly, such desires would endanger Prussia's relationship with Austria, which in the event of war with France was essential to Prussia's security. In the final analysis, Clausewitz believed that Prussia was too weak to support such a policy.[33] Thus, the federal military negotiations became a complicated and vexing issue because they involved Prussia's

30. Droysen, "Zur Geschichte der preussischen Politik," p. 89.

31. Gneisenau to Brühl, 31 May 1831, H. von Sybel, "Gneisenau und sein Schwiegersohn, Graf Wilhelm v. Brühl," pp. 278–279.

32. Gneisenau to Canitz, June 1831, GSA PKB, Rep. 92, v. Canitz, Nr. 3.

33. Clausewitz to his wife, 9 and 23 June 1831, Karl Schwartz, *Carl von Clausewitz*, 2:351, 359; and Paret, *Clausewitz*, pp. 403–405.

position in Europe and Germany, technical military considerations, and differences in political philosophy.

## CONTROVERSY OVER THE
## FOREIGN MINISTRY

The negotiations with the south Germans came to a momentary halt while the foreign ministry went through a period of uncertainty and reorganization. Bernstorff's health had been steadily declining for some time. On 18 April 1831, he told Frederick William that he wished to resign as Minister of Foreign Affairs.[34] The King reluctantly approved his request, but also said that he preferred to lighten Bernstorff's workload so that he might still remain in overall charge of Prussia's foreign policy.[35] Ignoring this option, Bernstorff thanked the King for approving his resignation and suggested that Werther would be the best man to succeed him. In addition, he indicated that Schönberg wanted to give up his position as director of the second division to be appointed to a position as *Oberpräsident*. Bernstorff nominated Eichhorn as Schönberg's replacement because "his outstanding capabilities and judgment have been proven in so many respects, and through his enthusiastic and forceful participation in the important and successful negotiations conducted by the Ministry of Foreign Affairs in recent times, he has earned the full claim to consideration and recommendation."[36] He added that Eichhorn should be promoted to *Wirklicher Geheimer Legationsrath,* with a raise in salary and a substantial housing allowance. Ancillon resented exclusion from Bernstorff's plans. On 27 April, he told Bernstorff that he did not want to serve under a new minister and preferred a post in Switzerland. Therefore, Bernstorff suggested to the King that perhaps the department of Neuchatel could be separated from the ministry and Ancillon made its head while still remaining as an independent advisor to the King. He also mentioned the possibility of an ambassadorial position for Ancillon in Switzerland.[37]

34. Bernstorff to Frederick William, 18 April 1831, ZSA Me, Rep. 2.2.1., Geheimes Civil Cabinet, Nr. 12909.
35. Frederick William to Bernstorff, 26 April 1831, ibid.
36. Bernstorff to Frederick William, 27 April 1831, ibid.
37. Ancillon to Bernstorff, 27 April 1831, and Bernstorff to Frederick William, 27 April 1831, ibid.

The King approved Bernstorff's plans for his successor and for the ministry. On 16 May 1831, Frederick William announced to the *Staatsministerium* that Werther would be Bernstorff's replacement and that Eichhorn would be made the director of the second division.[38] Bernstorff, however, was to remain as the senior cabinet minister in the area of foreign affairs and would continue to work in an advisory capacity.[39] Despite this last change, the ministry had been set up as Bernstorff had intended. He was especially happy over Eichhorn's increased responsibilities. At the end of May, he congratulated him. "Insofar as I have had the fortune to assist in the promulgation of the double distinction, I wish you to recognize it as only a weak and, in terms of my own feelings, inadequate recognition of your multifarious and consequential achievements by which you have, for far into the future, rendered a great service to the Prussian state and for which you have my undying gratitude."[40]

Unfortunately Werther was not eager to assume his new position, and he told Bernstorff he had doubts about his qualifications for the job. In June, he left Paris to discuss the matter personally with his chief, but Bernstorff was not able to convince him to change his mind. There is some evidence that Werther was bothered by the political friction in Berlin over the foreign ministry, and it is possible that Wittgenstein pressured him to refuse the appointment. We do know that Ancillon complained bitterly to Wittgenstein that Bernstorff was sacrificing him to Eichhorn and others. "The fate of foreign affairs and domestic politics as well lies in good hands," he wrote to Wittgenstein, "or I should say, it will lay in such hands if it depends upon you."[41] Whether Wittgenstein took any action on Ancillon's complaint is unknown. But Werther's refusal of the ministry had jeopardized Bernstorff's plans.[42]

Coincidentally, the King then presented a new proposal that Ancillon

38. Frederick William to Staatsministerium, 16 May 1831, GSA PKB, Rep. 90 C, III, 3.6; and Frederick William to Staatsministerium, 16 May 1831, GSA PKB, Rep. 90 C, III, 5.1.

39. Bernstorff to Maltzahn, 21 May 1831, ZSA Me, Rep. 81, Wien I, Nr. 143.

40. Bernstorff to Eichhorn, 31 May 1831, ZSA Me, Rep. 92, Eichhorn, Nr. 4.

41. See Droysen, "Zur Geschichte der preussischen Politik," p. 90; and Ancillon to Wittgenstein, 13 May 1831, GSA PKB, Rep. 192, Wittgenstein, V. 1, 15, 16. Also see Ancillon to Wittgenstein, 9 and 17 May in the same file.

42. Bernstorff to Frederick William, 30 May 1831, Frederick William to Bernstorff, 4 June 1831, Werther to Bernstorff, 26 June 1831, and Bernstorff to Frederick William, 27 June 1831, ZSA Me, Geheimes Civil Cabinet, Rep. 2.2.1., Nr. 12909.

should take over the political division, that is, become a second cabinet minister in charge of Prussia's European and German policy on a daily basis.[43] How much of the King's proposal was the result of pressure from ultraconservatives such as Wittgenstein and Duke Charles is impossible to tell, but they were clearly concerned, particularly over Eichhorn's new influence.[44] Bernstorff was reluctant to relinquish total administrative control of Prussia's foreign policy to Ancillon, so he countered the King's proposal with a new suggestion. Instead of making Ancillon a Minister of State, he could become a State Secretary with responsibility for the political section. But the task of conducting the correspondence with the German courts would be transferred to the second division, to be executed by Eichhorn under Bernstorff's direct supervision.[45] As soon as Ancillon learned of Bernstorff's modification of the King's proposal, he complained directly to Frederick William. He said it was unfair for him not to have full ministerial status as Werther was to have had, and it was unwise for him not to have control over German as well as European affairs. Bernstorff's wishing to divide the business of the ministry and to retain direct involvement in German affairs was inexplicable to him unless it was based on the personalities involved.[46]

The whole question of the reorganization of the ministry now became a major political issue. Bernstorff was trying to maintain the influence of those who favored an active and progressive policy in the Confederation; his restriction of Ancillon's activities was aimed at achieving this goal. The King finally approved Bernstorff's modification, although there is evidence that he was already becoming suspicious of the ministry's activities. On 1 August 1831, the new plan of operation went into effect.[47] Under this system, Bernstorff retained overall responsibility for the ministry, while Ancillon, under his guidance, was responsible for the

43. Frederick William to Bernstorff, 6 July 1831, ibid.

44. Duke Charles to Wittgenstein, 8 July 1831, GSA PKB, Rep. 192, Wittgenstein, V, 1, 15, 16; and Wittgenstein to Metternich, 12 June 1831, HHSA, Stk., Preussen, Karton 141.

45. Bernstorff to Frederick William, 9 July 1831, ZSA Me, Geheimes Civil Cabinet, Rep. 2.2.1., Nr. 12909.

46. Ancillon to Frederick William, 19 July 1831, GSA PKB, Rep. 192, Wittgenstein, V, 1, 15, 16.

47. Frederick William to Bernstorff, 25 July 1831, ZSA Me, Rep. 2.2.1., Geheimes Civil Cabinet, Nr. 12909; and Frederick William to Staatsministerium, 1 August 1831, GSA PKB, Rep. 90 C, III, 3.6.

correspondence with the European nations with full powers to sign. The second division under Eichhorn, with Bernstorff's more direct supervision, took care of German and commercial affairs. Bernstorff retained control over the personnel and financial policies of the ministry.[48]

There is no doubt that these changes introduced a certain split personality into Prussia's foreign relations, although, except for Prussia's relationship to Austria, Ancillon and Bernstorff agreed on many essential aspects of Prussia's European policy. The real area of disagreement between them revolved around Prussia's German policy. Thus, the institutional relationships within the foreign ministry were a tangible representation of the different sides of Prussia's foreign policy—a European policy that was cautious and desirous of peace, and a German policy that was progressive and somewhat innovative. Bernstorff formed the link between the two policies and their institutional manifestations.

Although Bernstorff had succeeded in maintaining the influence of those who desired a more progressive German policy, ultraconservatives within the Prussian government, with Metternich's support, were already launching a campaign to try to make Frederick William suspicious of his liberal advisors. On 14 July, the King traveled to Teplitz with Wittgenstein, where he met with Metternich's envoy, Werner. Metternich instructed Werner to argue forcefully for the closest possible relations between Russia, Austria, and Prussia to control the forces of revolution in Europe—a meeting of ambassadors in Vienna could maintain this alliance. In other words, Metternich was still trying to create his *point centrale* for the management of European affairs. Turning to Germany, the Chancellor's instruction discussed the necessity of Austrian and Prussian control of revolutionary impulses inside the Confederation. According to Metternich, the consolidation of Germany was a highly dangerous tendency. Many saw Prussia as actively participating in this process, while Austria was viewed as being foreign to this development. This evil, he said, must cease. The guiding principles for Germany were clear—the Confederation was a federation of princes not peoples, and Prussia and Austria must remain united in determining its policy. He suggested ongoing discussions in Vienna with the Prussian ambassador on German affairs, which would be the counterpart to the discussions of the three eastern powers on European affairs. In setting up these discussions, he saw

48. Bernstorff to Maltzahn, 30 July 1831, ZSA Me, Rep. 81, Wien I, Nr. 143.

Maltzahn as a useful tool for influencing the King. "Maltzahn," he said, "is in every way a splendid instrument. Whether he is viewed as such by his superiors is a question that I cannot answer. On this Prince Wittgenstein is better able to judge."[49] Thus, as he had tried to do in 1819, Metternich was attempting to convince the King that constitutionalist or nationalistic tendencies in Germany in which Prussia played a part were a threat to the German system.

In this first meeting with Werner, Frederick William expressed his concern over Germany's defensive weakness and said that Metternich was not sufficiently interested in the effectiveness of the federal military system. The King pointed out that the difficulties encountered over the question of military action by the Confederation in Luxemburg demonstrated that its capabilities left much to be desired. Werner replied that, on the contrary, Metternich was very attentive to federal military affairs, whereupon the King, softening his stand, indicated that, if this were the case, he would be interested in Metternich's ideas. The discussion then shifted to Prussia's relations with the south German princes. The King reportedly turned to Wittgenstein and said, "You know how often they have turned to me individually and have wanted to get me to establish an exclusively Prussian policy in Germany. That I will never do; it is against my fundamental principles for I believe one of the two great powers alone could never establish a wise system in Germany; only when both go hand in hand is this possible." The King expressed his distrust of constitutions and a free press and closed the audience with this comment to Werner: "The more [Metternich], in complete confidence, communicates his views to me on the specific questions and issues of the times, the better it will be for me."[50] Once again, the King displayed his innate timidity, and, by this opening to Metternich, he in effect invited the Austrian Chancellor to undermine the Prussian government.

The meeting at Teplitz reactivated the King's direct interest in Metternich's views and had an immediate effect on what might be called a

49. Only the part of the instruction dealing with European affairs was included in the printed collection of Metternich's papers. See Clemens Lothar Wenzel Fürst von Metternich-Winneburg, *Aus Metternichs nachgelassenen Papieren,* 5:190–197. The remainder is paraphrased somewhat haphazardly in Viktor Bibl, *Metternich in neuer Beleuchtung,* pp. 130–131. The original is in HHSA, Stk., Preussen, Karton 141.

50. Werner to Metternich, 30 July 1831, HHSA, Stk., Preussen, Karton 141.

procedural matter. Metternich had complained to Wittgenstein at Teplitz that "the [foreign] ministry is acting in many cases in a way that is different from the views of the King and from our own as well."[51] Metternich wanted to establish a direct channel between Frederick William and Vienna that circumvented the Prussian foreign ministry. Through Wittgenstein he was able to get the King to issue a Cabinet Order that not only endorsed discussions between the representatives of the three eastern powers in Vienna on European matters and between Prussia and Austria on German affairs, but, more importantly, ordered Maltzahn to submit his reports to Metternich for review before sending them to Berlin in order to be absolutely certain he had properly grasped Metternich's intent. These reports would be handled outside of normal diplomatic channels and would not be sent to the Ministry of Foreign Affairs; they would go directly to Frederick William to be personally opened by the King. Werner reported, "Prince Wittgenstein compliments himself that Your Highness will be entirely satisfied with this procedure."[52] Wittgenstein indicated that Maltzahn was already a faithful supporter of Metternich and that in this way "all ministerial intrigue shall be prevented, at least at the moment when your dispatches arrive."[53] In this atmosphere of increasing suspicion and tension, European events forced Bernstorff to move forward once again on the subject of the organization of the federal army.


## THE OPPOSITION OF AUSTRIA


On 4 August, the Dutch army invaded Belgium; by 11 August, the French, in response to Leopold's request for help, had begun their operation to eject the Dutch. Once again war seemed possible, and therefore sound defensive preparations in Germany became all the more pressing. On 8 August, Ludwig had told Küster that the German governments should not be lax in uniting for defensive purposes. He wanted to discuss Rühle's proposals again, and he asserted that as before "the military and political

51. Metternich to Wittgenstein, 12 August 1831, GSA PKB, Rep. 192, Wittgenstein, VI, 3, 1.2.3.
52. Werner to Metternich, 12 August 1831, HHSA, Stk., Preussen, Karton 141.
53. Wittgenstein to Metternich, 12 August 1831, ibid.

system of Bavaria rests upon the Prussian."[54] Under these circumstances, on 15 August 1831, Bernstorff sent a circular note to the south German courts. It began with a direct reference to the possibility of a war with France, despite the peaceful promises of the government in Paris. He then announced that he was very pleased with the success of Rühle's trip; there was complete unanimity between the various courts. After summarizing the major points of Rühle's mission and indicating Prussia's great contribution to the defense of Germany, he suggested that the next step was to hold a meeting among military representatives of the Seventh and Eighth Federal Army Corps, Prussia, and Austria, preferably in a smaller town such as Würzburg or Bayreuth.[55] In Bavaria, Ludwig immediately made plans to send General von Hertling to the upcoming conference.[56] Bernstorff also sent a copy of the circular dispatch to Maltzahn to show to Metternich and indicated his hope that the Austrian Chancellor would cooperate with this approach. He added that, in view of their responsibility for the defense of Germany, further hesitation was undesirable.[57]

No sooner had Metternich received word from Maltzahn than he immediately sent a blistering note to Werner complaining of the circular, arguing that it contradicted the positions he had made clear to Röder back in April. He believed that it was absolutely necessary that Austria and Prussia come to agreement on the question of the federal military before the matter was discussed with the representatives of the south German states. The King, he said, had two cabinets, implying that Bernstorff and others were working in opposition to the King's views, and he directed Werner to give this dispatch to Wittgenstein, who should present Metternich's complaints to the King.[58] He also decided to send General Clam-Martinitz to Berlin to discuss the matter with Prussian authorities.

By this time, Austrian officials were very sensitive to the political implications of the Prussian plan. As Spiegel reported from Munich, it was apparent that Bavaria and Württemberg were creating the strongest bonds

54. Küster to Frederick William, 8 August 1831, Chroust, *Gesandtschaftsberichte aus München: Abteilung III.,* 40:219–220.

55. Bernstorff to Küster, Salviati, Otterstedt, and Arnim, 15 August 1831, ZSA Me, Rep. 92, Witzleben, Nr. 111.

56. Wrede to Metternich, 4 September 1831, Bibl, *Metternich in neuer Beleuchtung,* pp. 240–241.

57. Bernstorff to Maltzahn, 21 August 1831, ZSA Me, Rep. 92, Witzleben, Nr. 111.

58. Metternich to Werner, 29 August 1831, HHSA, Stk., Preussen, Karton 141.

of unity—a similar phenomenon was developing between Baden, Hesse-Darmstadt, and Prussia—and that Bavaria was inclining itself more and more toward Prussia.[59] Thus, a political coalition of five powers dominating the population and territory of Germany seemed about to be reinforced by concrete military arrangements. In Berlin, Duke Charles, although he had favored a military reorganization of the Confederation, now attacked what he called "the Bernstorff-Eichhorn Opus"; he told Wittgenstein that the influence of this group of officials had to be eliminated. Unity with Austria was essential for Germany and Prussia.[60] Thus, the political implications of the plan had overridden his earlier concern for reform in the military structure of the *Bund*.

Clam-Martinitz arrived in Berlin on 16 September 1831. According to Metternich, the ostensible reason for his visit was the need to discuss sanitary measures to cope with the threat of cholera.[61] Shortly after his arrival, Clam briefly met with Bernstorff. From the outset, the Prussian minister said that he did not think Metternich's pretext of "sanitary measures" was very credible, and he intended to tell any diplomat who inquired that the discussions were about "federal matters." Bernstorff also indicated that Clam would have to discuss military details with Krauseneck, but Clam replied that the Emperor expected him to discuss these matters directly with Bernstorff. Clam then met with Ancillon, who, undercutting his own chief, explained that the missions of Röder and Rühle, as well as the 15 August circular, were not completely supported by the Prussian cabinet. He said that it would have been much better if the 15 August circular had been approved by Austria beforehand, and he apologized for Rühle's mission. On the next day, Clam met once again with Bernstorff, who explained that Rühle's mission was in response to the concerns of the south German courts and the influence of France and of parties inclined toward France in southern Germany. This action was taken in the interest of strengthening the Confederation, not in reducing the influence of Austria. Whether the south German states were right or wrong in turning to Prussia, they took that step voluntarily without any

59. Spiegel to Metternich, 3 September 1831, Chroust, *Gesandtschaftsberichte aus München: Abteilung II.,* 36:356–357.

60. Duke Charles to Wittgenstein, 4 September 1831, GSA PKB, Rep. 192, Wittgenstein, VI, 3, 1.2.3.

61. Metternich to Wrede, 23 September 1831, Bibl, *Metternich in neuer Beleuchtung,* pp. 244–245.

danger to the Confederation. He said that Austria was essential for the well-being of the *Bund*. The circular of 15 August was a preparatory statement meant to inaugurate definitive negotiations; the differences between Austria and Prussia were not insurmountable and could be worked out. When Clam voiced Austria's strong opposition to all phases of the plan, Bernstorff expressed surprise. On the basis of Röder's final report, he had concluded that Austria was not unconditionally opposed to Prussia's proposal. Clam replied that Austria wished above all to maintain supreme command over the Seventh and Eighth Federal Army Corps. Matters of deployment could be worked out later as time and circumstance required and should be settled by Austria and Prussia alone. Bernstorff said that, although he was not completely knowledgeable about military affairs, he believed that the differences could be resolved. Prussia was sensitive to Austria's concerns, but giving Austria the dominant position in these discussions was neither possible nor desirable, for the south German princes, particularly Ludwig of Bavaria, already had great mistrust for Vienna. Clam then told Bernstorff that the plan was not based on "military motives." Bernstorff asked, if the south Germans wanted to follow a retreat line toward the Main, did Clam mean that Prussia should refuse to approve? Clam answered yes, because it contradicted Austria's desires. Furthermore, if Berlin did not support Austria's position, it would be entirely excluded. Bernstorff retorted that not supporting an idea was not the same as totally excluding it from consideration. Clam replied that, if the goal of both countries was to work closely together, this "was an unfortunate position to observe." If the whole affair were purely a military matter, that would be one thing; but, if the south German states were intent on increased independence, then it was Prussia's duty to work with Austria to keep the south Germans away from such views. Bernstorff answered "that it was indispensable to recognize it was necessary to keep the south Germans in good spirits, not scaring away their ideas through stubborn opposition, but rather by making their efforts and sacrifices to a certain extent agreeable, to which after all they are entitled." He said that Austria was too critical of the plan to concentrate the south German forces on the Main. But Clam countered that the plan placed the Austrian military at a disadvantage in the Danube valley and had serious political consequences. The creation of a central corps out of the Seventh and Eighth Corps would make the south Germans more independent and that was not in the interest of the Confederation. Bernstorff closed the meeting by saying that he thought these differences could be worked out at the upcoming conference.

Bernstorff had not conceded a single point and, by stating that Berlin was going to be attentive to the interests of the south Germans, he confirmed Vienna's suspicions. Although Bernstorff stated that Austria's views would be welcome, he was not going to give them any special preference. Austria's ideas would have to compete on the basis of their merit. The perseverance with which Bernstorff defended the 15 August circular made Clam realize that the upcoming negotiations would be difficult. Clam had also met earlier with Wittgenstein, who agreed with the Austrian position, although he felt that Vienna was too condemnatory of the 15 August circular. Wittgenstein said that Bernstorff was still reliable, but the influence of Eichhorn, Rühle, and Krauseneck was very great and that they believed that Prussia "by proceeding in a constitutional sense should take the lead and so govern Germany."[62]

Bernstorff was highly suspicious of Clam. After the first meetings, he told Witzleben that he wanted Krauseneck and Rühle to take part in the discussions to strengthen his position.[63] Indeed, shortly thereafter, Krauseneck joined the meetings, a maneuver that Clam considered to be a victory for the Rühle-Eichhorn faction.[64] He was correct; if the Prussian military negotiator had been an associate of Wittgenstein and Duke Charles, Prussia's attempt to build a closer military relationship with the south would have been scuttled. Krauseneck, on the other hand, had reformist views. He had served on Blücher's staff in 1814 and later was a close associate of Boyen.[65]

On 19 September 1831, Clam met with Frederick William. Apparently supporting the position of Bernstorff and others, the King said that the southern states had to be convinced to take part in the defense of Germany. Using terminology almost identical to Bernstorff's, he added, "One had to do something in order to keep the south Germans in good spirits, since their participation was also necessary." Clam then began to develop one of the major tactics of his mission—creating suspicion in Frederick William's mind toward the intentions of the south Germans. Clam said

62. Clam to Metternich, 20 September 1831, HHSA, Stk., Preussen, Karton 141.
63. Bernstorff to Witzleben, September 1831, ZSA Me, Rep. 92, Witzleben, Nr. 111.
64. See resume of discussion between Clam and Krauseneck, 23 September 1831, and Clam to Metternich, 27 September 1831, HHSA, Stk., Preussen, Karton 141.
65. On Krauseneck, see [Felgermann, Major von], *General W. I. von Krauseneck*.

that their absolute independence appeared to the Emperor to be neither "politically advisable" nor "militarily necessary." This ploy was based on a bogus fear. No one in Berlin was advocating absolute independence for the southern states; in fact, the possibility that they might sign a separate agreement with France had been one of the original stimulants for Rühle's mission. The whole idea was to bind the south Germans more closely to the interests of Prussia and Germany, which clearly did not necessarily include those of Austria. Nevertheless, Frederick William seems to have been impressed by Clam's argument. The Austrian went on to say that the military plans of the south Germans were an undeniable attempt to emancipate themselves politically from the influence of the two great German powers. "Only in a firm agreement between Austria and Prussia can the means be found to stop this regrettable evil. The trust of the Emperor for Your Majesty is the foundation of his policy." For additional effect, Clam concluded that, in these times, "the preservation of the world lies in Prussia's alliance with Austria, and the trust of the Emperor for Your Majesty is unshakable." To this, Frederick William reportedly answered, "The Emperor can depend on me, and he certainly knows that."

Later in the day, Clam met with Witzleben. Referring to the 15 August circular, Witzleben immediately noted, "I had no part in it and in fact I have never even read it once." When Clam explained the contents of the document, the Prussian general replied, "I must repeat I had no responsibility whatsoever for the circular," but he agreed that it would have been better to have discussed the matter thoroughly with Austria before the circular was sent out. Witzleben said that the King was more dedicated than ever to close relations with Austria, and he would lament any attempt by the south Germans to isolate themselves from Austria. At a later meeting with Clam in early October, Witzleben added that, if Clam had difficulty coming to an agreement with Krauseneck, he was "convinced the King will certainly pay as careful attention to the concerns of the Austrians as to those of his own generals."[66]

The reasons for Witzleben's weak performance are unknown. Perhaps he had immediately detected that the King had been impressed by Clam's presentation and was reconsidering the policy pursued by Bernstorff, Eichhorn, Krauseneck, and others. In view of Witzleben's intimate connections with the entire project, it is difficult to believe that he still had not

66. Clam to Metternich, 9 October 1831, HHSA, Stk., Preussen, Karton 141.

read the circular one month after it had been sent. If these remarks represented Witzleben's true position, his defection from the progressive group on this issue seriously weakened the strength of the entire movement, for now there was no one on the King's personal staff who could argue the case for Bernstorff and his colleagues.

Returning to the Wilhelmstrasse from Charlottenburg after these discussions, Clam met with Bernstorff once again. Their conversation took "a somewhat painful course," Clam reported, for Bernstorff repeated his earlier position without modifications. The Austrian general concluded "that the desire for independence from Austria especially on the part of the south German princes and the secret encouragement of their efforts by a group in the Prussian government, and not military factors, is the actual basis for the opposition to our views. However, it is also undeniable that in the purely military sense the army here embraces the idea of a flank position on the Main." What he called the "Prussian-German faction" had gained influence over Bernstorff and the King, but he also felt that Austria's inaction in federal military affairs had left the field clear for Prussia.[67]

Metternich's dispatch, the complaints of Wittgenstein and Duke Charles, and the discussions with Clam had considerable impact on Frederick William's attitude. On 23 September, he issued a Cabinet Order that severely reprimanded his foreign minister for the 15 August circular and asked why he had never seen a draft of the document prior to its being sent; henceforth, no major document was to be sent out from the foreign ministry without the King's approval. According to Werner, Bernstorff attempted to explain to the King that Krauseneck had previously presented the ideas in the circular in a *Memoire* to the King. Frederick William said that he could not recall any such *Memoire,* and, in any case, the whole matter should have been discussed with Austria beforehand. Bernstorff, according to Wittgenstein, was surprised by the King's attitude, for, on the basis of a general report by Witzleben, he had probably assumed that the King had approved of the project.[68] Judging from the King's first comments to Clam, it seems likely that the King did in fact have at least a general knowledge of the contents of the circular, but now,

67. Clam to Metternich, 21 September 1831, ibid.

68. Werner to Metternich, 25 September 1831 (with copies of Frederick William to Wittgenstein, 2 September 1831, and Duke Charles to Wittgenstein, 4 September 1831), and Clam to Metternich, 27 September 1831, ibid.

in view of Austria's opposition, he had decided to change his mind and thus pretended that he was ignorant of the entire proposal.

About the same time that Clam learned of the King's displeasure over the 15 August circular, he had also gathered useful information from Duke Charles concerning the attitude of various figures within the Prussian government and military toward the south German plan. Duke Charles indicated that the maintenance of the line of the Main as well as the concept of a Main army was a well-established Prussian idea that was supported by the King and by what he called the independent Prussian faction (Duke Charles, Witzleben, Knesebeck, and Thile). The Prussian-German faction had seized this idea and, instead of thinking simply in terms of a Main army, wished to create a "mittel-teutsche" army, thereby connecting military considerations with their other well-known plans for Germany.[69] Clam also reported that Lottum and Ancillon supported Austria's position. Luxburg, the Bavarian minister, on the other hand, was working hard to maintain Berlin's commitment to the views of the 15 August circular.[70]

By October, Clam had adopted what he called his plan of operations: He would work with Lottum to postpone repeatedly the military conference until a firm understanding was established with Prussia, and he would attempt to debilitate and neutralize the Rühle plan by cooperating with Wittgenstein, Duke Charles, and Knesebeck against the combined efforts of the south German ambassadors and the Prussian-German faction.[71] Lottum, however, was not overly cooperative, and, while Duke Charles was very agreeable, he, like Lottum, noted that there were difficulties ahead. "The Prussian military," he said, "would not easily give up its defense of the Rühle plan," and he added that "the alliance between Rühle and the most influential south German military leaders is very strong and will be developed still more through connections between Eichhorn and the south German ambassadors."[72] The discussions then lagged somewhat because Bernstorff became ill in the middle of October.[73]

Meanwhile Metternich had had time to evaluate his special envoy's

69. Clam to Metternich, 26 September 1831, ibid.
70. Clam to Metternich, 9 October 1831, ibid.
71. Clam to Metternich, 14 October 1831, ibid.
72. Clam to Metternich, 19 October 1831, ibid.
73. Bernstorff to Clam, 17 October 1831, and Clam to Metternich, 22 October 1831, ibid.

reports. He agreed with Clam's assessment of the situation in Berlin. Rühle's plan was "the work of the Prussian-German and purely Prussian factions. The champions of the first of these groups subscribe to a Germany under Prussian hegemony; the doctrinaires of the second group have nothing but the campaign of 1806 and the Saale Valley in their minds." Clam had been correct to place his trust in Duke Charles, Wittgenstein, and Lottum.[74] Metternich added that he had long ago learned that talking to people like Armansperg and his ilk was a waste of time, and he no longer had anything to do with the south German courts. The same applied to people like Eichhorn and Rühle. He was still convinced that the King and even possibly Bernstorff did not really want this plan; what was essential, he said, was unity between Austria and Prussia. "All of this agitation by factions means only a loss of time—but a very regrettable loss of time. The enemy meanwhile moves forward with measured steps; the enemy is revolution."[75] By November, Clam had not succeeded in converting the Prussian negotiators to Austria's position.

Bernstorff's report to the King containing his formal reply to Clam-Martinitz and two additional policy papers restated the foreign ministry's position. On the basis of the initial discussions with Clam, Bernstorff told Frederick William that Austria was opposing the desires of the south Germans for political rather than military reasons. In his more detailed reply to Clam, which the King also read, Bernstorff indicated that the two courts were united in their desire to provide an effective defense for Germany; what they differed over was how to accomplish that goal. Obviously, the status of the Seventh and Eighth Corps was central to these differences. He said that he desired the best possible relations with Austria, but, even if the threat of war had passed, having a sound defensive plan was still a necessity. He felt that joint discussions were essential to meet the desires of the south German states and to make preparations for the eventuality of war. The policy papers attempted to counter Metternich's arguments; in particular, they refuted his opinion that Prussia's and Austria's roles as European powers were more important than their roles as German powers. Bernstorff and Eichhorn saw these two functions as being much more closely intertwined because, in the event of a French

74. Metternich to Clam, 9 October 1831, HHSA, Stk., Preussen, Karton, 140, f. 177–182.

75. Metternich to Clam, 30 October 1831, HHSA, Stk., Preussen, Karton 141.

war, an attack on Prussia automatically involved the Confederation. While it was true, as Metternich had pointed out in one of his papers to Berlin, that the military power of Prussia and Austria was far greater than that of the other German states, it was also true that, since the south German states would be in immediate danger from a French war and would play a key role in blocking a French invasion, special attention must be paid to their attitude. Austria's expectation that they would pull back against their own interests was unreasonable. The Austrian plan "would only make these states indolent and would separate them from the German cause. Prussia on the basis of the trust placed in it by them cannot recommend this course—it would contradict good sense and conscience."[76] The King did not indicate any disapproval of Bernstorff's policy statements at this time.

If Bernstorff could not be converted to Vienna's point of view, perhaps he could be circumvented. In early November, when Clam realized that he had failed in his mission, he had decided that he would have to get Ancillon and especially Knesebeck to pressure the King. Knesebeck, according to Ancillon, completely understood the secret aims of the German faction, which was composed of short-sighted Prussians who wanted to enlarge Prussia's influence in Germany and dedicated liberals who wanted to push Prussia toward constitutional rule.[77] Coincidentally, on 24 November 1831, Krauseneck was replaced by Knesebeck as the chief Prussian military negotiator with Clam.[78] How and why this took place at this particular time is not explained in the Prussian documents, but, from Clam's reports, it seems probable that the influence of Ancillon and Wittgenstein brought Knesebeck into the negotiations.[79] Metternich urged Clam to devise defensive plans of his own for Germany that were consonant with Austria's interests and could be used to counter Bernstorff's proposals; any new approaches should be kept secret from Bernstorff and his associates.[80] This new line of attack soon worked to Austria's advantage.

76. Bernstorff to Frederick William, 6 November 1831, ZSA Me, Rep. 92, Witzleben, Nr. 111.

77. Clam to Metternich, 8 November 1831, HHSA, Stk., Preussen, Karton 141.

78. Gneomar Natzmer, *Unter den Hohenzollern,* 2:61.

79. For example, see Clam to Metternich, 8 November 1831, HHSA, Stk., Preussen, Karton 141.

80. Metternich to Clam, 21 November 1831, ibid.

After some preliminary communications with Clam, Knesebeck sent the Austrian representative a plan for the creation of a central army made of 60,000 Austrians, 60,000 Prussians, and 60,000 federal troops from the south; this force was still based on a defense line along the Main, not the Danube valley. Prussia and Austria, he said, must stand together militarily and politically and must not let any third party come between them.[81] Knesebeck's approach had the great advantage of incorporating the south German troops into a Prussian-Austrian army, thereby avoiding giving the southern states any degree of independence, while at the same time retaining the defense line of the Main that was dear to the Prussian military.

Knesebeck's *Memoire* was not a private effort; he sent it to Clam with Frederick William's full knowledge and approval.[82] Yet Bernstorff, as Metternich had desired, knew nothing of Knesebeck's paper, for, in the discussions with Clam before the Austrian returned to Vienna for consultations with Metternich, Bernstorff merely spoke of the King's desire to settle all differences between Austria and Prussia on the question of the federal army.[83] The King did not inform him of Knesebeck's paper even when Bernstorff sent a circular dispatch for the south German courts explaining the nature of the negotiations with Clam to him for approval.[84] Probably the pressure of the ultraconservatives and the declining danger of war made Frederick William eager for compromise. While Knesebeck's plan satisfied the desires of the "Prussian military party," it sacrificed the political interests of the German-Prussian group and the south German states' independence from Austria, which had been an important part of the Rühle plan.

Clearly, Frederick William was no longer much concerned about public opinion in the south German states. In a note on 30 November 1831, he wrote, "Although there is still a moral danger, the prospects of an impending war have been greatly lessened. The powers and the German princes must therefore adjust their political and military measures in

---

81. Droysen, "Zur Geschichte der preussischen Politik," p. 119.

82. Clam to Metternich, 30 November 1831, HHSA, Stk., Preussen, Karton 141.

83. Clam to Metternich, 3 December 1831, ibid.

84. Droysen, "Zur Geschichte der preussischen Politik," p. 119; Bernstorff to Küster, 14 December 1831, ZSA Me, Rep. 81, Muenchen, Nr. IV a 4; and Bernstorff to Arnim, 14 December 1831, ZSA Me, Rep. 23.13 (Darmtsadt), Nr. 536.

accordance with the times."[85] As the danger of war declined, so did his interest in mobilizing the energies of the German people for a war of defense. He became more fearful of change and innovation, and his natural inclination to maintain the status quo reasserted itself. Most important of all, by exploiting this weakness of the King, Metternich had succeeded in separating him and his personal entourage from the advice and guidance of the more liberally inclined members of his own government. As Metternich put it, princely rule was gaining the ascendancy over government.

In January, Clam returned to Berlin, and negotiations were resumed. Once again, Bernstorff stated that Prussia would stand by its previous commitments to the south German courts.[86] Clam realized that, because of the Prussian foreign minister's obstinacy, the discussions would proceed no further in Austria's direction. Therefore, based on a suggestion by Ancillon, he made plans to approach Frederick William directly. On 5 February 1832, he told Metternich that only a direct appeal to the King, presented as the desire of Emperor Francis, would be successful.[87] On 27 February 1832, in response to this request, Metternich sent Clam a lengthy *Memoire* on German affairs for the King. Included in it was Austria's position on the military question. Metternich indicated that Austria was willing to base negotiations on the Knesebeck memorandum, except that he wanted the retreat line to be down the Danube valley, not along the Main. Clam presented this paper personally to Frederick William; Bernstorff never saw it. In numerous marginal notes, the King indicated his wholehearted approval of Metternich's draft. On 4 March, Clam wrote to Bernstorff that Knesebeck had returned Metternich's memorandum with the King's affirmative notes and that he was now sending this document to Bernstorff to serve as the basis for further discussions.[88] Bernstorff reacted immediately to the King's action and to the Austrian tactics. On the same day, he wrote to Frederick William,

> The Imperial Austrian General Count von Clam has sent to me the *Denkschrift* with the endorsement of Your Majesty's marginal statements and has requested that the negotiations be resumed on this basis.

85. Droysen, "Zur Geschichte der preussischen Politik," p. 118.
86. Ibid., p. 120; and Bibl, *Metternich in neuer Beleuchtung,* p. 163.
87. Bibl, *Metternich in neuer Beleuchtung,* p. 164.
88. Droysen, "Zur Geschichte der preussischen Politik," p. 124.

> Since I, in view of the turn and the form which these negotiations
> have taken, consider myself less suited than anyone else to continue with
> Count Clam in a manner satisfactory to Your Majesty, and since in my
> present state of poor health I am each day less able to conduct negotia-
> tions of this kind, please allow me to make the most humble request
> that it may please Your Majesty to release me from any further direct
> participation in the negotiations under discussion.[89]

Frederick William granted Bernstorff's request and added that he considered Metternich's *Denkschrift* to be "correct."[90] There is no doubt that
Bernstorff withdrew from the military discussions because he had been
circumvented, not primarily because his health was poor, as Treitschke
states. The meaning of Bernstorff's note to the King is clear. Moreover,
three weeks later, Bernstorff spoke bitterly to Trauttmannsdorff and attacked Metternich's participation in the whole affair. After the Austrian
minister brought up the federal military matter for discussion, Bernstorff
replied that, whatever Trauttmansdorff had to say to him was purely
academic because, as he already knew, he had withdrawn from the negotiations and no longer had any influence over them. Bernstorff then went
on to say that

> I cannot conceal that to me the course that Prince Metternich has chosen
> in this negotiation is absolutely shocking. A memoir was laid before the
> King about which I was informed after the fact, thereby separating the
> King from his ministry. I can tell you with complete frankness that I
> consider this procedure as not only completely unethical but also in no
> way in keeping with the relations that I have normally had with Prince
> Metternich in the past.[91]

Bernstorff took no further part in the military negotiations with Clam,
and Metternich had seemingly convinced Frederick William of the need
to abandon the military organization proposed by Rühle. In view of
Metternich's great efforts to disrupt Prussia's federal military plans, it is
paradoxical that, by the end of 1832, Austria agreed to an organization of

---

89. Bernstorff to Frederick William, 4 March 1832, ZSA Me, Geheimes Civil
Cabinet, Rep. 2.2.1., Nr. 13072.

90. Frederick William to Bernstorff, 12 March 1832, ibid.

91. Trauttmannsdorff to Metternich, 7 April 1832, HHSA, Stk., Preussen, Karton
142.

the federal military forces that corresponded very closely to Prussia's and the south Germans' desires. As a result of negotiations in Berlin between Clam, Knesebeck, Hertling, and Bangold in the end of May, and between those representatives and emissaries from the Ninth and Tenth Federal Army Corps beginning in August, it was agreed that the federal forces should be divided into three armies: one on the lower Rhine made up of 60,000 to 70,000 Prussian troops and the Tenth Federal Army Corps; a central army on the middle Rhine made up of 90,000 Prussian troops, 30,000 Bavarian troops, and the Seventh, Eighth, and Ninth Federal Army Corps; and a third army on the upper Rhine consisting of 150,000 Austrian troops. No Austrian troops were included in the middle army, the Main Valley was accepted by Austria as a possible line of retreat, and the question of a supreme commander was left open. In addition, because it was expected that it would take some time to mobilize the full strength of this force, a provisional army composed of the Seventh, Eighth, and Ninth Army Corps, 30,000 Prussians, and 70,000 Austrians would defend the Rhine frontier from Mainz to Basel until the permanent organization could be established.[92] The Austrians had in fact given in on most essentials. The question is why? It was this outcome to the Berlin talks that led Treitschke to believe the whole federal military question centered around resolvable technical military and procedural matters, but his understanding of the situation was incomplete.

The Austrians accepted this final arrangement for two reasons. First, the south German governments refused to agree to Metternich's organizational plans. Their perseverance led to compromise. Even the final contents of the Berlin protocol of 3 December 1832 were not entirely acceptable to them, and they never ratified the agreement.[93] Second, Bernstorff had been forced to resign as foreign minister in May 1832, the Six Articles had been passed, and a wave of reaction was sweeping Germany. With this kind of political atmosphere, Bernstorff out of the way, and Ancillon in his stead, Prussia's chances of following an active German policy and winning over the constitutional states of Germany were greatly diminished. Therefore, the military plans no longer posed a political threat, and Austria felt able safely to agree to an organization that was very similar to Röder's original December 1830 proposal. Treitschke denied that there

92. Droysen, "Zur Geschichte der preussischen Politik," pp. 126–131.
93. Billinger, "Metternich's Policy," p. 218.

was any connection between the military negotiations and Bernstorff's resignation, but he was mistaken.

The discussions over the organization of the federal military revealed Metternich's fear of Prussian leadership in Germany as well as his continued mistrust of reform conservatives. The south Germans demonstrated a desire for greater independence within the German Confederation and for improving and enlarging the community of interests that existed between the south and Prussia. In Berlin, the negotiations brought forth a bewildering conglomeration of differing opinions that often defied normal political categories. To be sure, ultraconservative absolutists such as Ancillon and Wittgenstein, who wished only to avoid alienating Austria, were against the ideas represented by the Rühle mission from the start. Other ultraconservatives, such as Duke Charles and Knesebeck, also wanted to retain Austria's good will, but they saw some virtue in the military features of Rühle's approach. The conservatives were joined in their belief in Austria's military importance by Clausewitz, a man of quite different political values who detested the ultraconservatives. The King was strongly inclined toward Austria as well, but in the beginning, when the threat of war was great, his desire to have a dynamic and forceful military organization supported by the population in Germany led him to tolerate the ideas of Bernstorff and others. As the threat of revolution and war passed, he became more reluctant to encourage such approaches and instead, out of political fear, emphasized the need to work with Austria.

There was almost as much variety among those who supported the Rühle mission. Rühle, Eichhorn, and Krauseneck believed in the military virtues of the plan and were also convinced that it would bring important political dividends of a liberal, slightly nationalist nature. Witzleben, on the other hand, supported some of their liberal-nationalist ideas and believed in the military advantages of the plan, but did not want to arouse Austrian opposition. Even the Austrians were able to distinguish these differences. As Count Anton Prokesch von Osten recorded in his diary on 14 November 1831, "General Witzleben is with Rühle with regard to domestic politics, but in foreign affairs he is neutral."[94]

Bernstorff's position was the least understood. For a long time, the

94. Grafen Anton Prokesch von Osten, *Aus den Tagebüchern, 1830–1834*, p. 111.

Austrians felt that he was being used by Eichhorn and Rühle. They were completely mistaken. His revisions of Eichhorn's drafts, his endorsement of Eichhorn to the King and in private communications, his furthering of Eichhorn's career, and his defense of the Rühle mission and the 15 August circular demonstrate that he believed in the policies of the so-called German faction. Still his outlook differed in important ways from some of his associates. He did not share their belief that Prussia should rapidly move in a constitutional direction; if Droysen is to be believed, he openly disagreed with Witzleben on this point.[95] The essence of Bernstorff's position rested on two points. First, Germany needed rational institutions for inner health and exterior strength. Prussia should promote the development of these kinds of arrangements, and he clearly viewed the Rühle plan as part of that development. He could not accept Austrian opposition to that kind of change. Second, he believed that, within Germany and Europe, Austria could not assume that Prussia would automatically support its position, most especially when it could not be demonstrated that that position was in the interest of either Prussia or the other German states. In other words, Prussia was a fully independent power and should not be taken for granted. Austria would have to conduct its own campaign for influence based on the beneficial contribution that its proposals might make to the operation of the German state system. Thus a redefinition of peaceful dualism was at the heart of Bernstorff's approach. Metternich wanted to base that dualism on Austria's interests and on the interests of reaction and status quo conservatism, while Bernstorff wanted to orient it toward Prussia's interests and the interests of reform conservatives and progressives throughout Germany.

The positions of Bernstorff and Witzleben were each inconsistent in their own way. Considering Metternich's attitude, the introduction of a constitution in Prussia and the creation of new arrangements in Germany could not be done with Vienna's cooperation. Opposition to Vienna was a logical consequence of Witzleben's stance on other issues, yet, probably because of his position with the King, he refused to acknowledge this point, which was an important weakness in the reform camp. Likewise, Bernstorff refused to accept the fact that Prussia could not expect the more liberal states within the Confederation to look to Berlin until the

---

95. Droysen, "Zur Geschichte der preussischen Politik," p. 88.

monarchy moved toward some form of representative government within Prussia. Just as resistance to Austria followed from Witzleben's position, constitutional rule, something Bernstorff disliked, was a natural extension of his views. These inconsistencies and the multitude of positions that existed in Berlin on the federal military question partly account for the confusing course of the negotiations.

# Chapter 10

✠✠✠✠✠✠✠✠✠✠✠✠✠✠

# Public Opinion
# and the Press

In his *Denkschrift* of 29 January 1831, Bernstorff stated that, if the government wanted to have a greater chance of influencing the educated public, it would have to use the press more effectively. Efficiency in government, domestic stability, and military strength all depended on the attitude of the population. He also suggested that the existing censorship laws be relaxed so that individuals of reliable political outlook could have greater opportunity to express their ideas. These two goals became the major objectives of his press policy during 1831 and 1832.

The Prussian government had been extremely lethargic in this area. Its only national press organ was the *Allgemeine Preussische Staatszeitung,* whose publication was supervised by Phillippsborn's office in the foreign ministry. Although it was the official paper of the state, it presented little that would stir a thinking individual to support the government. Was it possible to change the image of the *Staatszeitung?* There is no evidence that the foreign ministry made a conscious policy decision to publish more stimulating articles, but a number of such articles did suddenly appear in the paper in the early part of 1831.

The most notorious of these pieces were two articles written by a Major von Willisen. Writing in the 7 February issue of the *Staatszeitung,* he reacted to a moderate and pacific speech by Sebastiani to the French Chamber of Deputies. The article applauded Sebastiani's remarks and in a way endorsed the July Revolution by saying, "One may deplore the July Revolution as a revolution and may want to wish away the mistakes and blunders that it necessarily made, but the event itself means progress in the intellectual and ethical civilization of mankind." Should the French think of a war of conquest, on the other hand, "We Germans have learned, we have discovered that 'the first village is the entire *Reich*.' Therefore just set foot on our soil and you will see us seize our weapons as one individual."[1] Such vigorous sentiments had rarely been expressed in the paper.

On 13 March 1831, Willisen's second article appeared in the *Staatszeitung*. This one was also in response to an article in France that had been critical of Prussia's authoritarian political system. Willisen pointed out the distortions in the article, particularly its comment that Prussian citizens wanted a representative system of government. A draft of his article was sent to Frederick William for approval. The King made numerous changes in the piece, toning down its patriotic sentiment and progressive flavor. However, some of the King's corrections were not made clearly, and, when Witzleben returned the article to Willisen, he failed to tell the author to change two passages. Thus, the article as it appeared was not exactly what the King had approved.[2]

The piece first attacked the assertion that the Prussian people demanded a just constitutional system.

> Certainly one can assume that the nation wants guarantees that it will continue to move along the path of historical development which it has up to this time followed and to which its present tranquility can be attributed. For that reason, a Frenchman will never meet a Prussian who will say his country has no constitution; he may even reply that he possesses many things that are intrinsic to a good constitution and which the French lack.

Turning to foreign policy, Willisen stated that Prussia's foremost desire was peace; troop movements in the west were directed toward maintaining the security and order of Prussia's Rhineland province. Prussia was prepared to defend Germany—it had learned from the mistakes of 1806 and remembered the spirit of 1813, 1814, and 1815—but it did not want war. He concluded:

---

1. Paul Ritter, "Vier Briefe des Prinzen Wilhelm von Preussen (Kaiser Wilhelm I)," p. 204.
2. Ibid., p. 209.

Prussia has the sense of strength, which it has found in its moderation and in the support of all of Germany which this moderation has secured, and associated with this it feels it is the master of its decisions in all areas, [it is] in the fullest sense of the word—independent. In present times, conquests are made purely by moderation and wisdom. Any addition of territory is a more than doubtful blessing.[3]

There was nothing in the article that conflicted with the essential aspects of Prussia's European and German policy or with its attitude toward domestic politics. In fact, the article's emphasis on the moral leadership that Prussia exercised in Germany accurately caught the essence of Prussia's current German policy. Still, such thoughts had not normally appeared in the *Staatszeitung*.

The article received immediate attention throughout Germany; liberals in Hamburg and Saxony were said to have applauded its sentiments.[4] Ultraconservatives, on the other hand, were naturally highly critical. Duke Charles complained not only about Willisen's article, but about other pieces appearing in a paper that was the official organ of the government.[5] Trauttmannsdorff was also critical of such articles in the paper and felt that Bernstorff's censorship was too lax.[6] Ancillon and Metternich repeated these criticisms.[7] The King was upset because the final version of Willisen's article did not reflect his revisions. He ordered that the article be publicly repudiated.[8] Bernstorff, as the minister responsible for the paper, was expected to deal with these complaints.

With all of this clamor, Willisen wrote to the King, accepted full responsibility for his error, and said that he was willing to be punished. Nevertheless, he wanted the article to stand because its patriotic message had been so well received by the public. Bernstorff then met with Willisen personally and discussed the problems the article had created.[9] Bernstorff

---

3. *Allgemeine Preussische Staatszeitung,* Nr. 72, 13 March 1831.

4. Jordan to Wittgenstein, n.d. (sometime in March of 1831), and Metternich to Trauttmannsdorff, 25 March 1831, GSA PKB, Rep. 192, Wittgenstein, V, 2, 16.

5. Duke Charles to Wittgenstein, 16 March 1831, ibid.

6. Trauttmannsdorff to Metternich, 14 March 1831, ibid.

7. Ancillon to Wittgenstein, 18 March 1831, and Metternich to Trauttmannsdorff, 25 March 1831, ibid.

8. Ritter, "Vier Briefe," p. 209.

9. Ibid., p. 210.

settled the matter by placing the following retraction in the *Staatszeitung* of 20 March 1831:

> In view of the widespread and quite proper consternation that the article at the end of issue Nr. 72 of the *Allgemeine Preussische Staatszeitung* under the heading, the 12th of March 1831, has received, it has caused us to enumerate here that, although this article only expressed the views of an individual, a more strict examination of its contents would have precluded its acceptance in the *Staatszeitung*.[10]

The King's demands had been met, but the retraction was fairly mild. One conclusion must have been clear to Bernstorff from the Willisen affair: Under present circumstances, the *Staatszeitung* could not serve as a tool for effectively influencing the literate public of Prussia. Perhaps because of these difficulties, he turned to another alternative that had been already suggested to him by the influential, moderately liberal publisher, Frederick Perthes.

## The Historisch-politische Zeitschrift

In the fall of 1830, Perthes, a long-time friend of Bernstorff and an early adherent of Prussia's mission to unify Germany, developed the idea of a government-sponsored political magazine for Prussia. In a letter to Bernstorff in November, he discussed the ill effects of the liberal and radical press in Germany on public opinion. He suggested that the government needed to put forth a reliable and unbiased account of current politics to counter the distortions and falsehoods contained in accounts published elsewhere. "The poisoning of public opinion by the press," he told Bernstorff, "can be successfully combatted only through the press." Contained in his letter to Bernstorff was a plan for a *Historisch-politische Zeitschrift;* this periodical should contain a brief summary of current events, the transcripts of important speeches and noteworthy documents, biographical reports on significant political figures, reviews of important books, and clarifications of irresponsible or inaccurate accounts in other journals. The *Zeitschrift* was to be factual and objective in its approach. Its style, said Perthes, should be "attractive, with historical respectability,

---

10. *Allgemeine Preussische Staatszeitung,* Nr. 79, 20 March 1831.

candid and refreshing; compromising neither truth nor justice, but in order to win influence it should, especially at the beginning, not be shy of current topics of a liberal cast." The periodical was to appear every two weeks, and its editor "must be a Prussian patriot in the truest and highest sense" possessing the full confidence of the Ministry of Foreign Affairs.[11]

Although pressure of work and ill health kept Bernstorff from responding immediately to Perthes's suggestion, he brought the matter to the attention of Eichhorn, who in turn discussed the project with Savigny, Rühle, Krauseneck, and Witzleben.[12] Their reaction was favorable, and, after considerable delay, Bernstorff had Perthes invited to Berlin. He arrived on 18 August 1831. Although Bernstorff was out of town, Perthes immediately joined with other officials in setting forth the basic nature of the proposed journal. He also discovered that Wittgenstein, Ancillon, and Altenstein were not enthusiastic about the project. When Bernstorff returned to Berlin in the last week of August, he approved of Perthes's plan for a *Historisch-politische Zeitschrift,* and "he personally dismissed the objections of the three hostile gentlemen with the words, 'handled badly there can be problems with anything, even Prince Wittgenstein must have found that out.'" He told Perthes that "he retained the fullest confidence in a matter that Eichhorn will handle and that [Perthes] will promote."[13]

With the project finally approved, the first task was to find an editor. After the rejection of a more liberal candidate, Perthes suggested that Leopold Ranke and Eichendorff edit the new journal.[14] Bernstorff accepted this idea and presented the entire plan to Brenn and Altenstein. In his note, he analyzed the inadequacy of trying to influence public opinion solely by negative means. The journal, in contrast, would demonstrate initiative and would influence public opinion in a positive manner.

---

11. Clemens Theodore Perthes, *Friedrich Perthes Leben,* 3:333–337. Perthes once wrote to a friend, "It is not enough that her intentions and her administration are good. . . . It is not enough that Prussia is properly Prussian, she must also feel her coalescence with Germany. . . . The Prussian government must come before the public, she must lay aside her prudish fears and must enter into the public debate like a man," pp. 326–327.

12. Ibid., p. 337; Conrad Varrentrap, "Ranke's Historisch-politische Zeitschrift und das Berliner Politische Wochenblatt," pp. 46–47.

13. Perthes, *Friedrich Perthes Leben,* 3:346.

14. Perthes to Bernstorff, 5 September 1831, ZSA Me, AAI, Rep. 4, Nr. 258.

The new periodical was to have full government support, would investigate historical topics of current relevance, and would have an objective and practical, rather than theoretical, outlook. Like the *Hallesche Literatur-Zeitung,* it would be granted the right of self-censorship. Ranke and Eichendorff, who together combined great knowledge and government experience, seemed best suited for the important positions of editors.[15] In the end, however, Eichendorff did not participate in the venture, apparently because of some question involving his salary.[16] The other ministers approved of the idea, Perthes was authorized to move forward with the project, and Bernstorff officially offered Ranke the editorship at the end of October.[17]

Ranke accepted and immediately composed a detailed plan outlining the journal's purpose and contents. It should emphasize, he said, a practical definition of a state's interests and should explain the difference between "peaceful progress and actual liberalism, between intelligent preservation and reactionary attempts to retain the past." It should combine studies of contemporary history, particularly of the French Revolution and its aftermath, analyses of Prussian and German affairs, and historical accounts from any period that contributed to a true understanding of politics. Ranke's plan deemphasized the nationalistic tone that had been such an important part of Perthes's original concept and changed it from a magazine of current affairs to a journal that concentrated on sophisticated political analysis. Finally, Ranke indicated that the success of the journal would depend on its editor's having ready access to source materials and periodic discussions with government ministers to keep him well-informed about foreign and domestic developments.[18]

Bernstorff wholeheartedly approved of Ranke's plan of operations and told the young historian that

> the journal will only achieve its purpose if you make it your objective to impartially examine the political phenomenon of the present and the past,

15. Bernstorff to Brenn and Altenstein, 16 September 1831, ibid.

16. Eichendorff to Eichhorn, 19 November 1831, ibid.

17. Brenn to Bernstorff, 30 September 1831, Altenstein to Bernstorff, 20 September 1831, and Bernstorff to Perthes, 14 October 1831, ibid.; Varrentrap, "Ranke's Historisch-politische Zeitschrift," p. 52.

18. Ranke to Bernstorff, 1 November 1831 (this includes Ranke's prospectus for the *Historisch-politische Zeitschrift*), ZSA Me, AAI, Rep. 4, Nr. 258.

not according to the usual standards, that is, according to theoretical predilections as distinguished from actual scholarly methods, but according to their inner essence on the basis of a sober comprehension of practical interest, of what is necessary and feasible, to evaluate and interpret without thereby disputing such theoretical approaches, but much more through the recognition of that part of the truth that they may contain, and without fail to give expression absolutely to this unprejudiced truth as the product of rigorous investigation and a respect for the truth. The editors will ensure both of these functions because of the designated purpose of the journal and because of the special trust that will be bestowed upon them.[19]

With this challenging mandate, the journal began.

Ranke's development as a historian and an analysis of his theory of politics or history based on his writings in the *Historisch-politische Zeitschrift* are beyond the scope of this book.[20] I want to examine the journal in terms of its intended function as a mouthpiece for enlightened conservative elements inside the Prussian government. My main interests are the themes emphasized by the journal and the extent to which they corresponded to the official policies or intentions of this group of Prussian officials.

The first issue of the *Historisch-politische Zeitschrift* appeared in February 1832. Between 1832 and 1836, seven additional issues were published with decreasing frequency. The introduction to the first volume was a revised version of the plan Ranke had sent to Bernstorff on 1 November 1831 in which the political position of the periodical was clearly stated. It supported lawful progress, but opposed "drastic, destructive innovation," on the one hand, and blind adherence to the archaic, on the other.[21] Similar wording had been used in numerous diplomatic documents prior to that time. A vague national idea was also identified as an important theme, but it was treated gingerly. "The idea of the entire Fatherland will always be kept in mind," Ranke wrote. "Out of the homogeneity of our national existence, encompassing many differences in the particular,

19. Bernstorff to Ranke, 20 November 1831, ZSA Me, AAI, Rep. 4, Nr. 258.

20. See Theodore H. von Laue, *Leopold Ranke;* Otto Diether, *Leopold von Ranke als Politiker;* Friedrich Meinecke, *Cosmopolitanism and the National State,* pp. 203–217; George Iggers, *The German Conception of History,* pp. 63–89; and the very useful work by Rudolf Vierhaus, *Ranke und die Soziale Welt,* in which pages 146–155 treat the *Historisch-politische Zeitschrift.*

21. *Historisch-politische Zeitschrift* 1(1932):3.

will evolve necessarily a substantial unity of the whole.[22] The audience
for the journal was also explicitly identified, namely, well-meaning,
calm, and intelligent Germans who had the capacity and the inclination to distinguish the essence of things from their superficial appear-
ance.[23] Finally, the journal expected to be scholarly and objective in approach, setting as its goal "the comprehension of those important things
that a thoughtful contemporary could wish to learn in order to understand and fully experience his times not according to any particular
conception but according to their reality."[24]

Its issues brought together a diverse group of articles. None of them
were really as popular as Perthes had intended; most of the articles were
serious, rather scholarly discussions of topics or developments of special
interest to an understanding of the 1830s. For example, two articles that
discussed France also laid a sound foundation for understanding Prussia's
recent policy toward the July Monarchy. In "Frankreich und Deutschland," Ranke emphasized the different, equally legitimate national experiences of two neighboring peoples. The political and institutional
arrangements of both areas were the products of different historical
experiences. As he concluded, "Our precept is that every people has its
own politics." This was not only the historical reality, it was in accord
with the divine order. "God gave expression to the idea of humanity
through different kinds of states."[25] This meant, as Ranke made very clear,
that the Germans should not imitate French liberal political models, but
it also meant that French political arrangements had a legitimacy for the
French nation that Germans should respect.

In "Eine Bemerkung über die Charte von 1830," he turned his attention to the July Revolution. The revolution of 1830, according to Ranke,
was a further product of the intermixing of two very different traditions—
the monarchical and the constitutional—in modern France. Ranke pointed
out that the basic principles of the Charte of 1830 were already contained in
the constitution of 1815 and that the Charte was a logical consequence
of antipathy toward the Bourbons and a desire to permanently secure
those attributes of the French Revolution that had been sanctified in 1815.

22. Ibid., p. 6.
23. Ibid., p. 4.
24. Ibid., p. 8.
25. "Deutschland und Frankreich," ibid., p. 92.

Thus, Ranke considered the revolution of 1830 and the July Monarchy historically appropriate. This interpretation, which was very close to Bernstorff's in his *Denkschrift* of September 1830 on Prussian policy toward the new regime of Louis Philippe, could hardly serve as a justification for an antirevolutionary crusade to restore the Bourbon dynasty to power in France.

The articles in the *Historisch-politische Zeitschrift* on German affairs also adhered closely to the policies of the Prussian government. In the important article, "Ueber die Trennung und die Einheit von Deutschland," Ranke repeated the essential aspects of Bernstorff's *Denkschrift* of 29 January 1831 and his dispatches on Prussian policy toward the constitutional regimes in Germany. Tolerance of diversity must always be a characteristic of German politics. The constitutions granted to the south German states at the beginning of the Restoration were legitimate because these states needed to be united given their new territorial configurations after 1815. "So they turned, it was proper, it was unavoidable, to constitutions."[26] He was critical of how these constitutions operated —especially of the divisiveness that resulted from them—but not of their status or purpose. Turning to what he called the restored states— Brunswick, Electoral Hesse, and Hanover, which had been reestablished out of the Kingdom of Westphalia—he offered a fairly nonpartisan interpretation of the most recent upheavals in these countries. Looking to the cause of the unrest in 1830, he wrote, "Arbitrary acts will always call forth opposition. One ought not to be persuaded that a full restoration was possible at any time. As time passes, life actuates new manifestations that cannot be denied, that cannot be removed, and that cannot be suppressed."[27] He was critical of recent events in these three states, but he hoped that individuals of "judgment, good-intentions, ability, and inner fortitude" would be able to predominate.[28]

Turning to the two great German powers, Ranke made the only significant evaluation of contemporary Austria that appeared in the journal. In its entirety, he wrote: "Austria, made up of such different groups of Germans and Magyars, Slavs and Italians, must seek a unity based on

26. "Ueber die Trennung und die Einheit von Deutschland," ibid.; an explicit and approving reference is made to Bernstorff's *Denkschrift* in the "Politische Gespräch," published in 1836.
27. Ibid., p. 354.
28. Ibid., p. 355.

entirely different principles than those which a smaller, homogeneous state could employ; this unity must incorporate in a completely different way the individual parts, or else leave them to their autonomy."[29] After this brief and undynamic picture of Austria, Ranke proceeded to present a vigorous and attractive portrait of Prussia. Prussia was essentially German; its present strength was the product of reform and innovation early in the century, a revitalization of the state's energies in the interest of its own people that made a national constitution superfluous. Prussia's status in Europe was determined by its military power. Prussia was the defender of the German people on the continent. Ranke used this role as a rationale for maintaining the power of the state unrestricted by any constitutional apparatus. "This military power," he wrote, "has certain unrestricted needs; on a continuous basis it requires unity and strict subordination. An attack that was even partially successful could easily endanger the permanence of things and the general importance of the German element in the European community."[30] By asserting the primacy of foreign affairs and by emphasizing the controlled evolution of national institutions that were an expression of Prussia's particular historical experience, Ranke, like many in government at the time, sought to insulate Prussia from the effects of liberalism.

Did the existence of contrasting political systems in Germany mean that there was an unbridgeable difference between the constitutional and the absolutist states of the Confederation? On the contrary, Ranke felt that cooperation and greater unity between the different political entities of Germany was both desirable and necessary. Echoing Bernstorff's *Denkschrift,* he felt that there were three areas where the unity of Germany could be increased: military arrangements, the press, and commercial affairs. Turning to the first point, Ranke noted that states in the modern era showed an unmistakable tendency to concentrate their energies through more unified institutions in order to enhance their military power. Was Germany to stand alone against this trend? Fortunately, he argued, the German Confederation had made provisions for a federal army. But, he added, much remained to be done. In the event of an attack, how were these troops to be deployed, how should they operate? "It would be very desirable that these points should be settled so that at

29. Ibid.
30. Ibid., p. 360.

the crucial moment wearisome and delaying consultations would be avoided."[31] Only those in Berlin could really appreciate this veiled reference to the negotiations on the deployment of the federal army corps.

Ranke did not believe that freedom of the press was desirable, but he recognized that the Carlsbad Decrees were both extreme and provisional. As the products of reaction, they could not serve as the basis for comprehensive press regulations acceptable to all of Germany. He felt that an attempt should be made to free academic works from censorship; by academic works, he meant those that did not deal directly with contemporary political affairs, or were pamphlets, journals, or newspapers. "The expression of true thought ought to be free; the expression of trash should be prevented."[32] A successful press law had to be moderate and tolerant in its regulations, should concentrate on attacking real abuses, and be flexible enough to be compatible with the different internal political arrangements of the various German states. This allusion to a modification of the existing press regulations was based on the draft of a new press law for Prussia and Germany prepared by the foreign ministry, which Bernstorff presented to the *Staatsministerium* in February 1832.

Finally, Ranke turned his attention to commercial affairs. Ranke almost took it for granted that a unified system of tariffs would encourage trade and strengthen Germany. This idea was not fully developed in this article, but in his "Zur Geschichte der deutschen, insbesondere der preussischen Handelspolitik von 1818 bis 1828," in J. G. Hoffmann's "Das preussische Zollwesen," and in "Ueber den deutschen Zollverein" by Ludwig Kühne, the commercial and customs policy of Prussia received detailed coverage based on the extensive use of government documents.[33] Perhaps no subject received such comprehensive treatment in the entire journal as the question of the *Zollverein*.

In another article entitled "Die Theorie und die öffentliche Meinung in der Politik," Ranke examined the role of public opinion in politics. After a disjointed discussion, he concluded that the middle classes ought to develop opinions on public matters of special interest to them. It was

---

31. Ibid., p. 371.

32. Ibid. Also see the discussion of Rudolf Vierhaus, "Ranke's Verhältnis zur Presse," pp. 559–561.

33. The first and third articles, published in the second volume, appeared in 1833 and 1834.

important for the state to understand their desires; in this way, they would have a part in the activities of government. As he concluded, "No one can know better than they themselves, no one can express more effectively what is missing for them, what they want, and what is in accord with their needs."[34] An important task was to reconstitute the political *Stände,* which had become too intermixed, and out of the different middle *Stände* to make one *Mittelstand,* "which as such in its area of competence shall have its own rights and its own political power."[35] Here Ranke enumerated one of the frequent goals of the bureaucracy—the desire to reconstruct corporate society on a modern functional basis.

In the most famous essay published in the entire journal, "Die Grossen Mächte," Ranke described the essence of modern history as the interplay of the five great powers. This essay presented a clear formulation of the concept of the primacy of foreign affairs in the life of the state and a synthesis of international and national considerations in Prussia's approach to European politics. In addition, it forcefully asserted the full independence of each major European state. Subordination of any single state to another was in conflict with the dynamics of history; even the operation of a group of states in the same manner was undesirable. "The union of all must rest upon the independence of each single one."[36] Thus, in his treatment of the Restoration, Ranke made no mention of the Grand Alliance or of the eastern alliance, for, as shown by his discussion in the "Politisches Gespräche," he realized that these were only temporary arrangements brought on by exceptional and unique developments in the life of the European state system. His assertion of the full independence of each unit within the European community was in complete harmony with Bernstorff's philosophy of politics.

Two other articles, neither of them by Ranke, are worth noting. One was Clausewitz's "Ueber das Leben und den Character von Scharnhorst." It was an intense and persuasive description of one of the great leaders of the reform period, and it reminded the reader of the spirit, quality, and accomplishments of the Stein-Hardenberg era. Although the article, published posthumously, and the appendix written by Marie von Clausewitz were slightly edited by Ranke, the basic tenor of the piece was undam-

---

34. *Historisch-politische Zeitschrift,* 1 (1832):494.
35. Ibid., p. 495.
36. I have used Von Laue's translation in *Leopold Ranke,* p. 218.

aged. Marie von Clausewitz's glowing tribute to Scharnhorst, Gneisenau, and Clausewitz at the close of the appendix is still striking.[37] Perhaps by the 1830s, the achievements and personalities of the reform era had worked their way into the accepted official historical heritage of the Prussian state, but, on the other hand, there were also many still active at the court who considered that triumvirate to have been dangerous, irresponsible, and destructive. Thus, the publication of Clausewitz's article with its appendix clearly identified where the *Historisch-politische Zeitschrift* and its sponsors stood in the political spectrum of Prussia.

Although Ranke never addressed himself specifically to questions of local administration, one of the contributors to the journal did. In "Die Preussische Städteordnung," Savigny presented an interesting discussion of municipal self-government in Prussia in the early nineteenth century. The establishment of self-governing institutions in the towns of Prussia had been one of the major achievements of the Stein ministry. In 1831, this system of municipal government was revised, and, despite several important innovations that made the law more modern than before, the so-called *revidierte Städteordnung* of 17 March 1831 was more conservative, or at least more authoritarian, than the original ordinance promulgated by Stein in 1808.[38] However, the law was applied with the greatest forbearance and became applicable in only a small area of the kingdom. After a detailed discussion of the ordinances of 1808 and 1831, Savigny made a few more general observations. To some, he wrote, municipal self-government, which was a democratic idea, might seem to be in complete conflict with the idea of monarchical rule. However, Savigny concluded, "To say that an absolute antithesis exists between monarchy and the democratic elements of a governmental system is completely false." There are democratic elements in all societies, most especially in Germany. Only a short-sighted policy could ignore this fact. If these forces were given their own area in which to operate, "then it will be demonstrated that, far from being threatened by them, the monarchy can draw much more energy and life out of them."[39] Local government was the proper domain for

---

37. See Peter Paret, *Clausewitz and the State*, p. 409.

38. Heinrich Heffter, *Die Deutsche Selbstverwaltung im 19. Jahrhundert*, pp. 212–220.

39. [K. F.] v. Savigny, "Die preussische Städteordnung," *Historisch-politische Zeitschrift*, 1 (1832):405.

democratic rule. The tendency, he said, was to confuse constitutional government or republican government, which was not compatible with monarchical rule, with a democratic approach that was. Thus, to appropriate it for the bureaucratic regime, Savigny attempted to detach the idea of municipal self-government from constitutionalism. As in Ranke's discussion of public opinion, Savigny displayed the desire to compartmentalize the play of political forces among the middle class into a neatly defined and easily controlled area.[40]

The *Historisch-politische Zeitschrift* as a whole has not been considered a success. It never appealed to the wider audience Perthes intended it for, and he withdrew from the project after one year. Nor was it able to attract contributors from throughout Germany or even to any large extent from Prussia, as Ranke and others had hoped, despite the fact that Bernstorff officially wrote to all the *Oberpräsidenten* in Prussia asking them to encourage contributions to the journal from "academically educated men."[41] The journal's limited appeal reflected the approach of its editor, as well as the political approach of Bernstorff and his associates. An endorsement of representative institutions for Prussia was the key to wider support at home and throughout Germany, but obviously that alternative was not available to them. Tolerant of constitutions elsewhere and, in some cases (although not in the case of Bernstorff) harboring constitutional tendencies themselves, they knew the reality of the Prussian monarchy—anyone publicly displaying constitutional inclinations would be immediately removed from influence. To expect Ranke to produce some sort of wide-ranging liberal journal with a strong commitment to constitutional rule and the national cause was never within the realm of possibilities.

Despite its low-key, scholarly, and conservative approach, the *Historisch-politische Zeitschrift* ran into difficulty with the board of censors. After seeing the first issue of the journal, the board wrote to Bernstorff that it objected to freedom from censorship for the new periodical. According to one official, the laws of 18 October 1819 stated quite clearly that all periodicals were to be subject to censorship. The board could not permit exceptions.[42] Bernstorff replied that a precedent had already been set by

40. Heffter, *Die Deutsche Selbstverwaltung,* p. 216.
41. Bernstorff to Schön, Schönberg, Flottwell, Bassewitz, Merkel, Klewitz, Vincke, and Pestell, n.d. (1832), ZSA Me, AAI, Rep. 4, Nr. 258.
42. Raumer of Obercensur Collegium to Bernstorff, 7 March 1832, ibid.

the *Halleschen Literatur Zeitung,* which was free of censorship. In any case, Ranke's journal was self-censored, closely connected with the government, and under the supervision of the Ministry for Foreign Affairs. Therefore, the board's complaints did not apply.[43] The board was still not satisfied by Bernstorff's explanation. Self-censorship was not the same as true censorship, particularly in the case of a journal of political content. They demanded that the journal comply.[44] By this time, Bernstorff was out of office, but Eichhorn prepared another reply in July. He said that, according to Article IV of the censorship law of 18 October 1819, the Ministry for Foreign Affairs had the ultimate responsibility for the censoring of newspapers and periodicals of political content. Therefore, the ministry assumed full responsibility for the journal's content.[45] This draft was not finally approved by Ancillon until December 1832.[46]

Others have noted that the first issues of the *Historisch-politische Zeitschrift* bore closer resemblance to the original intent of the journal and were more specific and in a way adventurous in content. Later issues, on the other hand, were more theoretical in approach and innocuous in terms of day-to-day politics. Ancillon's appointment as Minister for Foreign Affairs may have contributed to this change. The problems with the censorship board may have caused a similar shift, and Ancillon's assumption of full responsibility for the journal's contents may well have made its editor more cautious. Still as a public expression of an enlightened bureaucracy, the journal was a success because it accurately reflected a large number of the views of this political body.

Moreover, it performed an additional function that has not yet been mentioned. Ranke's journal served to distinguish the political outlook of the Prussian government, particularly the foreign ministry, from the ultraconservative writings of another recent journal, the *Berliner Politische Wochenblatt,* which otherwise would have held a monopoly as the spokesman for conservatism in Prussia. Founded by Radowitz and Voss in 1831, edited by Jarcke and supported by the adherents of the Christian-German outlook such as Leopold and Ludwig von Gerlach, the *Berliner Politische Wochenblatt* attacked absolutism as a forerunner of revolution

43. Bernstorff to Obercensur Collegium, 14 April 1832, ibid.
44. Raumer to Bernstorff, 11 May 1832, ibid.
45. Eichhorn to Obercensur Collegium, July 1832, ibid.
46. Ancillon to Obercensur Collegium, 10 December 1832, ibid.

and rejected the European enlightenment in its entirety. The greatest inspiration for the journal was the first volume of Haller's *Restauration der Staatswissenschaft,* although there were significant doctrinal differences between Haller's work and the philosophy of the journal.[47]

The Prussian government tried to separate itself from this endeavor from the start. In September 1831, officials refused to let its organizers use the title *Allgemeine Staatsanzeiger* because it might imply some connection with the state.[48] Unlike the *Historisch-politische Zeitschrift,* it was not granted the right of self-censorship. Bernstorff was critical of the journal; for example, after Trauttmannsdorff had endorsed its outlook enthusiastically, Bernstorff replied that he "considered the articles to be too abstract and the end product prejudiced."[49] Ranke also tried to distance himself from the *Berliner Politische Wochenblatt,* as did Savigny, who noted that the *Historisch-politische Zeitschrift* "has nothing in common with the magazine of Jarcke and Radowitz."[50] Later in a letter to Jacob Grimm in October 1833, he criticized the whole undertaking in more detail. The occasion was Jarcke's departure as editor in order to replace Gentz, who had died, as Metternich's chief scribe. Savigny hoped that Jarcke's

> journal will now completely cease publication. . . . It is a sad observation that nothing arouses people so noticeably in turbulent times as falsehood passionately expressed, while the opponents of that are rejected as nonpartisan lovers of truth, averse equally to all extremes. Indeed not infrequently it is shown that this last way of thinking is attacked and persecuted by the extremes of both sides with greater energy than the outlook of their actual opponents.[51]

With few exceptions, the supporters of the *Berliner Politische Wochenblatt* were in turn critical of Ranke's effort.[52]

---

47. See Wolfgang Scheel, *Das "Berliner Politische Wochenblatt" und die politische und soziale Revolution in Frankreich und England;* Robert Arnold, "Aufzeichnungen des Grafen v. Voss-Buch über das Berliner Politische Wochenblatt"; and Meinecke, *Cosmopolitanism and the National State,* pp. 171–185.

48. Scheel, *Das "Berliner Politische Wochenblatt,"* p. 24.

49. Ibid., p. 31.

50. Savigny to Jacob Grimm, 13 December 1831, Adolf Stoll, *Friedrich Karl v. Savigny,* 2:442.

51. Savigny to Jacob Grimm, 27 October 1833, ibid., p. 459.

52. Scheel, *Das "Berliner Politische Wochenblatt,"* p. 43.

The more conservative philosophy of Jarcke's journal represented an advancing wave of political thought in Prussia, and, when Frederick William IV assumed the throne in 1840, this outlook attained ascendancy around the court in Berlin. The *Historisch-politische Zeitschrift,* on the other hand, ceased publication in 1836. Ranke had encountered difficulties producing the last volume, but the end also symbolized the passing of a generation of enlightened reformers who believed that the strength of a state lay in its moral energies as well as in its power, and who felt the need to constantly strive to bridge the gap between a changing society and monarchical authority. Despite its conservatism, the journal remains as an example of the willingness of enlightened members of the Prussian government to explain their policies and to provide a forum for public dialogue with articulate members of Prussian and German society. They did this to preserve their own position in times of change, but there was also a strong pedagogical element to their work; they wanted to educate the middle class in the ways of politics. They believed that, if sensible people understood the true value of the monarchy, they would voluntarily give the government their support. This aspect of Bernstorff's press policy is even more apparent when we turn to the question of press censorship.

## Bernstorff's Censorship Law

Throughout the period of the revolutionary crisis in Europe, especially in the early part of 1832, Bernstorff was aware of the need for some kind of comprehensive press law that would be acceptable and enforceable even in the constitutional states of southern Germany. In January, February, and March, a group of articles that appeared in the southern press extolled liberal or republican political values and attacked Frederick William III, Prussian absolutism in general, and Prussia's relationship with Russia. Many of these papers—such as the *Westbote,* the *Deutsche Tribune* and the *Speyersche Zeitung*—were located in the Bavarian Palatinate. For a variety of reasons, the government in Munich was unwilling to suppress them. In addition, the Diet of Baden had prepared a new press law that was to establish near-freedom of the press beginning on 1 March 1832; the new law was in conflict with the existing laws of the Confederation.

Bernstorff was critical of the excesses of the liberal press in the south, but he was hesitant to insist on severe measures and wanted to postpone a confrontation with the Diet in Baden over the new press law. Both matters, he felt, could more properly be taken care of by carrying out a comprehensive reform of the laws governing the press.[53] In the meantime, he told Küster to approach the Munich government in a conciliatory way and to urge them to control the situation themselves. Küster was to say that the Prussian government was already working on a new press law as the present situation certainly pointed out the necessity of new measures.[54]

Bernstorff's nonrepressive approach came in for considerable criticism. Nagler felt that he was lax, and Wittgenstein said that, unless drastic measures to control the German press were created, people would think that the government was weak.[55] In a letter to Frederick William, he said that Bernstorff was too concerned about preventing a split between the constitutional and nonconstitutional states of Germany.[56] The King in turn told Bernstorff to contact the governments of southern Germany and to demand that action be taken against the offenders in accordance with federal law.[57] Because of this pressure and the legal infractions involved, the foreign ministry condemned the Badenese press law as being in conflict with the laws of the Confederation and took a formal position against the excesses in Bavaria. Despite this action, Bernstorff attempted to maintain harmonious relations with Bavaria and tried to delay action against Baden until the new federal measures were announced for all of Germany, in order not to isolate and embarrass the government in Karlsruhe.[58]

The issue of press censorship had a disruptive effect on Prussia's German policy and, for Bernstorff, pointed up the urgent need for new press regulations within the Confederation. He and his ministry had already been occupied with this matter for nearly a year. On 18 February 1832,

53. For the political outlook of these papers, see Volkmann Eichstadt, *Die deutsche Publizistik von 1830,* pp. 151–152. The Badenese press law is discussed in Wolfgang von Hippel, *Friedrich Landolin von Blittersdorff, 1792–1861,* pp. 68–70. Also see Robert D. Billinger, Jr., "Metternich's Policy toward the South German States, 1830–1834," pp. 164–166.

54. Bernstorff to Küster, and Bernstorff to Nagler, 1 March 1832, GSA PKB, Rep. 192, Wittgenstein, V, 5, 41.

55. Nagler to Wittgenstein, March 1832, and Wittgenstein to Bernstorff, 28 February 1832; ibid.

56. Wittgenstein to Frederick William, 29 February 1832, ibid.

57. Frederick William to Bernstorff, 3 March 1832 (copy), ibid.

58. Bernstorff to Wittgenstein, 4 March 1832, ibid.; Trauttmannsdorff to Metternich, 14 April 1832, HHSA, Stk., Preussen, Karton, 142; and Hippel, *Friedrich Landolin Karl von Blittersdorff,* pp. 71–72.

Bernstorff submitted to the King a draft of a new Prussian press law that could also serve as a model for the federal level.[59] In the proposal, drawn up by Eichhorn, Bernstorff first outlined the difficulty of applying existing federal laws to constitutional states where national representative bodies existed, majority support was necessary for the smooth operation of governments, and freedom of the press was generally popular. The Carlsbad Decrees were too inflexible and therefore invited evasion. A major purpose of his draft was to avoid "a very hazardous political division between the constitutional and nonconstitutional states in Germany."

Bernstorff indicated that the constitutional states wanted to draft their own press laws, which presented the danger that they would come into conflict with the general interest of the Confederation and lead thereby to destructive divisions within Germany. In a significant passage, Bernstorff explained that Prussia needed to lead in the creation of a new policy toward the press; simultaneously, he indicated an essential purpose of Prussia's entire German policy:

> There is no doubt that it is Prussia's task to undertake such an effort so long as her policies, as up until now, remain directed toward mediating and harmonizing the political differences in Germany on the basis of her internal institutional arrangements, and toward cultivating the union of all German governments and peoples with each other and thereby strengthening the unifying bonds of the entire fatherland against external attack.

Prussia could accomplish this task by creating its own law with the Confederation's interests in mind. This is a prime example of Bernstorff's belief that the interests of Prussia should meld with those of Germany so that Prussia could serve as a model or a nucleus for the creation elsewhere in Germany of institutions that, while being flexible enough to account for individual differences in each state, would also be sufficiently uniform to contribute to the creation of a greater sense of unity within Germany. He noted that there was a desire for the freer play of public opinion throughout much of Germany—especially in Munich, Dresden, Karlsruhe, and Hanover. While these demands had some undesirable characteristics, "the existence of that opinion and the power that it exercises on people's attitudes is a fact." Prussia should therefore endeavor to create a more posi-

---

59. A draft of the law is contained in GSA PKB, Rep. 192, Wittgenstein, V, 5, 41.

tive environment for the expression of public opinion. The laws of 20 September 1819 were provisional laws; what was needed now was a set of definitive press regulations. As long as Germany was a literary and linguistic community, press affairs would not be purely local in nature. However, all the German states did not have to adopt the same principles in every detail; there must be "proper respect for the dissimilarities of their individual systems of government." The laws should only set forth certain guidelines; the details should be filled in by the individual states.

Bernstorff went on to say that obviously there were always some people who were intent on misusing the press and on sowing dissent, but, rather than resorting to purely negative measures, a sound press law should encourage sensible writers and journalists to participate in the process of influencing public opinion. The "moral weight" of their writings would be the surest way to neutralize the effects of those who wished to cause trouble. In order to create a more flexible system of press censorship, Bernstorff proposed restructuring the *Obercensur Collegium*. The new board would be made up of selected academics, officials from the school systems, and members of the high appellate courts, the Academy of Sciences, and the municipal city council of Berlin; when possible provincial authorities would also be included. The board would then become an autonomous body operating outside of government. The members of the board would be in an "independent position" and would bring together "different elements of society." "Free of any suspicion of narrow-mindedness, it would win and maintain general trust in its ability, impartiality, and independence, which would guarantee the same degree of respect and recognition by public opinion as its purpose necessarily demands."

In addition to restructuring the board of censors, the proposal set up new categories for censorship. Academic and artistic works would henceforth be free from censorship, and even book-length studies of politics would have the same privilege because it was felt that only serious-minded individuals would read an entire book on the subject. Newspapers, periodicals, and pamphlets of a religious or political nature would continue to be censored. However, in a complicated portion of the draft, the principles for censoring these kinds of materials were to be altered. First of all, there was a distinction between topics concerning foreign politics and those concerning domestic affairs. For example, news and analysis of developments inside a foreign country where absolute freedom of the press prevailed would be free of censorship so long as the German account was based on the periodical literature of the particular country with formal citations of the sources of the information. However, articles containing unsubstantiated opinion based on the author's views or on the reports of correspondents would be liable to censorship. The same principle applied to those German states where a degree of freedom existed. Information contained in opposition papers could be used if properly cited and presented with "strict impartiality." Articles that treated Prussian politics would be permitted

> a proper discussion of relevant information both in favor of and against the matter, so that not only praise of the government and of governmental affairs will be printed, which after all would harm the certain recognition of those things really worthy of praise; therefore, an absolute silence on domestic affairs will not be enforced because it could arouse for no purpose discontent that would disturb the harmonious connection between the education of the nation, interest in public affairs, and the government.

However, any direct references to specific officials or attacks on the character of an individual would be suppressed. This draft would be proposed to the entire Confederation after its adoption by the Prussian government.

This is perhaps the most interesting of all of Bernstorff's policy papers because it has some direct bearing on domestic politics. It shows most clearly that his view of the world differed sharply from that of a reactionary or status quo conservative. Bernstorff faced the future with a good deal of confidence. He retained a certain belief in human rationality and in the influence of moral forces. Within certain limits, he was not afraid of the truth, even though it might be contrary to his own political philosophy. What he was concerned with was distortion of the truth. The numerous references to the need for citing sources in journalistic accounts demonstrates almost scholarly standards, and his attempt to ensure reliable, responsible accounts of politics as opposed to purely congenial ones is evidence of some broad-mindedness and a willingness to compete in the political arena. To some extent, a freer press should aid in the political education of the public and provide a truer reflection of responsible public opinion.

For Bernstorff, a free press was not incompatible with an absolutist regime. In Denmark, freedom of the press had been part of his father's credo and had also played an essential role in creating government policy. These considerations no doubt influenced the basic philosophy of the law, although political concerns connected with the constitutional states and their relationship with Prussia provided the immediate impetus for its creation. The draft was carefully put together in order to accommodate the different political systems of the German Confederation. The board of censorship, made up of notables of each society, would reflect the interests of the educated elites of that society, and presumably each board would apply diverse criteria in enforcing censorship laws. As Bernstorff told Trauttmannsdorff, "There will be consequently a large number of nuances in the solution of this question, and it is to be expected just for this reason that in the discussions on the matter each state will want to make modifications that their local circumstances require."[60]

Bernstorff's proposal met with a chilly reception within the *Staatsministerium*. Kamptz attacked every respect of the proposal and concluded that concessions in press censorship were dangerous. He said that he had no faith in the good intentions of specific writers or in any positive influence that might be exerted on public opinion. "The censorship law of 18 October 1819 should remain unchanged," he wrote, "and should be maintained and enforced with vigor."[61] Altenstein and others criticized the law for being too liberal and too difficult to administer.[62] One official objected to the procedures outlined in the draft and to the motives behind them. He felt that Bernstorff gave too much latitude to the false liberalism of the times, and he objected to the notion of Prussia's attempting to move closer to the constitutional states.[63] Ancillon expressed his opposition to the draft to the King, and Duke Charles told Wittgenstein that the entire law was utterly fantastic and fortunately doomed to failure.[64] With this kind

60. Trauttmannsdorff to Metternich, 5 March 1832, HHSA, Stk., Preussen, Karton 142.

61. Votum by Kamptz, 18 March and 7 April 1832, Kamptz and Mühler to Bernstorff, 7 April 1832, GSA PKB, Rep. 192, Wittgenstein, V, 5, 41.

62. Votum by Sack, 4 March 1832, ibid.; and Rochow to Nagler, 17 April 1832, Ernst Kelchner and Karl Mendelsohn-Bartholdy, eds., *Preussen und Frankreich zur Zeit der Julirevolution*, p. 82.

63. Fr. Raumer to Wittgenstein, 29 February 1832, GSA PKB, Rep. 192, Wittgenstein, V, 5, 41.

64. Ancillon to Frederick William, n.d. (1832), GSA PKB, Rep. 192, Wittgenstein, VII, B, 1 and 2; and Duke Charles to Wittgenstein, 6 April 1832; Wittgenstein, V, 5, 41.

of opposition, there was little chance of getting the measure through the *Staatsministerium* and even less of its being approved by the King. In general, it was considered to have been a very liberal measure, and, as might be expected, Frederick William was opposed to it.[65] Bernstorff was unable to get the law approved, and, in the end, it was the last straw that led to his resignation as Minister of Foreign Affairs.

Bernstorff's press law represents his only major effort in the area of domestic reform. Censorship was properly in the domain of the foreign ministry, and a freer press in Prussia was central to Bernstorff's political philosophy. Bernstorff believed that more liberal press regulations made representative government unnecessary, because a freer press would inevitably involve the educated citizens of Prussia more directly in the life of the state and would encourage the government to appreciate and attend to their wishes. The same arrangement, made by progressive elements throughout Germany, particularly in the constitutional states, would help to prevent the development of the conviction that a dramatic difference existed between the governmental principles of Prussia and those of the constitutional states. Obviously, if Prussia were able to take the lead in introducing more liberal press regulations in the Confederation, it would also reap future dividends in Germany. Thus, a new press law, by partially meeting the liberal demands of the age, would give Prussia new stability and internal strength and would enable it to more effectively make moral conquests in Germany. The fact that even such a moderate and cautious bill, which still placed the control of the press in the hands of responsible elites in and out of government, aroused so much opposition on the part of ultraconservatives and others demonstrates that they were not willing to even slightly expand the political base of the monarchy. They contributed thereby to the creation of an ever-widening gap between government and progressive elements within society.

## BERNSTORFF'S RESIGNATION

The draft of the press law confirmed Austrian suspicions about Prussia's German policy. Werner reported extensively on its contents in

---

65. Rochow to Nagler, 27 May 1832, Kelchner and Mendelsohn-Bartholdy, *Preussen und Frankreich,* p. 93.

early March and emphasized that the purpose of the law was to create trust among the population and to ensure that the distance between the absolutist and the constitutional states would not increase. He noted that it would create serious problems for those who sponsored it and predicted that it would never be passed by the King.[66] Metternich left no doubt about his position on censorship: "Press affairs," he said, "are today the most important of all. . . . The best law implemented by any country is the Carlsbad law."[67] For Trauttmannsdorff, the press law symbolized the serious and dangerous differences that existed between the Austrian and Prussian approaches to German affairs. On 15 March, he sent an important dispatch to Metternich summarizing the seemingly unresolvable points of conflict between the two governments. Prussia had chosen, he said, to do "so much as nothing" to suppress revolutionary movements in Germany. In order to create a new reputation for the Confederation and to permit a closer study of federal affairs by the public, Bernstorff had suggested that the record of the Diet's proceedings should be made readily available. Frederick William's alleged comment on that proposal was, "Was the *Bundestag* supposed to be a university?" Trauttmannsdorff went on to say that the Ministry of Foreign Affairs had promised a new press law that would solve the problems plaguing the Confederation in this area. After great delay, it had been finally released, and, instead of being antidemocratic, it was antimonarchical. This draft was another drop in the constant stream of evidence that the proposals emanating from the Prussian foreign ministry in no way coincided with the views of Austria. It was very regrettable that Bernstorff supported these initiatives that were against Austria's interests, especially at a highly critical time when the closest attachment to Austria was called for. Bernstorff was convinced that the smaller German states must be protected against undue pressure, and many of Austria's well-conceived plans had foundered on his timid approach. What was this to lead to? Was Vienna to indulge the liberal and constitutional ideas of the lesser German states with untold consequences for the Confederation? In Trauttmannsdorff's opinion, there was no chance of the Prussian court's ever coming around to the views of Vienna "so long as the Ministry of Foreign Affairs has such a visible and adroit 'sanculotismus' in the person of Herrn von Eichhorn." As long as

66. Werner to Metternich, 4 March 1832, HHSA, Stk., Preussen, Karton 142.
67. Metternich to Wittgenstein, 27 March 1832, HHSA, Stk., Preussen, Karton 146.

this "proven Jacobin" continued to work on Prussia's German policy, no understanding between Prussia and Austria on federal matters was possible.

> The removal of this above-mentioned man from the direction of federal affairs would be the greatest gain for us; yes, it would be the indispensable condition for a better kind of relationship between the two courts. To separate Herrn von Eichhorn from Count von Bernstorff, who in the past has usually been a thoroughly proper man and a worker of rare intelligence, remains, however, a task that no one has yet risked accomplishing.

Not even Prince Wittgenstein, who in earlier times could have probably brought about such changes with ease, has dared to try, "for all those who take interest in the survival of the Confederation are regarded with the greatest mistrust." In view of these difficult circumstances, Trauttmannsdorff explained to Metternich that

> if Your Highness could work in this sense directly upon the King, or through Prince Wittgenstein, then our complaints to His Majesty would be heard and only then might we have the hope that a proper attitude in the German division would prevail, an attitude that would not always be ready with hostile envy to struggle against what Austria proposes in the common interests of Germany, that would not always try under the mask of greater liberality to vie for the favor of the lesser German princes, and in this way to supplant Austrian influence. . . . Who may exercise a greater influence upon His Majesty than precisely Your Highness through the mechanism of Prince Wittgenstein? The King wants to do the right thing, he must, however, at the same time be forced to do it, and then he will be content. Without this exterior pressure, a concern for the others presses upon him, an indulgence of the others, and everything will remain as before.[68]

It took Metternich several weeks to devise a way to follow Trauttmannsdorff's suggestion. Some time earlier (the exact date is not known), the Duke of Nassau had sent Metternich a copy of Bernstorff's *Denkschrift* of 29 January 1831. On 22 April 1832, Metternich sent a copy of the *Denk-*

---

68. Trauttmannsdorff to Metternich, 15 March 1832, HHSA, Stk., Preussen, Karton 142.

*schrift* to Wittgenstein with a cover letter. After making a few derogatory remarks about its author, Metternich told Wittgenstein: "I am giving to you, dear Prince, by the present letter the greatest proof of my personal trust that I am capable of conveying to you. Do with the same what you think is in the best service of the King. I do not separate his best interests from those of my own master. Both defend one cause; this is my cause and your cause and quite certainly that of the world." The people who have created Prussia's German policy, he said, are nurturing revolution and want to "mediatize the German Confederation."[69]

This letter was personally carried to Wittgenstein by Clam, and there is little doubt that it and its enclosure were effective. On 30 April, Bernstorff submitted his resignation to the King, citing poor health as the reason for the request.[70] A week later, Wittgenstein was so confident of Bernstorff's demise that he wrote to Metternich:

> I have presented Your Highness's esteemed letter of the 22nd of the previous month, together with the remarkable enclosure, to the King. His Majesty thanks Your Highness for this interesting disclosure and for this new proof of trust. I do not need to identify for Your Highness the pen that has written this piece; in the future it will no longer do harm in this manner. The influence that this man has exercised here is ended. You will hear more about this very shortly. I do not need to tell Your Highness that I completely share your views on this opus and its related purpose. It is the swansong of this clique.

Wittgenstein added that, if Metternich once again found that the policies of the Prussian ministry were not proper, "write to me. Your letters will always be presented to His Majesty, and in this way things will be again set right if they have been somewhat improper."[71]

Four days later, as Wittgenstein had anticipated, the King announced that he had accepted Bernstorff's resignation. Ancillon was immediately appointed as the new Minister of Foreign Affairs, but Bernstorff retained his seat in the *Staatsministerium* and was to remain informed on matters

69. Metternich to Wittgenstein, 22 April 1832, GSA PKB, Rep. 192, Wittgenstein, VI, 3, 1.2.3.

70. Bernstorff to Frederick William, 30 April 1832, ZSA Me, Geheimes Civil Cabinet, Rep. 2.2.1., Nr. 12909.

71. Wittgenstein to Metternich, 6 May 1832, GSA PKB, Rep. 192, Wittgenstein, VI, 3, 1.2.3.

of foreign policy.[72] Wittgenstein's role in Bernstorff's dismissal is apparent, and so is the fact that reasons of health alone do not account for Bernstorff's resignation. Bernstorff was in poor health, which made the burdens of his office especially difficult, but, as Trauttmannsdorff wrote, "Important though the poor state of his health was, probably discouragement and dissatisfaction determined his retirement from the ministry." Bernstorff, no doubt because of Wittgenstein's action and because of the way in which Knesebeck's *Denkschrift* had been handled earlier, realized that he no longer had the King's confidence. Frederick William was upset because he now viewed the contents of the *Denkschrift* in a new light and because he disliked its having gotten into the hands of someone outside of Prussia.[73]

The events leading up to Bernstorff's resignation were again described by Trauttmannsdorff in his first report to Metternich following Bernstorff's fall. His report shows that the cumulative effect of Bernstorff's total approach to German affairs had aroused opposition in Vienna and eventually also caused Frederick William to abandon his foreign minister. More than ten years ago, Trauttmannsdorff wrote, Bernstorff helped to implement the Carlsbad Decrees and believed in the closest possible relationship with Austria and in their joint administration of federal affairs. In recent times, however, he supported those who wanted to "find the greatness of Prussia in its complete separation from Austria's conservative views and looked in the direction of a policy whereby Prussia would assume leadership in Germany under the condition that it undertake the introduction of a new federal system based on entirely liberal principles." Leniency toward constitutional movements in Germany, the mission of General Rühle von Lilienstern, the 15 August circular, negotiations for the expansion of the *Zollverein*, Bernstorff's initiative in the area of press censorship (this last piece of work, put together by Eichhorn, found an especially poor reception, he said, due to its "thoroughly democratic tendencies"), his attitude toward the regulation of the press in Bavaria, and toward the implementation of more public access to the proceedings of the

72. Frederick William to Bernstorff, 10 May 1832, ZSA Me, Geheimes Civil Cabinet, Rep. 2.2.1., Nr. 12909; and Frederick William to Staatsministerium, 10 May 1832, GSA PKB, Rep. 90 C, III, 3.6.

73. Trauttmannsdorff to Metternich, 15 May 1832, HHSA, Stk., Preussen, Karton 142; Wittgenstein to Metternich, 6 May 1832, GSA PKB, Rep. 192, Wittgenstein, VI, 3, 1.2.3.

*Bund*—all stood in the way of a true understanding with Austria, and, on the basis of these undesirable characteristics of Prussia's German policy, Frederick William "also felt on his part the necessity to make a change."[74]

Metternich was the central figure in creating an atmosphere in which Bernstorff felt he could not continue his duties. As Werner had already written on 15 March 1832, Metternich's private communications with Ancillon and Wittgenstein "are making life difficult for Count Bernstorff and make his political death desirable (*den politischen Tod wünschenswerth*)."[75] As Metternich himself wrote to Wrede on 21 May 1832, "I have recently reported to you changes that would soon take place in Berlin, and in the meantime you will have found out that Count Bernstorff has resigned. You and I know how this happened. The affair proves how uninclined the King is to tolerate bad policies any longer. Today it is easier to proceed along the right path than was previously the case."[76]

No one doubted that Bernstorff's resignation would immediately affect the course of Prussia's German policy. Metternich told Clam at the end of May that the discussions on federal military affairs would be affected by what happened to the liberal party of Berlin, because Knesebeck would be much easier to work with than Bernstorff.[77] Hertling, the Bavarian negotiator, came to the same conclusion. He wrote to the head of his own government on 14 June 1832: "There can be no doubt that with the resignation of Bernstorff and the promotion of Ancillon a great, one could say an absolute, bending of Prussia to Austria has occurred."[78] Werner anticipated that progress would also be made in controlling the excesses of the Bavarian press now that Bernstorff was gone. Trauttmannsdorff added, "The consternation of the smaller German courts whose idol Bernstorff had become in recent times already proves that we can expect to have in Herrn Ancillon a warm defender of our views, who will make it his business to block as much as possible the penetration of liberal ideas into the affairs of the German Confederation."[79]

---

74. Trauttmannsdorff to Metternich, 15 May 1832, HHSA, Stk., Preussen, Karton 142.

75. Werner to Metternich, 15 March 1832, ibid.

76. Metternich to Wrede, 21 May 1832, Viktor Bibl, *Metternich in neuer Beleuchtung*, p. 315.

77. Metternich to Clam, 25 May 1832, HHSA, Stk., Preussen, Karton 146.

78. Hertling to Gise, 14 June 1832, Bay. GSA, MA 24 077.

79. Trauttmannsdorff to Metternich, 15 May 1832, HHSA, Stk., Preussen, Karton 142.

Metternich's and Trauttmannsdorff's efforts to change Prussia's German policy really had two targets. Bernstorff was one of them; the other was Eichhorn. In part, Bernstorff was undermined because he protected Eichhorn. The foreign minister's impeccable credentials and the King's respect for Bernstorff's work made him the perfect patron for the reformist official. As long as Bernstorff was in office, it was difficult to attack Prussia's German policy in general or Eichhorn in particular. Of course, the Austrians tended to underestimate or just refused to believe until near the end that Bernstorff actually believed in Eichhorn's ideas and that the guidelines for most of Prussia's reformist policies were in fact established by Bernstorff himself. In any case, no sooner had Bernstorff resigned than Metternich and Wittgenstein began to try to remove Eichhorn from office. Now that he was minister, Ancillon sometimes resented Metternich's meddling and did not always support his machinations within Prussia. Primarily because of the *Zollverein* negotiations, Eichhorn's dismissal proved to be impossible, but Metternich and Wittgenstein did succeed in neutralizing his influence in German affairs. On 19 June 1833, the King ordered that all instructions, dispatches, and notes dealing with the affairs of the Confederation, the individual German courts, and Vienna should be sent first to Wittgenstein and Lottum. Any objections they had to the views expressed in these documents were to be brought to the King's attention.[80] The ultraconservative absolutists had finally succeeded in gaining control over Prussia's German policy. Metternich's concept of princely authority had triumphed over Bernstorff's concept of government.

Thus, with Bernstorff's resignation, the reduction of Eichhorn's influence, and the death of Maassen, the dynamic antireactionary element in Prussia's German policy was lost. Since 1825, this movement for change had developed greater momentum, and, with the crisis of the 1830s, a coalition of reformist generals and officials attempted to bring about significant reform in Germany. The first impetus for this change was the *Zollverein* negotiations; around them there slowly built up a broader program with far-reaching political implications. Taken individually, the elements of Prussia's Germany policy under Bernstorff were modest in scope. However, had all aspects of this approach succeeded, Prussia's

---

80. For an early study on this and on Wittgenstein's role throughout the period, see Ludwig Dehio, "Wittgenstein und das letzte Jahrzehnt Friedrich Wilhelms III"; for the King's order, see Frederick William to Ancillon, 17 June 1833, GSA PKB, Rep. 192, Wittgenstein, V, 1, 15–16.

relationship to Germany would have been significantly altered. Berlin would have been clearly associated with the forces of progress within the Confederation, and her position in Germany, buttressed by the *Zollverein* and new military arrangements, would have surpassed that of Austria. Naturally, Metternich, in the interest of the state he served, should have resisted such a development. However, by blindly opposing change in Central Europe without offering any positive alternative to Prussia's policies, he fatally crippled a process that may have led in time to greater cohesiveness within the German state system. Certainly if the functionalist approach that Bernstorff propounded had continued, it would have rationalized political and economic relationships within Germany, which would have benefitted the German community, even if it did not ultimately lead to German unification.

The final defeat of Bernstorff's policies is another example of Prussia's uneven development. The broader program of reform and accommodation was destroyed. Only the original core, the *Zollverein,* was left. But now it was to operate for a time in an apolitical form as one of the last achievements of a generation of Prussian and German reformers. Economic developments continued, but the political structure of Prussia and Germany lagged farther and farther behind.

*Chapter 11*

✠✠✠✠✠✠✠✠✠✠✠✠✠✠

# Conclusion

After his resignation, Bernstorff was on the periphery of political life in Berlin.[1] As far as we know, he still supported the same policies he had advocated as foreign minister. When Metternich proposed a reestablishment of the conservative alliance of Russia, Austria, and Prussia, Bernstorff urged caution.[2] He continued to believe that Prussia should display a cooperative attitude toward British and French efforts to reach a definitive settlement of the Belgian question.[3] However, after 1832, as his health became worse, close attention to affairs of state was difficult. At the end of May 1834, he and his wife visited Denmark—something Bernstorff had wanted to do for many years. Their trip from Berlin to Copenhagen via Stintenburg was a sentimental journey, and they met many old friends as they slowly made their way northward. On 3 July, they arrived in Copenhagen, and the next day Bernstorff met with Frederick VI. During their stay, they went to Bernstorff Slot, site of the agrarian reforms of his father and great-uncle. In the fall, they returned to Berlin. In early 1835, Bernstorff became seriously ill. His condition worsened, and, by the end of March, it was clear that nothing could be done to save him. During these last days, he was visited by many relatives and close friends, including Eichhorn and Schönberg, who saw him shortly before his death. He died on 28 March 1835 at the age of sixty-five.[4]

1. Luxburg to Ludwig, 29 October 1832, Bay. GSA. MA III, Nr. 2610.
2. Heinrich von Trietschke, *History of Germany in the Nineteenth Century*, 5:400.
3. Charles Maurice de Talleyrand, *Memoirs of the Prince de Talleyrand*, 5:87n.
4. Gräfin Elise von Bernstorff, *Aus ihren Aufzeichnungen*, 2:250–258. Bernstorff

Bernstorff, like Münster and Talleyrand, had a political career that spanned the Revolutionary, Napoleonic, and Restoration periods in Europe. As we have seen, he was profoundly influenced by the enlightened tradition of his family, and, from 1797 to 1810, his approach to European politics was determined by this system of thought. After the bombardment of Copenhagen, which seemed to symbolize the lawlessness of the era, and the destruction of Denmark's domestic tranquility, Bernstorff became more conservative. If we speak of a general European reaction after 1815, in Bernstorff's case, we can also speak of a personal reaction against revolution and war. For him, it probably began around 1810 and lasted until 1825, although such periodization can never be precise. During these years, Bernstorff saw Denmark's position in Europe decline still further until, in 1814, the Danish federal kingdom as he knew it was defeated and torn apart. It is difficult to exaggerate the sense of failure he experienced at this time; the Denmark of his adolescence and early manhood—the Denmark of A. P. Bernstorff and the great reforms, of federal patriotism, neutrality and prosperity—had been transformed after the Treaty of Kiel into a prostrate state full of internal dissension. In his mind, the causes of Denmark's and Europe's problems were easy to identify. France, war, revolution—the involvement of the masses in politics, with the accompanying fall of monarchical and aristocratic rule, and disregard for international law and the traditions of Europe—seemed to account for many of the disappointments he experienced in mid-life. His work at the Congress of Vienna and at the congresses and conferences that followed may be viewed as an attempt to put the pieces of a broken Europe back together and to prevent a recurrence of the disastrous sequence of events that had first led Europe into a period of violence and upheaval.

Bernstorff reflected both the idealism and the conservatism of the years after the Congress of Vienna. But his work at Carlsbad, which represented a close affiliation with the paranoia of the period, led him to violate some of the basic convictions of his family. In 1819, Bernstorff did not display the sense of tolerance and respect for law typical of his father and great-uncle. However, he was not a complete reactionary during this period; he sometimes had misgivings about the course of action being pursued by Vienna and Berlin. But he was still one of the fearful, who

---

suffered from old age, gout, a nervous ailment of the back, and respiratory problems; however, the actual cause of his death is not indicated in the sources.

joined those Gneisenau called "the violent persecutors. . . . They accuse, arouse mistrust, collect statements, and poison them by their interpretations."[5] Whether Bernstorff aligned himself with reactionaries because he was new to the Prussian government and felt insecure, because the interests of the Prussian state might have made such a policy advisable, because of weakness of character, or because of the trauma of his life in the last decade is difficult to determine; probably all these factors contributed to this important phase in his life—the phase for which he is best remembered, namely, as Prussia's representative and Metternich's disciple at Carlsbad.

Still, his sense of judgment had not abandoned him entirely. He was not unalterably opposed to a Prussian constitution and believed that Frederick William should keep his promise to the people. At Vienna, Troppau, Laibach, and Verona, he was careful not to actively involve Prussia in antirevolutionary crusades that were not essential to the interests of his state. But, in general, he was a man of his age. He desired peace, order, and stability on conservative terms. He wanted a European community of nations ruled by the great powers on the basis of a respect for law, Christian values, and a disapprobation of war. Monarchical authority and rule by governmental elites would likewise guarantee domestic tranquility. Bernstorff was possessed by the fear that history would repeat itself and therefore adhered sincerely and with deep conviction to the conservative, repressive, yet also idealistic, approach to politics that characterized the years immediately after Napoleon's fall.

But, as the memory of war became less personal and more objective, Bernstorff slowly emerged from this strongly conservative phase of his life. This occurred partly because the mood in Berlin began to change around 1825, but his family tradition also provided a firm base to which he could return. There is no doubt that, in this last stage of his career, he still felt indebted to the rich political heritage of his family. As he told Ranke in the early 1830s, "For sixty years his family was identified with the politics of Denmark: his great-uncle, his father, he—all had followed the principle of conducting politics solely on the basis of *Wahrheit*."[6] His

---

5. Gneisenau to Princess Louise Radziwill, 22 October, 1819, G. H. Pertz and Hans Delbrück, *Das Leben des Feldmarschalls Grafen Neithardt von Gneisenau.* 5:379–380; and Peter Paret, *Clausewitz and the State,* p. 264n14.

6. Leopold von Ranke, *Tagebücher,* p. 279.

family tradition, the needs of Prussia, and those of Germany caused reformism to resurface in Bernstorff's approach to politics. Once again, he began to talk of the need for more rational arrangements in society; his attitude toward the participation of new elements of the nation in politics became more progressive. Above all, he felt that government had to move forward in accordance with his interpretation of the needs of a new age. In international affairs, his approach was now preeminently nonideological; he had achieved a firm grasp of the essential elements of the European situation and guided Prussian policy with a hand that was surer and more confident than at any time in his career. Bernstorff had grown as a man and as a diplomat; he is one of those individuals who did his best work late in life.

As foreign minister, Bernstorff became a moderate reformer, but he was still very cautious about political change. For example, representative government on a national scale was not entirely appropriate for Prussia because of the weakness of the middle classes, but other, equally backward German states did adopt rudimentary forms of parliamentary government, which over time provided citizens with a limited opportunity for political experience. Such a step forward would have been appropriate for Prussia in 1830. Although some of Bernstorff's closest associates such as Witzleben, Clausewitz, Rühle, and Eichhorn privately believed in such a system of government, he did not. The logical conclusion to his important *Denkschrift* of 29 January 1831 would have been a call for some kind of modest national representative assembly based on a very restricted franchise and with only consultative powers. In view of the way in which he was forced from office, Bernstorff may not have felt it was possible to advocate such a course. After all, even in its muted form, the *Denkschrift* was used to undermine his position at court. But, this does not eliminate the fact that Bernstorff was unwilling to weaken the power of government through the introduction of representative institutions.

Rather than involving the population directly in the political processes of the state, Bernstorff believed in the concept of government as an exclusive and independent entity. He was not a supporter of autocracy, but, like many other officials, he was enamored of the idea that the Prussian bureaucracy—as an elite based on talent, heritage, and class—was specially entrusted with the task of deciding the interests and needs of the population. Ultimately, they were accountable only to their own sense of responsibility, and all too often that sense was prejudiced by a desire to preserve their own status and power.

Furthermore, those reforms that Bernstorff supported were not always pursued with vigor. I suggested earlier that he lacked drive and intensity in his approach to politics. He was committed, responsible, and courageous enough to state his views even when they were unpopular, but he had little desire to lead others. In many ways, he was a passive individual who presented his ideas to the King, Metternich, and others as truths that he believed to be self-evident. He sometimes failed to realize that their objective validity might be irrelevant to the issue at hand. It is true that Bernstorff carried out well-conceived maneuvers to preserve the influence of progressive elements within government, but it still remains an open question whether the course of events in Berlin in 1831 and 1832 would have been different if he had taken his case to the King as forcefully as Wittgenstein and Metternich did. The King was weak and malleable. Perhaps if Bernstorff had been more skilled and energetic, he might have been more successful. However, although the King was weak, he was also cautious and fearful. He might have dismissed Bernstorff even earlier if he had been pressured to a greater extent. Bernstorff's difficult position was similar to Hardenberg's in 1819. His goals were less ambitious, but he had to face the opposition of the same international and domestic conservative forces. Moreover, because the European crisis was past, and because of the social backwardness of Prussia, Bernstorff's proposals did not carry any sense of urgency in the eyes of the King. Ultimately, Prussia's general characteristics were more decisive than Bernstorff's personal weaknesses in determining the final outcome of his policies in the 1830s.

Other aspects of his work also merit attention. For example, throughout his career, he believed that a firm sense of ethics should undergird the conduct of politics. This sense never deserted him completely, even during the crisis of 1819. Indeed foreign diplomats who dealt with Bernstorff overwhelmingly concluded that he was not only knowledgeable about European and German affairs but could also be trusted. In 1831, the Hanoverian reformer, Stüve, anticipating and regretting Bernstorff's retirement, expressed a general feeling when he wrote of Bernstorff: "To be sure an aristocrat, but a noble individual."[7]

---

7. Walter Vogel, ed., *Briefe Johann Carl Bertram Stüves,* p. 221.

history of Prussian foreign relations, but even the present limited study shows that it contained a number of significant developments and analytic relationships that take on a different cast in light of more extensive documentation.

It is now clear that Prussia's role in the European state system was not simply one of close affiliation with the eastern alliance. Prussian relations with the powers of Europe shifted in accordance with the realistically interpreted needs of the state. When Prussia was weakest, in the years 1818–1825, her relationship with Austria was especially close, though not subservient. Berlin's foreign policy also reflected the cooperative character of the international system during the period of the European congresses. At the time of the eastern crisis, Prussia increasingly assumed a non-aligned position in Europe, although its policies remained especially favorable to Russia. This shift resulted from Prussia's increased financial and economic stability, as well as from the nature of the conflict in the Near East and the opening up of the international system. During the early 1830s, Prussia worked effectively with Great Britain and the other powers to settle the Belgian crisis and in general devised a European policy that was sensitive to the concerns of the major states and still preserved Prussia's essential interests. It is accurate to speak of Prussian foreign policy as essentially conservative during these decades. But some differentiation should be made between the various phases of Prussian policy. The ideological basis for that policy should not be overemphasized, because solid reasons of state made a policy of caution advisable, and Prussia's constructive work within the Concert of Europe should be recognized.

In addition, the peaceful inclination of the government is noteworthy. Europe as a whole wanted to avoid armed conflict between the major powers (although this did not prevent France, Russia, and Austria from at times taking considerable risks), but Prussia also followed a pacific line because of its economic and financial problems and because it depended to a large extent on a citizen army. Regard for public opinion helped to make Prussia a defensive, rather than offensive, power. Similarly, the German Confederation was a defensive association, and, if Prussia had in part an army of citizens, then Germany partly had an army of states. The limited capacity of the relevant administrative structures meant that neither military force could be easily and quickly mobilized except in the face of foreign attack.

This period is also significant because of Prussia's German policy. The Congress of Vienna established a new system in Germany. In the years immediately after 1815, Prussia's relationship with this system shifted in accordance with the changing capabilities and interests of the state. During these years, issues that would be at the center of federal politics for the next half-century emerged and took clear shape. If, by 1813 and 1814, Prussia was viewed as a progressive force in Germany, there is no doubt that, by 1820, it had been severely compromised by its close involvement with the Carlsbad Decrees and its failure to adopt a constitution. But, as we have seen, the government tried to shed this repressive image after 1825 and, to some extent, succeeded until 1832. No one who reads the documents of the early 1830s can escape the general feeling that Prussia once again was displaying a progressive energy and, therefore, was beginning to exercise greater leadership within Germany. The success of the *Zollverein* is the most obvious manifestation of this new image, but Bernstorff's approach to the political uprisings in Germany in 1830, his advocacy of a more liberal press policy, his handling of the European crisis of 1830–1831, and Berlin's attempts to establish a more effective military organization within Germany were additional aspects of Prussian policy that earned the government the respect of some reformist elements. However, Prussia's continued failure to enact a constitution remained a fundamental obstacle in its attempt to project a more progressive image, and Bernstorff's reformist policies were an anemic version of the Prussian reformers' original program.

The idea that Prussia would make moral conquests in Germany also reappeared during this era. This approach continued to play a role until the time of Bismarck. Prussia did not want to conquer Germany by force. This was distasteful, as well as being inherently unrealistic. Only through mutual cooperation, through the erection of new relationships that were genuinely beneficial to the German community, would a new unity evolve, in which Prussia would play a leading but not a domineering role, and in which each state would retain much of its individuality. In addition to preserving Germany's interests in Europe, because it was voluntary and defensive, this community would play a constructive and peaceful role in international affairs. This concept has been discussed as an immature formulation of the nation and as an intermediate stage in the development of the modern German state. Yet this approach should not be assigned a lesser value because it was less successful than the approaches that characterized later periods of German history. Considering Prussia's limited resources, Witzleben, Bernstorff, Eichhorn, and others were being realistic as well as idealistic and cosmopolitan. A federal structure, defense apparatus, and national attitude faintly akin to that of the Swiss Confederation had much to commend it, as an alternative appropriate to the capabilities of Prussia and to the needs of Germany and Europe in the early nineteenth century.

This book has not been a study in domestic politics and internal administration, but external and internal policies were closely interrelated, especially for Germany, and to that extent we may gain some insights into this subject as well. The failure to enact a constitution in 1819 was a tragically missed opportunity, but it was consistent with developments elsewhere in Europe and, in view of Prussia's social backwardness, not surprising. Nor was it surprising that a substantial body of the Prussian military and bureaucracy should reassert itself in the 1820s as reaction throughout Europe became less virulent. Initially, these men felt that it was impossible to openly advocate fundamental political reforms, so they concentrated on enhancing Prussia's economic power in Germany and on enlarging Prussia's influence within the Confederation. Very shortly, however, both of these efforts acquired a political dynamic that led to more sensitive issues such as liberalization of press regulations in Germany. The progressive image that Berlin displayed in 1830 did not go unnoticed in Germany and Europe. Diplomats, officials, writers, and even two liberals—David Hansemann and Paul Pfizer—began to speak of Prussia's task of creating a more coherent political order in Germany. Pfizer and Hansemann held differing views on how a politically active Prussian nation could be integrated into the whole of Germany without endangering the individuality of the other states, but both were agreed that constitutional rule was a prerequisite for any leading role the German people might voluntarily assign to Prussia.[10]

Foreign observers saw this pattern of development in Germany as being entirely possible. As the British envoy to the German Confederation noted in 1831:

10. P. A. Pfizer, *Briefwechsel zweier Deutscher* (originally published in 1831); and for Hansemann's *Denkschrift*, "Über Preussens Lage und Politik am Ende des Jahres 1830," sent to Frederick William on 31 December 1830, see Joseph Hansen, ed., *Rheinische Briefe und Akten zur Geschichte der politischen Bewegung, 1830–1850*, pp. 11–81.

Prussia, or at least a great party in the Prussian Government, is supposed to be very ready to yield to the current and adopt modifications in the Laws of the Confederation more congenial to the Spirit of the age,— while Austria wishes to leave the Fabrick untouched. The Brunswick Question has proved the Austrian influence to be on the decline—and were Prussia now to profit of the opportunity and grant a Constitution to Her Subjects, she might probably by placing herself thus at the head of the Liberal Powers in Germany, find herself so strong in the Diet, that either she would be able to modify the Germanick Confederation after her own views, or would force Austria from its center and remodel it on a new basis with herself for its chief power. In either case she would be called upon to exert enormous influence in Germany.[11]

Bernstorff's modest program of reform had the potential to reach out to such men as Hansemann and Pfizer, and, in terms of its tolerant and rational approach to constitutional innovations, the press, and commercial and economic arrangements in Germany, it was attractive to those of moderately progressive political views. But without some semblance of parliamentary government, the gulf between these liberals and the regime could not be entirely bridged, and even they did not represent the views of most liberals on this issue at this time. For example, in 1832, Pfizer declined Ranke's invitation to contribute to the *Historisch-politische Zeitschrift* because Prussia had not yet introduced constitutional rule. And Cotta, who also believed that Prussia should assume the leadership of Germany, regretted that its lack of a constitution blocked the realization of this goal.[12]

Because Bernstorff's policies were inherently limited in scope, their appeal was reduced. But they were within the range of political possibilities, and they did manifest the prevalent belief that Prussia's interests and the interests of Germany were increasingly one and the same. The development of institutional responses to this community of interests that existed in Germany and the moral energies that this process would develop would help to create a more coherent federal political unit. Ranke alluded to this process in his writings in the *Historisch-politische Zeit-*

11. Cartwright to Palmerston, 17 July 1831, PRO F.O. 30/34.

12. Conrad Varrentrap, "Ranke's Historisch-politische Zeitschrift und das Berliner Politische Wochenblatt," pp. 67–74; and Erwin Hölzle, "Cotta, der Verleger und die Politik," *Historische Vierteljahrschrift* 29 (1934–1935):594.

*schrift,* and, as a result, Meinecke concluded that he looked "much farther ahead into the life of the national state . . . than did his limited contemporaries."[13] However, in reality Ranke's ideas on the organization of Germany were not exceptional; they were typical of the views held by many of the leaders in Berlin at that time. If Bernstorff's approach had been realized, Prussia's position in Germany would have changed, which might have given Prussian reformers the confidence and impetus to attempt additional innovations. Because Bernstorff underestimated Metternich's opposition, the Austrian Chancellor was able to combine forces with the neo-feudal elements at court to defeat Bernstorff's policies and to stifle the reawakened spirit of reform within Prussia.

The age of bureaucratic absolutism does not appear all that tranquil, nor does the bureaucracy's control over matters of high policy appear very dominant. Neo-feudal elements outside of the real apparatus of government had decisive influence. Such men as Wittgenstein, the Minister of the Royal Household; Duke Charles, the King's brother-in-law and commander of the guards; and even Ancillon, who because he had been the Crown Prince's tutor still had a special relationship to the court, were courtiers who had the ear of the King and could circumvent the normal institutions of government. Metternich exploited this anomaly to the fullest extent. As a result, Prussia affiliated with the Six Articles and with a reinvigorated eastern alliance; the *Zollverein* lost its political dynamic for the time being, Prussia lost her slightly progressive image, and the ability of the Prussian bureaucracy to act as a bridge between the needs of the times and the interests of the state was further damaged. This was unfortunate as well as ill-timed because, in contrast to 1819, Western Europe in the early 1830s was receptive to change. Its governments were dominated by conservative reformers who realized that, to preserve their political power, they had to expand their political base and slowly win over new elements of society. The adoption of some sort of modestly reformist program such as the one Bernstorff suggested would have been appropriate for Prussia; instead Prussia tended more toward the pattern of Austria and Russia. As Palmerston pointed out in 1832:

> I am afraid that Metternich is going to play the Devil in Germany with his six resolutions for the Diet. . . . *Divide et impera* should be

13. Friedrich Meinecke, *Cosmopolitanism and the National State,* p. 216.

the maxim of government in these times. Separate by reasonable concessions the moderate from the exaggerated, content the former by fair concessions and get them to assist in resisting the insatiable demands of the latter. This is the only way. . . . If Metternich would only leave people a little alone he would find his crop of revolutions which he is nursing up with so much care soon die away upon the stalk.[14]

In other words, there are positive and negative ways in which conservative elites can preserve their own status and power. The July Monarchy and the Reform Bill of 1832, which are examples of the former, contributed to the evolution of a more just political order in France and England. Metternich's approach, on the other hand, exemplifies the latter.

Bernstorff's approach obviously conformed to Palmerston's views; he even used some of the same arguments in his *Denkschrift* of 29 January 1831. He and his colleagues were reform conservatives; they were a link in a chain of moderate conservative groups and developments that stretches from the era of reform down to the *Wochenblatt* party of the 1850s and beyond. The lack of success of Germany's liberal and socialist movements has been and continues to be an issue of great interest and importance. Perhaps attention should also be devoted to the failures of moderate conservatives, who so often in other countries contributed constructively, if reluctantly, to the political development of their societies, but who in Germany were constantly pushed aside by a more virulent form of conservatism. Thus, Bernstorff's work in the years 1830–1832 is a modest chapter in the history of Prussia's faltering political development in the nineteenth century. Beginning in 1807–1808 with the ministry of Stein and continuing until the end of the century, Prussia and Germany repeatedly fell short of achieving political improvements that were necessary to keep them abreast of the social, economic, and intellectual changes that were occurring in Germany and Europe. This accumulation of lost opportunities, in which the failure of Bernstorff has a place, partly accounts for the acute problems encountered by Germany in the twentieth century.

14. Charles K. Webster, *The Foreign Policy of Palmerston, 1830–1841*, 1:226.

✠ ✠ ✠ ✠ ✠ ✠ ✠ ✠ ✠ ✠ ✠ ✠ ✠ ✠ ✠

# Bibliography

## I. Primary Sources: Unpublished Papers and Government Documents

### A. Zentrale Staatsarchiv, Merseburg (ZSA Me)

*Auswärtiges Amt: Sektion I. Politische Abteilung*

Politischer Schriftwechsel

AAI, Rep. 1, Nr. 23: Allgemeine Übersichten über die Verhältnisse der europäischen Politik. Memoires über diesen Gegenstand. 1829–1832.

AAI, Rep. 1, Nr. 26: Acta betr. die in Aachen und einigen anderen Orten des Grossherzogtums Niederrhein ausgebrochenen Volksunruhen und die dagegen ergriffenen Massnahmen. 1830–1835.

AAI, Rep. 1, Nr. 29: Acta betr. die durch die fortdauernden Rüstungen in Frankreich diesseits notwendig gewordenen Massnahmen. Febr.–Juni 1831.

AAI, Rep. 1, Nr. 31: La correspondance du Comte de Bernstorff avec le Prince de Hardenberg. 1818–1822.

AAI, Rep. 1, Nr. 32: La correspondance du Monsieur Ancillon avec le Comte de Bernstorff. 1818–1822.

AAI, Rep. 1, Nr. 44: Die Schreiben des Grafen von Bernstorff an den Herrn Ancillon aus den Jahren 1819–1833.

AAI, Rep. 1, Nrs. 824, 825, 826: Acta betr. die Intervention von Preussen und Württemberg in der Auseinandersetzungs-angelegenheit zwischen dem Königreich Bayern und dem Grossherzogtum Baden. Vol. 1. Juli–Dez. 1830. Vol. 2, 1830–1831. Vol. 3, 1831–1832.

AAI, Rep. 1, Nr. 889: Dänemark. Depeches du et au Sieur Darrest. 1 Jan.–7 Juni 1810.

AAI, Rep. 1, Nr. 917: Copenhagen. Correspondance avec la mission du roi. Jan.–Dez. 1818.

AAI, Rep. 1, Nr. 1134: Acta betr. die von England geschlossenen Handelsverträge mit den amerikanisch-spanischen Kolonien Mexico, Kolumbien, und Buenos Aires und die deshalb getroffenen Massnahmen der Grossen Mächte. März–Apr. 1825.

AAI, Rep. 1, Nr. 1377: Acta betr. die in Frankreich ausgebrochenen Unruhen. Die dagegen getroffenen Massnahmen. Das Neue Gouvernment in Frankreich unter der Regierung des Königs Ludwig Philipp I. 1830–1837.

AAI, Rep. 1, Nr. 1463: Acta betr. die durch die königliche Gesandtschaft in Hannover u. Braunschweig einzuziehenden Notizen über Einführung neuer Institutionen dort selbst. Feb. 1831.

AAI, Rep. 1, Nr. 1464: Die Unruhe in Göttingen u. Hannover Febr.–März 1831 betr.

AAI, Rep. 1, Nr. 1465: Die Verfassung des Königreichs Hannover Febr.–Juni 1831 betr.

AAI, Rep. 1, Nr. 1670: Acta betr. die Reise des Kurprinzen von Hessen von Cassel nach Berlin, dessen Differenz mit dem Kurfürsten. Die Verhältnisse der Kurfürsten. Jan. 1829–Nov. 1834.

AAI, Rep. 1, Nrs. 1793, 1794: Acta betr. die in Brüssel und an mehreren Orten von Belgien ausgebrochenen Volksunruhen. Die daraus entstandenen Verhältnisse. Die Londoner Konferenzen unter den Bevollmächtigen der fünf grossen Mächte. Der zwischen Holland und Belgien ausgebrochene Krieg (Intervention Frankreichs) Vol. 1, Sept. 1830–Febr. 1831. Vol. 2, Febr. 1831–Mai 1832.

AAI, Rep. 1, Nr. 2088: Memoire des Gesandten, Geheimen Staatsrats, Niebuhr über den Zustand des Königreichs Neapel. Juni 1823.

AAI, Rep. 1, Nr. 2259: Acta betr. das Benehmen und angebliche Äusserungen des Fürsten v. Metternich und anderer kaiserlich österreichischer Diplomaten über Russland und dessen Kaiser. 1828–1829.

AAI, Rep. 1, Nr. 2266; Correspondance avec le Prince de Metternich. 1823–1847.

AAI, Rep. 1, Nr. 2268: Acta betr. die in Wien zwischen den drei Mächten Preussen, Österreich, und Russland zu bildene Conferenzen über die Europäischen Angelegenheiten. 1831.

AAI, Rep. 1, Nr. 2333: Acta betr. die im Königreich Polen ausgebrochenen Revolution, und wegen der diesseits getroffenen Massregeln.

AAI, Rep. 1, Nr. 2990: Acta betr. die Fragen über der allierten Mächte Anerkennung der Spanischen Kolonien in Amerika.

AAI, Rep. 1, Nr. 3095: Acta betr. die ausserordentliche Sendung des General-Lieutenants Freiherrn v. Müffling nach Constantinople.

AAI, Rep. 1, Nr. 3210: Acta betr. die Opposition Württembergs gegen die Veronaer Kongress-Beschlüsse. 1823.

CENSUR

AAI, Rep. 4, Nr. 258: Acta betr. der Vorschlag des Buchhändlers Perthes zur Herausgabe einer historisch-politischen Zeitschrift. 1831–1840.

AAI, Rep. 4, Nr. 2352: Acta betr. die Ernennung des Grafen von Bernstorff zum Geheimen Staats- und Kabinettsminister und zum Chef des auswärtigen Departments. 1818–1835.

DEUTSCHER BUND

AAI, Rep. 5, Nr. 376: Acta betr. die bei der Bundestagsversammlung in Antrag zu bringende Erneuerung der Karlsbader Kongressbeschlüsse. Mai–Sept. 1824.

AAI, Rep. 5, Nr. 593: Acta betr. die Sendung des Generalmajors Freiherrn Rühle v. Lilienstern zu den süddeutschen Höfen wegen der Organisierung des Bundesheeres. März–Juni 1831.

AAI, Rep. 5, Nr. 592: Acta betr. die Sendung des Generals v. Roeder nach Wien wegen der Organisierung des deutschen Bundesheeres. Febr.–Mai 1831.

AAI, Rep. 5, Nr. 604: Acta betr. die in verschiedenen Gegenden Deutschlands vorgefallenen tumultarischen Volksaufläufe. Vol. 1, Sept. 1830–Mai 1832.

KONGRESSE, 1814–1834

AAI, Rep. 6, Nr. 335: Korrespondenz des Grafen von Bernstorff mit dem Grafen von Lottum.

AAI, Rep. 6, Nr. 338: Acta betr. die Verhandlungen des Karlsbader Kongresses. Aug.–Nov. 1819.

AAI, Rep. 6, Nr. 341: Acta betr. die Verhandlungen und Beschlüsse des Karlsbader Kongresses wegen der demagogischen Umtriebe. Aug.–Okt. 1819.

AAI, Rep. 6, Nrs. 344, 345: Die Berichte des Staats- und Kabinettsministers Grafen von Bernstorff an den König wegen der Konferenzverhandlungen am Kongress zu Wien. Vol. 1, Nov. 1819–1820. Vol. 2, März–Mai 1820.

AAI, Rep. 6, Nr. 356: Manualakten des Staats- und Kabinettsministers Grafen v. Bernstorff. 1819–1820.

AAI, Rep. 6, Nr. 376: Die Troppauer Kongressberichte an den König. Oct.–Dez. 1820.

AAI, Rep. 6, Nr. 378: Die Laibacher Kongressberichte an den König. Jan.–März 1821.

AAI, Rep. 6, Nr. 395: Rapports à Sa Majesté le Roi (Verona 1822). 1822–1823.

### Geheimes Civil Cabinet

Rep. 2.2.1., Nr. 12909: Immediate Vortrags Sache. Acta der Bureau Registi: Sr. Exc. des Herrn Staats Minister pp. Grafen von Lottum betr. das dienstentlassungs-Gesuch des Staats- und Kabinettsministers Herrn Grafen von Bernstorff.

Rep. 2.2.1., Nr. 13070: Des Herzogs Carl von Mecklenburg Denkschrift betr. kriegerische Zustände in Europa, Volkssouveränität, Organization des deutschen Bundes.

Rep. 2.2.1., Nr. 13072: Verhandlungen Bernstorffs mit Clam. Defensivstellung des deutschen Bundes.

Rep. 2.2.1., Nr. 13210: Carl v. Mecklenburg über das Einrücken der Franzosen in Belgien.

Rep. 2.2.1., Nr. 13291: Portugesischen Angelegenheiten. 1826–1830.

Rep. 2.2.1., Nr. 13311: Acta Secreta betr. der Ankauf von Verpflegungsmitteln für die Kaiserliche Russische Armee in Polen und dieserhalb zu leistende Geld-Vorschüsse.

Rep. 2.2.1., Nr. 13330: Acta betr. die spanischen Kolonien in Amerika. 1824–1825.

Rep. 2.2.1., Nr. 24584: Die Übersichten von den Resultaten der Finanzverwaltung, die Finanz-Abschlüsse. 1824–1831.

Rep. 2.2.1., Nr. 24741: Finanzsachen. 1818–1829.

Rep. 2.2.1., Nr. 24765: Berichte des Staatsministers Rother über Finanzangelegenheiten. 1831.

### Gesandtschaft Darmstadt

Rep. 23.13, Nr. 242: Umtriebe und Unruhe betreffend von Jahren. 1830–1835.

Rep. 23.13, Nr. 456: Zollvereins-Sachen.

Rep. 23.13, Nr. 536: Sendung des Generals Rühle v. Lilienstern. 1831–1832.

### Haus Archiv König Friedrich Wilhelm III

Rep. 49, E. I. a. 1: Die Auswärtigen Angelegenheiten in der Regierungszeit König Friedrich Wilhelms III gegenüber.

Rep. 49, B. VI, 33: Der neuen französischen Regierung zu befolgende Politik 1830. 1832.

*Gesandtschaft am deutschen Bundestag*

Rep. 75A, Nr. 451: Acta betr. die Anwendung und Erneuerung der Karlsbader Beschlüsse vom Jahre 1819.

Rep. 75A, Nr. 457: Acta betr. die in den Jahren 1831 und 1832 zwischen den Kabinetten zu Berlin und Wien stattgefundenen Berathungen wegen Massregeln zur Herstellung und Erhaltung der Ruhe in Deutschland.

Rep. 75A, Nr. 1081: Ansuchen der Prälaten der Ritterschaft des Herzogtums Holstein beim Bundestags.

Rep. 75A, Nr. 1218: Zollwesen, in specie Abschliessung eines Zoll- und Steuer Vertrags zwischen Preussen und Grossherzogtum Hessen und dessen Folgen.

*Preussische Gesandtschaften*

Rep. 81, Cassel, Lit. H., Tit. L., Nr. 1a: Zolleinigung und Zollanschluss von Kurhessen und Waldeck mit Preussen. 3 Jan. 1824–17 August 1838.

Rep. 81, Cassel, Lit. H., Tit. L, Nr. 1b: Den Austritt Kurhessens aus dem mitteldeutschen Zollverein. Aug. 1828–Juni 1833.

Rep. 81, London, Nr. 363: Rescripte an Bülow. 1828.

Rep. 81, London, Nr. 365: Rescripte an Bülow. 1829.

Rep. 81, London, Nr. 369: Rescripte an Bülow. 1830.

Rep. 81, Muenchen, Nr. IV a 1: 1830.

Rep. 81, Muenchen, Nr. IV a 2: 1831.

Rep. 81, Muenchen, Nr. IV a 3: 1832.

Rep. 81, Muenchen, Nr. IV a 4: Militärische Massregeln.

Rep. 81, Petersburg I, Nr. 107: Rescripte an v. Küster. 1825.

Rep. 81, Petersburg I, Nr. 109: Rescripte an v. Schöler. 1826.

Rep. 81, Petersburg I, Nr. 112: Rescripte an v. Schöler. 1827.

Rep. 81, Petersburg I, Nr. 114: Rescripte an v. Schöler. 1828.

Rep. 81, Petersburg I, Nr. 117: Rescripte an v. Schöler. 1829.

Rep. 81, Petersburg I, Nr. 120: Rescripte an v. Schöler. 1830.

Rep. 81, Petersburg I, Nr. 124: Rescripte an v. Schöler. 1831.

Rep. 81, Petersburg I, Nr. 127: Rescripte an v. Schöler. 1832.

Rep. 81, Stuttgart I, Nr. 20: Politische Immediatberichte des preussischen Gesandten zu Stuttgart. 1830.

Rep. 81, Stuttgart I, Nr. 21: Politische Immediatberichte des preussischen Gesandten zu Stuttgart. 1831.

Rep. 81, Wien I, Nr. 132: Erlasse an Hatzfeld u. Concepte von Berichten desselber an das Ministerium des Auswärtigen. 1824.

Rep. 81, Wien I, Nr. 137: Erlasse an Hatzfeld u. Concepte von Berichten desselber an das Ministerium des Auswärtigen. 1826.

Rep. 81, Wien I, Nr. 139: Erlasse an Hatzfeld u. Maltzahn. 1827.

Rep. 81, Wien I, Nr. 140: Erlasse an Maltzahn u. Concepte von Berichten desselber an das Ministerium des Auswärtigen. 1828.

Rep. 81, Wien I, Nr. 141: Erlasse an Maltzahn u. Conzepte von Berichten desselber an das Ministerium des Auswärtigen. 1829.

Rep. 81, Wien I, Nr. 142: Erlasse an Maltzahn u. Conzepte von Berichten desselber an das Ministerium des Auswärtigen. 1830.

Rep. 81, Wien I, Nr. 143: Erlasse an Maltzahn u. Conzepte von Berichten desselber an das Ministerium des Auswärtigen. 1831.

Rep. 81, Wien I, Nr. 144: Erlasse an Maltzahn u. Conzepte von Berichten desselber an das Ministerium des Auswärtigen. 1832.

*Nachlässe*

Rep. 92, Ancillon, Nrs. 2, 7, 61, 68, 75, 76.

Rep. 92, Eichhorn, Nrs. 4, 35, 37, 40, 55.

Rep. 92, Hardenberg, Nr. K. 32. 3/4.

Rep. 92, Müffling, Nr. B. 2.

Rep. 92, Rochow, Nr. A. III. 20.

Rep. 92, Witzleben, Nrs. 14, 20, 33, 67, 109, 111, 112, and 116.

### B. Public Record Office, London (PRO)

*Foreign Office* (F.O.)

German Confederation:
  30/24: Cathcart, Seymour, and Mandeville. 1824.
  30/28: Milbanke and Addington. 1828.
  30/29: Milbanke, Addington, and Chad. 1829.
  30/31: Chad. January–September 1830.
  30/32: Milbanke and Cartwright. February–December 1830.
  30/33: Cartwright. January–April 1831.
  30/34: Cartwright. May–July 1831.
  30/35: Cartwright. August–December 1831.
  30/37: Cartwright. January–April 1832.
  30/38: Cartwright. May–June 1832.
Prussia:
  64/114: Rose. August–December 1818.
  64/117: To Rose. 1819.
  64/118: Rose. January–April 1819.
  64/119: Rose. May–August 1819.
  64/120: Rose. September–December 1819.
  64/122: To Rose. 1821.
  64/123: Rose. January–April 1820.
  64/124: Rose. August–December 1820.
  64/127: Rose. January–June 1821.

64/128: Rose. July–December 1821.
64/131: Rose. January–April 1822.
64/132: Rose. May–August 1822.
64/133: Douglas and Rose. August–December 1822.
64/135: Rose. January–March 1823.
64/136: Clanwilliam. May–December 1823.
64/139: To Clanwilliam. 1824.
64/140: Clanwilliam. 1824.
64/143: Clanwilliam. 1825.
64/146: Clanwilliam. 1826.
64/147: Temple. 1826.
64/150: Clanwilliam and Temple. 1827.
64/153: To Brook-Taylor, Temple, Clanwilliam, and Seymour. 1828.
64/154: Temple, Seymour, Clanwilliam, and Brook-Taylor. 1828.
64/157: To Brook-Taylor and Seymour. 1829.
64/158: Brook-Taylor and Seymour. January–June 1829.
64/159: Brook-Taylor and Seymour. July–December 1829.
64/162: Brook-Taylor. January–June 1830.
64/163: Brook-Taylor. July–October 1830.
64/164: Brook-Taylor. September-December 1830.
64/166: To Chad. 1831.
64/167: Chad. January–February 1831.
64/168: Chad. 9–28 February 1831.
64/169: Chad. March 1831.
64/170: Chad. April 1831.
64/171: Chad. 1–22 May 1831.
64/172: Chad. 23 May–June 1831.
64/173: Chad. July–August 1831.
64/174: Chad. September–October 1831.
64/175: Chad. November–December 1831.
64/180: To Chad and Ambercrombie. January–August 1832.
64/182: Chad. April–July 1832.

## C. Österreichisches Staatsarchiv, Abteilung: Haus-, Hof-, und Staatsarchiv, Vienna (HHSA)

*Staatskanzlei (Ministerium des Äussern) (Stk.)*

Preussen:
   Karton 106: Berichte und Weisungen. 1818.
   Karton 109: Berichte und Weisungen. 1819.
   Karton 110: Berichte und Weisungen. 1820.

Karton 112: Berichte. 1821.
Karton 114: Berichte. 1822.
Karton 116: Berichte. 1823.
Karton 122: Berichte. 1826.
Karton 124: Berichte. 1827.
Karton 128: Berichte. 1828.
Karton 129: Berichte. 1828.
Karton 131: Berichte. 1829.
Karton 132: Weisungen. 1829.
Karton 135: Berichte. 1830.
Karton 136: Weisungen. 1830.
Karton 138: Berichte. 1831.
Karton 139: Weisungen. 1831$^{1-7}$.
Karton 140: Weisungen. 1831$^{8-12}$.
Karton 141: Briefwechsel Metternichs mit Wittgenstein und Kamptz. Sendung Werners nach Töplitz. Sendung Clam Martinitz (Berichte und Weisungen).
Karton 142: Berichte. 1832.
Karton 143: Weisungen. 1832$^{1-6}$.
Karton 144: Weisungen. 1832$^{7-12}$.
Karton 146: Briefwechsel Metternichs mit Wittgenstein und Kamptz. Sendung Clam Martinitz (Berichte und Weisungen).
Collectiania Borussica:
Nr. 4: 1819–1821.
Nr. 5: 1822–1824.
Nr. 6: 1825–1829.
Nr. 7: 1830–1832.

## D. Geheimes Staatsarchiv Preussischer Kulturbesitz, Berlin (GSA PKB)

*Staatsministerium*

Rep. 90, III, 3.6.
Rep. 90, III, 5.1.

*Nachlässe*

Rep. 92, Albrecht, Nr. 63.
Rep. 92, Canitz u. Dallwitz, Nr. 5.

*Wittgenstein*

Rep. 192, V, 1, 15, and 16: Betr. Personalien des Ministeriums für die Auswärtigen Angelegenheiten: Minister Graf Bernstorff, Minister Ancillon—Geschäftsverteilung. 1831–1833.

Rep. 192, V, 1, 17: Correspondenz mit dem Herzog Carl (von Meckl-Strelitz). März 1831.

Rep. 192, V, 2, 15: Den Aufsatz in der Gazette de France betreffend. Mai 1831.

Rep. 192, V, 2, 16: Betr. den Zeitungsartikel des Kammerherrn und Majors v. Willisens in der Staatszeitung vom 13. März 1831.

Rep. 192, V, 5, 39: Censur Angelengenheiten.

Rep. 192, V, 5, 41: Artikel in dem Westbothen betreffend März 1832. Neue Censur Vorschläge.

Rep. 192, V, 5, 47: Betr. den Geheimen Legationsrath späteren Minister der geistlichen Angelegenheiten. Dr. Eichhorn.

Rep. 192, VI, 3, 1.2.3: Briefe des K. K. Oesterr. Haus-, Hof-, und Staatskanzlers Fürsten von Metternich an den Fürsten zu Wittgenstein. Originals. Desgl. Schreiben des Letzteren an den Ersteren. Entwürfe. 1818–Juli 1832.

Rep. 192, VI, 4/I: Briefe des Fürsten zu Wittgenstein an den Kgl. Preuss. Gesandten in Wien, Grafen von Maltzahn.

Rep. 192, VI, 6, 1–2: Betr. die im September 1830 zu Braunschweig stattgehabte Regierungs-Veränderung. 1830.

Rep. 192, VII, B, 1 and 2: Acta Varia betr. Innen u. Aussenpolitik. 1813–1840.

Rep. 192, VII, K, 1(g): Königreich Belgien. 1831–1832.

Rep. 192, VII, K, 6(f): Betr. die demagogischen Umtriebe und geheimen Verbindungen in Deutschland.

## E. Rigsarkivet, Copenhagen (RA)

*Departementet for udenrigske anliggenders Arkiv* (DfuA)

Preussen Id: Korrespondancesager vedr. det danske Gesandtskab i Preussen, II.
Preussen II: Depecher 1817.
Preussen II: Depecher 1818.
Østrig Id: Korrespondancesager vedr. det danske Gesandtskab i Wien, I.

*Privatarkiver*

Bernstorffske arkiv:
Ober Ellguth 5127/2.
Ober Ellguth 5127/4.
Ober Ellguth 5127/7.

Ober Ellguth 5127/9.
Ober Ellguth 5127/18.
Ober Ellguth 5127/20.
Stintenburg 5128/48.
Stintenburg 5128/49.
Stintenburg 5128/50.
Stintenburg 5128/51.
Stintenburg 5128/52.
Stintenburg 5128/53.
Stintenburg 5128/54.
Stintenburg 5128/58.
Niels Rosenkrantz arkiv: 6128/1.

**F. Bayerische Haupstaatsarchiv, Abteilung II:**
**Geheimes Staatsarchiv, Munich (Bay. GSA)**

*Ministerium des Aüssern*

MA 24 076, 077: Militärkonferenzen zu Berlin über die Defensivaufstellung des Bundesheeres im Kriegsfalle. 1831. März–Juli 1832.
MA I, Nr. 402: Frankreich beabsichtigt die Neutralitäts Süd Deutschlands.
MA III, Nrs. 2598–2611. Preussen politische Korrespondenz. 1819–1833.

**G. Archives du Ministère des Affaires Étrangères,**
**Paris (A.M.A.E.)**

*Correspondance Politique (C.P.)*

Prusse, Vols. 274, 275, 276. 1830–1831.

**H. Niedersächsisches Staatsarchiv, Osnabrück**

Dep. 40b, von dem Bussche-Ippenburg, Nr. 89: Christian Günther von Bernstorff.

**I. Private Archives**

Gartow: Notes of Elise von Bernstorff.
Ippenburg: Various papers of Christian von Bernstorff, Elise von Bernstorff, and Elise von dem Bussche-Ippenburg gen. von Kessel.
Tegel: Papers of Heinrich von Bülow.
Wotersen: Papers of the Bernstorff family.

## II. PRIMARY SOURCES: PUBLISHED
## DOCUMENTS, MEMOIRS, AND LETTERS

Bailleu, Paul. "Aus dem letzten Jahrzehnt Friedrich Wilhelms III. Briefe des Königs an seine Tochter Charlotte, Kaiserin von Russland." *Hohenzollern-jahrbuch* 20 (1916):147–174.

Bernstorff, Gräfin Elise von. *Aus ihren Aufzeichnungen,* ed. Elise von dem Bussche-Kessell. 2 vols. Berlin, 1896.

Bobé, L. T. A., ed. *Efterladte Papirer fra den Reventlowske Familienkreds.* 7 vols. Copenhagen, 1895–1923.

Boyen, Hermann von. *Erinnerungen aus dem Leben des Generalfeldmarschalls Hermann von Boyen,* ed. F. Nippold. 3 vols. Leipzig, 1889–1890.

Brandt, Heinrich von. *Aus dem Leben des Generals der Infantrie z. D. Dr. Heinrich von Brandt.* 2 vols. Berlin, 1869.

Branig, Hans, ed. *Briefwechsel des Fürsten Karl August von Hardenberg mit dem Fürsten Wilhelm Ludwig von Sayn-Wittgenstein, 1806–1822.* Cologne and Berlin, 1972.

*British and Foreign State Papers, 1818–1819.* London, 1835.

Chodzko, Leonard. *Recueil des Traités, Conventions, et Acts Diplomatiques Concernant la Pologne, 1762–1862.* Paris, 1862.

Chroust, Anton, ed. *Gesandtschaftsberichte aus München, 1814–1848: Abteilung I. Die Berichte der französischen Gesandten.* Schriftenreihe zur bayerischen Landesgeschichte. Vols. 18–24. Munich, 1935–1937.

——. *Gesandtschaftsberichte aus München, 1814–1848: Abteilung II. Die Berichte der oesterreichischen Gesandten.* Schriftenreihe zur bayerischen Landesgeschichte. Vols. 33, 36–38. Munich, 1939–1942.

——. *Gesandtschaftsberichte aus München, 1814–1848: Abteilung III. Die Berichte der preussischen Gesandten.* Schriftenreihe zur bayerischen Landesgeschichte. Vols. 39–43. Munich, 1949–1951.

Clausewitz, Carl von. *Politische Schriften und Briefe,* ed. Hans Rothfels. Munich, 1922.

Colenbrander, H. T., ed. *Gedenkstukken der Algemeene Geschiednis van Nederland van 1795 tot 1840.* Part 10. *Regerring van Willem I, 1830–1840.* Vols. 40, 42, 44, 46, and 50. The Hague, 1918–1920.

Friis, Aage, ed. *Bernstorffske Papirer.* 3 vols. Copenhagen, 1904–1913.

Fürst, Julian, ed. *Henrietta Herz. Ihr Leben und ihre Erinnerungen.* Berlin, 1850.

*Handbuch über den Königlichen Preussischen Hof und Staat 1818.* Berlin, 1818.

*Handbuch über den Königlichen Preussischen Hof und Staat 1821.* Berlin, 1821.

*Handbuch über den Königlichen Preussischen Hof und Staat 1824.* Berlin, 1824.

*Handbuch über den Königlichen Preussischen Hof und Staat 1828.* Berlin, 1828.

*Handbuch über den Königlichen Preussischen Hof und Staat 1831.* Berlin, 1831.

*Handbuch über den Königlichen Preussischen Hof und Staat 1832.* Berlin, 1832.

Hansen, Joseph, ed. *Rheinische Briefe und Akten zur Geschichte der politischen Bewegung, 1830–1850.* Essen, 1919.

Kelchner, Ernst, and Mendelsohn-Bartholdy, Karl, eds. *Preussen und Frankreich zur Zeit der Julirevolution. Vertraute Briefe des Preussischen Generals von Rochow an den Preussischen Generalpostmeister von Nagler.* Leipzig, 1871.

Leitzmann, Albert; Gebhardt, Bruno; and Richter, Wilhelm, eds. *Wilhelm von Humboldts Gesammelte Schriften.* 17 vols. Berlin, 1903–1936.

Londonderry, Robert Stewart, Second Marquess of. *Memoirs and Correspondence of Viscount Castlereagh, Second Marquess of Londonderry,* ed. Charles Vane, Third Marquess of Londonderry. 12 vols. London, 1850–1853.

Martens, F. de. *Recueil des Traités et Conventions conclus par la Russie avec les Puissances étrangères.* 15 vols. St. Petersburg, 1894–1909.

Metternich-Winneburg, Clemens Lothar Wenzel, Fürst von. *Aus Metternichs nachgelassenen Papieren,* ed. Prince Richard Metternich-Winneburg. 8 vols. Vienna, 1880–1884.

Meusel, Friedrich, ed. *Friedrich August Ludwig von der Marwitz.* 2 vols. Berlin, 1908–1913.

Müffling, Friedrich Carl Ferdinand von. *Aus Meinem Leben.* Berlin, 1851.

Natzmer, Gneomar Ernst von. *Unter den Hohenzollern. Denkwürdigkeiten aus dem Leben des Generals Oldwig v. Natzmer.* 2 vols. Gotha, 1887.

Oncken, Hermann, and Saemisch, F. E. M., eds. *Vorgeschichte und Begründung des deutschen Zollvereins, 1815–1834. Akten der Staaten des deutschen Bundes und der europäischer Mächte.* Berlin, 1934.

Pallain, G., ed. *Correspondance Diplomatique de Talleyrand. Ambassade de Talleyrand à Londres, 1830–1834.* Paris, 1891.

*Papers Relative to the Affairs of Belgium. A. Protocols of the Conferences Held at London between the Plenipotentiaries of Austria, France, Great Britain, Prussia, and Russia.* London, 1833.

Pfizer, P. A. *Briefwechsel zweier Deutscher.* Stuttgart, 1911.

Pick, Albert. "Briefe des Feldmarschalls Grafen Neithardt v. Gneisenau an seinen Schwiegersohn Wilhelm v. Scharnhorst." *Historische Zeitschrift* 77 (1896):67–85, 234–256, and 448–460.

Prokesch von Osten, Grafen Anton. *Aus den Tagebüchern, 1830–1834.* Vienna, 1909.

Ranke, Leopold von. *Das Briefwerk,* ed. W. P. Fuchs. Hamburg. 1949.

————, ed. *Denkwüdigkeiten des Staatskanzlers Fürsten von Hardenberg.* 4 vols. Leipzig, 1877.

————. *Tagebücher,* ed. W. P. Fuchs and Theodore Schieder. Munich, 1954.

Rist, Johann Georg. *Lebenserinnerungen.* 3 vols. Gotha, 1880–1888.

Rühl, Franz. *Briefe und Aktenstücke zur Geschichte Preussens unter Friedrich Wilhelm III.* 3 vols. Leipzig, 1900.

*Russkoe Istorischeskoe Obshchestvo Sbornik.* Vols. 119, 122, 127, 131, and 132. St. Petersburg, 1904–1905, 1908, and 1910–1911.

Smolka, Stanislaw, ed. *Korespondencya Lubeckiego z ministrami sekretarzami stanu Ignacym Sobolewskim i Stefanem Grabowski.* 4 vols. Cracow, 1909.

Stein, Heinrich Friedrich Karl Freiherr vom und zum. *Briefe und Amtliche Schriften,* ed. Walter Hubatsch and Manfred Botzenhart. 10 vols. Stuttgart, 1957–1974.

Svarez, C. G. *Vorträge über Recht und Staat,* ed. Hermann Conrad and Gerd Kleinheyer. Cologne, 1960.

Sybel, H. von. "Gneisenau und sein Schwiegersohn, Graf Friedrich Wilhelm v. Brühl." *Historische Zeitschrift* 69 (1892):245–285.

Sydow, Anna von, ed. *Wilhelm und Karoline von Humboldt in ihren Briefe.* 7 vols. Berlin, 1806–1816.

Talleyrand, Charles Maurice de. *Memoires of the Prince de Talleyrand,* ed. Duc de Broglie. 5 vols. London, 1891–1892.

Varnhagen von Ense, Carl August. *Denkwürdigkeiten des eigenen Lebens.* 6 vols. Leipzig, 1871.

Vogel, Walter, ed. *Briefe Johann Carl Bertram Stüves.* Veröffentichungen der Niedersächsischen Archivverwaltung. Vol. 10. Göttingen, 1959.

Wellesley, Arthur, First Duke of Wellington. *Despatches, Correspondence and Memoranda of Field Marshal Arthur, Duke of Wellington, K.G.,* ed. Arthur Richard Wellesley, Duke of Wellington. 8 vols. London, 1867–1880.

Wellesley, F. A., ed. *The Diary and Correspondence of Henry Wellesley, First Lord Cowley, 1790–1846.* London, 1930.

Wittichen, Friedrich Carl, and Salzer, Ernst, eds. *Briefe von und an Friedrich von Gentz.* 3 vols. Munich, 1909–1913.

## III. SECONDARY SOURCES

Abel, Wilhelm. *Geschichte der deutschen Landwirtschaft vom frühen Mittelalter bis zum 19. Jahrhundert.* Stuttgart, 1962.

Albrecht, Curt. *Die Triaspolitik des Frhr. K. Aug. von Wangenheim.* Stuttgart, 1914.

Albrecht-Carrié, René. *A Diplomatic History of Europe,* rev. ed. New York, 1973.

————, ed. *The Concert of Europe.* New York, 1968.

Anderson, M. S. *The Eastern Question.* London, 1966.

Aretin, Karl Otmar Freiherr von. "Metternichs Verfassungspläne." *Historisches Jahrbuch* 74 (1955):718–727.

Arneth, Alfred Ritter von. *Johann Freiherr von Wessenberg.* 2 vols. Vienna and Leipzig, 1898.

Arnold, Robert. "Aufzeichnungen des Grafen v. Voss-Buch über das Berliner Politische Wochenblatt." *Historische Zeitschrift* 106 (1911):325–340.

Baack, Lawrence J. *Agrarian Reform in Eighteenth-Century Denmark.* University of Nebraska Studies, New Series, No. 56. Lincoln, 1977.

————. "State Service in the Eighteenth Century: The Bernstorffs in Hanover and Denmark." *The International History Review,* 3 (1979):323–348.

Baumgart, Peter. "Zur Gründungsgeschichte des Auswärtigen Amtes in Preussen, 1713–1728." *Jahrbuch für die Geschichte Mittel- und Ostdeutschlands* 7 (1958):229–248.

Baumgarten, Hermann. *Geschichte Spaniens vom Ausbruch der französischen Revolution bis auf unsere Tage.* 3 vols. Leipzig, 1865–1871.

Beer, Adolf. "Oesterreich und die deutsche Handelseinigungsbestrebungen in den Jahren 1817–1820." *Oesterreichisch-Ungarische Revue,* New Series, 3 (1887):277–311.

————. *Die österreichische Handelspolitik im neunzehnten Jahrhundert.* Vienna, 1891.

Bertier de Sauvigny, Guillaume de. *The Bourbon Restoration,* trans. Lynn M. Case. Philadelphia, 1966.

————. *Metternich and His Times.* London, 1962.

————. *Metternich et la France après le Congrès de Vienne.* 3 vols. Paris, 1968–1971.

Betley, Jan Andrzej. *Belgium and Poland in International Relations, 1830–1831.* The Hague, 1960.

Bibl, Viktor. *Metternich in neuer Beleuchtung.* Vienna, 1928.

Billinger, Robert D., Jr. "Metternich's Policy toward the South German States, 1830–1834." Ph.D. dissertation, University of North Carolina at Chapel Hill, 1973.

————. "The War Scare of 1831 and Prussian–South German Plans for the End of Austrian Dominance in Germany." *Central European History* 9 (1976):203–219.

Bindoff, S. T. "The Unreformed Diplomatic Service, 1812–60." *Transactions of the Royal Historical Society,* Fourth Series, 18 (1935):143–172.

Bismarck, Otto von. *Gedanken und Erinnerungen.* 2 vols. Stuttgart, 1898.

Böck, Hans Helmut. *Karl Philipp Fürst von Wrede als politischer Berater König Ludwig I von Bayern (1825–1838).* Munich, 1968.

Böse, Otto. *Die Enthronung des Herzogs Karl II von Braunschweig.* Braunschweig, 1935.

————. *Karl II, Herzog zu Braunschweig und Lüneburg.* Braunschweig, 1956.

Branchart, Albert. *Oesterreich und die Anfänge des preussisch-deutschen Zollvereins.* Marburg, 1930.

Brandt, Otto. *Geistesleben und Politik in Schleswig-Holstein um die Wende des 18. Jahrhunderts.* Berlin, 1925.

Branig, Hans. "Fürst Wittgenstein. Ein preussischer Staatsminister der Restaurationszeit." Unpublished manuscript.

————. "Die oberste Staatsverwaltung in Preussen zur Zeit des Todes von Hardenberg." *Jahrbuch für die Geschichte Mittel- und Ostdeutschlands* 13–14 (1965):182–199.

Breunig, Charles. *The Age of Revolution and Reaction, 1789–1850,* 2nd ed. New York, 1977.

Brinkmann, Carl. "Die Entstehung von Stourdzas 'État actuel de l'Allemagne.' " *Historische Zeitschrift* 120 (1919):80–102.

————. *Die preussische Handelspolitik vor dem Zollverein und der Wiederaufbau vor hundert Jahren.* Berlin, 1922.

Brockhage, Bernard. *Zur Entwicklung des preussischdeutsche Kapitalexports.* Leipzig, 1910.

Bruford, W. H. *The German Tradition of Self-Cultivation.* Cambridge, 1975.

Bulwer, Henry Lytton. *The Life of Henry John Temple, Viscount Palmerston.* 3 vols. London, 1870–1873.

Büssem, Eberhard. *Die Karlsbader Beschlüsse von 1819.* Hildesheim, 1974.

*The Cambridge History of British Foreign Policy, 1783–1919,* ed. A. W. Ward and G. P. Gooch. 2 vols. Cambridge, 1922.

Carr, Raymond. *Spain, 1808–1939.* Oxford, 1966.

Cecil, Lamar. *The German Diplomatic Service, 1871–1914.* Princeton, 1976.

Clapham, J. H. *The Economic Development of France and Germany, 1815–1914.* Cambridge, 1928.

Conrad, Hermann. *Die Geistigen Grundlagen des Allgemeinen Landrechts für die preussischen Staaten von 1794.* Cologne, 1958.

Conrady, E. von. *Leben und Wirken des Generals der Infantrie und Kommandirenden Generals des V. Armeekorps Carl von Grolman.* 3 vols. Berlin, 1896.

Contamine, Henry. *Diplomatie et Diplomates sous la Restauration, 1814–1830.* Paris, 1970.

Conze, Werner. "Vom 'Pöbel' zum 'Proletariat.'" *Vierteljahrschrift für Sozial und Wirtschaftsgeschichte* 41 (1954):333–364.

————, ed. *Staat und Gesellschaft im deutschen Vormärz.* Stuttgart, 1962.

Craig, Gordon. *The Politics of the Prussian Army, 1640–1945.* New York, 1956.

————. "The System of Alliances and the Balance of Power." *The New Cambridge Modern History:* Vol. 10. *The Zenith of European Power,* ed. J. P. T. Bury. Cambridge, 1960. Pp. 246–273.

Crawley, C. W. *The Question of Greek Independence.* Cambridge, 1930.

Cresson, W. P. *The Holy Alliance.* New York, 1922.

Curtiss, John Shelton. *The Russian Army under Nicholas I, 1825–1855.* Durham, N.C., 1965.

Dakin, Douglas. *The Greek Struggle for Independence, 1821–1833.* Berkeley and Los Angeles, 1973.

Degn, Christian. *Die Herzogtümer im Gesamtstaat, 1773–1830. Geschichte Schleswig-Holsteins,* ed. Volquart Pauls. Vol. 6. Neumünster, 1959.

Dehio, Ludwig. "Wittgenstein und das letzte Jahrzehnt Friedrich Wilhelms III." *Forschungen zur brandenburgischen und preussischen Geschichte* 35 (1923):213–240.

Demoulin, Robert. *La Révolution de 1830.* Brussels, 1930.

D'Haussonville, M. O. *Histoire de la Politique Exterieure du Gouvernement Française, 1830–1840.* 2 vols. Paris, 1850.

Diether, Otto. *Leopold von Ranke als Politiker. Historisch-psychologische Studie über das Verhältnis des reinen Historikers zur praktischen Politik.* Leipzig, 1911.

Dobmann, Franz. *Georg Friedrich Freiherr von Zentner als Bayerischer Staatsmann in den Jahren 1799–1821.* Kallmünz, 1962.

Doeberl, Michael. "Bayern und die wirtschaftliche Einigung Deutschlands." *Abhandlungen der Königlich Bayerischen Akademie der Wissenschaften Philosophisch-philogische und historische Klasse.* Vol. 29, Pt. 2. 1919. Pp. 3–117.

Dorow, Wilhelm. *Job von Witzleben. Mitteilungen desselben und seiner Freunde zur Beurtheilung preussischer Zustände und wichtiger Zeitfragen.* Leipzig, 1842.

Drewitz, Ingeborg. *Berliner Salons.* Berlin, 1965.

Droysen, Johann Gustav. "Zur Geschichte der preussischen Politik in den Jahren 1830–1832." In *Abhandlungen zur neueren Geschichte.* Leipzig, 1876.

Eckert, Christian. "Zur Vorgeschichte des deutschen Zollvereins. Die preussisch-hessische Zollunion vom 14. Februar 1828." *Jahrbuch für Gesetzgebung, Verwaltung und Volkswirtschaft im Deutschen Reich* 26 (1902): 505–556.

Eichstadt, Volkmann. *Die deutsche Publizistik von 1830: Ein Beitrag zur*

*Entwicklungsgeschichte der konstitutionellen und nationalen Tendenzen.* Historische Studien, Vol. 232. Berlin, 1933.

Elrod, Richard B. "The Concert of Europe: A Fresh Look at an International System." *World Politics* 28 (1975–1976):159–174.

Epstein, Klaus. *The Genesis of German Conservatism.* Princeton, 1966.

Erhardt-Lucht, Renate. *Die Ideen der Französischen Revolution in Schleswig-Holstein.* Neumünster, 1969.

Falke, Johannes. *Die Geschichte des deutschen Zollwesens.* Leipzig, 1869.

Feldbæk, Ole. "The Anglo-Danish Convoy Conflict of 1800." *Scandinavian Journal of History* 2 (1977):161–182.

———. *Dansk neutralitetspolitik under Krigen 1778–1808. Studier i regeringens prioritering af politiske og økonomiske interesser.* Copenhagen, 1971.

[Felgermann, Major von]. *General W. I. von Krauseneck.* Berlin, 1851.

Fischer, Wolfram. "The German Zollverein. A Case Study in Customs Union." *Kyklos* 13 (1960):65–89.

———. *Der Staat und die Anfänge der Industrialisierung in Baden, 1800–1850.* Berlin, 1962.

———. "Das Verhältnis von Staat und Wirtschaft in Deutschland am Beginn der Industrialisierung." *Kyklos* 14 (1961):337–363.

Franqué, Wolfgang von. *Luxemburg, die Belgische Revolution, und die Mächte.* Bonn, 1933.

Franz, Eugen. "Ein Weg zum Reich. Die Entstehung des Deutschen Zollvereins." *Vierteljahrschrift für Sozial und Wirtschaftsgeschichte* 27 (1934): 105–136.

Frauendienst, Werner. "Das preussische Staatsministerium in vorkonstitioneller Zeit." *Zeitschrift für die gesamte Staatswissenschaft* 116 (1960): 104–177.

Frensdorff, Ernst. "Der Berliner Schneideraufruhr im Jahre 1830." *Mitteilungen des Vereins für die Geschichte Berlins* 24 (1907):208–212.

Friis, Aage. *Die Bernstorffs.* Leipzig, 1905.

———. *Die Bernstorffs und Dänemark.* Bentheim, 1970.

———. "Holstens Indlemmelse i Danmark i Aaret 1806." *Historisk Tidsskrift,* Series 7, 6 (1905–1906):1–107.

Gagern, Friedrich von. *Das Leben des Generals Friedrich von Gagern.* 3 vols. Heidelberg, 1856–1857.

Gebhardt, Bruno. *Wilhelm von Humboldt als Staatsmann.* 2 vols. Stuttgart, 1899.

Gilbert, Felix. *Johann Gustav Droysen und die Preussisch-Deutsche Frage.* Beiheft 20 der Historischen Zeitschrift. Munich and Berlin, 1931.

Gillis, John R. *The Prussian Bureaucracy in Crisis, 1840–1860.* Stanford, 1971.

Griewank, Karl. "Preussen und die Neuordnung Deutschlands, 1813–1815."

*Forschungen zur brandenburgischen und preussischen Geschichte* 52 (1940): 234–279.

———. *Der Wiener Kongress und die Europäische Restauration, 1814/15,* 2nd ed. Leipzig, 1954.

Grimsted, Patricia Kennedy. *The Foreign Ministers of Alexander I.* Berkeley and Los Angeles, 1969.

Gronemann, Werner. *Die Haltung Preussen in der belgischen Frage, 1830–1832.* Berlin, 1928.

Guichen, Eugène, Vicomte de. *La Révolution de Juillet 1830 et l'Europe.* Paris, 1916.

Gulick, E. V. "The Final Coalition and the Congress of Vienna, 1813–15." In *The New Cambridge Modern History:* Vol. 9. *War and Peace in an Age of Upheaval, 1793–1830,* ed. C. W. Crawley. Cambridge, 1965. Pp. 639–667.

Haake, Paul. "Die Errichtung des preussischen Staatsrat im März 1817." *Forschungen zur brandenburgischen und preussischen Geschichte* 27 (1914): 247–265.

———. *Johann Peter Friedrich Ancillon und Kronprinz Friedrich Wilhelm IV von Preussen.* Berlin, 1920.

———. "König Friedrich Wilhelm III, Hardenberg, und die preussische Verfassungsfrage, I." *Forschungen zur brandenburgischen und preussischen Geschichte* 26 (1913):171–221.

———. "König Friedrich Wilhelm III, Hardenberg, und die preussische Verfassungsfrage, II." *Forschungen zur brandenburgischen und preussischen Geschichte* 28 (1915):175–220.

———. "König Friedrich Wilhelm III, Hardenberg, und die preussische Verfassungsfrage, III." *Forschungen zur brandenburgischen und preussischen Geschichte* 29 (1916):305–369.

———. "König Friedrich Wilhelm III, Hardenberg, und die preussische Verfassungsfrage, IV." *Forschungen zur brandenburgischen und preussischen Geschichte* 30 (1917):317–365.

———. "König Friedrich Wilhelm III, Hardenberg und die preussische Verfassungsfrage, V." *Forschungen zur brandenburgischen und preussischen Geschichte* 32 (1920):109–180.

Haas, Arthur G. *Metternich, Reorganization, and Nationality, 1813–1818.* Wiesbaden, 1963.

Hammer, Karl, *Die Französische Diplomatie der Restauration und Deutschland, 1814–1830.* Stuttgart, 1963.

Hampe, Karl. *Das belgische Bollwerk.* Stuttgart and Berlin, 1918.

Haussherr, Hans. *Hardenberg: Eine politische Biographie.* Cologne, 1963.

———. "Hardenbergs Reformdenkschrift Riga 1807." *Historische Zeitschrift* 157 (1938):267–307.

———. "Stein und Hardenberg." *Historische Zeitschrift* 190 (1960):267–289.

Heffter, Heinrich. *Die Deutsche Selbstverwaltung im 19. Jahrhundert.* Stuttgart, 1969.

Henche, Albert. "Die Karlsbader Konferenzen nach den amtlichen Berichten und der vertraulichen Briefen des Frh. von Marschall an den Herzog Wilhelm von Nassau." *Annalen des Vereins für Nassauische Altertumskunde und Geschichtsforschung* 59 (1939):83–100.

Henderson, W. O. "Christian von Rother als Beamter, Finanzmann und Unternehmer im Dienste des Preussischen Staates, 1810–1848." *Zeitschrift für die gesamte Staatswissenschaft* 112 (1956):523–550.

——. *The Zollverein.* Chicago, 1959.

Hillebrand, Karl. "Die Berliner Gesellschaft in den Jahren 1789 bis 1815." In Karl Hillebrand, *Unbekannte Essays,* ed. Hermann Uhde-Bernays. Bern, 1955. Pp. 13–81.

——. *Geschichte Frankreichs (1830–1871).* 2 vols. Gotha, 1877.

Hinsley, F. H. *Power and the Pursuit of Peace.* Cambridge, 1967.

Hintze, Otto. "Das preussiche Staatsministerium im 19. Jahrhundert." *Gesammelte Abhandlungen,* ed. Gerhard Oestreich. Vol. 3. *Regierung und Verwaltung.* Göttingen, 1967. Pp. 530–619.

——. "Prussian Reform Movements before 1806." In *The Historical Essays of Otto Hintze,* ed. Felix Gilbert. New York, 1975. Pp. 64–87.

Hippel, Wolfgang von. *Friedrich Landolin von Blittersdorff, 1792–1861.* Stuttgart, 1967.

Hoermann, Liselotte von. *Der bayerische-badische Gebietsstreit (1825–1832).* Historische Studien, Vol. 336. Berlin, 1938.

Hoffman, Kurt. *Preussen und die Julimonarchie, 1830–1834.* Historische Studien. Vol. 288. Berlin, 1936.

Holborn, Hajo. *A History of Modern Germany, 1648–1840.* New York, 1964.

——. *The Political Collapse of Europe.* New York, 1951.

Holm, Edvard. *Danmark-Norges Historie fra den store Nordiska Krigs Slutning til Rigernes Adskillelse, 1720–1814.* 7 vols. Copenhagen, 1891–1912.

Hölzle, Erwin. "Cotta, der Verleger und die Politik." *Historische Vierteljahrschrift* 29 (1934–1935):576–596.

Howard, Michael. *Studies in War and Peace.* New York, 1971.

Huber, Ernst Rudolf. *Deutsche Verfassungsgeschichte seit 1789.* 4 vols. Stuttgart, 1957–1969.

Iggers, George. *The German Conception of History.* Middletown, Conn., 1968.

Ilse, L. F. *Geschichte der deutschen Bundesversammlung.* 3 vols. Marburg, 1861–1862.

——. *Die Politik der beiden Grossmächte und der Bundesversammlung in der kurhessische Verfassungsfrage vom 1830 bis 1860.* Berlin, 1861.

Janssen, Johannes. *Friedrich Leopold Graf zu Stolberg.* 2 vols. Freiburg, 1877.

Jungfer, Thaddäus. *Die Beziehungen der Julimonarchie zum Königreich Polen in den Jahren 1830/31.* Lissa, 1909.

Kaehler, Siegfried A. *Wilhelm von Humboldt und der Staat.* Munich and Berlin, 1927.

Kamlah, Irmgard. *Karl Georg Maassen und die preussische Finanzreform von 1816–1822.* Halle, 1934.

Kapp, Friedrich. "Die preussische Pressegesetzgebung unter Friedrich Wilhelm III, 1815–1840." *Archiv für die Geschichte der deutschen Buchhandels* 6 (1881):185–249.

Kessel, Eberhard. "Zu Boyen's Entlassung." *Historische Zeitschrift* 175 (1963): 41–54.

Kielmannsegg, Peter, Graf von. *Stein und die Zentralverwaltung 1813/1814.* Stuttgart, 1964.

Kissinger, Henry. *A World Restored.* New York, 1957.

Kitchen, Martin. *A Military History of Germany.* Bloomington, 1975.

Klein, Ernst. "Funktion und Bedeutung des preussischen Staatsministeriums." *Jahrbuch für die Geschichte Mittel- und Ostdeutschlands* 9–10 (1961):195–261.

———. *Von der Reform zur Restauration. Finanzpolitik und Reformgesetzgebung des preussischen Staatskanzlers Karl August von Hardenberg.* Berlin, 1965.

Kleinheyer, Gerd. *Staat und Bürger im Recht. Die Vorträge des C. G. Svarez vor dem Kronprinzen (1791–92).* Bonn, 1959.

Kliewer, Eberhard. *Die Julirevolution und das Rheinland.* Cologne, 1963.

Koselleck, Reinhard. *Preussen zwischen Reform und Revolution. Allgemeines Landrecht, Verwaltung und soziale Bewegung von 1791 bis 1848.* Stuttgart, 1967.

Koser, Reinhold. "Die Gründung des Auswärtigen Amtes durch König Friedrich Wilhelm I. im Jahre 1728." *Forschungen zur brandenburgischen und preussischen Geschichte* 2 (1889):161–197.

Kossok, Manfred. *Im Schatten der Heiligen Allianz. Deutschland und Latein Amerika, 1812–1830.* Berlin, 1964.

Kraehe, Enno E. *Metternich's German Policy.* Princeton, 1963.

Lannoy, Fl. de. *Histoire Diplomatique de l'Indépendance Belge.* Brussels, 1830.

Laue, Theodore H. von. *Leopold Ranke: The Formative Years.* Princeton, 1950.

Lauren, Paul Gordon. *Diplomats and Bureaucrats.* Stanford, 1976.

Lefebvre, Georges. *The Coming of the French Revolution,* trans. R. R. Palmer. Princeton, 1947.

Leslie, R. F. *Polish Politics and the Revolution of November 1830.* London, 1956.

Levis Mirepoix, Emmanuel de. *Le Ministère des Affaires Étrangères.* Angers, 1934.

Liddell Hart, B. H. "Armed Forces and the Art of War: Armies." In *The New Cambridge Modern History:* Vol. 10. *The Zenith of European Power,* ed. J. P. T. Bury. Cambridge, 1960. Pp. 302–330.

Linderberg, Fernando. *Staatsminister Andreas Peder Bernstorff.* Kolding, 1886.

Lingelbach, William E. "Belgian Neutrality: Its Origin and Interpretation." *The American Historical Review* 39 (1933):48–72.

Linvald, Axel. *Kronprins Frederik og hans Regering, 1797–1807.* Copenhagen, 1923.

Mager, Wolfgang. "Das Problem der Landständischen Verfassungen auf dem Wiener Kongress 1814/15." *Historische Zeitschrift* 217 (1973):296–346.

Mann, Golo. *The History of Germany since 1789.* New York, 1970.

Markert, Werner. "Preussisch-russische Verhandlungen um einen europäischer Sicherheitspakt im Zeichen der Heiligen Allianz." In Werner Markert, *Osteuropa und die abendländische Welt.* Göttingen, 1966. Pp. 145–158.

Marquardt, Frederick D. "Pauperismus in Germany during the Vormärz." *Central European History* 2 (1969):77–88.

Marriot, John A. R. *The Eastern Question.* London, 1940.

Marriot, John A. R., and Robertson, C. G. *The Evolution of Prussia.* Oxford, 1937.

Mayr, Josef Karl. *Geschichte der österreichischen Staatskanzlei im Zeitalter des Fürsten Metternich.* Vienna, 1935.

———. *Metternichs Geheimer Briefdienst, Postlogen und Postkurse.* Vienna, 1935.

Meinecke, Friedrich. *The Age of German Liberation, 1795–1815,* ed. Peter Paret. Berkeley and Los Angeles, 1977.

———. *Cosmopolitanism and the National State.* Princeton, 1970.

———. *Das Leben des Generalfeldmarschalls Hermann von Boyen.* 2 vols. Stuttgart, 1896–1899.

———. *Preussen und Frankreich im 19. und 20. Jahrhundert.* Munich, 1918.

Meisner, Heinrich Otto. "Zur neueren Geschichte des preussischen Kabinetts." *Forschungen zur brandenburgischen und preussischen Geschichte* 36 (1924): 46–52.

Menn, Walter. *Zur Vorgeschichte des deutschen Zollvereins. Nassaus Handels- und Schiffahrtspolitik vom Wiener Kongress bis zum Ausgang der süddeutschen Zollvereinsverhandlungen, 1815–1827.* Greifswald, 1930.

Molden, Ernst. *Die Orientpolitik des Fürsten Metternich, 1829–1833.* Leipzig, n.d.

———. *Zur Geschichte österreichisch-russischen Gegensatzes; die Politik der europäischen Grossmächte und die Aachener Konferenzen.* Vienna, 1916.

Møller, Erik. "England og Danmark-Norge i 1807." *Historisk Tidsskrift,* Series 8, 3 (1910–1912):309–422.

Morley, Charles. "The European Significance of the November Uprising." *Journal of Central European Affairs* 11 (1951–1952):407–416.

Müller, J. *Die Polen in der öffentlichen Meinung Deutschlands, 1830–1832.* Marburg, 1923.

Näf, Werner. *Abrüstungsverhandlungen im Jahre 1831.* Berner Untersuchungen zur allgemeinen Geschichte. Vol 2. Bern and Leipzig, 1931.

————. *Zur Geschichte der Heiligen Allianz.* Berner Untersuchungen zur Allgemeine Geschichte. Vol. 1. Bern, 1928.

Nichols, Irby C., Jr. *The European Pentarchy and the Congress of Verona.* The Hague, 1971.

Nørregård, Georg. "Christian Bernstorffs afsked med Danmark." *Jyske Samlinger,* New Series, 5 (1959):43–60.

————. *Danmark og Wienerkongressen, 1814–1815.* Copenhagen, 1948.

————. *Efterkrigsår i dansk udenrigspolitik, 1815–24.* Copenhagen, 1960.

————. *Freden i Kiel, 1814.* Copenhagen, 1954.

————. "Mødet på Hardenberg 1816." *Lolland-Falsters historiske Samfunds Årbog* (1955):46–58.

Obermann, Karl. *Deutschland vom 1815–1849.* Berlin, 1967.

Paret, Peter. "An Anonymous Letter by Clausewitz on the Polish Insurrection of 1830–1831." *The Journal of Modern History* 42 (1970):184–190.

————. "Bemerkungen zu dem Versuch von Clausewitz, zum Gesandten in London ernannt zu werden." *Jahrbuch für die Geschichte Mittel- und Ostdeutschlands* (1978):161–172.

————. *Clausewitz and the State.* New York, 1976.

————. *Yorck and the Era of Prussian Reform, 1807–1815.* Princeton, 1966.

Perthes, Clemens Theodore. *Friedrich Perthes Leben.* 3 vols. Gotha, 1855.

Pertz, G. H., and Delbrück, Hans. *Das Leben des Feldmarschalls Grafen Neithardt von Gneisenau.* 5 vols. Berlin, 1864–1880.

Petersdorff, Hermann von. *Friedrich von Motz, eine Biographie.* 2 vols. Berlin, 1913.

Phillips, Walter Alison. *The Confederation of Europe.* London, 1920.

Pinckney, David H. *The French Revolution of 1830.* Princeton, 1972.

Pope, Dudley. *The Great Gamble.* London, 1972.

Porch, Douglas. *Army and Revolution. France, 1815–1848.* London and Boston, 1974.

Price, Arnold. *The Evolution of the Zollverein.* Ann Arbor, 1949.

Prokesch von Osten, Anton, Freiherr von. *Geschichte des Abfalls der Griechen vom Turkischen Reiche.* 6 vols. Vienna, 1867–1880.

Reinermann, Alan J. "Metternich and Reform: The Case of the Papal State, 1814–1848." *The Journal of Modern History* 42 (1970):524–548.

———. "Metternich, Italy and the Congress of Verona, 1821–1822." *The Historical Journal* 14 (1971):263–287.

Riasanovsky, Nicholas V. *Nicholas and Official Nationality in Russia, 1825–1855.* Berkeley, 1959.

Richter, Franz. *Das europäische Problem der preussischen Staatspolitik und die revolutionäre Krisis von 1830 bis 1832.* Leipzig, 1933.

Ringhoffer, Karl. *The Bernstorff Papers. The Life of Count Albrecht von Bernstorff.* 2 vols. London, 1908.

———. *Ein Dezenium preussischer Orientpolitik zur Zeit des Zaren Nikolaus (1821–1830).* Berlin, 1897.

Ritter, Gerhard. *Staatskunst und Kriegshandwerk.* Vol. 1. Munich, 1965.

———. *Stein: Eine Politische Biographie.* Stuttgart, 1958.

Ritter, Paul. "Vier Briefe des Prinzen Wilhelm von Preussen (Kaiser Wilhelm I)." *Deutsche Rundschau* 134 (1908):187–217.

Robertson, William S. "Metternich's Attitude towards Revolutions in Latin America." *Hispanic American Historical Review* 21 (1941):538–558.

———. "Russia and the Emancipation of Spanish America, 1816–1826." *Hispanic American Historical Review* 21 (1941):196–221.

Rodriguez, O., Jaime E. *The Emergence of Spanish America, Vincente Rocafuerte and Spanish Americanism, 1808–1832.* Berkeley, 1975.

Roloff, Gustav. "Die Neuorganisation des Ministeriums des Auswärtigen von 1798–1802." *Forschungen zur brandenburgischen und preussischen Geschichte* 7 (1894):97–111.

Romani, George T. *The Neapolitan Revolution of 1820–1821.* Evanston, Ill., 1950.

Rosenberg, Hans. *Grosse Depression und Bismarckzeit.* Berlin, 1967.

Rothenburg, Gunther E. "The Austrian Army in the Age of Metternich." *The Journal of Modern History* 40 (1968):155–165.

Roussakis, Emmanuel N. *Friedrich List, the Zollverein, and the Uniting of Europe.* Bruges, 1968.

Ruppenthal, Roland. "Denmark and the Continental System." *The Journal of Modern History* 15 (1943):7–23.

Ryan, A. N. "The Causes of the British Attack upon Copenhagen in 1807." *English Historical Review* 68 (1953):37–55.

Sasse, Heinz. "Zur Geschichte des Auswärtigen Amts." *Mitteilungsblatt der Vereinigung der Angestellten des Auswärtiges Dienstes* 4 (1960):105–118.

Scharff, Alexander. *Schleswig-Holstein in der Europäischen und Nordischen Geschichte.* Veröffentlichen der Schleswig-Holsteinische Universitäts-gesellschaft, New Series, Nr. 16. Kiel, 1955.

Scheel, Wolfgang. *Das "Berliner Politische Wochenblatt" und die politische und soziale Revolution in Frankreich und England.* Göttingen, 1964.

Schiemann, Theodore. *Geschichte Russlands unter Kaiser Nikolaus I.* 4 vols. Berlin, 1904–1914.

———. "Die Sendung des Feldmarschalls Diebitsch nach Berlin." *Zeitschrift für Osteuropäische Geschichte* 1 (1911):2–22.

Schmalz, Hans W. *Versuche einer gesamteuropäischen Organization, 1815–1820.* Berner Untersuchungen zur allgemeinen Geschichte. Vol. 10. Aarau, 1940.

Schmoller, Gustav. *Das preussische Handels- und Zollgesetz vom 26. Mai. 1818.* Berlin, 1898.

Schnabel, Franz. *Deutsche Geschichte im Neunzehnten Jahrhundert.* 4 vols. Freiburg, 1948–1951.

Schnieder, Hans. "Das Attentat des Apothekers Lönig auf den Präsidenten Ibell (1819)." *Quellen und Darstellungen zur Geschichte der Burschenschaft und der deutschen Einheitsbewegung* 5 (1920):153–170.

Schroeder, Paul W. *Metternich's Diplomacy at Its Zenith, 1820–1823.* Austin, 1962.

Schwartz, Karl. *Leben des Generals Carl von Clausewitz.* 2 vols. Berlin, 1878.

Scott, Ivan. "Counter Revolutionary Diplomacy and the Demise of Anglo-Austrian Cooperation, 1820–1823." *The Historian* 34 (1972):465–484.

Simon, Walter. *The Failure of the Prussian Reform Movement, 1807–1819.* Ithaca, N.Y., 1955.

———. "Variations in Nationalism during the Great Reform Period in Prussia." *American Historical Review* 59 (1953–1954):305–321.

Spielmann, C. "Regierungspräsident Karl von Ibell über die preussiche Politik in den Jahren 1830 u. 1831." *Annalen des Vereins für Nassauische Altertumskunde und Geschichtsforschung* 28 (1896):61–95.

Srbik, Heinrich Ritter von. *Metternich: Der Staatsmann und der Mensch.* 3 vols. Munich, 1925–1954.

Steckhan, Gertrud. *Preussen und die Neuorientierung der europäischen Staatengesellschaft auf dem Aachener Kongress 1818.* Berlin, 1934.

Stern, Alfred. *Geschichte Europas seit den Verträgen von 1815 bis zum Frankfurter Frieden von 1871.* 10 vols. Berlin, 1894–1924.

———. "L'Idée d'une Représentation Centrale de l'Autriche conçue par le Prince de Metternich." *Revue Historique* 31 (1886):313–326.

Stoll, Adolf. *Friedrich Karl v. Savigny.* 2 vols. Berlin, 1927–1929.

Taylor, A. J. P. *The Course of German History.* New York, 1962.

Temperley, Harold. *The Foreign Policy of Canning, 1822–1827.* London, 1925.

Tenner, Edward Harvey. "Popular Disorders in Germany, 1830–1833." Ph.D. dissertation, University of Chicago, 1972.

Thaulow, Th., and Bro Jørgensen, J. O. *Udvalgte Breve, Betænkninger og Optegnelser af J. O. Schack-Rathlous arkiv, 1760–1800.* Copenhagen, 1936.

Thielen, Peter G. *Karl August von Hardenberg, 1750–1822.* Cologne, 1967.

Thierfelder, Hildegard. "Rother als Finanzpolitiker unter Hardenberg, 1778–1822." *Forschungen zur brandenburgischen und preussischen Geschichte* 46 (1934):70–111.

Thimme, Paul. *Strassenbau und Strassenpolitik in Deutschland zur Zeit der Gründung des Zollvereins, 1825–35.* Beihefte zur Vierteljahrschrift für Sozial und Wirtschaftsgeschichte 21 (1931).

Tilly, Richard. "The Political Economy of Public Finance and the Industrialization of Prussia, 1815–1866." *Journal of Economic History* 26 (1966):484–497.

Treitschke, Heinrich von. "Die Anfänge des deutschen Zollvereins." *Preussischer Jahrbücher* 30 (1872):397–466, 479–571, and 648–697.

———. "Aus den Papieren des Staatsministers von Motz." *Preussische Jahrbücher* 39 (1877): 398–422.

———. *History of Germany in the Nineteenth Century,* trans. Eden and Cedar Paul. 7 vols. New York, 1915–1919.

Treue, Wilhelm. *Wirtschaftzustände und Wirtschaftpolitik in Preussen, 1815–1825.* Berlin, 1937.

Varrentrap, Conrad. "Ranke's Historisch-politische Zeitschrift und das Berliner Politische Wochenblatt." *Historische Zeitschrift* 99 (1907):35–119.

Vierhaus, Rudolf. *Ranke und die Soziale Welt.* Münster, 1957.

———. "Ranke's Verhältnis zur Presse." *Historische Zeitschrift* 183 (1957): 543–567.

Vogler, G., and Vetter K. *Preussen, Von der Anfangen bis zur Reichsgründung.* Berlin, 1970.

Wallenberger, Margaret Kruse. "The Revolutions of the 1830s and the Rise of German Nationalism." Ph.D. dissertation, Radcliffe College, 1962.

Weber, Eberhard. *Die Mainzer Zentraluntersuchungskommission.* Karlsruhe, 1970.

Webster, Charles K. *Britain and the Independence of Latin America, 1812–1830.* 2 vols. London, 1938.

———. *The Congress of Vienna, 1814–1815.* New York, 1966.

———. *The Foreign Policy of Castlereagh, 1812–1822.* 2 vols. London, 1963.

———. *The Foreign Policy of Palmerston, 1830–1841.* 2 vols. New York, 1969.

———. "Palmerston, Metternich and the European System, 1830–1841." *Proceedings of the British Academy, 1934* (London):125–158.

Weniger, Erich. *Goethe und die Generale der Freiheitskriege.* Stuttgart, 1959.

Westphal, Otto. "System und Wandlungen der auswärtigen Politik Bayerns in den ersten Jahren Ludwigs I." In *Staat und Volkstum* (Festgabe für Alexander von Müller). Munich, 1933. Pp. 355–366.

Woynar, Karl. "Oesterreichs Beziehungen zu Schweden und Dänemark, vornehmlich seine Politik bei der Vereinigung Norwegens mit Schweden in den Jahren 1813 und 1814." *Archiv für oesterreichische Geschichte* 77 (1891):377–537.

✠✠✠✠✠✠✠✠✠✠✠✠✠✠

# Index

## G

## H

## Z